Architecture and Ugliness

Architecture and Ugliness
Anti-Aesthetics and the Ugly in Postmodern Architecture

Edited by
WOUTER VAN ACKER
AND THOMAS MICAL

BLOOMSBURY VISUAL ARTS
LONDON • NEW YORK • OXFORD • NEW DELHI • SYDNEY

BLOOMSBURY VISUAL ARTS
Bloomsbury Publishing Plc
50 Bedford Square, London, WC1B 3DP, UK
1385 Broadway, New York, NY 10018, USA
29 Earlsfort Terrace, Dublin 2, Ireland

BLOOMSBURY, BLOOMSBURY VISUAL ARTS and the Diana logo are trademarks
of Bloomsbury Publishing Plc

First published in Great Britain 2020
Paperback edition published 2021
Selection and editorial matter © Wouter Van Acker and Thomas Mical, 2021

Individual chapters © their authors, 2021

Wouter Van Acker and Thomas Mical have asserted their right under the Copyright,
Designs and Patents Act, 1988, to be identified as Editors of this work.

Cover design: Eleanor Rose
Cover image © Pixabay

All rights reserved. No part of this publication may be reproduced or
transmitted in any form or by any means, electronic or mechanical,
including photocopying, recording, or any information storage or retrieval
system, without prior permission in writing from the publishers.

Bloomsbury Publishing Plc does not have any control over, or responsibility for, any
third-party websites referred to or in this book. All internet addresses given in this
book were correct at the time of going to press. The author and publisher regret any
inconvenience caused if addresses have changed or sites have ceased to exist, but can
accept no responsibility for any such changes.

A catalogue record for this book is available from the British Library.

A catalog record for this book is available from the Library of Congress.

ISBN: HB: 978-1-3500-6823-0
PB: 978-1-3502-3670-7
ePDF: 978-1-3500-6824-7
eBook: 978-1-3500-6825-4

Typeset by Newgen KnowledgeWorks Pvt. Ltd., Chennai, India

To find out more about our authors and books visit www.bloomsbury.com
and sign up for our newsletters.

CONTENTS

List of figures viii
List of contributors xii

Introduction: Retracing the ugly and the anti-aesthetic as a productive force in postmodern architecture 1
Wouter Van Acker

1 Ugliness, the anti-aesthetic and appropriation: With some remarks on the architecture of ARM 19
   John Macarthur

2 On ugliness (in architecture) 39
   Bart Verschaffel

PART ONE Ugly and monstrous 57

3 Instrumentalizing ugliness: Parallels between High Victorian and Brutalist architecture 59
   Timothy M. Rohan

4 Monstrous becomings: A minor cartography 77
   Heidi Sohn

5 Traces of ugliness in Bofill's *Les espaces d'Abraxas* 95
   Thomas Mical

6 Post-communism and the monstrous: Skopje 2014 and other political tales 107
Mirjana Lozanovska

7 Here be monsters 125
Andrew Leach

8 To make monsters 137
Caroline O'Donnell

PART TWO Ugly and ordinary 151

9 'Ugly': The architecture of Robert Venturi and Denise Scott Brown 153
Deborah Fausch

10 Camp ugliness: The case of Charles W. Moore 175
Patricia A. Morton

11 Architecture in El Alto: The politics of excess 193
Elisabetta Andreoli

12 The critical kitsch of Alchimia and Memphis: Design by media 209
AnnMarie Brennan

13 The immediacy of urban reality in post-war Italy: Between neorealism's and Tendenza's instrumentalization of ugliness 223
Marianna Charitonidou

14 Ugliness as aesthetic friction: Renewing architecture against the grain 245
   Lara Schrijver

15 Ugliness, or the cathectic moment of modulation between terror and the comic in postmodern architecture 257
   Wouter Van Acker

Index 279

FIGURES

I.1 Table of comparison between Venturi and Rauch's Guild House and Paul Rudolph's Brutalist Crawford Manor from *Learning from Las Vegas* (1972). Venturi, Robert, Denise Scott Brown and Steven Izenour, Learning From Las Vegas, revised edition, Table, page 102, © 1977 Massachusetts Institute of Technology, by permission of the MIT Press. 4

1.1 Ashton Raggett McDougall (ARM)'s design of a black Villa Savoye for Australian Institute of Aboriginal and Torres Strait Islander Studies (AIATSIS), 2001. Photograph by John Gollings. 29

1.2 ARM, St Kilda Town Hall interior (1994). Photo courtesy of ARM Architecture. 30

3.1 William Butterfield, Keble College Chapel, Oxford (1873–6). Wikimedia Commons. Photo by David Iliff. License: CC-BY-SA 3.0. 60

3.2 Kallmann, McKinnell and Knowles, Boston City Hall (1962–8). Photo by Timothy M. Rohan. 66

5.1 Ricardo Bofill, *Les espaces d'Abraxas*, Paris, 1983. Photography by Fred Romero. 96

6.1 The Telecommunications Centre by Janko Konstantinov, 1974–79. Photograph by Mirjana Lozanovska, Skopje 2013. 110

6.2 Map of the implementation of Skopje 2014, illustrating the 'masking' strategy of thin architectural interventions on the north bank of the Vardar River. Image reconstruction by Ali Rahimi. Photographs by Mirjana Lozanovska. Google Earth – Mage © 2018 Digital Globe. 114

6.3 The Macedonian Opera and Ballet, 1979, architects Štefan Kacin, Jurij Princes, Bogdan Spindler and Marijan Uršič. Photograph by Mirjana Lozanovska, Skopje 2007. 117

7.1 Antonio Fantuzzi, after Rosso Fiorentino, The Enlightenment of Francis I, *c.*1542 Etching, 30.9 × 42.6 cm. © Trustees of the British Museum. 126

7.2 Proteus-Glaucus, Sacro Bosco, Bomarzo. Gardens designed by Pirro Ligorio, *c.* 1551–2. Photograph by Andrew Leach. 127

8.1 James Stirling, Michael Wilford and Associates, Neue Staatsgalerie, Stuttgart, 1977–84. Redrawn with site by CODA. 140

8.2 Bloodline, CODA, 2010. Above: 1:10 model and 1:1 mock-up presented in 'Self-Consuming' an exhibition at Tjaden Experimental Gallery, Cornell, supported by the CCA and the College of Architecture, Art, and Planning, as well as by Akademie Schloss Solitude and Elise Jaffe + Jeffrey Brown. Photographs by CODA. 144

8.3 Party Wall, MoMA/PS1 Young Architects' Program, CODA, 2013. View from dance floor. Photograph by Brent Solomon. 145

8.4 Urchin, CODA, 2016. Photograph by Joe Wilensky. 146

9.1 Venturi and Short, North Penn Visiting Nurse Association Headquarters, 1961, Ambler, Pennsylvania. Photograph by George Pohl, provided by Venturi, Scott Brown and Associates, Inc. 160

9.2 Venturi and Rauch, Brighton Beach Housing Competition, 1967, Brooklyn, New York, site model. Photograph provided by Venturi, Scott Brown and Associates, Inc. 161

9.3 Venturi, Rauch and Scott Brown, Gordon Wu Hall, 1982, Princeton University, Princeton, New Jersey. Photograph by Tom Bernard, provided by Venturi, Scott Brown and Associates, Inc. 166

9.4 Wu Hall, entry and keystones. Photograph by Tom Bernard, provided by Venturi, Scott Brown and Associates, Inc. 167

10.1 Moore Lyndon Turnbull Whitaker/Moore–Turnbull, Sea Ranch Athletic Club #1, Sea Ranch, California, 1966, interior of locker room with supergraphics by Barbara Stauffacher Solomon. Courtesy author. 182

10.2 Moore Lyndon Turnbull Whitaker/Moore–Turnbull, Charles Moore House, New Haven, Connecticut, 1966, rear facade. *House and Garden*, 133, no. 1 [January 1968]: 110. Courtesy John T. Hill. 184

10.3 Moore Lyndon Turnbull Whitaker/Moore–Turnbull, Charles Moore House, New Haven, Connecticut, 1966, 'Ethel' at the kitchen. *House and Garden*, 133, no. 1 [January 1968]: 115. Courtesy John T. Hill. 185

11.1 Freddy Mamani Silvestre, El Tren Diamante, El Alto, Bolivia. Photo by Alfredo Zeballos. 194

12.1 Nathalie Du Pasquier, 'Interior', Drawing, 1982–3. 210

12.2 Alessandro Mendini, 'Kandissi' sofa, Alchimia 1979. ©Atelier Mendini. 216

13.1 a and b Torre Velasca (1950–8) by Ludovico Belgiojoso, Enrico Peressutti and Ernesto Nathan Rogers (BBPR). Photo by Marianna Charitonidou, 13 June 2018. 229

13.2 Plan of the Tiburtino district, Rome, 1949–54. The main architects of the project were Ludovico Quaroni and Mario Ridolfi. Other architects who worked on this project were Carlo Aymonino, Mario Fiorentino, Federico Gorio, Maurizio Lanza, Piero Maria Lugli, Giulio Rinaldi, Michele Valori, Carlo Aymonino, Carlo Chiarini, Sergio Lenci, Carlo Melograni, Gian Carlo Menichetti and Volfango Frankl. Credit: Associazione archivio storico Olivetti, Fondo Quaroni Ludovico, Serie Progetti e corrispondenza, fasc. 130. 235

13.3 Mario Ridolfi and others, Quartiere Ina-Casa Tiburtino a Roma. Lotto B, case con ballatoio, riproduzione fotografica. Courtesy Accademia Nazionale di San Luca, Roma. Archivio del Moderno e del Contemporaneo, Fondo Ridolfi-Frankl-Malagricci, www.fondoridolfi.org. 236

15.1 Robin Boyd, cover of *The Australian Ugliness*, 1960. © Estate of Robin Boyd, courtesy Robin Boyd Foundation. 259

15.2 Sebastiano Serlio, The Comic Scene, from Sebastiano Serlio, *The First [-Fift] Booke of Architecture* (1475–1554; London: Stafford, Simon, 1630), scanned from Columbia University Libraries. 263

15.3 Peter Corrigan, House for Mr and Mrs Kevin McCarthy, Melbourne, built in 1967; compared to Robert Venturi's house for his mother, Philadelphia, 1963. Originally published in *Architecture in Australia* February 1972. 266

15.4 Edmond & Corrigan, Building 8, RMIT University, Melbourne, Victoria (1990–4). Photograph by John Gollings, courtesy of Gollings Photography Pty Ltd. 268

CONTRIBUTORS

Elisabetta Andreoli is an architectural and art historian and documentary maker. She organized the *Lina Bo Bardi* exhibition at the Royal Institute of British Architecture in 1994. Together with Adrian Forty she co-edited *Brazil's Modern Architecture* (2005). She published *Bolivia Contemporanea* (2012) and *The Architecture of Freddy Mamani Silvestre* (2014).

AnnMarie Brennan is Senior Lecturer of Design Theory in the Faculty of Architecture, Building and Planning at the University of Melbourne. She teaches architectural history, theory and design studio subjects and her research focuses on twentieth- and twenty-first-century architecture, with interests in the political economy of design, machine culture, Italian design, the history of computing and media and architecture.

Marianna Charitonidou is a lecturer and a postdoctoral fellow at ETH Zürich at the Chair of the History and Theory of Urban Design of the Institute for the History and Theory of Architecture (gta) (project: "The Travelling Architect's Eye: Photography and the Automobile Vision"), National Technical University of Athens (project: "The Transformations of 'Greekness' as a Device for Exploring Post-colonial Culture") and Athens School of Fine Arts (project: "Constantinos A. Doxiadis and Adriano Olivetti's Post-war Reconstruction Agendas").

Deborah Fausch is an architect and architectural historian and theorist whose writings on modern and contemporary architecture and urbanism, and especially the works of Robert Venturi and Denise Scott Brown, have appeared in many journals and essay collections.

Andrew Leach is Professor of Architecture at the University of Sydney School of Architecture, Design and Planning, where he is also Associate Dean, Research. He writes on contemporary issues in the fields of architectural history, theory and criticism. Among his books are *Manfredo Tafuri* (2007), *What Is Architectural History?* (2010) and *Rome* (2017).

Mirjana Lozanovska is Associate Professor at Deakin University. Her research deploys multidisciplinary theories of space to examine migration, mobility and exchange in architecture and the city. Her books include

Migrant Housing: Architecture, Dwelling, Migration (2019) and *Ethno-Architecture and the Politics of Migration* (2016). Mirjana is co-editor of *Fabrications: JSAHANZ*.

John Macarthur is Professor at the University of Queensland where he is Chair of Research in the School of Architecture. His research focuses on the intellectual history of architecture, the aesthetics of architecture and its relation to the visual arts. He is the author and editor of numerous books including *The Picturesque: Architecture, Disgust and Other Irregularities* (2007).

Thomas Mical is Dean and Professor of Architecture at Jindal Global University, India. His research focuses on the historical, qualitative and transformative attributes of spaces, with interest in the logical and sensory models and processes used in the production of spaces, and how these spaces then produce meanings and identities.

Patricia A. Morton is Associate Professor in the Media and Cultural Studies Department at the University of California, Riverside. She is the author of *Hybrid Modernities: Architecture and Representation at the 1931 International Colonial Exposition in Paris* (2000). Her current project, *Paying for the Public Life*, focuses on work by Charles W. Moore.

Caroline O'Donnell is the Edgar A. Tafel Associate Professor and director of the M.Arch. program at Cornell University. She is the sole principal of the design practice CODA: Caroline O'Donnell Architecture. Her first book, *Niche Tactics: Generative Relationships Between Architecture and Site*, was published in 2015.

Timothy M. Rohan is Associate Professor at the University of Massachusetts, Amherst. His research focuses on European and American modernism, especially of the post-Second World War era, on subjects ranging from brutalism to disco architecture. He is the author of *The Architecture of Paul Rudolph* (2014).

Lara Schrijver is Professor in Architecture Theory at the University of Antwerp Faculty of Design Sciences. Her research focuses on twentieth-century architecture. She is the author of *Radical Games* (2009) and co-editor of *Autonomous Architecture in Flanders* (2016) and the annual review *Architecture in the Netherlands* (2016–19).

Heidi Sohn is Associate Professor of Architecture Theory at the Architecture Department of the Faculty of Architecture, TU Delft. Her main areas of investigation include genealogical inquiries of postmodern and post-human theoretical landscapes. She is co-editor of *Critical and Clinical Cartographies: Architecture, Robotics, Medicine, Philosophy* (2017).

Wouter Van Acker is Associate Professor of Architectural History and Theory at the Université libre de Bruxelles (ULB). He is director of *hortence*, ULB's research centre for architectural history, theory and criticism. His research focus is the history of epistemology and aesthetics in architecture in the twentieth century.

Bart Verschaffel is Professor of Architectural Theory and Criticism at Ghent University. He publishes in the fields of architectural theory, aesthetics and philosophy of culture. Book publications include *Architecture Is (as) a Gesture* (2001), *À propos de Balthus* (2004) and *Nature morte, portrait, paysage* (2007).

INTRODUCTION

Retracing the ugly and the anti-aesthetic as a productive force in postmodern architecture
Wouter Van Acker

To say that a building is ugly is to make an aesthetic judgement, a critical act that points out that a building fails to meet the social or professional expectations we have of architecture as an aesthetic object, deviates from the standards of taste or goes against our interests. Such a judgement expresses a sense of inconvenience or discomfiture. The category of the ugly is, as Adorno reminds us, a 'canon of prohibitions' because the ugly, when found in an artwork, 'opposes the work's ruling flaw of form' and is aesthetically dissonant.[1] The fact that the ugly often enforces normative aesthetic behaviour is illustrated by stylistic guidebooks, common in the nineteenth and early twentieth centuries, that show examples of architecture in 'good' or 'bad taste' on opposite pages.[2] The ugly is a counterexample to illustrate what one should avoid. Aesthetic education in architectural taste prompts a behavioural reaction to looking away from ugliness, to have it cleaned, neutralized, covered up or even demolished. The aim of these aesthetic reflexes is to terminate as quickly as possible the experience of the ugly, favouring a subjective indifference over any cultivation of interest regarding the object of ugliness.

Architectural scholarship is not immune to this cultural defence mechanism of looking away from things that transgress normativity and disrupt the order of things. This might explain to some extent why the role that ugliness has played in the conception of postmodernism has received little attention in architectural histories, and is even absent from most theories of postmodernism.

Yet interest in the theme of ugliness, part of a recent 'return to beauty' in the field of art theory and practice, has been growing since the 1990s.[3] If judgements of beauty were dismissed from art and architectural criticism during the heyday of modernism (and postmodernism), the 'venus in exile' is back and now finds itself caught in a complex field of aesthetic and anti-aesthetic positions.[4] In a complex world where conditions and attributes are increasingly fleeting or in question, it is curious that the theme of ugliness can have its own place.

While the present volume necessarily positions itself within this recent 'return to beauty' and aesthetics, its focus is demarcated in time by a return to the postmodern response to the avant-garde sentiment that rejected aesthetic rewards of pleasure and empathy and sought to establish a 'beauty of ugliness reclaiming for art everything in human experience that artistic representation had previously rejected'.[5] The post-war sentiment, as Alexander Alberro reminds us, was expressed by Adorno when he stated that 'to write poetry after Auschwitz is barbaric'.[6] It seems difficult to imagine how the world appeared so profoundly ugly after the First and Second World Wars, as Adorno observed, that art gave up on beauty. In his *Aesthetische Theory* (1970) Adorno called for an art that faces the terror that had been chased from the temple of beauty:

> Art must take up the cause of what is proscribed as ugly, though no longer in order to integrate or mitigate it or to reconcile it with its own existence through humor that is more offensive than anything repulsive. Rather, in the ugly, art must denounce the world that creates and reproduces the ugly in its own image, even if in this too the possibility persists that sympathy with the degraded will reverse into concurrence with degradation.[7]

Art that valued beauty over critique in the post-war period became questionable, whereas the experience of negativity or disgust became relevant to articulate our orientation in the world designed and built under these shifting conditions.

Certainly one of the most important publications in the field of art and cultural history that orients this recent interest in the ugly, as part of the 'return to beauty' since the 1990s, is Umberto Eco's *On Ugliness* (2007) – the follow-up volume of his *History of Beauty* (2004) – which illustrates with multiple pictures how the concept of the ugly and the grotesque have changed in painting and visual culture over time. In a similar compilation, Stephen Bayley's *Ugly: The Aesthetics of Everything* (2011) provides us with an iconographic atlas of the ugly.[8] Andrei Pop and Mechtild Widrich's *Ugliness: The Non-Beautiful in Art and Theory* (2013) is probably the first scholarly effort in art theory to explicitly come to terms with the aesthetics of the ugly in the work of the early-twentieth-century avant-garde.[9]

Pop and Widrich also published an English translation (2015) of the first philosophical treatise on ugliness, *Aesthetik des Hässlichen* (1853) by Karl Rosenkranz. Nathalie Heinich, Jean-Marie Schaeffer and Carole Talon-Hugon's edited volume *Par-delà le beau et le laid* (2014) defines twelve values used in the evaluation of an experience of art by both the public as well as professionals.[10] Mojca Küplen's *Beauty, Ugliness, and the Free Play of Imagination* (2015) devotes two chapters on the problem of ugliness and its relation to disgust in Kant's aesthetics as exposed in the *Critique of the Power of Judgment*. And in *Ugliness: A Cultural History* (2015), Gretchen E. Henderson reveals, in a wide range of examples of cultural imagination, from antiquity to the present, how concepts of 'ugliness' and synonyms of the 'ugly' have helped re-evaluate the cultural borders between 'us' and 'them'.[11]

This growing body of scholarly inquiry into beauty and ugliness within the field of aesthetics is slowly but steadily finding its way into the field of architecture. The recently published special issue of *Le Visiteur* (2017) on the complex relation between the ugly and the beautiful is a good example,[12] as is *San Rocco*'s issue on 'pure beauty' (2017). The editorial of the latter noted that 'nobody talks about beauty. Nobody dares. (Or, at least, not in architecture; if you are in the soap business, then it's another story).'[13]

The most important architectural writings on the ugly are Mark Cousins's three-part article 'The Ugly' in *AA Files* (1994–5), John Macarthur's *The Picturesque: Architecture, Disgust and Other Irregularities* (2007) and his other articles that address ugliness in relation to eighteenth-century theories of the picturesque, architectural Brutalism and the work of Lyons architects,[14] and most recently Timothy Hyde's book *Ugliness and Judgment: On Architecture and the Public Eye* (2019). The latter book investigates debates on ugliness in seven contested social contexts in Great Britain, from John Wood the Elder in the eighteenth century to Prince Charles' advocacy of neoclassical architecture in the 1980s. Through these episodes Hyde argues that ugliness signals the participation of the architectural profession in societal judgements that are resolved through legal and institutional mechanisms of norms, laws and customs rather than through the aesthetic dimension of architecture – which is the primary focus in this anthology.[15]

What differentiates the essays in this volume from the architectural writings on ugliness mentioned earlier is an effort to retrace both theoretically and historically how the ugly and the anti-aesthetic have been a *productive* force in postmodern architecture. The authors of this volume share an interest in coming to terms with the twists and turns of the psyche of postmodern architects who took pleasure in exploring aesthetic transgressions beyond the field of the beautiful, or who sought to appropriate uneasy complexities and troublesome contradictions bound to the real, and who wilfully designed buildings in a field of cultural production considered a no-go area for the generation of modernists before them.

102 *UGLY AND ORDINARY ARCHITECTURE*

Table 1. Comparison of Guild House and Crawford Manor

Guild House	Crawford Manor
An architecture of meaning	An architecture of expression
Explicit "denotative" symbolism	Implicit "connotative" symbolism
Symbolic ornament	Expressive ornament
Applied ornament	Integral expressionism
Mixed media	Pure architecture
Decoration by the attaching of superficial elements	Unadmitted decoration by the articulation of integral elements
Symbolism	Abstraction
Representational art	"Abstract expressionism"
Evocative architecture	Innovative architecture
Societal messages	Architectural content
Propaganda	Architectural articulation
High *and* low art	High art
Evolutionary, using historical precedent	Revolutionary, progressive, anti-traditional
Conventional	Creative, unique, and original
Old words with new meanings	New words
Ordinary	Extraordinary
Expedient	Heroic
Pretty in front	Pretty (or at least unified) all around
Inconsistent	Consistent
Conventional technology	Advanced technology
Tendency toward urban sprawl	Tendency toward megastructure
Starts from client's value system	Tries to elevate client's value system and/or budget by reference to Art and Metaphysics
Looks cheap	Looks expensive
"Boring"	"Interesting"

FIGURE I.1 *Table of comparison between Venturi and Rauch's Guild House and Paul Rudolph's Brutalist Crawford Manor from* Learning from Las Vegas *(1972). Venturi, Robert, Denise Scott Brown and Steven Izenour,* Learning From Las Vegas, *revised edition, Table, page 102, © 1977 Massachusetts Institute of Technology, by permission of the MIT Press.*

Many scholars will note that the important temporal and conceptual reference point for this approach (and key to this volume) is the attribution of an operative function to the notion of the 'ugly' in *Learning from Las Vegas* (1972). In the second part of that book, entitled 'Ugly and Ordinary Architecture, or the Decorated Shed,' Robert Venturi, Denise Scott Brown and Steven Izenour pose architecture that is 'distinctly conventional in image as well as substance or, rather, ugly and ordinary' in opposition to the heroic and original architecture of megastructures and Brutalism. Philip Johnson and Gordon Bunshaft described Venturi and Rauch's fire station in Columbus as 'ugly and ordinary'.[16] Because architecture is culturally conditioned as an aestheticized object, the anxiety that a building might fail aesthetically and be perceived as ugly is deeply rooted within the range of possible practices of architectural modernism and urbanism. But instead of being offended by these critiques, Venturi, Scott Brown and Izenour found that their critics 'did catch the spirit' of their work. Just as early modern architects had appropriated the conventional vocabulary of industrial architecture, *Learning from Las Vegas* made the argument that by 'withholding judgement', rather than all too quickly dismissing the new commercial vernacular as ugly, much could be learned from it. In a table (Figure I.1) and in photographs on opposite pages, they compare ironically Venturi and Rauch's 'ugly and ordinary' Guild House (1963) to Paul Rudolph's 'heroic and original' Crawford Manor (1966).

Learning from Las Vegas exemplifies the way the concept of the ugly surfaces at key moments in the discourse on postmodern architecture without having been theorized as aesthetic or anti-aesthetic. It raises the question of how the architectural instrumentalization of ugliness in postmodernism is bound up with shifting critical values: contradiction over clarity, the ordinary over originality, pop culture over elitism, surface over depth, humour over seriousness, dirtiness over cleanness. Some architects deliberately employ these changes of polarity in response to the shifting contexts, and the shifting reception, of modernism in the late modern period.

The anti-aesthetic: Ugliness and the aesthetics of self-reflexivity

Coming to terms with the role that ugliness played in postmodern architecture, that of resistance to being reduced to the purely aesthetic, necessarily drives us to Hal Foster's *The Anti-Aesthetic* (1983).[17] This publication is still read in universities as 'a historical document, a moment in the history of reactions against Modernism' in practices that emerged in the 1970s and finally gave way to other forms of resistance in the late 1990s.[18] During a seminar in 2013, when he looked back at this publication, Foster situated the anti-aesthetic in the shift away from a modernist paradigm. This paradigm, legible in conceptual art practices of the neo-avant-garde, was exemplified by Clement Greenberg's argument that an aesthetic judgement of a work in the present was to be based on its 'quality'. This value was challenged by Donald Judd's notion that a work only needed to be 'interesting', displaced in turn by the value of 'criticality' and superseded more recently by the so-called revival of 'beauty', 'affect' or 'celebration'.[19] The diversity of the loosely related set of texts in *The Anti-Aesthetic* deliberately mirrors the widely divergent discourse on postmodern culture that converges on an anti-modernist moment in the historiography of postmodernist criticism. In a text like Craig Owens's 'The Allegorical Impulse', the themes of 'appropriation' and 'hybridization' are advanced as subjects within a set of discontinuities and continuities between aesthetics and anti-aesthetics, modernism and postmodernism, that is more complex than its rhetoric suggests.[20] Extending what Peter Bürger had noted on the relation between the late and historical avant-garde, one could argue that the anti-aesthetic in art and architecture was the next step of rebelling in self-reflexive practice against the institutional, discursive framework that guarded disciplinary autonomy and formalism, returning to a desire to be a thing in the world of the living.[21]

The prefix 'anti' in *The Anti-Aesthetic* denoted that the Kantian model of subjective taste had become problematic in a world where mass mediation coexisted with multiple cultures. 'Anti' stands for a dissociation of a privileged aesthetic realm from the sphere of the social and the political. According to Foster,

> 'Anti-aesthetic' also signals that the very notion of the aesthetic, its network of ideas, is in question here: the idea that aesthetic experience exists apart, without 'purpose,' all but beyond history, or that art can now effect a world at once (inter)subjective, concrete and universal – a symbolic totality. Like 'postmodernism,' then, 'anti-aesthetic' marks a cultural position on the present: are categories afforded by the aesthetic still valid?[22]

In the Kantian tradition, aesthetic judgements are assumed to be disinterested and to aspire to universal validity; the *sensus communis*, or the common faculty of taste, is in this regard foundational. A generalized 'third person' is presumed to confirm the validity of an aesthetic judgement because it is conceived as an aesthetic claim that is made public and therefore demands others to confirm this conclusion of aesthetic (dis)pleasure – others who are capable of speech and of disagreeing. For Kant, a judgement of beauty presupposes a unity in its conception of the social. This directedness of judgement towards others guarantees the objective form of the aesthetic judgement of beauty or ugliness through a form of subjectivity guided by community sense. In the postmodern context addressed by the research for this volume, we can see how commercial culture and populism slide into this category.

This conception of subjectivity in the original project of aesthetics has become problematic in the postmodern condition that is driven by what Jameson calls 'total culturalization', a society that integrates a pluralistic and relativist conception of the social as a blend of subcultures and minorities that have diverging social and political interests and affiliations. The fragmentation and collapse of the *sensus communis* has become clearly visible since the advent of various social media sites where we are constantly compelled to judge what we like and dislike, to confirm our interests and to form different communities or interest groups that share a judgement of what that group deems worthy of attention.[23]

At the same time, the anti-aesthetics of postmodernism are surprisingly Kantian in that its aesthetics addressed not the privileged world of art but the everyday world. And it is not always acknowledged that the conditions of everyday life were rapidly transforming in the timeframe of the postmodern. From the perspective of Kantian aesthetics, beauty (and implicitly also the ugly) is an aesthetic judgement that can be made not only of art or architecture but potentially about all things, all species and all environments, in a set time and context. Art or architecture do not have a privileged position as objects of the aesthetic attitude; it is the real world that is the legitimate object of aesthetics. Precisely because everything can become the object of aesthetic contemplation, architecture with or without architects, 'nonpedigreed' or pedigreed, with or without artistic pretensions, is a potential object of an aesthetic sensation of pleasure or displeasure. It is this widening of the aesthetic registers of postmodern anti-aesthetics, pushing modernist art and architecture from the exceptional pedestal of high culture to engage with the banal, everyday economy and cultural reality, that makes the anti-aesthetic project, up to a certain degree, very Kantian.

To the extent that the anti-aesthetic aligns with an increasing willingness for designers (and the public) to embrace the ugly, trivial and informal aesthetics and the messiness and glossiness of a commodified, mediated culture, the anti-aesthetic put a halt to the traditional aesthetic project. Ugliness rightly has no place in Kant's *Critique of the Power of Judgment* – ugliness is only mentioned once in relation to explaining disgust as the true negative of aesthetics. But as Alix Cohen argues, there is also a case to be made for the existence in Kant's theory of judgements of impure and pure ugliness. 'Impure ugliness' is that which is distasteful and which contravenes our interests – whether these interests are conceptual, emotional, personal or moral. 'Pure ugliness' in Kant's aesthetics could then posthumously be defined as the positive opposite to beauty.[24] If we contemplate a building that produces a feeling of aesthetic displeasure, and that we judge is exquisite in its ugliness, this judgement can be aesthetically disinterested, as in the case of 'pure beauty'. Like a painting in a museum, we can say of a building that it is ugly, and we express a purely aesthetic experience of displeasure that is caused by a counterplay of the imagination and understanding. This sensation of aesthetic and cognitive disharmony can potentially be found to be fascinating or mind-boggling. It is in that sense that Rosenkranz observed of the ugly, in contrast to the beautiful:

> Beautiful is, as Kant rightly states, what pleases apart from all interest; thus ugly is what displeases apart from all interest. The disharmonic can in fact arouse our interest without being beautiful; this we call interesting. Something devoid of internal contradiction we will not call interesting. The simple, light, transparent are not interesting; the great, sublime, sacred are above such expression; they are more than merely interesting. But the complicated, contradictory, amphibolical, and therefore the unnatural, the criminal, the strange, even the lunatic, are interesting. The seething restlessness in the boiling pot of contradiction has a magical attraction.[25]

In Kantian aesthetics, these forms of pure and impure ugliness arouse a sensation of displeasure, which in theory leaves open the possibility of finding pleasure in the displeasure of ugliness because of its captivating or significant qualities;[26] a possibility that appealed in particular to the anti-aesthetic explorations in postmodern art and architecture.

The 'cross-pollenization' and historical interlacing of the anti-aesthetic impulse and Kantian aesthetic theory converged in the postmodern moment in a self-conscious positioning of architecture within history, epitomized in the values of criticality and the interesting.[27] The new anti-aesthetic regime demanded a self-reflective critical stance to be operational at multiple levels: putting to the test the traditional decoupling of the aesthetic experience from non-aesthetic social and political concerns, as well as the sacred values such as 'disinterested pleasure', 'free play' and 'distance' that constitute the autonomy of high art. The new anti-aesthetic regime confronted the appropriation of an aesthetic appreciation of non-architecture in a cultivated autonomy of art and architecture, acknowledging its coexistence with a pervasive world of design, a world in which all things, species and even behaviour are subject to aestheticization and radical commodification.

In the present time, architect Joshua Prince-Ramus gives a straightforward example of how ambiguous anti-aesthetic and aesthetic dynamics continue to hold our relationship to ugliness in its grips:

> What do you do when you stand before a client and you have based your argument on beauty and they say 'I think it is ugly'? YOU ARE SCREWED. It is much more powerful to know what you think is beautiful and be able to justify it [a project] on issues that simply have nothing to do with that.[28]

A critical practice in architectural design that mobilizes its relationship with and positions itself consciously within architectural criticism mirrors a conflation of aesthetic choices with reflexivity.[29] The criticism of ugliness then becomes an act of explanation and interpretation rather than judgement.³⁰ This attitude is well captured by Miuccia Prada:

> If I have done anything, it is to make ugly appealing. In fact most of my work is concerned with destroying – or at least deconstructing – conventional ideas of beauty, of the generic appeal of the beautiful, glamorous, bourgeois women. ... The investigation of ugliness is, to me, more interesting than the bourgeois idea of beauty. And why? Because ugly is human.³¹

Within the series of publications on the theme of ugliness that have appeared in the field of literary, cultural, art and architectural history and theory, this volume turns to ugliness not so much as a publicly constructed aesthetic judgement but as a resource essential in critical architectural practice – an anti-aesthetic judgement that has been internalized as a critical operation in different modes of the postmodern design process.

The ugly, the ordinary and the monstrous

The chapters in this volume are diverse, but for efficiency they have been grouped in two parts: the first part deals with stronger forms of the ugly by relating it to the category of 'the monstrous'; the second part deals with weaker forms of the ugly that interact with the aesthetic register of the 'ordinary'. The two parts move in two different directions: the first part appraises architectural thought and production that tend towards the sublime, formlessness and the impure, while the second part deals with architects' practice and agency in realizing in concrete form an inherent desire to escape ugliness as a habitual characterization and naturalization of the built environment as mundane, conventional, stereotyped or generic.

In tandem, these directions, from the ugly to the ordinary or the monstrous, are bound in the questioning of architecture's normative aesthetic expectation to be representational. A useful starting point to address how the issue of representation relates to the role that ugliness plays in postmodern architecture is Mark Cousins's three-part article 'The Ugly' in *AA Files* (1994–5). Cousins comes to terms with the spatial characteristics of distance in the relational movement between the object and the subject of ugliness. The ugly, according to Cousins, problematizes the representational relation in the double existence of each object, namely as an exterior and an interior:

> The exterior is the representation of the object for the subject, and therefore includes much which is 'inside' the object. The interior is the existence of the object and therefore can include anything on the 'outside' of

the object which has not been submitted to a regime of representation. It is in this sense that ugliness arises as and when the interior of the existence of an object exceeds, for a subject, its representational exterior.[32]

The relationship between the exterior and interior of a person, a thing or building is mediated through a face, a surface or a facade. We expect that the surface of an object tells us the character and purpose of that object, that a face expresses what goes on in someone's head, and that a facade reflects the life inside a building. If the face no longer expresses the inner life of a thing or a person, it becomes superficial, a mere 'sur'-face – skin-deep. Above all, ugliness lacks depth. Beauty, on the other hand, requires a sense of profoundness or depth that reflects aspects of inner beauty. What can be deduced from Cousins's work is that ugliness in architecture emerges when this representational logic is broken up, because of excess – the interior erupts over the exterior, matter dominates over form – or, its inverse, because of the impossibility or absence of expressiveness.

The logic of excess goes in the direction of the monstrous and can be understood through Mary Douglas's analysis of dirt: 'Where there is dirt there is system. Dirt is the by-product of a systematic ordering and classification of matter, in so far as ordering involves rejecting inappropriate elements.'[33] Dirt is not dirty in itself but becomes dirty when it no longer occupies the place that has been assigned to it. Dirt is the big enemy of the house, interpreted as a system to allocate things to places so that we can live in order and peace. A house that is maintained in good order requires that dirt is removed and that matter which 'is out of place' is put back into the place where it belongs. Dust, as a variation of 'the formless', empties the form and destabilizes propriety in architecture. In its formlessness, as Teresa Stoppani has shown in her reading of Bataille, dust is an enemy of the modernist dream of transparency and cleanliness.[34] The formless breaks down the relationship between form and matter by creating disorder in all taxonomies, as Rosalind Krauss and Yve Alain Bois stated when reviewing how this category had been used productively in art between 1930 and 1975.[35]

The monstrous as an inversion of the representational order between the interior and exterior also figures in several of the typologies of architectural horror explored by Joshua Comaroff and Ong Ker-Shing in *Horror in Architecture*.[36] The Centre Pompidou in Paris (1977) figures as an example of such an inversion in the typology of the 'incontinent object' that is defined by an anarchic, 'scatological' exposure of the technical intestines of architecture; Luigi Moretti's Church of the Concilio Sancta Maria Mater Ecclesiae (1965) illustrates Comaroff and Ker-Shing's typology of 'solidity, mass, stereotomy' – an architecture that becomes all inside and articulates its outside as if it was a cavern.[37] The horrid in architecture, they argue, crops up when the conventional mode of abstraction in architecture fails. Numerous examples, they say, of architectural monsters can be found in attempts to domesticate new large-scale programmes such as skyscrapers, shopping malls, large event halls or hotel resorts that become cities in themselves, violently colliding with traditional historical types and languages of composition. Like Frankenstein's monster whose limbs are stitched together, we can find in *Horror in Architecture* examples of strange spatio-temporal juxtapositions: in radical eclecticism as promoted by Jencks, in renovations or historical revisions, or in the mixing of different cultural registers in a sort of *cadavre exquis*. As Denis Gigante notices, Frankenstein 'is only *too* real'; he exceeds representation.[38] And once this monster invades the social order, he consumes it; once ugliness as the aesthetically repressed steps out of the margins and into the daylight, it disrupts the social system of aesthetic expectations of how to appear in public space, leaving only a trace of disorder.

In combining seemingly mutually exclusionary categories, monstrous ugliness as a disequilibrium or imbalance of ratios can also unfold in the mode of the grotesque.[39] In the grotesque, registers usually kept apart collapse: human, animal, mineral, and vegetable; nature and technology; the rational and the irrational. The grotesque consists of bodies that merge and fuse with the world and, in its state of becoming, lacks precise borders. Ugliness and the grotesque are both founded on a disunity that refuses classification, an unstable incongruity of 'both/and', and an aggressive juxtaposition of opposites such as high/low, private/public, human/animal or familiar/unfamiliar – it is the proximity of these dual categories in one instance, without a dialectic convergence, that creates the tension and irresolution of the aesthetics.

At the other end of the spectrum of the ugly we find architecture that engages with the ordinary as a 'linguistic mask, speech in a dead language', to use Jameson's words. Much postmodern architecture flirted with kitsch in accepting a collapse of the modernist ideology of minimalist-industrial style and revamping a prior eclecticism of all the styles of the past as pastiche.[40] Kitsch and camp in the post-war period aesthetically cultivated the artificiality and theatricality of design, encapsulated in the 'ultimate Camp statement: it's good because it's awful'.[41] For Gillo Dorfles, kitsch or 'the world of bad taste' enjoys the degeneration of 'serious' art to a comic state of forgery.[42] To the extent that monsters appear in the ordinary, they appear here as funny rather than scary. The humour in the blog *McMansionHell* and the publication and blog of *Ugly Belgian Houses* (2015), populated with photographs of extraordinarily ugly houses found, respectively, in the American and Belgian suburbs, owe much to how the images of their facades are captioned with punning aphorisms, revealing the naiveté of the unrestrained architectural imagination of its inhabitants. The ugly is found through irony in the failure to blend in, in its errant ordinariness.[43]

The aesthetic experience of a collapse of the boundaries of the object between interior and exterior, matter and form, representation and existence, is doubled in the relation to the subject of ugliness. The stronger and weaker forms of ugliness have their counterpart in what we may call *Ugly*

Feelings, after Sianne Ngai's book.[44] 'Ugly feelings' such as envy, paranoia, irritation, animatedness or what she calls stuplimity (a mix of shock and boredom), originate from uneventful moments that, she argues, produce a meta-feeling of uncertainty '*about* what one is feeling', confusion about the objective or subjective status of that feeling. This 'affective indeterminacy' and disconcertedness is an attribute we can project on the relationship between the object and the subject of ugliness.[45] This weakness is confirmed in John Macarthur's analysis of Udevale Price's theory: 'Ugliness alone is merely disagreeable; by the addition of deformity, it becomes hideous; by that of terror it may become sublime.'[46] Ugliness itself is not striking; it needs to be combined with deformity to strongly arouse attention, and to potentially trigger disgust.

Ugliness requires distance, whereas the feeling of disgust presupposes proximity and immediacy. Sufficient distance, the critical distance of creator or audience from the work under analysis, is essential for the higher senses to discern the 'artful deception' that structures the aesthetic experience. In the sensation of disgust, by contrast, a lack of distance makes it impossible to distinguish art from nature or illusion from reality. In disgust both collapse and leave the subject no room and no time to reflect on how the artwork is associated with and dissociated from reality. The sensation of the real or imagined object of disgust immediately intrudes upon the subject, triggering an equally violent defence mechanism to throw back out what threatens to contaminate our inner being. Curiously, the spatiality and temporality of ugliness is quite different. The experience of the ugly, as of the beautiful in eighteenth-century aesthetics, aligns the 'distance'-associated senses of sight and hearing.[47] By contrast, as Moses Mendelsohn observed, disgust, or *Eckel*, can only be experienced by the 'dark' proximity-related senses of 'taste, smell, and touch', while 'artistic imitation labors solely for the more lucid senses, namely sight and hearing'.[48]

Cases and themes of architectural ugliness and the anti-aesthetic

Because it is in the nature of ugliness to be censured or negated, much subterranean labour in the 'carceri' of the discipline of architectural history remains to be done. The role that ugliness, the ugly and the anti-aesthetic have played in the intermingled processes of the conception, production and reception of postmodern architecture has yet to be examined. This volume consists of chapters that address an understanding of architectural ugliness through theoretical argumentation as well as more focused historical studies that reveal disturbing complications in the archives of architectural history.

In the first chapter in this book, 'Ugliness, the Anti-Aesthetic and Appropriation: With Some Remarks on the Architecture of ARM', John

Macarthur disentangles the anti-aesthetic beyond simple antinomies of beauty, pointing out how it either took form as a scepticism of aesthetic judgement, implying a valuation of the discursive over the sensory, or took form as a proper negative aesthetic attitude. Situating the discourse on the anti-aesthetic in parallel with the emergence of postmodernism as theorized by Jencks, deconstructivism and critical architecture, Macarthur then looks at the positivity of ARM's architectural anti-aesthetics.

Bart Verschaffel's philosophical discussion of ugliness, in the chapter 'On Ugliness (in Architecture)', complements Macarthur's historical contextualization of the post-war discourse on the ugly and the anti-aesthetic. Relying on a reading of Rosenkranz, Kant and Valéry, among others, Verschaffel considers what a proper aesthetic appreciation of the ugly is and how it is different from a conception of taste or moral judgement. After having established an aesthetic definition of the ugly, he asks if something like ugliness can exist in architecture, and if so, how. He concludes that the aesthetic object that is architecture, when it tends to become monstrous, triggers a fear that can be aesthetically controlled and recuperated, but architecture can also succeed aesthetically, at a weaker register, when taming the ugly to a state of ordinariness. Verschaffel's essay thus sets out the two axes, the monstrous and the ordinary, that give this volume its structure.

The first section, on the ugly and the monstrous, opens with Timothy M. Rohan's chapter, 'Instrumentalizing Ugliness: Parallels between High Victorian and Brutalist Architecture'. With its focus on Brutalist ugliness, it is the overture for the other contributions in this volume that focus on anti-heroic, postmodern architecture. An analysis of John Summerson's 1945 reappraisal of the High Victorian architecture of William Butterfield provides a useful perspective for the debates about the preservation of the Brutalist architectural heritage in the Anglo-American world, as both High Victorian and Brutalist architecture have been derided as ugly. Rohan also discusses how Summerson's use of the term 'ugliness' informed Alison and Peter Smithson's value of a raw authenticity in the 1950s, the ethical dimension of Brutalism.

Heidi Sohn's chapter, 'Monstrous Becomings: A Minor Cartography', provides an anti-essentialist reading of the cultural category of the ugly and 'the monster' as a way in to understand how the monstrous functions in society as an aesthetic category. Leaning on feminist theory that deals with 'posthuman teratology' and on Deleuze and Guattari's philosophy of becoming, Sohn offers an understanding of the expressions and practices of monstrosity in architecture by addressing the disruptive and affective forces of the monstrous. Going well beyond traditional postmodern interpretations of the monstrous within the framework of the sublime, the chapter traces the ontological liminality of the monstrous and its capacity to produce forms of subjectivity that are described as unstable, nonrepresentable and metamorphic interactions of a multitude of intensive 'machines'.

The next two chapters in this section each dissect a specific project through the lens of the monstrous. Thomas Mical, in 'Traces of ugliness in Bofill's *Les espaces d'Abraxas*', reconsiders the effects of monumentality and the domesticity of social housing in the Abraxas complex. He relates this landmark of postmodernism's neoclassical ugliness to the 'social ugliness' that emerged from the Reagan–Thatcher–Mitterrand neo-liberal collapse of social support. Mirjana Lozanovska's chapter, 'Post-communism and the Monstrous: Skopje 2014 and Other Political Tales', recounts how the appearance of what was once a socialist city has been aggressively encapsulated recently in historicist facades and neoclassicist scenery. The Brutalist architecture built in the period following Kenzo Tange's 1965 master plan for the Macedonian capital was effaced systematically during the post-communist renovation plan called Skopje 2014.

Andrew Leach's 'Here Be Monsters' and Caroline O'Donnell's 'To Make Monsters' wrap up the section on the ugly and the monstrous, by projecting the monstrous to two different directions in history: to architectural histories of mannerism on the one hand, and to an ongoing practice of designing monsters on the other. Leach inspects the post-war historiographical judgement of mannerist architecture of the sixteenth century as ugly. He looks at how such a judgement, made by historians of architecture in the twentieth century, affected the revival of the classical tradition. O'Donnell, in contrast, explores how the 'fugly' informs the niche tactics of the architectural practice CODA, to the point where the firm aspires to create 'hopeful monsters'. Tracing a path through biological theories of evolution and genetic mutations, the essay outlines examples of that firm's environmentally responsive architecture.

The volume's second section, on the ugly and the ordinary, opens with Deborah Fausch's chapter entitled '"Ugly": The Architecture of Robert Venturi and Denise Scott Brown'. Fausch investigates Venturi and Scott Brown's deadpan sensibility for the ugly and the ordinary, illustrated in *Learning from Las Vegas*, in relation to the techniques of British and American Pop Art that were meant to reveal the communication structures of commercial culture. She questions to what extent their search for inspiration in vernacular and popular building culture continues a modernist strategy of using the ugly and the ordinary as an agent of shock and revolutionary action.

The four subsequent chapters deal with the position held by the ugly and its close ties with the ordinary in specific cases of postmodern architecture. In 'Camp Ugliness: The Case of Charles W. Moore', Patricia A. Morton examines the camp ugliness of Charles Moore's house in New Haven (1966) and his other works in relation to theories that define camp's detached aesthetic vision of the world, by which the aesthetic redemption of ugliness as beauty occurs at the same time as a controlled reduction back to a state of excessive ugliness. Elisabetta Andreoli shifts the focus to the colourful buildings that Freddy Mamani realized since the late 1990s in the Andes in Bolivia. Andreoli's 'Architecture in El Alto: The Politics of Excess' shows that the eccentricity and glossy facades of the 'new Andean' architecture should be understood in a context of folklore, capitalist urban politics, commercial funfair culture and traditional indigenous patterns. AnnMarie Brennan revisits the texts and debates on Italian postmodern design culture of kitsch in her essay 'The Critical Kitsch of Alchimia and Memphis: Design by Media', looking at the appropriation of media effects by designers such as Alessandro Guerriero, Ettore Sottsass Jr. and Alessandro Mendini. She explains that what they ironically called the 'New International Style' acknowledged the undeniable hegemony of modernism while at the time merged that hegemony with a 'New' antithesis of modernist beauty: the banal but affective aesthetic of advertisements that only succeed if media emotionally reproduce desire and emotion. Marianna Charitonidou looks at the way in which ugliness was discussed in relation to the post-war urban reality of reconstruction by other Italian protagonists such as Ernesto Nathan Rogers, Ludovico Quaroni and Aldo Rossi, in her chapter 'The Immediacy of Urban Reality in Post-war Italy: Between Neorealism's and Tendenza's Instrumentalization of Ugliness'.

The volume is brought to a close by two chapters. Lara Schrijver's essay, 'Ugliness as Aesthetic Friction: Renewing Architecture against the Grain', reviews moments in the history of modernist architecture when a sense of the ugly functioned as a mechanism of friction that challenged our standards of aesthetic taste and beauty. Finally, Wouter Van Acker, in 'Ugliness, or the Cathectic Moment of Modulation between Terror and the Comic in Postmodern Architecture', reshuffles the two axes of the ordinary and the monstrous that structure this volume by introducing another binome to which these are closely allied: that of the comic and the terrible. This last chapter discusses how the discourse on the 'ugliness' of the rapid suburbanization by modernists like Robin Boyd or Peter Blake contributed to staging the post-war suburban landscape as a scene of horror and terror. This discourse was conducive to a cathectic displacement in aesthetic registers of the comic – relying on irony, satire and wit – in the work of Robert Venturi, Peter Corrigan and Rem Koolhaas.

Together the chapters shed light on divergent frames of the aesthetic problem, both as a historical and a theoretical question. The driving engine for this manifold inquiry is simply if and how ugliness can be of interest to architecture; or more precisely, how architecture can make good use of ugliness when its own dynamics are characterized by disunity and contradiction, by a deviation from normativity, and by being experienced as a 'mixed sensation' of pleasant and unpleasant feelings that can be intellectually more interesting than simple enjoyment. This volume offers many tools and approaches to assist the reader to come to terms with ugliness in architecture. It adopts a range of post-formalistic means to generate a deliberate interplay between the inner and the outer, the representational and the material, the organic and the inorganic – all sorts of pathological kernels and aberrations. This volume also digs deeper into that historical context to precisely articulate the range of postmodern aversions and slippages in the psyche of the beholder-critic, the creator-architect and the wider collective subjectivity today identified as the 'multitude'.

Notes

1 Theodor Adorno, *Aesthetic Theory* (London: Continuum, 1997), 60. See especially the third chapter of this volume, 'On the Categories of the Ugly, the Beautiful and Technique'.
2 Edward Leonard, *Bouwen in het Dorp en op het Land* (Antwerpen: De Sikkel, 1928).
3 Two notable publications that are exemplary in questioning the traditional philosophical doctrine of aesthetics are Jean-Marie Schaeffer, *Adieu à l'esthétique* (Paris: Editions Mimésis, 2016) and Jacques Rancière, *The Politics of Aesthetics* (London: Bloomsbury, 2013).
4 Mario Vargas Llosa, as quoted in Wendy Steiner, *Venus in Exile: The Rejection of Beauty in Twentieth-Century Art* (New York: Free Press, 2001).
5 Ibid., xv.
6 Alexander Alberro, 'Beauty Knows No Pain', *Art Journal* 63, no. 2 (2004): 37–43.
7 Adorno, *Aesthetic Theory*, 64.
8 Umberto Eco, *On Ugliness* (New York: Rizzoli, 2007); Stephen Bayley, *Ugly: The Aesthetics of Everything* (London: Fiell, 2011).
9 Andrei Pop and Mechtild Widrich, *Ugliness: The Non-Beautiful in Art and Theory* (London: I.B. Tauris, 2013).
10 Nathalie Heinich, Jean-Marie Schaeffer and Carole Talon-Hugon, eds, *Par-delà le beau et le laid. Enquêtes sur les valeurs de l'art* (Rennes: Presses Universitaires de Rennes, 2014).
11 Gretchen E. Henderson, *Ugliness: A Cultural History* (London: Reaktion Books, 2015).
12 Karim Basbous, 'Le beau et le laid', *Le Visiteur* no. 22 (2017): 5–7.
13 Matteo Chidoni, 'Editorial', *San Rocco* 13 (2017): 3–6, 3.
14 John Macarthur, *The Picturesque: Architecture, Disgust and Other Irregularities* (London: Routledge, 2007); John Macarthur, 'Brutalism, Ugliness and the Picturesque Object' in *Formulation Fabrication – The Architecture of History:* Proceedings of the Seventeenth Annual Conference of the Society of Architectural Historians Australia and New Zealand (Wellington: SAHANZ, 2000), 264. See also John Macarthur, 'The Butcher's Shop: Disgust in Picturesque Aesthetics and Architecture', *Assemblage* 30 (1996), and John Macarthur, 'Ugliness and Romanticism in the Work of Lyons Architects' in *More: The Architecture of Lyons 1996–2011*, ed. Lyons (firm) (Fishermans Bend: Thames and Hudson, 2012).

15 Timothy Hyde, *Ugliness and Judgment: On Architecture in the Public Eye* (Princeton, NJ: Princeton University Press, 2019).

16 Robert Venturi, Denise Scott Brown and Steven Izenour, *Learning from Las Vegas: The Forgotten Symbolism of Architectural Form* (Cambridge, MA: MIT Press, 1977), 128.

17 The following two publications have been the basis for this discussion of the anti-aesthetic James Meyer and Toni Ross, eds, 'Aesthetic/Anti-Aesthetic', special issue, *Art Journal* 63, no. 2 (2004); James Elkins and Harper Montgomery,eds, *Beyond the Aesthetic and the Anti-Aesthetic* (University Park: Pennsylvania State University Press, 2013).

18 James Elkins, 'Introduction' in *Beyond the Aesthetic and the Anti-Aesthetic*, ed. Elkins and Montgomery, 1.

19 Hal Foster, in *Beyond the Aesthetic and the Anti-Aesthetic*, ed. Elkins and Montgomery, 35.

20 Originally published as Craig Owens, 'The Allegorical Impulse: Toward a Theory of Postmodernism', *October* 12 (1980): 67–86.

21 Peter Bürger, 'Avant-Garde and Neo-Avant-Garde: An Attempt to Answer Certain Critics of Theory of the Avant-Garde', *New Literary History* 41, no. 4 (2010): 695–715; Hal Foster, 'What's Neo about the Neo-Avant-Garde?' *October* 70 (1994): 5–32.

22 Hal Foster, 'Postmodernism: A Preface' in *The Anti-Aesthetic. Essays on Postmodern Culture*, ed. Hal Foster (New York: Bay Press, 1983), xv.

23 Sianne Ngai, *Our Aesthetic Categories: Zany, Cute, Interesting* (Cambridge, MA: Harvard University Press, 2012), 42.

24 Alix Cohen, 'Kant on the Possibility of Ugliness', *British Journal of Aesthetics* 53, no. 2 (2013): 199–209.

25 Karl Rosenkranz, 'Aesthetic of Ugliness', *Log* no. 22 (2011): 101–11, 109.

26 Mojca Küplen, 'The Aesthetics of Ugliness – A Kantian Perspective', *Proceedings of the European Society of Aesthetics* vol. 5 (2013): 260–79. See also Mojca Küplen, *Beauty, Ugliness, and the Free Play of Imagination* (Cham: Springer, 2015).

27 Meyer and Ross, 'Aesthetic/Anti-Aesthetic: An Introduction', *Art Journal* 63, no. 2 (2004): 20–23, 23.

28 Mark Foster Gage and Joshua Prince-Ramus, 'Fool's Game', *Perspecta* 4 (2008): 102.

29 K. Michael Hays, 'Critical Architecture: Between Culture and Form', *Perspecta* 21 (1984): 15–29; Jane Rendell, 'Critical Architecture: Introduction', *Journal of Architecture* 10, no. 3 (2005): 227–8.

30 Pierre Machery, *A Theory of Literary Production*, trans. Geoffrey Wall (London: Routledge, 1978); Ngai, *Our Aesthetic Categories,* 112–13.

31 As quoted in Adam Geczy and Vicki Karaminas, *Critical Fashion Practice: From Westwood to Van Beirendonck* (London: Bloomsbury, 2017), 64.

32 Mark Cousins, 'The Ugly, Part II', *AA Files* 29 (1995): 3–6, 3.

33 Mary Douglas, *Purity and Danger: An Analysis of Concepts of Pollution and Taboo* (London: Routledge & Kegan Paul, 1966), 36, quoted in Johannes Scanlan, *On Garbage* (London: Reaktion Books, 2005), 42.
34 Georges Bataille, 'Dust' in *Encyclopaedia Acephalica*, ed. Georges Bataille, et al. (London: Atlas Press, 1995), 42–3; Teresa Stoppani, 'Dust Revolutions: Dust, Informe, Architecture (Notes for a Reading of Dust in Bataille)', *Journal of Architecture* 12, no. 4 (2007): 437–47.
35 Yve Alain Bois and Rosalind E. Krauss, 'Communiqué de presse: L'Informe: mode d'emploi', Exposition 22 mai-26 août 1996, Le Centre Georges Pompidou (1996); Yve Alain Bois and Rosalind E. Krauss, *Formless* (New York: Zone Books, 1997).
36 Joshua Comaroff and Ong Ker-Shing, *Horror in Architecture* (Novato, CA: ORO editions, 2013).
37 Ibid., 127 and 190.
38 Denise Gigante, 'Facing the Ugly: The Case of "Frankenstein"', *ELH* 67, no. 2 (2000): 565–87.
39 On the grotesque, see Geoffrey Galt Harpham, *On the Grotesque. Strategies of Contradiction in Art and Literature* (Aurora, CO: The Davies Group, Publishers, 2006); and Justin D. Edwards and Rune Graulund, eds, *Grotesque* (London: Routledge, 2013).
40 Fredric Jameson, *Postmodernism, or, the Cultural Logic of Late Capitalism* (Durham: Duke University Press, 1991).
41 Susan Sontag, *Notes on Camp* (New York: Penguin Random House, 2018), Statement 58.
42 Gillo Dorfles (ed.), *Kitsch: The World of Bad Taste* (New York: Universe Books, 1975).
43 Kate Wagners's blog, *McMansion Hell*, https://mcmansionhell.com [accessed 17 May 2019]; Hannes Coudenys, *Ugly Belgian Houses: Don't Try This at Home* (Gent: Borgerhoff & Lamberigts, 2015). See also Hannes Coudenys's blog, *Ugly Belgian Houses*, at https://uglybelgianhouses.tumblr.com [accessed 15 May 2019].
44 Sianne Ngai, *Ugly Feelings* (Cambridge, MA: Harvard University Press, 2005).
45 Ibid., 17.
46 Price, as quoted in Macarthur, 'Brutalism, Ugliness and the Picturesque Object', 264. See also Macarthur, 'The Butcher's Shop'.
47 Winfried Menninghaus, *Disgust: The Theory and History of a Strong Sensation* (Albany: State University of New York Press, 2003), 39.
48 Ibid., 38.

CHAPTER ONE

Ugliness, the anti-aesthetic and appropriation: With some remarks on the architecture of ARM

John Macarthur

Introduction

In a recent essay on Australian architects ARM Architecture (formerly Ashton Raggatt McDougall), Charles Jencks claimed a critical role for ugliness in architecture.[1] In doing so he cited the famous essay by John Summerson on the ugliness of the buildings of nineteenth-century architect William Butterfield.[2] To praise ugliness as an affront to norms of good taste, as a 'sensuous beastliness', has much the same meaning today as it did when Summerson wrote in the 1940s, or indeed that it had for Butterfield. A claim is made that a certain kind of aesthetic demandingness can challenge and unsettle norms, with the aim of forcing art and architecture to progress and evolve. In architecture the techniques of mal-proportion, incompleteness, pattern overwhelming form, abrupt changes of scale, appropriations of the vernacular and inelegant detailing are pretty much continuous from the Gothic Revival, through Brutalism to postmodernism, to the more critical architecture of today. But the word 'ugly' did not have a place in the postmodernism of the late twentieth century when ugliness, along with beauty and aesthetics as a whole, were under erasure as an uncritical presumption that the essence of human subjectivity could be found in perceptual experience.

This is the time of the 'anti-aesthetic' when Jencks's account of architecture as a popular language, and the journals *Oppositions*' and *Assemblage*'s account of it as a very difficult theoretical one, each assumed that architecture was a matter of meaning, or its impossibility: of critique of architecture's professional autonomy or, alternatively, a claim that architecture's formal autonomy could be a critique of instrumental modernity. Either way it was a turn away from thinking of architecture as something found in sensory experience to a matter of meaning or, rather, semiosis, where architecture transmitted, negotiated and critiqued pre-existing culture. An agonistic attitude to aesthetics was a familiar part of the critical stance of postmodernism, because of the identification of aesthetics with the normalization of modernism under capitalism. The kind of universalization of modernist design principles promulgated by institutions such as New York's Museum of Modern Art, or the United Kingdom's Design Council, opened a space for a critical practice within the arts. Confronting the normalizing program of modernist 'good taste' was no longer just a matter of cliché busting within art and design discourse but could claim a wider politics of confronting the vested interests in the promotion of modernity.

Critical postmodernist practice was an aspect of a wider anti- or post-humanist moment in the humanities academy guided by landmarks such as Louis Althusser's critique of humanist Marxism, Roland Barthes and Jacques Derrida's studies of the construction of subjectivity in texts, and Michel Foucault's historicizing of the forms of governing persons and populations. By the 1980s, to decry something as being ugly was seen as naïveté, a failure to realize the complexities of subject formation. The epithet 'ugly', like beauty, implied that phenomena were experienced at some essential ahistorical level that could be found beneath the social and cultural construction of discourse. Critics of the oppressive regime of essentialism were not interested in ugliness but were instead readers of Hal Foster's highly influential collection *The Anti-Aesthetic: Essays on Postmodern Culture* of 1983.[3] Alongside essays by the well-known figures of Rosalind Krauss, Jurgen Habermas, Jean Baudrillard and Fredric Jameson, it contained subsequently influential essays by younger writers; Douglas Crimp's 'On the Museum's Ruins' and Craig Owen's 'The Discourse of Others: Feminists and Postmodernism'. Foster's introduction, along with Crimp, and Owen's and Krauss' other publications from this period produced a loose concept of the 'anti-aesthetic' that the title had advertised. Architects, like myself, bought the book in part because it also contained Kenneth Frampton's essay 'Towards a Critical Regionalism'.[4] Earnest readers of architectural theory did their best to place architecture in this wide spectrum of postmodern thought where resistance to the architectural hegemony of the metropole was said to be part of a wider critique of the instrumentalization of the enlightenment, and the 'otherness' of non-metropolitan architecture could be read as the end of a normative culture of modernism. How these typical themes of architectural postmodernism were related to institutional critique in the visual arts and the 'othering' of women artists, and were against 'aesthetics', was harder to interpret at the time. With some historical distance it is indeed surprising that anyone thought that critical regionalism was anti-aesthetic.

An anti-aesthetic artist or architect was nevertheless producing things that would once have been called ugly. And the comportment of those who employed these techniques has much in common with Aristotle's description of the power of the artist to take something ugly and render it pleasing or in post-Romantic terms 'interesting' in representation.[5] But there are also crucial differences, which unfold from the question of whether art can also be ugly. The ugly is the antonym of natural beauty, but it is also the base material that can be transformed by art and which then distinguishes the beauties of art and nature. Ugliness' difference with beauty starts to come undone in the trichotomy of beauty and ugliness in nature, and an exclusively beautiful art. If we introduce a fourth term, a kind of artistic ugliness, an anti-aesthetic, then a complex matrix opens.

In a common-sense understanding, 'anti-aesthetic' might be a true scepticism about the existence of a faculty of aesthetic judgement; in the politics of culture it might be an attempt to raise the value of 'meaning' and discursive construction over the sensory; or, third, it could be a negative aesthetics where the previous possibilities are enacted as ploys and feints in a fundamentally aesthetic understanding of the affectivity of the ugly. All these are in fact at play in the late twentieth century and this chapter will attempt to distinguish them as concepts as well as the fact that they have been confused and overlaid, a confusion not resolved in the current return to respectability of 'aesthetics'. A main task in disentangling ugliness and the anti-aesthetic is to do with the relation of the discourses of architecture and the visual arts in postmodernism; and here also lies the critical potential of re-entangling these terms today. In what follows I claim that the artistic strategy of appropriation adds a further dimension, a new problematic to the other issues of a negative aesthetics and the refusal of aesthetics per se. As historical understanding of postmodernism grows we should also understand that ugliness today has no choice but to admit that, while Butterfield might be an ancestor, it is the child of the anti-aesthetic.

Anti-aesthetic in the visual arts

While 'the anti-aesthetic' is not a thing well known in architecture, it is a moderately well-defined term of visual arts discourse. In the introductory essay to the book of that name Foster writes:

> 'Anti-aesthetic' is the sign not of a modern nihilism – which so often transgressed the law only to confirm it – but rather of a critique which

destructures the order of representations in order to reinscribe them. 'Anti-aesthetic' also signals that the very notion of the aesthetic, its network of ideas, is in question here: the idea that aesthetic experience exists apart, without 'purpose', all but beyond history, or that art can effect a world at once (inter)subjective, concrete and universal ... More locally, 'anti-aesthetic' also signals a practice, cross-disciplinary in nature, that is sensitive to cultural forms engaged in a politic.[6]

In a slightly earlier publication, Owens described what distinguished postmodern practice: 'Appropriation, site specificity, impermanence, accumulation, discursivity, hybridization – these diverse strategies characterize much of the art of the present and distinguish it from its modernist predecessors.'[7] Such art was political, either explicitly so by attacking dominant ideologies or implicitly in rejecting modernist claims to art's autonomy. The affirmation of culture was seen as hiding social distortions and the idea of the subject experiencing their own putative autonomy in aesthetic judgement as a privileging of the bourgeois subject. Foster has recently described what he, Owens, Crimp and other younger writers associated with the journal *October* were against in their 'anti-aesthetics'.

What bothered us about aesthetic discourse à la Kant was this: ... it did seem to be a space of mediation, but one that was concerned above all with reconciliation – of judgments of fact and judgments of value, in the first instance, but soon enough of other kinds of conflicts and contradictions, too. That's what bothered us: we construed the aesthetic as a space of resolution – of subjective integration and social consensus – and we wanted to question this conciliatory dimension. Certainly the art practices that had come to interest us were pledged against this kind of reconciliation.[8]

For Foster et al. 'the aesthetic' so described was implicit in Clement Greenberg's ideas of art's autonomy lying in the specificity of its medium, the telos of which was the formalism of post-war American abstract painting. Here the proposition of a judgement of sensory experience implied a set of formal qualities – of purity, object-coherence, autonomy from setting and a primary address to the visual sense – that were the opposite of Owen's description of the qualities of postmodern visual art. A formal, visual modernism founded on invariable aesthetic sensibilities was challenged by a discursive, politically engaged art of the postmodern that rejected modernism's claims to an authority found in aesthetics.

While 'anti-aesthetic' is an apt description of the unpleasing aspects of much international avant-gardism, in the terms of the opposition described earlier, it is largely an artefact of American academic debates that swirled around the journal *October* in the 1980s and 1990s.[9] It is the concept of an anti-aesthetic from the *October* circle that has had substantial, wide and long-lasting effects. As James Elkins has described more recently, the opposition passed from its brief life in theory and criticism into being a term of art practice that

> divides art instruction around the world. Every department of art, every academy, every art school of sufficient size, from Chongqing to Bogotá, from Vancouver to Ljubljana, has some classes, studios, and departments that are mainly dedicated to political and identity issues, and others where students attend to techniques and media. The division runs deep, and permeates the world of art instruction.[10]

Elkins wrote this in the introduction to a seminar published as the book *Beyond the Aesthetic and Anti-Aesthetic* in 2013. In this seminar Foster discusses his original book with a number of interlocutors, which has the effect of historicizing and reinvigorating the term – aiming to return it from being a landmark in the pedagogic territory that Elkins describes to being a usable theoretical term. Why the anti-aesthetic was due for this renovation is partly due to the return to prominence of beauty as a concept and value, again in American art history circles, from the 1990s.[11] Ranging from a classical 'return to order', to a debunking of the theoretical pretensions of discursive art forms, to properly aesthetic attempts to understand the relation of sense and affect, the return of beauty has also occasioned a return of the anti-aesthetic, or at least the critique of beauty it supposed. Alexander Alberro's evocatively entitled essay 'Beauty Knows no Pain' argues forcefully that 'beauty', in the name of a future reconciliation of individual experience with universal values of truth, denies any engagement of artworks with the world as it is.[12] He also points out that 'beauty sells' and that, as much as metaphysics, the art market and the increasing commodification of culture have been responsible for the rise of beauty. Beauty might not be used in quite the same way in architecture, but the rise of palatable neo-modernism is not unconnected to the post-critical turn.

The title of Elkins's seminar suggests a project of going 'beyond' the dichotomous terms of aesthetic and anti-aesthetic in some sublation of their opposition, or deconstruction of their mutual dependence.[13] More direct is James Meyer and Toni Ross's earlier suggestion in 2004 that we might understand 'aesthetics' beyond the beauty question in considering its critical potential.[14] In Ross's subsequent response to Elkins's seminar, she suggests that Jacques Rancière's concept of the politics at stake in changes to sensibility can make this shift.[15] If we followed Rancière in thinking that art can shift the distribution of what can be sensed, the critical function of art lies neither in the values of beauty, or ugliness, nor in opposing these attributions of value in an anti-aesthetics. Rather, the politics of aesthetics lies in shifts in human acuity, in offering new or differently arranged objects or qualities of sense to which such values are attached.

If the above can suffice for a summary of what the anti-aesthetic was, and why it is significant again with the increasing use of beauty and ugliness as descriptors in visual culture, we can now turn to architecture to see where these terms have and have not matched in recent history and current debates.

Ugliness and aesthetics in architecture

Surprisingly, the term 'anti-aesthetic' did not get taken up as an important trope in architecture discourse. Nevertheless, Foster's book circulated among readers of theory in architecture, and Owen's description of strategies of 'appropriation, impermanence, accumulation, discursivity, [and] hybridization' works reasonably well for much architecture of the late twentieth century. But examining these similarities first requires accounting for substantial differences between architecture and the visual arts, which explain why 'anti-aesthetic' does not chime in architecture, despite the inspiration anti-aesthetic art gave to postmodern architecture. What complicates things is the modernism/postmodernism break and what aesthetics has to do with it. Modernism in architecture has a different if intersecting narrative with the modernism of the visual arts, and hence anti-aesthetic did not map from the visual arts onto architecture.

A first confusion is that much of postmodern architecture was anti-aesthetic in the simpler sense of rejecting the idea that any identifiable category of aesthetic experience underlay the vagaries of taste in building. For a whole strand of the architectural profession postmodernism meant architecture at last acknowledging it had no role instructing and educating the public on the form of building but should instead merely reflect popular taste. More sophisticated versions of this idea drew on Pierre Bourdieu's sociological critique of aesthetics and his refusal of Kant's distinction of aesthetic pleasure from simple enjoyment.[16] From such a point of view the anti-aesthetic that concerns us here would be 'aesthetic'.

The second confusion is that those architects who, like Foster et al., saw postmodernism as a positive program to succeed modernism, had a somewhat different target to the visual arts theorists. Thus, an architectural anti-aesthetics would have meant something quite different. The hegemony of modernism in architecture lay in the supposition that it arose from rational structure and the expression of function produced by technological developments. If it was beautiful it was so on account of this truth, not in some Kantian reconciliation of the rational subject with their sensory experience. An aesthetic account of this theory lies in Hegel's aesthetics, which holds that beauty lies not only in artistic creativity but also in the truth of the contents that are given to it to express. Modernist architecture shared the values of purity of form of modernist visual art, and postmodern architects were cousins of Foster et al. – but the aesthetic theory that valorized the formal purity that they both opposed was different.

A separate, culturalist humanist strand of architectural thought, critical of the technocratic instrumentalism of modernism and Hegelian teleology would also stand outside the problematic of the anti-aesthetic. This strand is what Mark Jarzombek has called 'aesthetic experientialism'; a stew of scraps of empathy theory and phenomenology which claims that architecture creates sensory experiences of space that cause affects at such a level of immediacy that architecture might as well be anterior to culture.[17] Though more often described as a 'poetics' or as 'phenomenology' this is aesthetics in the narrow sense of pleasure and displeasure at the richness or paucity of sensory experience without necessarily requiring the moment of judgement where Kant thought we reflected on our sensations and balanced aesthetic ideas with rational concepts. This is an essentialist account of subjectivity, which typically calls on archetypes of building and continuity with pre-modern forms, and which leaves no way to account for cultural difference or historical change except in terms of degrees of recognition of human essentials.[18] Aesthetic experientialism is generally opposed to the constructivist flavour of modernism and is associated with attempts to define an 'other modernism' of humanist values, often associated with Alvar Aalto, among others. This 'aesthetic experientialism' or 'phenomenology' has been a dominant aesthetic theory of architecture for most of the second half of the twentieth century, and, thus in architectural discourse, the closest thinking to aesthetics properly understood was opposed to modernism, not identified with it. In a wider view we can also say that this kind of aesthetic naturalism is opposed to art. Just as a technocratic view of architecture distanced itself from art, the aesthetic experientialist discourse supposed that architecture spoke directly to the aesthetic faculty just as nature does and is thus superior to 'art' with its codes, precedents and competences.

The last difference between architecture and the visual arts around what an 'anti-aesthetic' might mean brings us back to the kind of challenging ugliness that Summerson observed in nineteenth-century neo-Gothic ghastliness, and which Jencks thinks relevant now.[19] This did not develop out of an opposition to beauty but rather in the picturesque, an aesthetic category, one that was typically experienced as mixed with beauty.[20] Significantly, one of the principal picturesque theorists, Uvedale Price, had a theory of ugliness that influenced architecture, particularly in the value given to directness and the distaste with refinement of detail that mid-twentieth-century Brutalists shared with nineteenth-century neo-Goths.[21]

Price held that certain ugly and distorted forms could be incorporated into art, and thus showed the power of the artist to transform empirical experience. But he distinguished between ugliness, which he defined as a lumpish lack of form, from distortion, a kind of excessive forming that did not result in whole form, because of breaks, decay or the unruliness and insubordination of parts of the form. Quoting Virgil, Price describes ugliness with the Latin word 'informe'. With this, he means much of what George Bataille meant in his better-known use of the term 'informe', but without the value that the latter put on transgressiveness.[22] For Price it is only objects which combine ugliness and deformity that are beyond the possibility of aestheticization. It is these principles of Price's, originally devised to show how peasants' cottages and ruined abbeys could both be picturesque despite their differing social status, and their being ugly on the one hand and distorted on the other. It is this picturesque ugliness, an added piquancy to beauty that worked through the nineteenth century to the architecture of today.

We now think of the picturesque as naively affecting and distastefully saccharine, but in the early nineteenth century its play with the appropriation of vernacular buildings was seen as a radical affront to good taste. But beyond the associations of poverty and un-learnedness, vernacular buildings also showed the way to concepts of unclosed form observed in the successive additions and varieties of construction material. John Nash and Humphry Repton had proto-functionalist accounts of building form that had nothing to do with rural poverty, and by the 1830s JC Loudon, AWN Pugin and others were able to conceptualize this in writing. The picturesque concept of building form is that the overall three-dimensional form of the building should not be apparent from any one point of view, requiring the viewer to attend to successive visual experiences.

It is important to remember these eighteenth-century origins of architectural ugliness, because they complicate the binary with beauty. Variously thought of as a kind of beauty with differing empirical causes, or, as an aesthetic quality other than beauty that we typically experience as mixed with beauty, picturesqueness does not stand in a binary relation with beauty as does the sublime of Edmund Burke or Kant, nor is it a critique of sensorial pleasures as with the postmodern anti-aesthetic.[23] The picturesque was an attempt to make a sensory account of the varieties of aesthetic pleasure and to invent formal strategies, which, as Heinrich Wölfflin wrote, pitch visual form against object form.[24] In the late eighteenth century, ugliness was barely a pejorative, having none of the meaning of earlier religious values in representing evil or corruption, nor the transgressive colour that romantics and avant-gardists gave to disgust and abjection.[25] Ugliness was just useful information about sensory experience that could be shared and compared in forming a standard of taste. But by the time of Butterfield and Ruskin, influenced by romanticism, this play of disconnectedness between perception and cognition of building form had become a positive discordance carried in the building surface with the applied patterning of polychrome brickwork, and a positive denigration of any closure of building form.[26]

Nineteenth-century architects were self-aware about an aesthetics of the ugly that derived from the picturesque as we can read in Robert Kerr's warning against it, in *The English Gentleman's House* of 1864.

> There has been growing up an incredible worship of the Ugly. ... Chiefly on account of the preposterous practice of counterfeit with which the Classicism of the last generation of architects is so much identified ... and also to some extent on account of that prevailing feebleness which came to be the ultimate destiny of their borrowed refinement, certain it is that reaction that has taken the form of those qualities which are the readiest reverse of such deceptiveness and imbecility. Hence the introduction of a love for undisguised honesty in the first place, however crude, – and, in the second, for masculine simplicity, however unrefined; for unaffected construction, in other words, and unaffected form, both in their extremes; for Gothic models, therefore, because, however rough-and-ready, they are truthful and sincere, – and for the Ugly, because, however odd, it has at least not the weakness of being feminine.[27]

Kerr adds a note to this discussion in which he satirizes the earnestness of a young architect who we might take to be a pupil of Butterfield. The architect rails against the elegance required by popular taste:

> I don't know so much about that elegance; I rather think I should object to it. You may laugh; but I confess I like a thing to be ugly! I do indeed; now and then I like to see a thing downright ugly! This elegance of yours is all very well, but I call it feebleness. You don't see it in nature. I like a building to stand up; with a sort of – 'what shall I call it?'; – Let us say brusquerie – a contempt! of fastidiousness.

Edwardian philosopher Bernard Bosanquet – an admiring reader of Ruskin – argued that aesthetic ugliness, such as that praised by Kerr's young architect, was in fact a kind of beauty. Bosanquet, one of the principal British Hegelians, and translator of Hegel's lectures on aesthetics, followed Bernardo Croce's idea that aesthetics lay in affective responses to artistic expressiveness. Bosanquet argued that much that we would call ugly expressed nothing and could not be aesthetic, so the phenomenon of a taste for ugliness must be explained otherwise.[28] Bosanquet argued that this was a matter of aesthetic difficulty. When Kerr's young architect complains about elegance, this would be in Bosanquet's terms 'easy beauty'. This is not necessarily a pejorative term for Bosanquet; facile or easy beauty is beauty just the same, but it does not require the kind of aesthetic education and concentration needed to appreciate difficult beauty. Nevertheless Bosanquet is, ultimately, arguing against a facile concept of beauty.[29] In this respect Bosanquet's argument is like that of Ruskin's distinction of a higher, noble picturesque over easy sensuous pleasures. Bosanquet argues that the term ugly, when used aesthetically, describes the failure of the imagination of some observers to cope with the level of difficulty involved. Difficulty he finds falls into three classes of intricacy, tension and width. Tension refers to the level of concentration and commitment to the aesthetic experience of difficult subjects, typically tragedy. Intricacy, or elaborations of form at a minor scales, was commonly thought to be one of the empirical causes of picturesqueness. 'Width', however, is closer to the core of Price's idea of the picturesque. Bosanquet's difficult 'width', like Price's picturesque, is a matter of the tragi-comic (both refer to Shakespeare). In Bosanquet's theory this difficulty is a test of the aesthetic subject's ability to experience the banal alongside high themes; he even makes a case for formlessness being a kind of difficult beauty.[30] Thus, ugliness, particularly in art, was held to be a more challenging form of beauty. The only true ugliness, Bosanquet argues, is failed attempts at beauty in art; there is no ugliness in nature, only in insincere and affected art.[31]

Bosanquet's attempt to explain away ugliness as difficult beauty has had little uptake in philosophical aesthetics, but the antinomy of the facile and the difficult has been greatly influential in cultural practice. Bosanquet had, in retrospect, given terms to what made the savage and changeful comportment of Butterfield's buildings different to the empirical distaste of Hume or Price. His implicit critique of facile beauty becomes programmatic in architectural Brutalism, as discussed by Timothy Rohan in this volume. When, in his seminal 1955 essay Reyner Banham connects Brutalism with *arte povera* and *tachism*, we have something like an anti-aesthetic in architecture, but one that Banham was to decry in his book on the topic a decade later, and which in a subsequent essay he identified as the 'revenge of the picturesque'.[32] There is one more step in this cartoon of a history of architectural ugliness, and it has to do with postmodernism and particularly the practice of appropriation.

ARM and appropriation

The cultural logic of making 'ugly' buildings, such as those of Neutelings Riedijk, ARM, MVRDV, Lyons or FAT, and numerous others is, then, clear enough: such buildings oppose beauty, or, more specifically, facile beauty. Even though the word 'beauty' is rare in architecture today, it is clear that ugliness aims to jab a pin in the idea that sensory pleasure at building crosses place, culture and time, and that such pleasure is unmediated by precedent. However, described this way there is little difference between ugliness now and that of the nineteenth century, between Butterfield's All Saints Margaret Street and MVRDV's Rotterdam Markthal, or ARM's Geelong Library. Butterfield's 'coltish negligence' and 'agonies of discord' lay in the Gothic revival's critique of the slavish rule following of classicism, just as its medievalist references were a critique of the mercantile capitalism of the time. Such buildings might be more simply described by Bosanquet's 'difficult beauty'.

However, it is also the case that the ugliness of some, better, contemporary architecture, such as that of ARM, opposes a 'reconciled' architecture,

FIGURE 1.1 *Ashton Raggett McDougall (ARM)'s design of a black Villa Savoye for Australian Institute of Aboriginal and Torres Strait Islander Studies (AIATSIS), 2001. Photograph by John Gollings.*

and in that it has much common with the anti-aesthetic of the visual arts. It does this by refusing the idea that architecture could have an agreed social licence where its rules and principles fold neatly into the economy of land and building, and that, consequent on this, the experience of architecture rises above the interests and conflicts in which buildings are made. If we return to Owen's list of the strategies of postmodern art, 'appropriation, site specificity, impermanence, accumulation, discursivity, hybridization',[33] all of these have precedents in nineteenth-century architecture, but understanding one of these in more detail, 'appropriation', and the kind of theft and misplacement that this involves, can take us beyond picturesque ugliness into a fuller account of a contemporary architectural anti-aesthetic.

Nineteenth-century architects made explicit borrowings from Gothic, Tudor and vernacular forms that were intended to be recognized as such, but this is something different from the 'appropriation art' that Owens is referring to. ARM is well known for incorporating references and representations of famous buildings, and the everyday into their work. From the black version of the Villa Savoye (Figure 1.1) forming a facade of the Aboriginal and Torres Strait Islander Studies Institute in Canberra, to the Melbourne Recital Hall taking its form from the Styrofoam packaging of a laptop computer, to Finlandia Hall making up an internal street at St Kilda Town Hall (Figure 1.2), to the McDonald's yellow arches appearing on their public housing refit, ARM's appropriations are not licences claimed and then granted from an honoured common culture. As founding partner Ian McDougall has recently reflected on the firm's beginnings:

FIGURE 1.2 *ARM, St Kilda Town Hall interior (1994). Photo courtesy of ARM Architecture.*

It was also the start of that tendency where everyone was photocopying everybody else's images. You know, paintings and whatever, the start of that thing, saying, 'hey, wait a minute, you've just, you're supposed to get copyright release to use those famous images, to publish them.' And people would just go ahead, appropriating imagery. We had something of this attitude to the international canon. It was an attempt to create a language not by formal replication, but by working within a cultural framework that was shared, but also disrespected. It was almost like play acting within the agreed cultural structures and seeing what they revealed from our own mongrel upbringing in Australia. ... Our work is displaced from THERE; it is always an EXOTICA or a COPY – or both.[34]

Again in retrospect, McDougall reflected:

You know there is some nervous giggling when you discuss the issue of the copy. But the proposition of the copy as an artistic and intellectual act is incredibly complicated, about what constitutes a copy, what's the origin of it, historical precedents all that sort of stuff. People say 'oh, that's just a copy.'

Howard Raggatt continued this reflection:

And a beautiful form of the copy is the translation, with jokes and cultural implications and all of that's written in one book in one language; you transfer it to another language and people think that they are reading some German existentialist, *nicht wahr?*[35]

A certain rambunctious nationalism is a part of ARM's strategy of appropriation. A celebration of the fact that Australian cars were copies of American cars, and that the Parliaments and banks were copies from the classical canon, meant a freedom from the typical Australian yearning for cultural validation. Similarly, realizing that applying Aldo Rossi's concept of urban memory meant acknowledging that Australian colonial cities were themselves copies of European cities made for a different urbanism, one that need not fall into the claims of authenticity made for the historical European city, or for a critical regionalism.

Appropriation is not simple theft; it opens wider issues of meaning and property, and in the case of ARM, appropriation is frequently in the mode of the revenge of a subaltern culture. At the base of the concept of appropriation property rights are being violated or ignored, with insufficient respect given in the taking or the new use. The firm's unbuilt project for the Australian Centre for Education Research at Monash University (*c.*1989) collaged together Le Corbusier's Villa Savoye with Phillip Johnson's Glass House, Aldo Rossi's Modena Cemetery and a section of Ronaldo Giurgola's Australian Parliament. Howard Raggatt wrote of the project:

> The strategy explored is to exaggerate quotation and influence to the point of default. Like a new text made up, not of poignant or esoteric quotations ... but instead of quotations, texts taken whole, torn out slabs and added chapters from elsewhere but also rewritten originals and new bits in between to suit. And operating just as happily with cringing servility or whole hearted homage as with self-conscious taunting, or infantile gestures of defiance.[36]

ARM's practice grew out of strategies of collage already well established in architecture which was geared up by the wider availability of photocopiers and the arrival of digital design in the 1980s, and with that a 'new ease and irresponsibility in copy and paste'.[37] ARM most often call this aspect of their strategy 'copying'. It is common in architectural discourse to also call it, 'referencing', 'sampling' or 'pastiche'. I am consistently returning to the term 'appropriation' because of the etymology of the word in 'proper' and 'property', both which concepts are targets of ARM's critique, and which show the wider importance of this issue in architecture.[38] Appropriation is the action of taking property to one's self, the implication being that, prior to the act, that the thing was not one's property. Appropriation is, thus, unlike the polite neutrality of 'referring', always a question of whether the taking is 'proper', or theft. While the immediate issue here is cultural property, there is no edge or boundary that stops this issue of cultural propriety opening out onto 'real property', the condition of building. More specifically, I am arguing that this kind of cultural violence in architecture drew in part of the valency of the word appropriation in the visual arts and more broadly in postmodernism.

In his commentary on his 1982 'copy' of Adolf Loos's House for Tristan Tzara (Grosvenor Street House, South Yarra), McDougall references Sherry Levine, the artist around whom the aesthetic category of appropriation arose.

> We were always interested in mass media, pop iconography and the blurring of media's strategies into art, anathema to the cult of original genius. Like Sherry Levine, we were looking for strategies that challenged the self-importance of the creative superman.[39]

Appropriation strategies in both architecture and the visual arts arise out of the longer history of collage. Collage is affecting by creating a weak totality of form, which is at risk of imploding as the collaged materials continue to reference their original state. But this is a contract, however tense, between material that is available, typically the detritus of everyday life and a present task in art. This contract is rewritten by artists of the late 1970s and 1980s such as Sherry Levine and Richard Prince and other artists working in the lineage of Marcel Duchamp's ready-mades, who appropriated images whole or in great chunks, and images, that in Levine's case, already have the status of art.

In exhibiting a photograph of Weston's famous photograph of his son Neil, copied not from the original but from an exhibition poster, Levine asks fundamental questions of authorship, the patrimony of Western art going back to the trope of male beauty in classical times, copyright law and what drives us to see an image. Douglas Crimp, who curated the exhibition that showed this work, and was first to conceptualize this appropriative practice, unfolds the problem thus:

> Levine has said that, when she showed her photographs to a friend, he remarked that they only made him want to see the original. 'Of course,' she replied, 'and the originals make you want to see the little boy, but when you see the boy, the art is gone.' For the desire that is initiated by that representation does not come to closure around that little boy, is not at all satisfied by him. The desire of representation exists only in so far as it will never be fulfilled, insofar as the original must always be deferred. It is only in the absence of the original that representation may take place.[40]

ARM's practice of explicit copying and distortion is notorious in Australia, and is frequently taken to be a humorous debunking of the architectural canon and a joke played on ill-informed clients. But it also draws on the seriousness with which Levine, Crimp, Rosalind Krauss and others understood the linguistic turn in the language of images and problems of understanding a work, or a culture as a whole, through a concept of origin. When in 1994 at St Kilda Town Hall, ARM rebuilt sections of Aalto's Finlandia Hall in such a way that it produced an anamorphic image of an onion dome, or built a version of the Vana Venturi house that had been stretched on a photocopier, they practice all the irony, death-of-the-author rhetoric of postmodernism, and a critique of origin like that of Levine. But, importantly, the historical trajectory of the things appropriated is in no way subordinated to a present task, we could say that the success of such works lies in Aalto and Venturi not knowing that they formed the flash of a constellation in Melbourne. Appropriation in this sense does not honour a context so much as eat it up. Rather than name a place and set of precedents as proper to a work and reduce their difference to an identity, however momentary, the appropriative strategy of postmodernist architects 'others' the appropriated works, producing alterity out of the familiarity of the canon. The physical fact and the intellectual impossibility of Aalto breeding with Johnson in the project for St Kilda, or Le Corbusier with Daniel Libeskind in the National Museum of Australia, makes a strong critique of architecture's pretension to conceptual coherence.

The results of ARM's appropriative practice are inventive, surprising and possess the unclosed formal qualities of nineteenth-century 'ugliness'. But they are unclosed at another level where appropriation is anti-aesthetic as Craig Owens explained it in 1980:

> Modernist theory presupposes that mimesis, the adequation of an image to a referent, can be bracketed or suspended, and that the art object itself can be substituted (metaphorically) for its referent. This is the rhetorical strategy of self-reference upon which modernism is based, and from Kant onwards it is identified as the source of aesthetic pleasure ... this has become increasingly difficult to maintain. Postmodernism neither brackets nor suspends the referent but works instead to problematize the activity of reference. When the postmodernist work speaks of itself, it is no longer to proclaim autonomy, its self-sufficiency, its transcendence; rather, it is to narrate is own contingency, insufficiency, lack of transcendence.[41]

It is this lack of transcendence, which is something other than abasement, that characterizes ARM's work. Apart from the games of appropriation that we have been following we should also note the striking directness of their semantics. One thinks of the Marion Library spelling out the name Marion on the facade, or the red-stained shell craters at the Melbourne's Shrine of Remembrance for its war dead. But these blunt messages combined with a ruthless appropriation of the high canon are not intended to be lacking in refinement merely as a lesson to an effete architectural culture. Rather they are something like the breadth of Bosanquet's difficult beauty. As Owens writes, they exist at that moment where we might expect to separate out a direct aesthetic experience from the building, from its use and meaning, its play with architectural codes and precedents, but cannot. For Kant and Friedrich Schiller this moment of the autonomy of the beautiful object is also a personal self-becoming. The mechanism of this putative transcendence lies in forgetting the work's contested patrimony and unresolved values; it lies in the illusion that the building 'knows no pain'. Against such an illusion Raggatt writes that ideas are the ugly ducklings that shit in the nest of architecture, they are what acts against the building being finished on time, on budget and with a resolution of form and materials that will allow it to be handed over to sensuous experience.[42]

The ugliness of appropriation

Undoubtedly, as Umberto Eco's anthology *On Ugliness* shows, the past produced many things that we would want to call ugly. But reading this as a history of an idea that transcends time and place suggests an overly familiar story in which ugliness is the proper antonym of a transcendental beauty, a kind of explanation of beauty.[43] From our present encounters with the ugly we can trace a genealogy of ugly things in the past, but this does not mean that there can be coherent history of the adventures of ugliness that culminate in the present.[44] The entanglement of ugliness with the theory of picturesque and neo-Gothic architecture tells us something about why confronting beauty with an anti-aesthetic was not a topic of architectural discourse in the 1980s; but it doesn't tell us how architecture drew on the strategy of appropriation so much identified with the critique of beauty.

Currently there is a renewed interest in aesthetics in art and architecture that can be characterized in the re-emergence of minor aesthetic categories, such as monstrous, dainty, dumpy, gory, picturesque, disgusting, interesting, zany, cute and so on, might each be of use in differentiating formal and affecting qualities of a work.[45] Shorn of any evaluative role each provides an opportunity to unpack the historical circumstances in which they arose. The renewed interest in the ugly as such a predicate is unsurprising. But just as we cannot make a properly historical account of ugliness, neither can it be easily instrumentalized as a critical term – it cannot easily slip onto the list of predicates for describing the aesthetic qualities of artworks.[46] How can ugliness not recall a metaphysics of beauty? And having done so how can it not narrate their dirty romance? Understanding ugliness through its more immediate genealogy in the anti-aesthetic shows us that even where word itself is under erasure, ugliness reintroduces questions of the ontology of art where they are least wanted and most in the way. If, as postmodernists thought, all cultural artefacts are iterations within the cultural field, and there is no beauty or ugliness, then to be affected by the sensuous experience of a building or artwork is an ugly manoeuvre, a form of theft, a taking to one's self of a common property. It is harder, since the anti-aesthetic ploys of appropriation, to think that there could be some beautiful mastery of ugly things or a history that explains some honourable trussle with the ugly that each generation has experienced in their own way. There is no proper place for ugliness, nor any property to be had in it.

Notes

Research for this chapter was funded in part by the Australian Research Council Discovery Project. DP160101569.

1 Charles Jencks, 'ARM at Risk: The Historical Context' in *Mongrel Rapture: The Architecture of Ashton Raggatt McDougall*, ed. Mark Raggatt and Maitiü Ward (Melbourne: Uro Publications, 2015), 1313–18. Jencks also mentions ARM in Charles Jencks, *The Story of Postmodernism: Five Decades of the Ironic, Iconic and Critical in Architecture* (Chichester: John Wiley, 2012), 215.

2 John Summerson, 'William Butterfield: Or, the Glory of Ugliness' in *Heavenly Mansions: And Other Essays on Architecture* (London: Cresset, 1949), 159–76.

3 Hal Foster, *The Anti-Aesthetic: Essays on Postmodern Culture* (Washington, DC: Bay Press, 1983).

4 This was the more theoretical formulation of the idea that Frampton also published as 'Prospects for a Critical Regionalism', *Perspecta*, 20 (1983): 147–62.

5 Aristotle, *Aristotle Poetics* (Ann Arbor: University of Michigan Press, 1970), 48b12-19, 20.

6 Foster, *The Anti-Aesthetic*, xv.

7 Craig Owens, 'The Allegorical Impulse: Toward a Theory of Postmodernism', *October* 12 (1980): 67–86. Craig Owens, 'The Allegorical Impulse: Toward a Theory of Postmodernism Part 2', *October* 13 (1980): 58–80. Quotation from Part 2, 75.

8 James Elkins, ed., *Beyond the Aesthetic and Anti-Aesthetic* (University Park: Penn State University Press, 2013), 26.

9 To an extent they happened in a territory established by Rosalind Krauss and Michael Fried's differing views on what an art historical account of modernism told contemporary practitioners. Cf. David Raskin, 'The Dogma of Conviction', in *Rediscovering Aesthetics: Transdisciplinary Voices from Art History, Philosophy, and Art Practice*, ed. Francis Halsall, Julia Jansen and Tony O'Connor (Stanford, CA: Stanford University Press, 2009), 66–74.

10 Elkins, *Beyond the Aesthetic and Anti-Aesthetic*, 2.

11 See, for instance, Arthur C. Danto, *The Abuse of Beauty: Aesthetics and the Concept of Art* (Chicago, IL: Open Court, 2003). Umberto Eco, ed., *History of Beauty* (New York: Rizzoli, 2004). Dave Hickey, *The Invisible Dragon: Essays*

on Beauty (Chicago, IL: University of Chicago Press, 2009). Elaine Scarry, *On Beauty and Being Just* (Princeton, NJ: Princeton University Press, 2001). We could also speculate that such reflections are caused by the 'post-theory' turn in the humanities where speculative theory has been replaced by the history of such speculations.

12 Alexander Alberro, 'Beauty Knows No Pain', *Art Journal* 63, no. 3 (2004): 36–43.

13 Elkins, *Beyond the Aesthetic and Anti-Aesthetic*, 16.

14 James Meyer and Toni Ross, 'Aesthetic/Anti-Aesthetic: An Introduction', *Art Journal* 63, no. 2 (2004): 20–3.

15 Toni Ross, 'The Elusive "Beyond" of the Aesthetic and Anti-Aesthetic' in *Beyond the Aesthetic and the Anti-Aesthetic*, ed. James Elkins (University Park: Penn State University Press, 2013), 159–63.

16 Pierre Bourdieu, *Distinction: A Social Critique of the Judgement of Taste* (Cambridge, MA: Harvard University Press, 1984).

17 Mark Jarzombek, 'De-Scribing the Language of Looking: Wölfflin and the History of Aesthetic Experientialism', *Assemblage*, 23 (1994): 29–69. Mark Jarzombek, *The Psychologizing of Modernity: Art, Architecture, and History* (Cambridge: Cambridge University Press, 2000). Also see Jorge Otero-Pailos, *Architecture's Historical Turn: Phenomenology and the Rise of the Postmodern* (Minneapolis: University of Minnesota Press, 2010).

18 Issue 42 of the journal *Log* (2018) entitled 'Disorienting Phenomenology' is an interesting attempt at a critical appraisal and tentative resurrection of this strand of architectural theory, one that would not assume a universalized subject and which would take proper account of Husserl and Merleau-Ponty's complex understanding of perception and cognition.

19 Charles Jencks, 'What Is Radical Post-Modernism?', *Architectural Design* 81, no. 5 (2011): 14–17; Jencks, *Story of Postmodernism*.

20 I use the word 'minor' advisedly in this context and have only the space to allude to the discussion of arguments for more descriptive aesthetic predicates, that might undo some of metaphysical claims that seem inseparable from beauty. For example, Arthur Danto's interest in the 'dainty' and the 'dumpy'; or Sianne Ngai's in the zany, cute and interesting, Sianne Ngai, *Our Aesthetic Categories: Zany, Cute, Interesting* (Cambridge, MA: Harvard University Press, 2012).

21 Uvedale Price, *Essays on the Picturesque: As Compared with the Sublime and the Beautiful and On the Use of Studying Pictures for the Purpose of Improving Real Landscape*. 3 vols. (London: J. Mawman, 1810). On this aspect of the picturesque, see my John Macarthur, *The Picturesque: Architecture, Disgust and Other Irregularities* (London: Routledge, 2007).

22 Price quotes Virgil's description of Cyclopes as 'Monstrum horrendum, informe, ingens, cui lumen ademptum', Virgil and R. D. Williams, *The Aeneid* (Basingstoke: Macmillan, 1972), 111, 658; Georges Bataille, 'Formless' in *Visions of Excess: Selected Writings, 1927–1939*, ed. Allan Stoekl (Minneapolis: University of Minnesota Press, 1985), 31.

23 The first is Richard Payne Knight's theory, the second, Uvedale Price.

24 Heinrich Wölfflin, *Principles of Art History: The Problem of the Development of Style in Early Modern Art*, edited and with essays by Evonne Levy and Tristan Weddigen, trans. Jonathan Blower (Los Angeles, CA: Getty Research Institute, 2015).

25 This chronology follows Winfried Menninghaus, *Disgust: Theory and History of a Strong Sensation*, trans. Howard Eiland and Joel Golb (Albany: State University of New York Press, 2003).

26 On Ruskin's concepts of surface, see Anuradha Chatterjee, *John Ruskin and the Fabric of Architecture* (London: Routledge, 2018).

27 Robert Kerr, *The English Gentleman's House: Or, How to Plan English Residences, from the Parsonage to the Palace; with Tables of Accommodation and Cost, and a Series of Selected Plans* (London: John Murray, 1864), 383–5.

28 Bernard Bosanquet, *Three Lectures on Aesthetic* (London: Macmillan, 1915); Bernard Bosanquet, 'The Æsthetic Theory of Ugliness', Proceedings of the Aristotelian Society 1, no. 3 (1889–90): 32–48; Dale Jacquette, 'Bosanquet's Concept of Difficult Beauty', *Journal of Aesthetics and Art Criticism* 43, no. 1 (1984): 79–87.

29 Ibid., 112.

30 Using the German term *Unform*. This is again close to Price's notions of the ugly where he describes it 'informe' character, taking the term from Virgil's description of Cyclops.

31 Ibid., 106, 108.

32 Peter Reyner Banham, 'Revenge of the Picturesque: English Architectural Polemics, 1945–1965' in *Concerning Architecture: Essays on Architectural Writers and Writings Presented to Nikolaus Pevsner*, ed. John Summerson (London: Allen Lane, The Penguin Press, 1968), 265–73.

33 Owens, *Allegorical Impulse*, 75.

34 Ian McDougall, 'Culture Mining' in *Italy/Australia: Postmodernism in Translation*, ed. Silvia Micheli and John Macarthur (Melbourne: Uro Publications, 2018), 165.

35 Ian MacDougall and Howard Raggatt in Raggatt and Ward, *Mongrel Rapture*, 706.

36 Howard Raggatt, "Fringe de Cringe" (RMIT Master of Architecture by Project, 1993) reproduced in Raggatt and Ward, *Mongrel Rapture*, 222–80, 225.

37 McDougall, *Culture Mining*, 165.

38 Also see my John Macarthur, 'Visual Appropriation and Property in the Theory of Humphry Repton' in *The Geography of Law: Landscape, Identity and Regulation*, ed. William Taylor (Oxford: Hart, 2006), 49–64.

39 Ian McDougall, in Raggatt and Ward, *Mongrel Rapture*, 42.

40 Douglas Crimp, 'The Photographic Activity of Postmodernism', *October* 15 (1980): 91–101, 98.

41 Craig Owens, 'The Allegorical Impulse: Toward a Theory of Postmodernism Part 2', *October* 13 (1980): 58–80, 79–80.

42 Howard Raggatt, 'IP' in Raggatt and Ward, *Mongrel Rapture,* 360–1.
43 Umberto Eco, ed., *History of Beauty* (New York: Rizzoli, 2004). Umberto Eco, ed., *On Ugliness* (New York: Rizzoli, 2007).
44 More precise studies of monstrosity and the grotesque in the early modern period show a particular, differentiated history of what we might still want to call, in retrospect, 'ugly'. Mark Dorrian, 'On the Monstrous and the Grotesque', *Word and Image* 16, no. 3 (2000): 310–17; Luke Morgan, 'The Monster in the Garden: The Grotesque, the Gigantic, and the Monstrous in Renaissance Landscape Design', *Studies in the History of Gardens & Designed Landscapes: An International Quarterly* 31, no. 3 (2011): 167–80.
45 See, for instance, the panel discussion of aesthetic predicates in Elkins, *Beyond the Aesthetic and Anti-Aesthetic*, 51–89. Ngai, *Our Aesthetic Categories.* 'Interesting' is as well as its popular use as a descriptor has a complex history in its descent from German Romanticism. See Peter Osborne, *Anywhere or Not at All: Philosophy of Contemporary Art* (London: Verso, 2013). On 'interesting' in architectural andragogy, see Mark Dorrian, 'What's Interesting? On the Ascendency of an Evaluative Term', *Architecture and Culture* 4, no. 2 (2016): 173–84.
46 Mark Cousins in his influential seminar at the Architectural Association and later publications made a psychoanalytical account of the ugly, which would explain the difficulties in instrumentalizing ugliness. Cousins links ugliness to death, that is, the conscious fear of which, and the contradictory subconscious denial of which, then explains the sense in which ugliness is a fundamental misplacement. Cousins's substantive definition of ugliness goes beyond the usual simple deconstruction of the beauty–ugly binary but offers little to those who want to see how that binary, with all its blindness, has driven moments in the fragmented history of ugliness in architecture. Mark Cousins, 'The Ugly [part 3]', *AA Files* no. 30 (1995): 65–8; Mark Cousins, 'The Ugly [part 2]', *AA Files*, no. 29 (1995): 3–6; Mark Cousins, 'The Ugly [part 1]', *AA Files*, no. 28 (1995): 61–4.

CHAPTER TWO

On ugliness (in architecture)
Bart Verschaffel

The aesthetic gaze

In philosophical aesthetics, a branch of knowledge that developed from the Enlightenment onwards, the aesthetic experience is considered to be a natural faculty. It is assumed that the aesthetic approach and the aesthetic gaze are perpetually and universally accessible to all, and that aesthetic judgement is part of the more general workings of our cognitive faculties. It is undeniably true that the appearance of things – form, patterns, colour, luminosity – naturally influences everything that we perceive and experience, feel and do. We are responsive to shapes and can recognize rhythms and colour combinations. This awareness of form can, however, be framed in many different practices and modes of experience. It has no autonomous existence per se as 'the aesthetic experience'. The aesthetic approach implies an appreciation of the initial and immediate appearance of things, whereby the visual aspect of an object is somehow disconnected from its function, value and meaning. Likewise, an aesthetic experience presupposes that an object's immediate appearance is isolated and given independent consideration. This bears an extraordinary, sophisticated and profoundly artificial relationship to reality. The acceptance of such an experience, and even more fundamentally its availability, is far from evident. A society and its culture must, after all, permit and tolerate this abstraction: focusing exclusively on appearances while disregarding an object's value and function often feels inappropriate and can, on occasion, be downright disrespectful or outrageous. An aesthetically abstracting attitude can offend multiple kinds of political, moral or religious engagement with the subject matter. Isolating and appreciating appearances, regardless of their moral value or usefulness, is therefore a cultural and social issue. The concrete manner – the codes and settings – through which a disinterested or dispassionate gaze is made possible and accessible varies. And even when aesthetic detachment is an accepted disposition, it inevitably remains a question of individual attainment. It is also a social or 'class' issue. But none of this precludes a more general discussion of the logic and conditions pertaining to the aesthetic gaze and experience.

The aesthetic experience is one of constant evaluation using terms that are generally positive or negative – in other words, 'pleasant' or 'unpleasant'. Yet we possess an extensive vocabulary that allows us to describe the generically (un)pleasant with greater precision. Appreciating something as beautiful and pronouncing it ugly are but two examples. The choice of the appropriate register seems to depend upon the specificity of both the senses and the object. For example, we do not speak of a beautiful jam but a delicious one; a bouquet can be pretty, but music is neither pretty nor delicious; a sea breeze can be fresh, as can a colour or a face, but we do not speak of fresh furniture; a sound might be soft or harsh but not handsome; we can have a handsome face but not a handsome apple; we speak of a gorgeous light but would not describe a smell or taste in such a way and so on. Appreciating something as beautiful or stating that it is ugly appears to be connected with the senses of isolation and distance, with the auditory and visual, and only exceptionally and fleetingly with the senses of proximity, such as taste and smell.[1]

The aesthetic gaze isolates and evaluates the immediate visual impression that something makes. It is therefore related to, and can be induced by, the specific way in which the object presents itself: the circumstances pertaining to its perceptual presence. It implies that the 'dark' senses of smell, taste and touch are circumvented by physical distance or obstacles, and that perception and attention are channelled towards Riegl's 'pure visuality'. The object of our gaze can be coded as 'spectacle' or 'performance', thus as something enacted or played, which implies that it is somehow unreal or belongs to an alternative reality. It is only intended to be viewed. The apparatus of 'showing' and 'exhibiting' focuses the attention, and both frames and isolates an object, thereby detaching it from the world. This has the effect of neutralizing the engagement that would automatically be engendered through physical proximity. The codes can be communicated, while physical distance can be imposed by a wide range of devices, including shop windows, plinths, dishes, frames or windows, glass plates and viewpoints; or, in the theatre, by the proscenium that separates the audience from the 'unreal' space of the performance. Acts of showing or exhibiting might range from simply pointing at something to baptizing it as 'art'. The most important means of establishing aesthetic distance – so that we are confronted with pure visuality and, at the same time, a form of unreality – is (and always will be) *the image*, or representation by similitude. Both performances and images readily lend themselves to aesthetic appreciation. Anyone who has internalized the aesthetic approach will find themselves able to look at almost anything as they would a performance or picture – just as one can listen to ambient noise as a kind of music. The distance that allows one to see something 'aesthetically' might only belong to *the eye of the beholder*, therefore, and merely be a question of attitude and perspective. One could, in principle, assess anything from an 'aesthetic' perspective. But this form of appreciation would still appear to require a variety of conditions that are not mental but concrete – devices, attitudes of the body, distances. And we also tend to concur that it is both wrong and inappropriate to treat *everything* as an aesthetic object.

On beauty and ugliness (in general)

Beauty and ugliness are neither opposites nor two extremes of a continuum. To say that something is not beautiful does not automatically mean that it is ugly, and to pronounce something as not ugly does not equate to it being beautiful. To declare something beautiful or ugly is to deploy one of two distinct forms of aesthetic appreciation, each one of which similarly privileges and isolates an object, thereby setting it at an aesthetic distance. They are both opposed, therefore, to all that is 'normal'. Aesthetic appreciation, whether positive or negative, is a form of individualization: both appraisals accord the object a status that transcends the ordinary or normal, or the 'not-ugly' and 'not-beautiful'.[2] A beautiful or ugly object differs from the myriad of aesthetically neutral things that sink into the quagmire of ordinariness. The beautiful and the ugly are both *outstanding*, albeit in vastly divergent ways and for opposite reasons. An experience of beauty differs radically from an encounter with ugliness, and the issues at stake are completely different.

The aesthetic experience is orientated towards immediate impressions and presupposes that the act of contemplation detaches an object's appearance from its existence and agency in the world vis-à-vis its origin, meaning, value, function, purpose and so on. Experiencing as beautiful a spring day or a landscape, a melody or a physique, and expressing this perception, implies that one is impressed by the mere appearance or (visual) inexhaustibility of what is seen or heard; any vested interest or intention to profit does not factor into the impression, nor does any comparative assessment against established criteria (such as the idea of perfection or moral considerations). I would argue, however, that this 'disinterested pleasure', as Kant terms it, is structurally associated with another element. This is our amazement that beauty is, in fact, *real*: 'A thing of beauty is improbable – and exists.'[3] Crucially, beauty is always 'new' and exceptional, and therefore unexpected. It takes us by surprise, and this is due to its incomprehensibility and deviation from our expectations of normality. The Kantian 'subjective universality' that characterizes aesthetic judgement thus expresses this claim that something *is*, in fact, genuinely beautiful, that is, that the judgement goes beyond individual preferences or tastes. An experience of beauty is akin to a *broadening of reality*. And because the manifestation of beauty presents a paradox – being both implausible and yet irrefutably real – reality outshines the things we both already know and can imagine. The experience of beauty, therefore, entails far more than a simple delight in appearances: it always involves a revelation or a *discovery*. Beauty functions as an ontological threshold. But the discovery is made through a coincidental, fortunate encounter: one needs to be present at a specific time and place for beauty to be seen or heard. The certainty that beauty actually exists is based purely upon a subjective, personal and unique experience. It privileges both a moment and an individual.[4] Beauty is thus existentially anchored and can mark someone's life. The so-called judgement of beauty, therefore, does not articulate a verifiable opinion as to a state of affairs. Nor does it pretend to any scientific description of reality, which relates to the objective properties of objects. It belongs to a language-game of a completely different order. To judge something as beautiful is to bear *witness:* it is the statement of a universal truth as revealed to one person via a unique and private experience.[5]

Classical aesthetics posited ugliness as a negative principle and examined whether it might dissolve within something beautiful (thus lending beauty a specific 'colouring') and, if it did, by what means this occurred. Twentieth-century philosophical reflections on themes such as the 'formless' and the 'abject', and which are concomitant with developments in modern and contemporary art, have greatly contributed to the insight that ugliness cannot be defined in only negative terms or merely reduced to an absence of beauty. Ugliness is a thing unto itself; it has an independent status.

Beauty triumphs over the ordinary and augments that which already exists. The *Wohlgefallen* (aesthetic pleasure) is coupled with an affirmation of this surprising enrichment of reality. Ugliness, by contrast, is not 'new'. It does not amaze, surprise or transcend the world that we already know. Instead, it cleaves to the 'normal world' and is immediately identifiable. Ugliness is permeated by a primitive resistance or force that predates the known world. It is an unwelcome *revenant*. Enlightenment theories of aesthetics assumed, as they did for beauty, that ugliness is a natural and primary mode of being (for objects) or experience (for humans). Everything was believed to be either beautiful or ugly to a greater or lesser extent, and thus experienced as such, with the many guises of ugliness and beauty individually linked to specific feelings and emotions. Attempts were made to identify and classify the many kinds of ugliness and to correlate them with the responses they engendered. The experience of ugliness, however, is even more specific and quite distinct from that of beauty, because it is – pace what Kant might think – not ugliness as such that elicits rejection or disgust. Aesthetic appreciation – the ability to apprehend something as ugly and give it a name – already involves the processing and mastery of primary emotions and reactions that *precede* the aesthetic. Ugliness is the alarming aesthetic mode of appearance for everything that erupts from below and disrupts the ordinary or normal or, in short, our whole, life-sustaining world. From ugliness there emanates a threat of the monstrous and a risk of contamination by the formless.

Normality is threatened, disturbed or ruptured in two radically different ways: by the monstrous or terrifying – Rosenkranz uses the word *Abform* (deformity) – or by the formless or disgusting, which he called *Ungestalt* (formlessness).[6] Admittedly, one can easily conjure up disgusting monsters. But the monstrous, as such, is not disgusting, and the formless is not, per se, terrible and frightening.

The monstrous is 'a deviation from nature', says Rosenkranz, the fruit of 'an efficient cause that claims omnipotence, a will that strives to compete with nature, and a tortured and dominant matter'.[7] It is therefore 'uncanny',[8] while also proving the fragility of form and the uncertainty of order. The monstrous 'runs against', or is contrary to 'nature', or to put it better, 'against what has been naturalized'.[9] It is the ill-proportioned and deformed, the result of uncontrolled, disorganized genesis, and it engenders and incites capriciousness and excess. It is the advent of chaos. Monsters, as Lucretius described them, are primordial remnants of the original chaos that still lurks beneath the wafer-thin crust of what we call the natural order, or man-made normality. The ultimate example of monstrosity is clearly the deformed human figure (Rosenkranz calls it 'the ugliest ugly').[10] Monstrosity is dangerous. It threatens ruin and destruction, spreads panic, paralyses or petrifies and causes all in its path to flee. The monstrous *graiae* – the triplet sisters of the fearsome gorgons Medusa, Skylla and Echidna – are Horror (Enyo), Terror (Deino) and Destruction (Persis).[11]

Formlessness, on the other hand, is vague, viscous and glutinous, weak, decayed, diseased and rotten, with the most pungent variants being bodily secretions (the abject). One only has to think of Georges Bataille's squashed spider or worm. At its core, says Rosenkranz, is 'Verwesen' (putrefaction), or organic decay: not dying or dead, but 'das Entwerden des schon Toten' (the decomposition of the already dead). The human body reverts to waste or remains. Teeming, nameless, soulless life: 'We are more disgusted and repulsed by the appearance of life in what is already itself dead.'[12] A lack of form transmits negativity; an encounter with the formless is contagious, sticky and contaminating: it attacks the *Gestalt* and identity, provokes revulsion and disgust, makes one recoil and retch; it must be kept at bay. All contact must immediately be remedied by purification, cleansing, disengaging and vomiting, or through (ritual) laughter.[13]

A direct confrontation with the monstrous or the formless invokes archaic and automatic responses that precede every possible form of aestheticization or experience of ugliness: the actual confrontation with a heinous creature, or pus, for example, will never directly inspire a judgement of ugliness or aesthetic appreciation. Rather, they provoke primary reactions and operations that neutralize the imminent threat. All societies develop a culture to deal with these situations. Religions in particular offer many solutions, including myths and a whole host of ceremonies and magical practices, from exorcisms, ritual insults and cursing, to sacrifices, purification or simply 'laughing it off'. It took centuries of arduous effort to wrest theatrical and visual forms of representation from their original religious contexts and, furthermore, to sufficiently divest them of their magical aspects. In so doing, performances and images could be finally put to artistic use – not only as a way of playing with meaning (probably the first and ultimate type of artistic work) but also as a method of isolating appearances and offering them up for aesthetic appreciation. The difficult and profoundly artificial base operation of aestheticization, therefore, does not primarily preclude, contrary to expectation, the finding of beauty in ugliness. What it does imply is that something monstrous or disgusting can successfully be kept at arm's length and subjected to scrutiny, whereupon it becomes innocuous, or *merely ugly*, that is, practically harmless and perhaps even ridiculous. The *sight* of what is effectively monstrous or disgusting therefore becomes, in the worst case, just unpleasant: a lingering emotion associated with the origin of this ugly appearance. Rosenkranz notes that a painting depicting the raising of Lazarus is powerless to convey the human stench of death: the viewer 'is only forced to *think* of the superficial beginning of decay'.[14] Elsewhere, he refers to the fresco of the *Triumph of Death* in the Campo Santo of Pisa, a detail of which depicts a noble hunting party pinching their noses as they ride past a corpse in an open grave: 'We see this well enough, but we do not smell it.'[15] Indeed, to find something hideously ugly already presupposes an aesthetic distance, one that has terminated the primary automatic reactions. The detachment implied by an experience of ugliness, therefore, is much more complicated, ambiguous and tainted than an encounter with beauty. It conceals a greater involvement and deeper significance than is associated with the latter, whereby the engagement presupposes a disinterested contemplation; one that is related to the gift of a life-changing moment and the unexpected discovery that follows.

It is possible that, just as with beauty, the isolation and contemplation of ugliness occurs through *the eye of the beholder*. Yet because the experience of ugliness does not commence with disinterest, but originates from a primary, *pre-aesthetic* involvement, it is much more problematic. A specific disposition of the attention will rarely suffice. Special resources and singular contexts, such as the arts, seem necessary to the successful neutralization and reduction of the impending monstrosity or invading formlessness. Once distilled to a mere image or appearance – reduced to pure visuality and unreality – it can be aesthetically appreciated and deemed (merely) ugly. Here, the effective medium par excellence is undoubtedly 'representation', or the image/likeness. Perhaps the paralysing, lethal or contagious potency of the monstrous and disgusting can never be fully neutralized, but an image can tone it down just enough for it to be viewed. Their powers can be captured and imprisoned when reflected in a picture or performance. This is the *medusa strategy*.

Rationalist and ahistorical aesthetic theories mistakenly interpret the emotions involved in disliking an unpleasant picture as a response (or reaction) to ugliness itself. Our dealings with ugliness – the aesthetic rejection – are always existentially loaded, motivated by other concerns and somewhat archaic. Ugliness can even *fascinate:* something of the ancient and well known, which remains suppressed and concealed, shines through. We know very well that ugliness is about things that we are familiar with but don't want to know about. The aesthetically distant relationship with the ugly always cloaks a specific stance towards the monstrous and/or disgusting. 'The intricate, the contradictory, the amphibious, and therefore even the unnatural, the criminal, the strange, even the mad' is always somehow secretly interesting. We are *implicated.* A hint of obscenity hangs over the ugly.[16] And the reverse might also be true. Rosenkranz was probably right to say that everything phallic, though venerated by religion, is ugly when viewed aesthetically and so cannot be idealized/aestheticized: 'All phallic gods are ugly'.[17] The primordial question is not, therefore, whether something ugly can still be rendered as somehow beautiful. Ugliness, as such, is already the result of the aestheticization of the monstrous or disgusting. But it still lends a frisson to works of art when added in small doses. The different and more primal level at which this engagement occurs is the very reason that its (carefully controlled) appearance in art can be far more gripping and intense than the presence of beauty. The ever-ambiguous satisfaction that one feels at the sight of (a successful artistic representation of) ugliness – such as, for example, in one of the variations of the sublime, or as an ingredient of the picturesque or fantastic – is not derived from the pleasantness of its pure appearance but from the realization that a risky enterprise has succeeded. It is not the appearance, as such, that we admire, but the triumph of the depiction: we are amazed that the hideous-monstrous and/or disgusting – which we would never dare to confront – has been tamed through visualization and can now be viewed with detachment. Artworks can, it would seem, keep the monster in check and produce complex, equivocal experiences in which unease at the sighting of a dangerous enemy is mingled with gratification at its imprisonment and a sense of relief.

Aesthetic objects

Architecture, as with all that we are able to sense or perceive, can also be approached and appreciated in aesthetic terms. And this independently of any other meanings that people might ascribe to a building, or of their expectations that it should, for example, be functional or agreeable. The way in which a building 'sounds' or feels can certainly contribute to a general sense of pleasantness or unpleasantness and, as such, these qualities can be integrated into the architectural experience. Architectural beauty or ugliness, on the other hand, is something that is *seen*. What does it mean to isolate a building's visual appearance and to *contemplate* this initial impression independently of any other considerations, such as the structure's usefulness, function or meaning? What are the consequences for a building that is experienced and judged as being beautiful or ugly? What are the possible conditions for this, and what does it affect?

How buildings or the built environment are *perceived* is a matter of great complexity. The architectural experience is a total experience.[18] Above all else, it is one that compresses and synthesizes multiple sensory impressions and synesthetic connections – sight, sound (acoustics) and touch (sensing the floor beneath one's feet and the relationship between materials), an awareness of air and light, of how a building breathes or smells – into an overall estimation. This results in a *final* opinion, albeit one that has been gradually constructed from varied perspectives, the latter typically gained by following a particular route, and through an accumulation of moments. Usually, the object of this architectural experience is itself a composite object that boasts an interior and exterior, a complex spatiality and its own surroundings. The experience thus demands a 'narrative' (or at least a scenario). Only very exceptionally can it be reduced to a single impression. To a great extent, the architectural experience is also an immersive one: 'We are, we move, we live inside the work of man!'[19] The aesthetic appreciation of an immersive experience is typically made in *sensory terms* (strong, impressive, captivating …). The act of contemplation – a focus on the visual and its appreciation or dismissal as beautiful or ugly – involves both a comparison and distance. It is certainly possible, perhaps even essential, for an architectural work to anticipate the possibility that it will be *viewed* in purely aesthetic terms. This might, for example, be evident because it possesses a face or facade, and itself looks (back), or is constructed using the laws of perspective. It is evident, however, that this self-awareness structurally presupposes that a form of representation – a (design) drawing, film or photograph, or model – literally frames and isolates the visual, privileges certain viewpoints and 'objectifies' the building. Every assessment of beauty implies that a building will somehow – at least in the mind's eye – be depicted or photographed.

All in all, this means that aesthetic appreciation, and *a fortiori* aesthetic judgement, necessitates an adaptation or transformation, and even a *reduction*, of the architectural experience. And furthermore, it suggests that the overall experience or perception of architecture is also itself only one of the factors that determines architectural quality. Should not architecture, in the first place, be well made or durable, usable or comfortable, useful or meaningful? But architecture can indeed be experienced, viewed and appreciated in aesthetic terms.

We are culturally conditioned to view a building as *an aesthetic object*. This implies an expectation that it should be good as well as comfortable, but it should also possess a minimum degree of aesthetic quality.[20] The assumption is, therefore, that a building will have a visual aspect. It is normal and thus *usual* that buildings, like faces and hairstyles, coats and houses, table settings, seats, railway stations, fireworks and stamps, are (also) beautiful to behold. The same cannot be said of machine parts or surgical equipments, nappies, paint pots, garbage bags or a house fire. This does not mean that one cannot look at such things aesthetically, or that is impossible to experience them as beautiful per se. Nevertheless, it would seem inappropriate to judge or experience them in such a manner. The aesthetic assessment of an aesthetic object is not, however, an expression of having experienced beauty. Whether an object 'behaves itself', or in other words, is seen to conform to the norms and expectations associated with a particular *class* of object, is a matter of taste. Knowing that something is generally regarded as an aesthetic object will determine whether or not it can justifiably be considered beautiful or ugly, as will the act of making an aesthetic judgement. But nothing is fixed. One can *know* that something is considered beautiful, can both see and affirm this quality, but without *experiencing* beauty. And one can inappropriately experience something as beautiful or ugly without it being an aesthetic object. When the appropriate, metered attractiveness that is expected of a particular type of object is found wanting – as in architecture, for example – it is then considered banal. The banal or trivial, however, remains correct. The object is not deformed in this case but is regarded as disappointing. It goes without saying that what is considered to be an aesthetic object, and what is seen as aesthetically appropriate in a given time or culture, is constantly shifting and subject to great debate. Are men's hands 'aesthetic objects' and should they be adorned with rings, nail polish or tattoos? Can a chamber pot be beautifully painted? Should public buildings be more opulent than domestic homes? The banal or disappointing, however, remains within the parameters of the *normal*. It is not ugly.

Ugliness in architecture

Can architecture be ugly? Normality is not a natural given. A society must perform intensive and strenuous symbolic work – the continual sorting, separating, fixing, cleaning and restoration of meanings – to construct a precarious normality that is familiar and reassuring. For this, initial appearances must also be 'in order', being *kalos* (full-grown) and *agathos* (non-malodorous), or clean and conforming to type. After all, normality is threatened by the deformed or monstrous, and by the unclean and disgusting. Ugliness – unlike that which is simply devoid of attractiveness and is thus perceived as banal – seems to fulfil an anthropologically ancient function of aesthetic quality: ugliness signals the threatening intrusion of the monstrous or disgusting into the world. It indicates that something is 'wrong'. Can architecture, in this sense, be ugly and *alarming*?

Dozens of websites publish lists of what is thought to be ugly architecture, and these buildings can be subdivided into various categories. In the first place, there are structures so slapdash and lacking in form that they cannot even be called banal. It would appear that these buildings were never considered to be aesthetic objects and, as a result, no thought was ever given to their visual evaluation. Like an unwashed and dishevelled man who strolls down the street in his pyjamas, the ugly building *stands out*. Perhaps the very opposite is also true? A second category includes the buildings that have had too much care lavished upon them and are trying too hard to be beautiful. Exaggerated forms, a riot of colour or an excess of ornamentation can make a building seem kitschy or vulgar. A third group of ugly buildings are the mistakes and failed jokes. These structures form another category: the anthropomorphic facade is given a nose and eyes and looks, quite literally, like a face; a Flemish triple-facade house resembles a Spanish hacienda; a garage is decorated with Doric columns and a fronton; an office building assumes the guise of a machine; a house combines the typology of a medieval donjon with that of a farmhouse and so on. A fourth group mainly suffers from a problem of scale: the building is not the right size and either looks like an enlarged model or a doll's house. The Altar of the Fatherlands (Altare della Patria) is a gigantic typewriter.[21] Another building is a scarecrow or gadget, either too big or too small, ginormous or diminutive, deformed or misshapen. For all these reasons, it is thought to be 'abnormal'. These forms of ugliness – with the exception of dilapidated buildings – are variations on a gentler kind of monstrosity. But looking through the examples of so-called ugly architecture on professional websites, it becomes clear that none of these buildings are *alarmingly* ugly. Ugly buildings are not *Dirty Beasts* but *Big Friendly Giants*.[22] Their ugliness is more ridiculous than it is frightening: 'It is hard to be abominable in the art of architecture.'[23]

Beauty invokes wonder: it is an excess and a quality that transcends everything that we already know of the world. Ugliness, on the other hand, fails to surprise and is recognized. It reminds us of the monstrosity that we thought we'd evaded, or the disgust from which we hoped we'd been saved. To experience beauty, or to judge something as beautiful, is to affirm its existence. An object that is deemed to be ugly loses its raison d'être or, at the very least, there is a sense that it should have been different. The *intrinsic positivity* of architecture makes it impossible for a building to be genuinely and radically ugly in such a way and, as a result, it cannot become the object of an authentic experience of ugliness. After all, architecture is not intended to exist separately from the world or manifest itself as an exceptional, amazing and unexpected apparition. It is supposed to be part of the 'normal world'. Architecture *succeeds* when it is ordinary and commonplace. And the ordinary appears to have the ability to neutralize and absorb much of what the aesthetic eye could find ugly, to make it banal and thus normal. Even the most slipshod, kitschy and failed structure can still be equated (in other and more essential aspects) with a *successful* building. An ugly building also *endures*: it is always a sufficiently robust and usable construction. And when a building effectively fails, its ugliness is the least of the problems. The ugliness of architecture is always incidental and, therefore, never essential.

A second reason why a certain form of architectural ugliness is neither problematic nor alarming but, on the contrary, normal and even appropriate, follows on from the fact that a building, unlike a work of art, continues to labour. When making an effort, a lack of elegance is acceptable. A building is a muscleman and its appearance and beauty are secondary considerations. First, it must demonstrate *firmitas*, character and strength, and only then *venustas*. Classical facades were decorated with ugly *telemons*, *rustica* and Doric columns, all of which supported the lighter superstructure and feminine Corinthian order. The ugliness of Brutalism, with its roughness, lack of civility and absence of intentionality, and which pits an image of the primitive power of materials against the ideality of form, is beautiful in a masculine way.[24] Finally, when a well-made, successful and beautiful building ages and deteriorates, and the architecture does not fail but is merely diminished by time and circumstances, and when design decisions and architectural form are only gradually overruled by nature, this ugliness remains acceptable. Its faded beauty is even found to be picturesque or ruinously beautiful.

The issue of (appropriate) beauty, banality and ugliness is clearly different for private homes and commercial premises than for public and cultural buildings. The upper and lower limits of what is deemed appropriate and normal for the initial appearance of a public building are clearly higher. After all, it must – and especially at first sight – distinguish itself from private architecture and the freely accessible, informal space of daily traffic and work. For this, and almost like a monument, it must stand apart from its surroundings and radiate its presence. To this end, it is appropriate and even necessary for the initial appearance to be aesthetically pleasing. It is worth noting, however, that new public buildings tend to spark a great deal of controversy and resistance. In almost all cases, the debate concerns their outward appearance. Only very rarely do such discussions focus on sustainability, usefulness or cost. In an open letter published in *Le Temps* in 1887, several hundred artists and intellectuals protested against the 'useless and monstrous' tower that Gustave Eiffel was building: 'We come, writers, painters, sculptors, architects, passionate lovers of the beauty of Paris which was until now intact, to protest with all our strength and indignation, in the name of the little-known French taste, in the name of threatened French art and history, against the erection, in the heart of our capital, of the useless and monstrous Eiffel Tower.'[25] James Ensor opposed the new St Peter's Station in Ghent, built for the world exhibition of 1913, and viewed it as an example of architectural degradation. Public buildings – the Eiffel Tower, the Centre Pompidou or the Très Grande Bibliothèque in Paris, or the Palace of Justice by Poelaert and the Koekelberg Basilica in Brussels, the Stadshal in Ghent or the Port House in Antwerp – often spend years being decried as ugly and are frequently given satirical names. But after a while, they are adopted and accepted, and to such an extent that their demolition would provoke an equally loud outcry. This suggests that it is easy to perceive any new large-scale construction project as 'monstrous' and for the very reason that it brutally alters – and thus threatens – the normal and familiar environment.

When architecture somehow – and always relatively innocently – alarms or fails aesthetically, and thus is considered ugly, it evokes the monstrous rather than the disgusting.[26] Authors who write about ugliness in architecture always have variations of the monstrous in mind. John Macarthur, however, also discusses the theme of the disgusting in his work on picturesque architecture. Nevertheless, like Kant and almost the whole tradition of aesthetics, he assumes that ugliness is the source, or cause, of aversion or disgust, while on the contrary, it is precisely the opposite: ugliness contains a form of aestheticization that already neutralizes the monstrous and disgusting. The appreciation of ugly architecture as picturesque or sublime relates almost exclusively to the monstrous-ugly, and not (if at all) to the repulsive-ugly.[27] In any case, it is difficult to build *radically* ugly architecture – that is, architecture that effectively generates an actual 'experience of ugliness'. And it is nigh on impossible to design and build disgusting architecture. One can easily imagine nausea-inducing, dirty and disgusting *places*, contaminated by blood, waste, mucilaginous or turbid moisture, or puke, or filled with a vague cold shadow that lurks in the dark and hides in the depths of the earth. One can invoke troubling or disgusting things by association, by means of organic or anthropomorphic forms or pale colours. But this has nothing to do with disgusting architecture. Repulsive structures (e.g. formless, limp or flaccid, semi-living or half-dead biomorphic buildings) are artistic inventions; they exist only as *paper architecture* or as decor.

Can architecture be beautiful?

If not of ugliness, can architecture be the object of an authentic experience of *beauty*? Can an experience that interrupts life and suspends the everyday, that captures our full attention and confronts us with something absolutely and incomprehensibly extraordinary, be something that is completely improbable but at the same time, and contrary to all expectations, apparently real? Can architecture – like the Socrates of Valéry's *Eupalinos* – not speak but sing? When a building effectively becomes the object of an experience of beauty, and the phrase 'that is beautiful' becomes an *exclamation*, it is no longer about the assessment of an aesthetic object. The architectural work is not then situated alongside, or compared with, its own kind but experienced as an exception. It becomes an example of the kinds of extraordinary, unclassifiable objects – certain paintings, musical passages, landscapes or faces, for example – of which each life certainly holds a small collection. However, given the specificity and structure of the architectural experience, it does not seem easy for architecture to be *outstanding* in this way. What kind of architecture are we talking about, and in which circumstances? Is this what Le Corbusier encountered during his visit to Le Thoronet, or what certain visitors seem to experience when they see, for example, Giotto's Campanile, the Barcelona Pavilion, the villas of Palladio, the Brion Cemetery by Scarpa or the Bruder Klaus Field Chapel by Zumthor?

As a case study of what it means to experience architectural beauty, I would like to quote a passage from a unique document. The *Relazione della fabbrica*, written in 1638 by the Spanish monk-builder Fra Juan di San Buenaventura, is a report about the building of Borromini's church of San Carlo alle Quattro Fontane.[28] The priest notes in Italian-Spanish that the place of worship was immediately greeted with 'great applause' and visitors came from Germany, Flanders, France, Spain, Italy and even India, 'because of the praise they had heard in distant and foreign countries' about 'the splendour, beauty and architecture of the church'. The report continues: 'Every day we see people from these countries who come to visit the church as a result of the praise and glory that has reached them.' Father Juan describes the behaviour of the visitors who 'do nothing but look up and turn around'. He explains that this is because 'all parts of the church accord with each other and the eye is led from one element to another'. The church – a chapel in fact – is a composite unity that captivates the eye. The Fathers watch the church from the gallery and witness how the visitors 'spend a long time looking and cannot stop, they are speechless'. Their eyes were never sated but, on the contrary, the more they looked the more they wanted to see. The visitors would return 'many times, day after day'. The author concludes: 'Why? The longer they looked at the church, the greater their desire to see it more fully.' The sight of the church was said to 'pare che suspende il lor intelletto'. It would seem as though the visitors took leave of their senses.[29]

What the author is describing here is an authentic experience of architectural beauty. These visitors do not assess the correctness of an aesthetic object or gauge the extent to which San Carlino corresponds to what is aesthetically expected of a church, and in which manner. The visitors do not admire a church but architecture – a building reduced to its initial appearance or to pure visuality and, in this case, to a very limited number of images, or views, regardless of the programme or any other meaning. Borromini's San Carlino does indeed lend itself well to an experience of beauty, unlike many or most other buildings and churches: it is a small building and its initial appearance can be summed up in two or three aspects. However, to experience beauty makes one forget the function of the building, which is something that remains inappropriate in religious terms. Eye-catching beauty might perhaps be appropriate and useful for a building belonging to a cult. But what if the experience of beauty makes one forget that one is in a church, and the believer becomes a visitor who no longer prays but admires the architecture? The experience of beauty then has a secularizing effect. The author of the *Relazione*, who is clearly aware of the problem, tries to legitimize the encounter with beauty (and thus beauty itself, and the effort and investment she demands), by interpreting it as a harbinger of the *visio dei*: the inexhaustibility of the experience of beauty and the rapture evoke the coming of heavenly glory.[30] It is a tried and tested argument, but not very credible when the experience of beauty is even divorced from an appreciation of the architecture as such: the chapel here becomes a *case* of '*something* exceptionally beautiful', similar to a painting or a melody.

As a second case study, I cite two texts by Paul Valéry, each of which points in a completely different direction, but both of them indicating a way in which architecture can be a miraculous thing and the object of a late-modern – and therefore somewhat sublime – experience of beauty. In his pseudo-Socratic dialogue *Eupalinos*, Valéry lets the architect confess that he has built the 'elegant chapel' for passers-by only 'as something small, four columns, a very simple style', after 'the particular proportions' of his loved one, a 'souvenir of a clear day in my life'. The harmony experienced by the passer-by is not derived, in the classic Platonic sense, from the eternal, essential forms shining through in the transitory and sensory world, but from a kind of idealization: not of an 'objective' ideal body but the private and uncanny presence of a particular *objet de désir*. The 'inexplicable grace' of the building comes from the latent and infinite desire that it harbours, which 'opens' the object, and gives it a perspective: 'It vaguely awakens a memory that cannot end.'[31] In one of his scattered notes containing aphorisms related to architecture, Valéry generalizes this idea: 'But if an architecture which resembles, in relation to the sense of sight, nothing of man (or else some other harmony, so exact that it is almost as painful as a dissonance) brings you to the brink of tears, this dawning effusion that you feel struggling out of your incomprehensible depths is of an infinite value, for it teaches you that you are sensitive to objects entirely indifferent and useless to your person, to your history, your interests, to all the matters and circumstances that circumscribe you as a mortal.'[32] There is the soft and warm side of the architecture, that of shelter, habitation and domesticity, but there is also the hard and strange side, the side of the constant, the indifferent, the confrontational resistance of stone and natural perfection. In addition to the hint of longing and ambiguity, there is an 'inhuman' core to architecture that – like music – brings distance and infinity inside: 'Architecture and Music make us think of something quite other than themselves; they are in the midst of this world like the monuments of another world; or, if you will, like the examples, disseminated here and there, of a structure and duration that are not those of beings but those of forms and of laws.'[33]

In both cases, experiencing beauty in architecture involves the opening up of a kind of infinity. With San Carlino, it concerns the inexhaustible visual splendour of the architectural object that miraculously exists and does not fit into the ordinary world. In the case of Valéry, it is about the soft, postmodern sublimity of the ambiguous figures of desire and the materiality and resistance that open up to a reality beyond the mortal, one that is liberated from human self-involvement. Burke and Kant were right to believe that while architecture can be correctly beautiful, it will always struggle to evoke infinity or be sublime. Architecture that makes an impression such as San Carlino is indeed rare. Even more exceptionally, architecture can be the object of a beauty experience. But then one will probably learn more about beauty than about architecture. Man can rightly question the relevance of such an experience of beauty to architectural criticism. To quote Diderot:

> 'Sensibility, when it is extreme, is no longer discerning; everything moves it without discrimination. One will tell you coldly: "That is beautiful." The other will be moved, transported, intoxicated ... He will stammer; he will find no expressions which render the state of his soul ... The happiest of the two is undoubtedly the latter. Who is the better to judge? That's another matter.'[34]

Translated from the Dutch by Helen Simpson.

Notes

1 On this problem, see John Dewey, *Art as Experience* (New York: Perigee, 1934), and for a discussion on the so-called ordinary aesthetics, which invokes Dewey's 'pragmatic' aesthetics, see, amongst others, Joseph Kupfer, *Experience as Art: Aesthetics in Everyday Life* (New York: State University of New York Press, 1983). Thomas Leddy, *The Extraordinary in the Ordinary: The Aesthetics of Everyday Life* (Peterborough: Broadview Press, 2012).

2 Karl Rosenkranz, *Ästhetik des Hässlichen* (Stuttgart: Reclam, 2007), 190–203.

3 Translated from the French, from Paul Valéry, *Cahiers, II*, Bibliothèque de la Pléiade (Paris: Gallimard, 1974), 962.

4 Paul Valéry provides a striking description of the intimacy and seclusion associated with an experience of beauty in the section 'London Bridge' in *Tel Quel*, in Paul Valéry, *Oeuvres II*, Bibliothèque de la Pléiade 148 (Paris: Gallimard, 1984), 512–14.

5 This is a recapitulation of the argument that I originally developed in 'Fatale waarheid. Bemerkingen bij het esthetisch oordeel en de schoonheidservaring' (2008), included in the anthology Bart Verschaffel, *De zaak van de kunst: Over kennis, kritiek en schoonheid* (Ghent: A&S Books, 2011), 113–26.

6 Rosenkranz, *Ästhetik des Hässlichen*, 12.

7 Translated from the French, from Gilbert Lascault, *Le monstre dans l'art occidental: Un problème esthétique* (Paris: Klincksieck, 2004), 21, 24–5.

8 Ibid., 24–5.

9   Mark Dorrian, 'On the Monstrous and the Grotesque', *Word and Image* 16, no.3 (2000): 310–16, 310.
10 Translated from the German, from Rosenkranz, *Ästhetik des Hässlichen*, 12.
11 For the literature on the monstrous, see, in addition to Lascault (with extensive bibliography), David Leeming, *Medusa in the Mirror of Time* (London: Reaktion Books, 2013), and Jean Clair, *Medusa: Contribution à une anthropologie des arts du visuel* (Paris: Gallimard, 1989).
12 Translated from the German, from Rosenkranz, *Ästhetik des Hässlichen*, 294.
13 The writings of Georges Bataille were essential to the introduction of the formless (and disgusting) as a theme in art and art theory. He, in turn, drew upon anthropological studies of primitive religions and rituals, especially on the subject of 'purity' (Mary Douglas, Emile Durkheim, Mircea Eliade, Roger Caillois). The most important overview and first conceptualization of the artistic use of 'formless', before it became concentrated upon the physical and abject, is the exhibition catalogue: Yve-Alain Bois and Rosalind Krauss, eds, *L'informe: Mode d'emploi* (Paris: Centre Pompidou, 1996); Yve-Alain Bois and Rosalind Krauss, eds, *Formless: A Users Guide* (New York: Zone Books, 1997). The couple of pages that Rosenkranz dedicated to the subject are certainly *grundlegend* (fundamental); about 'Das Ekelhafte' (The Disgusting) see Rosenkranz, *Ästhetik des Hässlichen*, 293–303. A recent survey is Winfried Menninghaus, *Ekel: Theorie und Geschichte einer starken Empfindung* (Frankfurt am Main: Suhrkamp, 2011).
14 My emphasis, translated from the German, from Rosenkranz, *Ästhetik des Hässlichen*, 297.
15 Translated from the German, from Rosenkranz, *Ästhetik des Hässlichen*, 295.
16 Rosenkranz, *Ästhetik des Hässlichen*, 104.
17 Rosenkranz, *Ästhetik des Hässlichen*, 223.
18 It is difficult to find serious and focused texts on this subject. In addition to Valéry's essential *Eupalinos ou L'architecte*, there is Peter Zumthor, *Atmospheres: Architectural Environments, Surrounding Objects* (Basel: Birkhäuser, 2006). Another useful work is Tonino Griffero, *Atmospheres: Aesthetics of Emotional Spaces* (London: Routledge, 2014).
19 'Eupalinos ou l'architecte', in Valéry, *Oeuvres II*, 101.
20 Roger Scruton has defended the idea that art may have the right to bruise and provoke people but that architecture must be mannered and do what is expected of it. Cf. Roger Scruton, *The Classical Vernacular: Architectural Principles in an Age of Nihilism* (New York: St Martin's Press, 1994). In the same vein, Christian Illies and Nicholas Ray recently argued that since man needs beauty and nobody can avoid architecture, architecture is morally obliged to provide accessible beauty: Nicholas Ray, 'An Aesthetic Deontology: Accessible Beauty as a Fundamental Obligation of Architecture', *Architecture Philosophy* 2, no. 1 (2016): 63–82.
21 For a discussion of the monstrous *Altare delle Patria* in Rome, see Terry Kirk, 'Monumental Monstrosity, Monstrous Monumentality', *Perspecta* 40 (2008): 6–15.

22 On 'friendly monsters', see also the contribution by Caroline O'Donnell in this volume.
23 Translated from the German, from Rosenkranz, *Ästhetik des Hässlichen*, 52.
24 See John Macarthur, 'Brutalism, Ugliness and the Picturesque Object' in *Formulation Fabrication: The Architecture of History: Proceedings of the Seventeenth Annual Conference of the Society of Architectural Historians* (Wellington: SAHANZ, 2000), 259–66.
25 Translated from French, from Jean-Louis-Ernest Meissonier, et al., 'Protestation des artistes contre la tour de M. Eiffel', *Le Temps*, 14 February 1887.
26 For a rare example of the disgusting turned beautiful, see Paul Valéry's story about the fascinating beauty of the colours of fish innards floating in the sea, in 'Inspirations méditerranéennes', in his 'Essais quasi politiques', *Oeuvres I*, Bibliothèque de la Pléiade (Paris: Gallimard, 1957), 1084–98. Cf. my essay 'Omtrent het lelijke', *De Witte Raaf* no. 185 (2017): 1–3.
27 John Macarthur, *The Picturesque: Architecture, Disgust and Other Irregularities* (London: Routledge, 2007).
28 Juan María Montijano García, *San Carlino alle Quattro Fontane di Francesco Borromini nella 'Relazione della fabrica' di fra Juan di San Buenaventura* (Milan: Il Polifilo, 1999), 71–3.
29 Translated from the Spanish/Italian, from 'Montijano García, *San Carlino alle Quattro Fontane*, 71–3.
30 Montijano García, *San Carlino alle Quattro Fontane*, 73.
31 Translated from the French, from Valéry, 'Eupalinos ou l'architecte', 92.
32 Translated from the French, from the chapter 'Mélange', in Valéry, *Oeuvres I*, 339.
33 Translated from the French, from Valéry, 'Eupalinos ou l'architecte', 105.
34 Translated from the French, from the chapter 'Essai sur la peinture', in Denis Diderot, *Oeuvres*, Bibliothèque de la Pléiade, 25 (Paris: Gallimard, 1978), 1170.

PART ONE
Ugly and monstrous

CHAPTER THREE

Instrumentalizing ugliness: Parallels between High Victorian and Brutalist architecture

Timothy M. Rohan

High Victorian buildings – especially those by William Butterfield – and Brutalist ones were often compared to one another in post-Second World War, Anglo-American architectural discourse. Though they seem dissimilar, commentators regularly compared the size, scale and material qualities of the hard-surfaced, monumental buildings of those two centuries. What has been overlooked is how frequently the word 'ugly' appears as the common denominator in those comparisons; it is one that alerts us to questions about aesthetics and semantics in these discussions. In his guide to the buildings of Oxford from 1967, Nikolaus Pevsner memorably claimed that William Butterfield's High Victorian Keble College (1868–82) (Figure 3.1) and a nearby newly built Brutalist building (Philip Dowson for Arup Associates, Denys Wilkinson Building, 1967) exemplified how ugliness had been the 'ideal' for their respective eras.[1] Describing ugly as an ideal may confuse the early-twenty-first-century reader who knows ugly only as a pejorative adjective, but Pevsner was in fact knowingly drawing upon a famous usage of this term that redefined ugly as a positive descriptor, which related High Victorian and Modern architecture to one another in long-term, consequential ways.

Pevsner's usage of ugliness can be directly traced to an important article of the late 1940s by John Summerson, 'William Butterfield, or the Glory of Ugliness'.[2] As is apparent from its title, Summerson transformed ugly,

FIGURE 3.1 *William Butterfield, Keble College Chapel, Oxford (1873–6). Wikimedia Commons. Photo by David Iliff. License: CC-BY-SA 3.0.*

making it glorious and admirable. He did so in order to win new appreciation for the work of Butterfield, a High Victorian architect whose buildings had until then been decried as ugly and not deemed worth preserving. Summerson's agenda in the article concerned both preservation's and architecture's future and ugliness served as the pivot between the two. By redefining ugliness, Summerson reimagined Butterfield as an architect bravely defiant of his day's conventions about ideal beauty in a way that inspired young British architects in the post-war era. In effect, Summerson made Butterfield a model for how to become a Brutalist.

Beginning with Summerson's article, this essay traces how ugliness was instrumentalized in post-war architectural discourse to advance and critique Brutalism in Britain and America. Tracing ugly's usage therefore helps in understanding how the New Brutalism of Britain – an architecture of strong attitudes but relatively small-scale bearing – related to the large-scale, monumental concrete Brutalism of post-war America. The intertwined semantic arc of Brutalism and ugliness leads from 1940s Britain to 1960s America; it associates Butterfield's buildings with significant British and American Brutalist examples such as the Hunstanton School (Peter and

Alison Smithson, 1949–54) and the Boston City Hall (Kallmann, McKinnell and Knowles, 1962–8). It involves historians, pundits and critics ranging from Summerson to Reyner Banham, Philip Johnson and Peter Collins.

They instrumentalized ugliness, knowingly nudging and redefining ugliness over time to define, promote, transform and ultimately undermine Brutalism. In these discussions, ugliness was therefore not a fixed aesthetic category, but a powerfully changing or evolving one. Brutalism is often considered a nearly mute architecture of bold forms, raw materials and surface articulation with a strong overall image, especially as Reyner Banham defined it. However, it was not just an architecture of sensation. Language was as important for Brutalism as it was for its successor, postmodernism, which is usually associated with theoretical texts and wordplay. The Deutsches Architekturmuseum's 'SOS Brutalism' exhibition of 2017 surveyed this architecture globally and revealed as many differences as similarities suggesting that 'Brutalism' was cohered by its name and the attendant adjective ugliness.[3] Unravelling the knots that tie these words, buildings, ideas and people together reveals that Brutalism was not just an ethic, or aesthetic, or style as was claimed in the past and today but a semantic phenomenon, an aspect that must be openly reckoned with as the fate of Brutalist buildings castigated as ugly in the twenty-first century is being decided upon today.

From epithet to encomium

One of the most historically informed of architectural styles, Brutalism developed in part out of twentieth-century reconsiderations of the past as has been noted. The Smithsons drew upon Rudolf Wittkower's analysis of Renaissance geometry and their own research into the British industrial vernacular architecture. John MacArthur has shown how the nineteenth-century picturesque informed Brutalism.[4] But out of all of these precedents, John Summerson's reconsideration of the High Victorian architect William Butterfield was the historical inquiry which most powerfully inspired Brutalism, as Elain Harwood noted some time ago.[5]

Writing in 1945, Summerson knew that there was no way of changing the widely held conviction that High Victorian architecture was irredeemably ugly, a pronouncement delivered by tastemakers of the 1920s and 1930s from neo-traditionalists to modernists. So Summerson instead smartly drew upon this characterization of Butterfield in order to change the concept of ugly, rehabilitate the architect's reputation and thus save his buildings, many of which had been damaged in the Second World War. Bomb-damaged Victorian buildings were often demolished in post-war London. Damaged or not, Victorian architecture was poorly regarded during these years for polemical reasons. To make a case for Modern architecture, its proponents had regularly attacked the Victorian. In Britain and America, functioning, intact Victorian landmark buildings of the nineteenth and early twentieth centuries were routinely found aesthetically unappealing and obsolete and therefore condemned. Summerson was as much a preservationist as he was a historian; these concerns are among the multiple agendas at work in his eloquent article which makes up a vital strand in the DNA of Brutalism.

To build his case for Butterfield, Summerson astutely exploited the Freudian dimension of the interwar period's relationship with the High Victorian. Epitomizing his generation's mixed feelings about the era, Evelyn Waugh lovingly described a large, uncomfortable Butterfieldian-style country house in his popular novel *A Handful of Dust* (1934) only to have its unhappy twentieth-century chatelaine exclaim in exasperation about it, 'I do wish that it wasn't all, every bit of it, so appallingly ugly.'[6] Ugliness was expressed here with obdurate materials used in an all-encompassing fashion – qualities that would later be seen as characteristic of Brutalist ugliness. The materials also had a moral dimension. The encaustic tiles, meters of varnished woodwork and polychromed brickwork manifested the High Victorian's uncompromisingly moral superiority. In Waugh's book, their soft, breakfast-in-bed, cocktail-swilling, fox-trotting interwar descendants found that ethical stance oppressive, knowing they could never live up to it. Understanding how completely ugliness was already associated with Butterfield and the High Victorian, Summerson accepted this characterization and adroitly shifted its semantics, boldly claiming that it was the best quality of Butterfield's buildings. He said, 'All Butterfield's churches are to a greater or less degree ugly. And in almost all there is power and originality transcending the ugliness.'[7] Summerson 'spun' ugliness, infusing the epithet with 'power and originality' to make it an encomium positive and worthy of emulation.

Summerson proceeded to make Butterfield over into a brave original who did not follow the aesthetics or conventions of his era's architecture. A devout Christian, Butterfield's ethics guided him to building with an aesthetics expressive of the truth of structure and materials, making him more like a builder or mechanic than an architect. This quality was admired in 1945 by egalitarian, left-leaning modernists (like Summerson) who disdained the effeteness of the elite architect who did not know how to lay a brick. Summerson's Butterfield had none of the nostalgia or sentimentality of the typical Gothic revivalist or his successor, the Arts and Crafts architect. He did not conform to any rules or agendas. Butterfield distorted scale and conventional proportions to make buildings with strong visual qualities, whose discordant notes protested against the prettiness of the eighteenth- and early-nineteenth-century Gothic Revival and the laboured, respectful archaeological earnestness of the institutional Gothic of mid-century. Butterfield's Gothic distorted precedents in a fashion truer to the inventiveness of the builders of the Middle Ages and therefore closer to the medieval 'grotesque' as theorized by John Ruskin. Introducing brick to the largely stone fabric of Oxford, Butterfield's Keble College struck discordant notes that erupted forcefully amid the historic university. Summerson thought these discordances shocked, surprised and even disgusted the senses and therefore were authentic and real sensations. As Mark Cousins has explained, ugliness in architecture is usually considered to be anything discordant in terms of scale, form and materials which threatens an environment imagined to be cohesive, such as historic Oxford.[8]

Quaint environments held no appeal for Summerson's Butterfield. He tolerated no ideal beauty, conventional prettiness or tastefulness. Summerson said, 'The first glory of Butterfield is to me, his utter ruthlessness.'[9] Summerson thought that Butterfield's ruthlessness was what made his approach honest, authentic and ethical. Revealing that his article concerned the future as much as the past, Summerson warned that pretty tastefulness might again dominate Britain after the Second World War but hoped that Butterfield's example would inspire architecture in the dawning post-war era.

Exemplifying what Manfredo Tafuri later called 'operative criticism', Summerson's article was not a measured historical account but a call-to-arms for an ethically based, post-war British modernism inspired by nineteenth-century architecture.[10] Butterfield scholar Paul R. Thompson said in 1971 that Summerson's characterization of Butterfield was in fact historically inaccurate but tremendously influential for the post-war generation of scholars and modernist architects who believed Butterfield was 'a pioneer of the modern movement, a New Brutalist a hundred years ahead of his time'.[11] The article was widely available and frequently read and cited because it was included in Summerson's 1949 collection of essays, *Heavenly Mansions*, which was regularly reissued and is still in print today. An important part of the collective consciousness of British post-war architecture, Summerson's 'William Butterfield; or the Glory of Ugliness' became the Ur-text for Brutalism.

The New Brutalism

Though Summerson had warned against it, pretty tastefulness nevertheless dominated Britain immediately after the Second World War. Organized to raise spirits in the depressed post-war years, the Festival of Britain in 1951 showcased an officially sanctioned British modernism tastefully coloured by the friendly tones of the Swedish 'New Humanism' with shades of the eighteenth- and nineteenth-century picturesque to make it even more congenial.

The originators of the 'New Brutalism', Alison and Peter Smithson, thought the festival immoral for deliberately downplaying contemporary realities, even if they were grim. War-time rationing of food in Britain did not end until 1954. To show how everyday life and aesthetics could interact productively, they mounted the exhibit, the *Parallel of Life and Art* (1953) at the Institute for Contemporary Art. 'Life' was exemplified by discordant, non-ideal objects found in the real or industrial world, including advertising images, while 'art' was represented by works with a rough-edged, unpremeditated quality, such as photos of canvases by Jackson Pollock and Alberto Burri. The Smithsons did not call these things ugly, but their critics did. Reyner Banham remembered that reviewers 'complained of the deliberate flouting of the traditional concepts of photographic beauty, of a cult of ugliness, and "denying the spiritual in Man".'[12]

The Smithsons elaborated upon this 'cult of ugliness' in their buildings pursuing a strategy which eventually became the 'New Brutalism'. Initially undefined by them, it was a forthright attitude strikingly similar to the one attributed by Summerson to Butterfield. They did not cite Summerson's article, nor did they have to; it was a common reference point for their contemporaries. The New Brutalism was predicated upon references familiar to those who knew them from the drafting rooms of British architecture firms and schools. At first the New Brutalism circulated across drawing boards just as a name whose origins have been traced to everything from Peter Smithson's middle name (Brutus) to the *beton brût* of Le Corbusier. But it was Smithsons' verbal wordplay – the surprising redefining of the negative term 'Brutal' to make it a positive one – that was significant. Their transformation of brutal was a semantic strategy or operation similar to Summerson's redefinition of ugly.

The Smithsons also practiced the New Brutalism in a manner remarkably similar to the way Summerson described Butterfield practicing architecture. They emphasized construction, materials and an ethical basis, albeit one informed by the *brut* or raw authenticity emphasized by French existentialism rather than the moralizing of Victorian Christianity.[13] In their Hunstanton School (1949–54) they expressed brick, steel, concrete and mechanical equipment in a forthright manner appreciated by critics as realistic and therefore truthful and ethical. Exposing the plumbing struck an incongruous note. Though they bore no direct physical or material resemblance to one another, Hunstanton had the overall consistent qualities and hardness of Butterfield's buildings. Summerson understood and acknowledged these similarities. Referencing the title of his own article about Butterfield, Summerson himself said the school displayed 'an acceptance of building materials and equipment in the raw, a *Butterfieldian glorying* in the smell of the shop'.[14] Others noticed this as well. An unattributed critique of 1954 from *The Architectural Review* likened the Hunstanton School to Butterfield's St Margaret's Church and praised it for its 'ruthlessness', an essential term for Summerson's characterization of Butterfield.[15]

Banham emphasized this quality when he defined the 'New Brutalism' in the 1955 article for *The Architectural Review* that introduced it to modernist discourse internationally. Making the New Brutalists sound even more ruthless than Butterfield, Banham said their attitude was characterized by 'its brutality, its *je-m'en-foutisme*, its bloody-mindedness'.[16] He further defined the New Brutalism with characteristics found in the Hunstanton Project that emphasized truthfulness: 'legible' expression of plan, structure and materials. In addition to these basic ones, Banham introduced 'Image' as a final aesthetic characteristic. Characterized by Banham as 'anti-beauty in the classical aesthetic sense of the word', it could be anything with a strong, immediately apprehensible image from the domed Renaissance church at Todi, Italy, to the 1954 Cadillac convertible, to a painting by Jackson Pollock.[17] Beyond Hunstanton, the 'New Brutalism' in architecture was exemplified for Banham by relatively small-scale brick structures with some roughened, seeming artless concrete detailing, such as Louis Kahn's Yale University Art Gallery (New Haven, CT, 1950–4). After the article was published, the New Brutalism was applied to other brick and concrete buildings, like Stirling and Gowan's Ham Common Housing in London (1955–8).

Believing that Banham's foregrounding of the aesthetics of Brutalism was reductive, the Smithsons attempted to define it themselves several times. Obviously alluding to how Banham had discussed it stylistically, they wrote in 1957, 'Brutalism tries to face up to a mass-production society, and drag a rough poetry out of the confused and powerful forces which are at work. Up to now Brutalism has been discussed stylistically, whereas its essence is ethical.'[18] It was striking how they emphasized words and poetics – essentially language – over aesthetics and images. By foregrounding ethics, they reiterated and expanded upon the agenda for Modern architecture in Britain laid out by Summerson in his 1945 article about Butterfield.

American Brutalism

In 1962, the young architects Gerhard Kallmann and Michael McKinnell encountered Philip Johnson in New York soon after it was announced that they had won the competition for the Boston City Hall (1962–8) with their partner Edward Knowles (Figure 3.2). As an anecdote about this encounter later told by McKinnell demonstrates, the landmark example of American Brutalism has been praised and maligned as ugly nearly from the moment the design was revealed. Johnson called out to Kallmann and McKinnell, 'Ah! I'm so happy for you two young boys who have won this competition. Absolutely marvellous. I think it's wonderful. And it's so ugly!' Because he was British-born and educated, McKinnell was familiar with the semantics of the New Brutalism and understood that Johnson's remarks were positive. He later said of them, 'We thought that was the greatest praise we could get.'[19]

A key figure for modernist architecture discourse and an important if unacknowledged one for Brutalism, the erudite Johnson correctly understood the British etymology of the New Brutalism, having commented on the Hunstanton School when it was first published in *The Architectural Review* in 1954.[20] In a 1961 issue of the American journal, *Architectural Forum*, he said the New Brutalism was an 'attitude, not a style, not even

FIGURE 3.2 *Kallmann, McKinnell and Knowles, Boston City Hall (1962–8).*
Photo by Timothy M. Rohan.

a way of forming ... For form the brutalists are apt to bring us great concrete beams ... and tiny windows funny shaped, scattered in great brick walls. Much inside and outside movement, and a great many pieces of concrete exposed.'[21] Johnson had in mind what were typically cited as examples of the New Brutalism, which were fairly simply brick buildings with roughened concrete detailing such as Stirling and Gowan's Ham Common Housing (London, 1955–8).

But Johnson also changed the concept of Brutalism when he explained it to American audiences by emphasizing form and concrete – a material that American architects were shifting to in the late 1950s and early 1960s as they left behind the steel and glass of the International Style to achieve a new monumentality appropriate for the grandeur of the post-war *Pax Americana*. During the transatlantic migration of the term, the adjective 'new' was dropped from New Brutalism and the emphasis shifted from socially based ethics to individualistic dynamism and action – qualities found as well in Summerson's characterization of Butterfield. A new type of dynamic, plastic, monumental architecture in concrete was already in formation by the late 1950s in America. Rather than calling it Brutalism, Gerhard Kallmann had called it 'Action Architecture' in a 1959 article that cited the New Brutalism as defined by Banham and the Smithsons.

Educated in Britain where he lived and worked until he emigrated to the United States in 1948, Kallmann's vocabulary revealed his familiarity with British architectural discourse of the 1940s and 1950s. He said that the new 'Action Architecture' had 'violent' qualities, using many of the same adjectives that Summerson had employed to describe Butterfield's architecture, though he never cited the 1945 article. But Kallmann also clearly had in mind the dynamism and power of American Action Painting or Abstract Expressionism and the overall American cultural and social emphasis upon individualism. He married the two together, to suggest a dynamic architecture of 'harsher esthetics [sic] than that of the present modish eclecticism'.[22] As in Summerson's article about Butterfield, Kallmann's 'Action Architecture' critiqued present-day aesthetics based upon traditional concepts of beauty, as exemplified by the classically informed Romantic Modernism of post-war American architects such as Edward Durrell Stone, Minoru Yamasaki and others.

The British-born Canadian academic and critic Peter Collins knowingly referenced all these textual antecedents which had informed the design of the Boston City Hall in his review of it for *Progressive Architecture* in 1963.[23] Construction had not yet begun, so his assessment was based upon published drawings of it. Demonstrating how ideas flowed through the shared Anglo-American discourse about architecture, Collins's review appeared nearly simultaneously in British and American journals.[24] This discourse was also shared at the personal level. The critic and the architects of the city hall knew each other well. Michael McKinnell had been Collins's student at the University of Manchester, where the critic had been an instructor before emigrating to Canada.

Collins drew British and American architecture together in his criticism, thus assisting in the blurring of the lines between British and American Brutalism. Citing Summerson's article about Butterfield and quoting liberally from Kallmann's call for an action architecture, Collins linked the two respective texts together when he called Butterfield an 'action architect'. Having already been recast as a proto-Brutalist, Butterfield was now made into something resembling a post-war American architect.[25] Collins's reference to Butterfield was one of the rare direct acknowledgments of the role that Summerson's article played as the Ur-text of Brutalism.

However, Collins's critique of the Boston building was not a positive one. Given to hyperbole in his criticism, Collins wondered if the new city hall with all its striking discordances and levitating masses was 'simply the architecture of William Butterfield raised to the terrifying dimensions of the atomic age'.[26] Collins's negative characterization of the civic structure's large-scale and imposing presence as a manifestation of the 'atomic age' suggested geopolitical tensions. The British resented how the Americans had achieved hegemony over Modern architecture – even seizing Brutalism – just as they had achieved political hegemony with their nuclear weapons. The linchpin between the New Brutalism and American Brutalism, the Boston

City Hall was for the British a mushroom cloud symbolizing American dominance of world architecture.

Other British critics were unhappy with how Brutalism had become large-scale monumental architecture in America. In 1966, Reyner Banham would himself express disappointment about how the 'Johnson, Johansens and Rudolphs of the American scene' had transformed Brutalism into a style larger, more monumental and more aesthetic than his 'New Brutalism'. Banham made this remark in the conclusion to his book, *The New Brutalism: Ethic or Aesthetic?*[27] In it, Banham both denied that Brutalism was one single coherent international style and yet promulgated this notion with the book, an international survey of Brutalism which remained one of the few sources on the subject until the twenty-first century. In 1955, 'Image' had been one of his original criteria for defining Brutalism, but he dropped it in his book because he thought Brutalism had become too aesthetic. He noted that the word 'Brutalism' had been instrumental in what had degenerated into a style even for the British, who by the 1960s practiced it as a monumental concrete architecture much like that of their American counterparts.[28]

During the 1960s, unfavourable and favourable comparisons continued to be made between the High Victorian and Brutalism. At the dedication of Paul Rudolph's Yale Art and Architecture Building in 1963, Nikolaus Pevsner famously dismissed this landmark example of monumental American concrete Brutalism, unflatteringly comparing it to the earlier home of the school of fine arts, the nearby High Victorian building, Street Hall by Peter Wight (1864). But Pevsner favoured few American buildings, again probably reflecting British dismay about American hegemony. He complemented Street Hall but also belittled it as 'provincial' compared to the work of Butterfield.[29] In contrast, Yale architectural historian George Hersey delighted in finding precedents for Brutalism in the High Victorian. Writing of the High Victorian Connecticut State Capital (Richard Upjohn, Hartford, CT, 1872–8), Hersey said that its 'spiked gables, its tall faceted roofs, its squarely locked masses and its big-volumed, downlit interior wells' constituted 'an old brutalism' that anticipated the new post-war Brutalism of the Boston City Hall. The American High Victorian legitimized the monumental Brutalism of the *Pax Americana*.[30]

Much of this negative criticism of American buildings by British critics was cleverly oblique. Collins cited passages from Summerson's Butterfield article to suggest that it was ugly in the most negative of ways – though he never said this outright himself. Knowing well that ugly had been used positively by Summerson, Collins admitted that it was a subjective notion by invoking Victor Hugo's remarks about how nothing in the world was 'ugly in the sight of God'. Collins said that the architects of the City Hall also saw the notion of beauty as a subjective one and thought that this was problematic. He said,

It is undeniable that the term 'beauty' is a purely relative humanistic notion. The problem is going to be whether or not the citizens of Boston will be satisfied with letting God be the judge; because there seems to be little doubt that their new city hall is unlikely to be beautiful in the traditional sense of the word, and it will be interesting to see how human critics will decide what precisely are its aesthetic merits when it is completed, and how relevant these are to the world in which we live.[31]

Ground had not yet been broken for it, but Collins anticipated future debates in his review about the aesthetics of the Boston City Hall.

Recovering Brutalism and ugliness

Despite some open scepticism about its appearance, the Boston City Hall was initially accepted upon its completion in 1968 as a symbol of a new and progressive modernist city rebounding after years of urban problems caused by deindustrialization and internal political deadlocks. However, the Boston City Hall's reputation declined during the 1970s and into the twenty-first century in what proved to be a classic trajectory for Brutalist buildings chiefly caused by lack of care, changing tastes, and politics. Ugliness used as a pejorative greased the track which seemed to be leading the building to an unavoidable encounter with the wrecking ball. To be sure, the Boston City Hall was a challenging building. Its entrances and interior spaces were complex, and pedestrians found its enormous plaza alienating. But deferred maintenance beginning in the 1970s, overcrowding of office spaces and unsympathetic remodelling of its modernist interiors all made it appear dirty and disorderly and therefore uglier.[32] In addition to discordances, dirtiness is often seen as a characteristic of ugliness as is the 'indeterminacy' of a space like the City Hall Plaza.[33] As modernism fell out of favour, the City Hall's lack of readily apparent context with nearby smaller-scaled, traditional brick buildings for which there was a growing regard also made it seem discordant, especially after the successful restoration of the nearby eighteenth-century market, Faneuil Hall (1742 and later; restored by Benjamin Thompson Associates, 1979), into a 'festival' shopping complex that became a model for similar ones nationwide.

Symbolic of a progressive modernism allied with progressive government, the Boston City Hall's reputation suffered as the backlash grew against the ambitious but often heavy-handed and poorly implemented governmental policies of the post-war era. The City Hall was the centrepiece in a larger downtown urban renewal effort which demolished the decaying buildings of a red-light district that had long embarrassed Boston. Illustrating how quickly opinions can change and nostalgia grow, by the late twentieth century its demolition was mourned and big government and modernism blamed for its destruction. Drawing upon these anti-government and anti-modernist sentiments, during his long term in office (1993–2013), the popular mayor of Boston, Thomas Menino, became an outspoken critic of the City Hall. He regularly claimed it functioned poorly and was outmoded and ugly. He repeatedly called for demolishing the Boston City Hall, selling the site and building a new city hall in a renewal district outside the city centre favoured by him.[34]

Brutalist civic buildings like the Boston City Hall are often threatened in the twenty-first century by politicians, like Menino, who draw upon growing anti-government sentiment in order to dismantle post-war institutions and privatize them, their policies, and their programs, often reflecting neo-liberal policies or more personal outright attempts to seize political power. Brutalist critics seek to demolish post-war monuments in part because they seek to undermine the post-war period's progressive agenda of making democracy accessible to all. In the 2010s, politicians succeeded in largely dismantling and disastrously rebuilding Paul Rudolph's Orange County Civic Centre (Goshen, NY, 1963–71). They began by belittling it with the usual charges made against Brutalist buildings: it was ugly, overly complex, dirty and discordant with the traditional buildings of the town. The building's supporters replied that the building was not only architecturally significant but also fostered civic values. Rudolph's complex lobby encouraged encounters between the public and politicians. Its legislative chamber made politicians engage with one another face to face and reach a resolve even if there was some discomfort during the exchange. Nevertheless, county officials deliberately deferred maintenance and repairs to make the building seem unappealing and ultimately succeeded it implementing a renovation that effectively eliminated its most inclusive public spaces.[35]

Reporting about the controversial renovation in the *New York Times* in 2015, Michael Kimmelman defended the building stating, 'Rudolph's design was about openness, transparency, and accountability.'[36] Kimmelman quoted one advocate for the building who said its original openness was a 'daily rebuke to how legislators "now run the county ... That's why they really hate it".' The Orange County case reveals that this type of antagonism and ill-will are shot through with a psychological uneasiness, one concerning anxieties about a failure to live up to a previous generation's achievements that recalls the early-twentieth-century's antipathy towards the High Victorian.

Hoping that such antipathies will lessen with time, modernist preservationists often claim that appreciation for Brutalist buildings will soon develop as it did for the High Victorian. Forty years after she had first positively reviewed the Boston City Hall, Ada Louise Huxtable in 2009 defended it from its latest critics by pointing out how its predecessor – a Victorian structure that had been reviled in the 1950s – had been saved, renovated to become a fashionable restaurant, and was now well liked in Boston. She concluded that public opinion would eventually favour the Brutalist city hall as well. She said, 'Tastes change as surely as the seasons, only it takes a little longer.'[37] Ugliness, preservation and generational conflict keep the High Victorian and Brutalism engaged with one another in a dialectical relationship that continues to haunt the rhetoric about these buildings long after Summerson's remarks about Butterfield.

Semantics continue to play a key role in attempts to improve the reputation of Brutalism. As is evident from the title of Barnabas Calder's book *Raw Concrete: The Beauty of Brutalism*, he explains with great fervour why he finds Brutalism beautiful in order to counter the perception that it and concrete are ugly.[38] Other supporters of Brutalism have sought to recast or rebrand it positively by changing its name. In Boston, organized admirers of Brutalism actively tried to change the vocabulary used in discussions about monumental concrete buildings by replacing 'Brutalism' with the term 'Heroic' – a reference to the optimistic, heroic ambitions of the post-war era. It is a particularly adroit turning of a phrase since it also recalled how the authors of *Learning from Las Vegas* had used 'Heroic' in an ironic fashion to critique Brutalist buildings.[39]

Advocates for Brutalism often ally it with contemporary architecture. The two justify each other. Peter Chadwick appealingly, if loosely, juxtaposes Brutalist structures with new buildings by prominent architects from around the world in his very popular collection of photographs, *This Brutal World*.[40] Examples beyond Chadwick's book confirm that it is largely the aesthetics of Brutalism that appeals to contemporary architecture. Appropriately for a museum devoted to the work of a 1960s American artist, Allied Works Architecture invokes the boldness of Brutalist massing and the surfacing techniques of Rudolph with their Clifford Still Museum (Denver, CO, 2011). But it is not the same as the Brutalism of the past. Though its raw concrete and striking forms suggest a 'ruthlessness' that can pass for an ethical stance, this is largely an aesthetic ode to brutalism with little of the spatial or material challenges of the buildings it is modelled upon. Inside, it is like most other new museums.

Indeed, the true ethical stance of Brutalism lay in how its buildings completely stimulated users through their all-encompassing ugliness of image, surface and space to engage with the world in the critical manner that is at the heart of the larger modernist project. Timothy Hyde has shown in his analysis of the Brutalist South Bank Centre in London (LCC Architects Department, London, 1961–7) that the discordant qualities of space, surface and even the irritating ones such as stains often used to define Brutalism's ugliness are its valuable ones. Hyde concludes that ugliness is more 'generous' than the beautiful because it accepts the discordant, non-ideal aspects of the contemporary world.[41]

Because it is inclusive, ugliness is more appropriate for the twenty-first-century, which struggles with all aspects of diversity. Ugliness should therefore be emphasized as Brutalism's best, not worst characteristic. Very little holds Brutalism together aside from its name and its ugliness which should be further explored to save and understand buildings that are worth calling Brutalist. Proponents should engage more deeply with the semantics that have always defined Brutalism.

Brutalism and ugliness should be taken back by the advocates of this architecture, much as Summerson did when he redefined Butterfield's ugliness as glorious, but with greater historical accuracy. In doing so, the ethical aspects of Brutalism could resurface to inspire the present. This may seem like a difficult task, but it is not impossible if one remembers how once derogatory words such as queer and gay have been recuperated and became sources of empowerment precisely because they raised ethical questions. Such a semantic move has a precedent in architecture. Referring to the purported uncouthness of a German barbarian tribe, Gothic was initially a derogatory term for buildings of the Middle Ages, but it was recovered during the Enlightenment and instrumentalized to open architecture up to rich and myriad possibilities beyond the idealism of classical beauty. Eventually, the Gothic Revival led to Butterfield's imaginative efforts. Semantically complex, Gothic is also a model for reworking Brutalism because it has multiple, related definitions beyond architecture, describing everything from a type of novel to a subculture. Words are powerful and flexible and can carry multiple meanings at once. By substituting semantic for ethical, the Smithsons' definition of the New Brutalism could serve as a modest, inspirational maxim for how to change the language used to discuss this architecture: 'Up to now Brutalism has been discussed stylistically, whereas its essence is semantic.'[42]

Notes

1 Jennifer Sherwood and Nikolaus Pevsner, *The Buildings of England: Oxfordshire* (Harmondsworth: Penguin, 1974), 227.

2 John Summerson, 'William Butterfield, or the Glory of Ugliness' in *Heavenly Mansions and Other Essays on Architecture*, ed. John Summerson (New York: W. W. Norton, 1963). The US-based Norton Books has published it continuously since 1963. Summerson's article was part of an issue of *The Architectural Review* devoted to examining the Victorian Gothic. It was originally titled 'Act 3: Christian Gothic. Scene 1: William Butterfield', *Architectural Review* 98, no. 588 (December 1945): 166–72.

3 Oliver Elser, Philip Kurz and Peter Cachola Schmal, *SOS Brutalism: A Global Survey* (Zurich: Park Books, 2017). Organized jointly by the Deutsches Architekturmuseum and the Wüstenrot Stiftung, 9 November 2017–2 April 2018.

4 John MacArthur, 'Brutalism, Ugliness and the Picturesque Object' in *Formulation Fabrication – The Architecture of History: Proceedings of the*

Seventeenth Annual Conference of the Society of Architectural Historians, Australia and New Zealand (Wellington, NZ: Society of Architectural Historians, Australia and New Zealand, 2000), 259–66.

5 Elain Harwood, 'Butterfield and Brutalism', *AA Files* 27 (1994): 39–46.
6 Evelyn Waugh, *A Handful of Dust* (New York: Dell Publications, 1964), 45.
7 For convenience, all quotations are drawn from article as it appears in the widely available Norton edition. Summerson, 'William Butterfield, or the Glory of Ugliness', 167.
8 For my summary of what is considered ugly in architecture, I have drawn upon Mark Cousins, 'The Ugly [part 1]', *AA Files* 28 (Autumn 1994): 61–4; Mark Cousins, 'The Ugly [part 2]', *AA Files* 29 (Summer 1995): 3–6; Mark Cousins, 'The Ugly [part 3]', *AA Files* 30 (Autumn 1995): 65–8.
9 Summerson, 'William Butterfield, or the Glory of Ugliness', 172.
10 Manfredo Tafuri, 'Operative Criticism' in *Theories and History of Architecture*, ed. Manfredo Tafuri, trans. G. Verrecchia (New York: Harper & Row, 1980), 141–70.
11 Paul R. Thompson, *William Butterfield* (Cambridge, MA: MIT Press, 1971), 3.
12 Reyner Banham, 'The New Brutalism', *The Architectural Review* 708 (December 1955): 356.
13 For how Brutalism is informed by existentialism, see Sarah Williams Goldhagen, 'Freedom's Domiciles: Three Projects by Peter and Alison Smithson' in *Anxious Modernisms: Experimentation in Postwar Architectural Culture*, ed. Sarah Williams Goldhagen and Rejean Legault (Cambridge, MA: MIT Press, 2001), 75–96.
14 John Summerson, 'Introduction' in *Ten Years of British Architecture*, ed. John Summerson (London: Arts Council, 1956), 11. My emphasis.
15 Unattributed, 'School at Hunstanton, Norfolk', *Architectural Review* 116 (September 1954): 152.
16 Banham, 'The New Brutalism', 357.
17 Ibid., 358.
18 Alison and Peter Smithson, 'The New Brutalism', *Architectural Design* 27 (April 1957): 113.
19 N. Michael McKinnell, 'Concrete Is Patient' in *Heroic: Concrete Architecture and the New Boston*, ed. Mark Pasnik, Michael Kubo and Chris Grimley (New York: Monacelli Press, 2015), 309.
20 Philip Johnson, 'Notes on Hunstanton', *Architectural Review* 116 (August 1954): 148–52.
21 Philip Johnson, 'Architecture – Fitting and Befitting', *Architectural Forum* 114 (June 1961): 87.
22 Gerhard Kallmann, 'Action Architecture', *Architectural Forum* 111 (October 1959): 133.
23 Peter Collins, 'Critique', *Progressive Architecture* (April 1963): 146. This was a revised and expanded version of a review by Collins originally published in *The Manchester Guardian*, 13 September 1962, 6.

24 Other scholars have seen architectural publications as sites for the transatlantic discourse about Brutalism during the post-war period. Réjean Legault, 'The Trajectories of Brutalism: England, Germany and Beyond' in *SOS Brutalism: A Global Survey*, ed. Oliver Esler, Philip Kurz and Peter Cachola Schmal (Zurich: Park Books, 2017), 20–5. See also Joan Ockman, 'The American School of Brutalism: Transformations of a Concrete Idea' in *Brutalism: Contributions to the International Symposium in Berlin: 2012*, ed. Dorothea Deschermeirer (Zurich: Park Books, 2017) 105–16.

25 Collins, 'Critique', 146.

26 Ibid.

27 Reyner Banham, *The New Brutalism: Ethic or Aesthetic?* (London: Architectural Press, 1966), 135.

28 Banham, *The New Brutalism: Ethic or Aesthetic?*, 10.

29 Nikolaus Pevsner, 'Address Given at the Inauguration of the New Art and Architecture Building of Yale University, 9 November 1963', *Journal of the Society of Architectural Historians* 26 (March 1967): 4–7.

30 George Hersey, 'Replication Replicated, or Notes on American Bastardy', *Perspecta* 9/10 (1965): 211–48. Sketches of the Boston City Hall also appeared in this issue of *Perspecta*, Kallmann, McKinnell and Knowles, 'The New City Hall at Boston: A Portfolio of Sketches and Drawings', *Perspecta* 9/10 (1965): 265–80.

31 Collins, 'Critique', 146.

32 For a complete history of the Boston City Hall, see Brian M. Sirman, *Concrete Changes: Architecture, Politics, and the Design of Boston City Hall* (Amherst: University of Massachusetts Press, 2018). See especially chapter 4, 'An Evolving Reputation', 136–81.

33 Mark Cousins, 'The Ugly, Part 1', 63. Drawing upon Cousins's remarks about dirtiness and staining, Timothy Hyde also shows how the 'indeterminacy' of the Brutalist South Bank Arts Centre (LCC Architects Department, London, 1961–7) has harmed its reputation in his article 'Piles, Puddles and Other Architectural Irritants', *Log* 27 (Winter/Spring 2013): 67–79.

34 Sirman, *Concrete Changes*, 173–5.

35 For a complete history of the controversial and unsympathetic of Rudolph's Orange County Civic Center, see Mark Byrnes, 'An Architectural Rescue Gone Wrong', *Citylab* (29 August 2017), https://www.citylab.com/design/2017/08/an-architectural-rescue-gone-wrong/537975/.

36 Michael Kimmelman, 'Landmark's Last Hope for Rescue', *New York Times*, 4 March 2015, C1.

37 Ada Louise Huxtable, 'Boston New City Hall: A Public Building of Quality', *New York Times*, 8 February 1969. Huxtable, 'The Beauty in Brutalism, Restored and Updated', *Wall Street Journal*, 25 February 2009.

38 Barnabas Calder, *Raw Concrete: The Beauty of Brutalism* (London: William Heinemann, 2016).

39 Mark Pasnik et al., *Heroic*. Robert Venturi, Denise Scott Brown and Steven Izenour called 'heroic' Paul Rudolph's Brutalist Crawford Manor (New Haven, CT, 1962–6) in *Learning from Las Vegas. The Forgotten Symbolism of Architectural Form* (Cambridge, MA: MIT Press, 1972), 102.

40 Peter Chadwick, *This Brutal World* (London: Phaidon, 2016).

41 Hyde, 'Piles, Puddles and Other Architectural Irritants', 79.

42 Alison and Peter Smithson, 'The New Brutalism', *Architectural Design* 27 (April 1957): 113.

CHAPTER FOUR

Monstrous becomings: A minor cartography
Heidi Sohn

Encounters with ugliness and the monstrous

This chapter addresses the problematic aesthetic category of 'the ugly' as applied to architecture and other phenomena of sensory perception through the equally problematic cultural category of 'the monster'. The ugly and the monster both occupy marginal positions in the production of knowledge, where they both tend to be trivialized, dispatched as a simple matter of (bad) taste or a fancy of the imagination.[1] They certainly have received only peripheral attention in contemporary architectural discourse.[2] The ugly and the monster, however, recur in the arts and in popular culture, spilling over into aesthetic theory and cultural analysis alike, where they are not considered frivolous categories. They are relevant precisely because of their marginal, uncomfortable status: unresolved, undefined, ambivalent, unfinished or 'grotesque', continuously transforming. They are essentially unclassifiable, and this resistance alone is what has kept thinkers busy trying to capture and describe some of their formal or structural characteristics for millennia.

While the ugly and the monster are not constitutive of each other, or even necessarily related, they do share several characteristics. Herman Parret, for instance, writes that ugliness 'is formless and lacks internal structure, balance and symmetry. The ugly is not complete, it deviates from the norm.'[3] This coincides almost verbatim with recurrent 'evaluative' descriptions of the monster as abnormal: whether incomplete, excessive, formless, deformed, unstable, ambiguous and/or chaotic, the monster always deviates. Yet anything can be a monster, and anything can be ugly, depending on the particular context and the interpretative framework from which we depart. As David Skal writes, 'Speak of monsters and you're soon speaking about all kinds of things.'[4] One could assume the same applies to the ugly. This would indicate that the ugly and the monster are more than unclassifiable categories; they are unstable, category-destroying *concepts*. Refusing to be reduced to any one essence, substance, class, thing or meaning, they operate from a sort of 'ontological liminality',[5] from where they often wreak havoc upon aesthetic canons and conventions, on the one hand, and – as in the case of the monster – disrupt the order of things and uproot entire structures of knowledge on the other.[6] Referring specifically to the monster, Asa Simon Mittman, for instance, argues that as a concept it 'calls into question our … epistemological worldview, highlights its fragmentary and inadequate nature, and thereby asks us … to acknowledge the failures of our systems of categorization'.[7] In this sense, the ugly and the monster, while arguably liminal and 'minoritarian', are always already much more powerful, rather than simply banal, laughable, or insignificant.

Both the ugly and the monster are conventionally considered sensorial – and primarily visual – phenomena;[8] but this is complicated further through their understanding as (embodied, or incorporeal) manifestations of something 'else': an underlying or anterior, pre-individual, pre-personal 'force field', whose impact approaches extreme thresholds (e.g. of horror or ecstasy) and which cannot be announced, measured or represented. This impact is often explained through psychoanalytic frameworks as psychosomatic symptoms that in many cases conceal, occlude or repress their underlying causes or origin. This threatens the integrity, purity and consistency of predefined and preconceived ideas of what constitutes essential entities: Being, the self, the subject and so on. As such, they embody deepseated psychic fears and anxieties usually associated with lacunae and excess embedded within the unconscious, and which trigger somatic sensations. Through (psycho)analysis, or the reading and interpretation of symptoms (signs), and therapy, it is possible to reveal and work through the aetiology (cause) of a particular anxiety. However, the root cause of anxiety may not always be related to a graspable object, or pinned down in stable spatiotemporal coordinates, as would be the case of arachnophobia: the spider itself does not cause horror; instead, its presence embodies and represents an underlying, non-graspable and unknowable primal fear. In this sense, the monster and the ugly function as examples of 'the tangible means by which the unspeakable force of the monstrous is brought into being'.[9] Yet, as Patricia MacCormack points out, the monster is never an entity or even an object.[10] In an effort to normalize or neutralize it, we tend to objectify it as an effect and a cause of the monstrous. It would take a lengthy formulation to explain these complex mechanisms here, so for the sake of brevity, it should suffice to say that even when the ugly or the monster are objectified, there is always a remainder – an excess – left over in the process that cannot be captured. This excess is always disruptive and explains why the ugly and the monster are necessarily distressing and scandalous.

The ugly and the monster do not necessarily need to be visual or tangible to be perceived, though. Even when they are rendered invisible we can determine their presence through retroactive causality, that is, mediated through their immediate effects.[11] In this sense, liminal ontological concepts such as the ugly or the monster tend to evoke that which is beyond or outside representation, perception, thought or imagination and which causes disgust, as Denise Gigante writes of the ugly in her article on Frankenstein.[12] In addition to this, both terms refer to all that which provokes convulsion because it has been infused with excessive 'affectiveness', or affective power, as Mark Dorrian writes of the monstrous and the grotesque in certain art forms.[13] Perhaps even stronger yet, they embody all that which cannot be located or grounded and expressed in physiological, psychological or spatiotemporal units or parameters, and which thus produces a sense of vertigo.[14]

Jeffrey Jerome Cohen argues that the monster – like time, wind or oxygen – does not necessarily hold any tangible materiality, and hence cannot always be grasped. Yet, because we vividly perceive its effects, and take these effects as evidence of its presence, 'we postulate agency and cause'.[15] He writes that 'the effects of the monster are undeniable: a spur to self-protection; an insistent impulsion to narrative; a catalyst to fear, to desire, and to art'.[16] These effects may be either unproductive or productive, or both, but they are always affective: they hold the power to affect and to be affected – that is, to produce effects and, thus, to affect material reality. Agential power can be restrictive (*potestas*), but understood as *potentia*, the agency of the monster – while not necessarily reproductive, engendered or viable[17] – is nonetheless affirmative and empowering, and thus creative, productive, vital and generative.[18]

It may be wise to pause here to mention a crucial issue before we move further into the turbulent dimension of the monstrous. The term 'ugly' should not be conflated with ugliness, any less than the 'monster' with monstrousness (or the monstrous); ugliness should not automatically be extrapolated to the monstrous either. Nevertheless, these notions are here cautiously related in that they refer – in different degrees and in different registers – to much more than formal, structural or systemic abnormality, otherness and difference. When taken to their extremes, they become unintelligible: insensible, imperceptible, indiscernible and not fully present. They allude to all sorts of abstract conceptual phenomena: the unrepresentable, the unnameable, the unthought and the unknown, the chaotic, the yet-to-come and so on. As such they always already exceed aestheticization, and as such they always resist representation.[19] In other words, while it may be possible to capture, objectify and neutralize the monster through visualization and representation, regardless of whether it is ugly or not, 'what is truly monstrous is that which stands outside the processes of representation or articulation', as Alexa Wright reminds us.[20] Along the same line, but speaking of ugliness,

Gigante refers to the ugly as the 'raw unaestheticised stuff of humanity' that 'threatens not only the subject, but the entire system of symbolic representation'.[21] Parret discusses the distinction that Kant draws between the colossal and the monstrous in his *Critique of Judgement*, writing that 'while the *colossal* incites a feeling of the sublime, the *monstrous* paralyzes and impairs the mind and this is precisely what the *ugly* does. Maybe there are degrees of ugliness but the "ultimate ugliness," the monstrous eliminates even the possibility of an aesthetic experience.'[22]

The *monstrous*, understood as the 'ultimate ugliness', as the 'uglier than ugly',[23] is radically outside human cognition, perception and experience. Allen Weiss notes in this regard that 'a true monster will be remembered for the *shock* it produces, breaking all chains of association'.[24] It always delivers a blow to the system: it is a shock to *thought*. In this sense, it is not the ugly or the monster that in their aberrancy or abnormality threaten existing categories of knowledge and resist control but rather that which cannot be thought, that 'which presents itself as a horizon for thought itself'.[25] In short, the encounter with the monstrous is an encounter with the possibility of something unthought that nevertheless somehow demands immediate attention.[26]

In his philosophical analysis of the horror genre (in both film and literature), Eugene Thacker refers to the unthinkable as the 'unnameable thing': not as the unknown (mystical) or not-yet known (the scientific) but as that which presents the possibility of life through a radically *inhuman* logic.[27] Referring to the horror science fiction of P. H. Lovecraft, Thacker claims that what the 'unnameable thing' does is to effectively annihilate human categories of thought such as 'matter and form, actual and potential, origin and finality, growth, decay, and organisation'.[28] Elsewhere, Thacker discusses the horror film genre through 'creature-feature films'. He contrasts the monster as an abomination of nature that still retains an element of familiarity with the unnameable 'creature' as an aberration of thought, in which the monster is contextualized 'in terms of *ontology* (form-without-matter, matter-without-form) or in terms of onto-theology (the spiritual abject, the oozing abstraction)'.[29] These 'creatures' point towards a form of 'life-after-life that highlights *conceptual* aberrations'.[30] While Thacker's concepts of the 'teratological noosphere'[31] or his 'entelechy of the weird'[32] may be difficult to digest, what they point at is nevertheless significant: from a radical anti-anthropocentrism that shuns not only all forms of humanism but which also rejects even post-human possibilities – where not only the human but also the monster is dethroned – the monstrous becomes a zone where aesthetic experience is not only impossible and unthinkable, but entirely irrelevant. In this archaic and alien dimension teeming with unnameable things and creatures, the emphasis on the non-representational, *inhuman* angle of the monstrous is nonetheless brought into full view through 'affective contamination'.[33] The encounter with the inhuman-monstrous opens up a zone of disassociated, multifarious origins and trajectories. It is the gateway to a cacophonous, chaotic zone of indiscernibility: the 'pandemonic space' of the multiple, noisy, 'furious sea of non-individuated, non-harmonized relations: the necessary but neglected background of thought, of life'.[34] Paradoxically, the connection to life via death or non-existence is what makes the monstrous vital.

The monstrous, if anything, causes cognitive interference: it forces us to rethink our trusted positions and to question the solidity of conventional theoretical and discursive frameworks and methodologies. This opens the conditions of possibility for a non-anthropocentric, non-binary and non-representational horizon upon which new concepts may be created. This is in itself the realm for creative experimentation, and as Rosi Braidotti reminds us, 'experimenting with thinking is what we all need to learn'.[35]

Monstrous becomings: Process ontologies and cartographic experiments

Psychoanalytical, representational and ontological approaches that anchor the monstrous to anthropocentric positions based on ideas of Being, of essence, identity and meaning, as well as on constructed preconceptions about what constitutes normality and order from an anthropomorphic and anthropological perspective, although very valuable in their own right, do not reveal much more than that judgement is dependent on perception; that perception is socially, culturally and historically constructed (thus prone to change according to each context); and that – as in the case of psychoanalysis – perception is structured according to oppositions and polarities.[36] Thacker's horror-concept philosophy and his ontologically deviant 'unnameable creatures', on the other hand, have comparable but inverse effects: the incommensurable, unthinkable Outside, or the radically inhuman, might be just too alien and detached to even matter.

To remain operative, liminal ontological concepts such as the ugly or the monster allude primarily to issues of 'difference'. Difference, however, is neither exclusively nor necessarily anthropocentric and anthropomorphic, neither dichotomous nor bipolar. Rather, it is *processual*, *performative* and *relational*. Difference is never static: it originates in process and practice rather than in fact.[37] It emerges through metamorphosis and movement, not from stable categories. It always precedes fixed points or subject positions, because difference emerges in the first place through cuts and through interference. As such, difference may be seen as a germinal, plastic concept that refers to a phenomenon that is deeply rooted in change and transformation, and as such, it always carries a productive force. Difference is then reconfigured from a binary opposition that functions in terms of 'different from' to an action that sets off a process of becoming.[38] The point here is not the 'what' of this becoming but rather the 'how'. This is a crucial aspect of process ontologies, where *telos* and meaning are not of essence. What matters is '*how* we change the way we make meanings'.[39]

This would apply to the ugly and the monster as well. The monster understood as a vessel of difference in perpetual change, as Cohen reminds us, is always at the threshold of becoming,[40] and as such, it always opens more possibilities than it forecloses.[41] In this sense, the monster mutates from being a discrete object, a 'punctum in space and time',[42] a problematic, constructed category or an unstable concept, to become instead a force field or line of flight that escapes conventions, subverts established orders and hence always promotes change. At times, it sketches the contours of that which was always already there but was not recognized, thus rendering visible the invisible. Sometimes it announces the emergence of the new, or assists in its birthing. By focusing not only on its disruptive, transgressive and dysfunctional powers but also on its vitality and productivity, namely on its generative, creative and affirmative potentials, we may shift away from discussions on the monster itself – or from any liminal ontological category for that matter – to the *monstrous as process*. The monstrous is understood here not as that which is humanly unthinkable per se, and hence completely inaccessible, but as a process of becoming. Through theorizations of 'the changeless nature of the process of change itself',[43] through an ontology of becoming, it is possible to liberate the monstrous as a trajectory or vector: a force or desire that animates not only figures and metaphors of the monster but which stirs (within) literally everything.[44] This perspective, in its investment with the changing nature and affective potential of concepts, subjects, objects and matter alike, hinges on the idea that the monstrous is a constitutive and vital force in the human and non-human production of the world, thus opening it up to materialist and pragmatic concerns.

This acknowledges the emergence of a horizon of possibility where cartographic experimentation and theoretical speculation become an occasion for thought and practice that may lead away from logics fixed on identity, reflection, reason and self-containment, and towards what Elizabeth Grosz refers to as the 'logic of invention'. In reference to Gilles Deleuze and Félix Guattari's 'machinic assemblage',[45] Grosz writes that the logic of invention is expansive, ramifying and expedient, producing techniques, solutions, effects and descriptions, rather than rules, premises, conclusions or arguments.[46] In the absence of a hierarchy of Being, pre-ordained order or central organization of plan, the creation of a machinic assemblage follows the 'imperative of endless experimentation, metamorphosis, or transmutation, alignment and re-alignment'.[47] In practice this would mean a process of distributed agency among human and non-human participants, a creative process independent of the normative directives of mastery. The human is one more element in the complex interplay of practice: a practice that does not reveal exclusively but also realizes a particular kind of movement. The realization of such movement, Grosz writes, includes the conditions as well as the *effects* of making.[48]

In this regard, Brian Massumi writes that movement is a consequence of the encounter of different speeds, intensities and forces, which include the human being and the body.[49] He uses the example of carpentry as a sort of 'machinic assemblage' where the encounter of different but interacting materials (wood), tools (plane) and the human (the artisan) sets off a 'hand-to-hand combat of energies'[50] that produces form but in unexpected, dynamic ways. What emerges from the interaction and integration of multiple vectors and heterogeneous elements is a 'diagram of a process of becoming'.[51] In his formulation of 'inventive connections', the focus is on the ways in which *affect* may be diagrammatically related to movement, expansion, relay and process, informing the manner in which the body can connect with itself and with the world.[52] We cannot foresee this diagramming in advance, map it or even translate it as prototype. Since it is contingent to a specific situation, we can never know in advance what it will produce.[53] Diagramming as a mode of composition encompasses a 'new dynamic range [that] outlines itself in the in-between: a fusion as potential relations of movement and rest, mapping a mutant trajectory never before travelled'.[54] In other words, diagramming reveals the contours of a monstrous becoming: understood not as the striving towards a concrete thing, a discrete object, noun or adjective, but as a relational *material process* in which creative and disruptive potentials and agencies are unleashed and reconfigured.

This holds particular importance for material-discursive practices such as architecture, which, as Marco Frascari reminds us, is an entanglement of artistic sensibility and scientific rationality, and which as such cannot be explained by demonstrative reasoning or by the scientific method alone.[55] Experimenting with other narratives and cartographies may provide a glimpse of just how the monstrous is always already latent in architecture, in its practice and its theorization. In what follows, I will trace the contours of a minor cartography in Greek mythology and use the objects that surface in the myths of Daedalus as a thread by which to unravel itinerant, mutant trajectories of the monstrous in architecture. Let's begin with Ariadne and her well-known ball of yarn.

Machinic assemblages: Mechanical cow/white bull/human hand

The myth of Ariadne and her thread is a derivative of one of the most popularized and enduring stories of ancient Greek mythology: the Minotaur and the labyrinth.[56] Lured by the trope of the labyrinth and by the disciplinary affinity with Daedalus, most architects are familiar with the storyline. Less familiar are the entanglements and interactions between the human (and non-human) and the myriad of curious artefacts and monstrous 'things' that populate the plot. Asterion, or the Minotaur, is the hybrid product of the monstrous 'aberrant nuptials' between Queen Pasiphae and a magnificent white bull, mediated by a mysterious mechanical cow. The labyrinth in the dungeons beneath the Knossos Palace serves the double purpose of hiding the monstrous hybrid from the public eye while functioning as a chaotization machine processing enemy prisoners and sacrificial maidens through digestion into Minotaur excrement.[57] A subtle yet effective thread eventually leads to the destruction of the monster, as well as to the ultimate escape of Theseus and Ariadne. Daedalus and his son Icarus, for their part, rely on the famous pair of wings in their epic airborne retreat from Crete, and we all know the consequences of Icarus's hubris. Also less known are Ariadne's *chorós* (dance floor) located on the palace grounds not far from the labyrinth and the fact that both the *chorós* and the labyrinth were engraved on Achilles' magical shield, which appears (and disappears) in another myth. Or that upon their arrival in the sacred island of Delos, Ariadne and Theseus engage in a cryptic 'crane dance',[58] and that at the time, *chorós* meant both the 'thing' and the 'act' (dance floor and dancing), thus folding Delos and Crete through the modulation of movement. Or that Daedalus had to seek refuge in Crete for the murder of his nephew over alleged copyright infringements and the plagiarism of a particularly important instrument: the prototype for the drafting compass.[59]

All these curious artefacts and 'things' are only a few among many objects that animate this and other Greek myths and which under particular conditions were classified as a *daidalon* or *daidala*. In very rough terms, a *daidalon* was a type of machinery – a machinic assemblage, perhaps – composed of all sorts of implements and diverse artefacts, including large-scale infrastructural, naval and architectural works, furniture, domestic appliances, textiles, tools, instruments, life-like sculptures, jewels, ships, even glue. And while less common, *daidala* could also contain certain enigmatic defensive weapons (Achilles' armour and shield, or Hades' invisibility helmet, being some of the best-known examples in this category), as well as other objects with less evident or obtuse functions (such as the infamous wings, the weird mechanical cow or the disorienting labyrinth). *Daidala* also included intangible, immaterial 'things' such as performed choreographies and theatrical plays. However, not just any mundane object could aspire to the status of a *daidalon*. A *daidalon* was composed of mutating, dynamic sets of 'otherworldly', wonderfully luminous, valuable and quasi-divine tangible (and intangible) works of fine craftsmanship and excellent execution[60] that in their articulation and relation revealed quite unusual traits and produced equally peculiar effects. Particularly interesting was a *daidalon*'s relationship to the godly. Mythological Greek gods were divine by virtue not of their genesis (which they shared with human mortals) but rather of their 'immortality' (*athanatoi*), for their unending 'appearingness', mutability and ability to be remade.[61] The facility for appearing, momentarily disappearing and then reappearing under different guises was one of the basic qualities of divinity, a trait that is commonly attributed to the monstrous as well. Like the gods and the monstrous, the *daidalon* appeared, yet because it was so proximate it continuously withdrew without ever entirely disappearing.

But in order to appear a *daidalon* first had to be invented; it had to be thought of and made, and while it was entirely uncertain how it would interact with other *daidala*, with the gods or with other human and nonhuman 'things', thus leaving their *affective* potential undisclosed, the fact that it would produce *effects* was not. The *daidala* exceeded the 'things' that were articulated within and through them. They also surpassed, and deviated from, the functions for which they were created. Endowed with mysterious powers, they provoked effects that were not always calculable or predictable, which more often than not led to chaos rather than order. These crafty artefacts and the assemblages they formed produced much more than what they were initially intended for, and they did so by deviating from a prefixed *telos* or premeditated overarching plan. Believed to enchant, seduce and immobilize those who beheld them, the *daidala*, these 'marvelous machines',[62] revealed more than the vigour, health and power of well-made artefacts. As Lian Chang writes, they could convey opaqueness and enclosure, 'providing something with a new and deceptive veneer'.[63] Hence, a *daidalon* was also a ploy: false, deceiving and often fake not only in its formal appearance or physical materiality but also in its deviant, subversive, dysfunctional potential (recall Pasiphae's mechanical cow that functioned as prosthetic camouflage pod to induce human–bovine intercourse, and its monstrous interspecies outcome). This would bring a *daidalon* close to the contemporary understanding of a 'deviant object'.[64] In general terms, a deviant object swerves – or, as Timothy Morton says, 'veers' – against the normative order of things, or behaves irregularly, playing out in a variety of patterns, noise, aberrancy, redundancy, mutation and so on. In short, a 'thing' that deviates, turns or moves 'not simply from our (human) idea of it, but from other entities' models, conceptions, plans, frameworks' shows how 'movement is part of being a thing, ... such that a thing deviates from itself, just to exist'.[65] Like the deviant object the monstrous also veers – slants away, so to speak – 'disturbingly poised between activity and passivity'.[66] This calls into question the long-standing problem of objects (passive) and subjects (dynamic, agential), challenging the assumption that humans are 'the gods of artefacts', fully capable of putting things together by determining their motion, by discerning 'what is apt, fitting, beautiful, and ugly',[67] and instead drawing from desire as the driving force or vector of becoming in the production of novel 'things' and new subjectivities. In this sense, as a deviant object the *daidalon* always contains the traces and movements of the monstrous: of non-anthropocentric, non-instrumental, inhuman forces that cannot be artificially or cognitively perceived and assembled, nor fully captured or controlled. Yet, precisely because of their affective capacities, they open up a space of possibility for the new, the unexpected or the novel to emerge. The machinic assemblage of daidala generated much more than physical objects or ingenious artefacts: it unleashed earthly disruptions and cosmic chaos; it engendered monsters, heroes and semi-gods; it sparked myths of epic proportions. In short, it produced original creations in the world.[68]

Pushing this idea a little further, it is possible to think of the *daidalon* as the machination of the artificer, the sorcerer or the magician and not as the result of the vision and intervention of the expert, some master architect of rules, truth, authority and order. This would bring us closer to understanding the production of such *daidala* as a 'minor practice' – artisanal rather than technical or even architectural production. Here we would have to call Daedalus to the stand to make our case. In the Western tradition Daedalus is considered the prototypical architect in Greek mythology, fully capable of manipulating and controlling the material world and the cosmos, orchestrating and arranging socio-spatial relations and instilling order from chaos. This corresponds neatly to 'arche-thinking': the Platonic understanding of hylomorphism, or 'the doctrine that production is the result of an (architectural) imposition of a transcendent form on chaotic and/or passive matter'.[69] These 'grand roles' of vision and command, not only of form over matter but also of expert knowledge over artisanal know-how, are commonly attributed to (or appropriated by) architects in general. But, arguably, Daedalus had achieved a higher status as King Minos's master builder as a demiurge (which in contemporary parlance would amount to something of a 'starchitect') not for his powers of cosmic arrangement, his technical knowledge or *technē*, but for his intimate knowledge of *crafts*, most notable in his outlandish inventions and rich variety of *daidala*. Seen not as a noun or 'thing' but rather from its etymological root, a *daidalon* is the substantive complement of the verbs to manufacture, make, forge, weave and make visible[70] actions that already point to the importance of having a 'knack' or intuition for handiwork and the sensitivity for the aesthetic and the artisanal, and not exclusively for the rational and technical.

Significantly, as Indra Kagis McEwen writes, in the early Greek view it was precisely the knowledge of how to *make things* that had brought humankind out of the bestial into a civilized state. Thus, a demiurge was basically not only a public maker, someone whose work belonged to the public realm, but also someone who also understood this work as more than tedious labour, brute, obedient muscle power or compliance with established knowledge. Instead, he knew how to fabricate 'things' by elevating the *experience* and *practice* of making over its *rules* and *techniques*.[71] In this sense a demiurge was someone who veered, not only from a Platonic, Aristotelian or even Heideggerian understanding of the superiority of technical knowledge over artisanal and aesthetic sensibility,[72] but also according to the forms implicit in matter; the 'maker' and the 'thing made' engaged in a sort of 'mutual veering', or attunement.[73] A demiurge was a craftsman, aware that forms are 'not pure but already laden with "variable intensive affects" and thus tied to "material traits of expression"'; someone who surrendered not to the visions, plans and commands of a master architect, but instead to the demands of dynamic matter.[74] This suggests that an artisanal, aesthetic sensitivity means more than simply working in proximity with materials, or even a form of intimate material knowledge (of wood, leather, cloth, etc.). It implies *kairos*, or 'stochastic *technē*', 'the experience of embodied skill and an ability to recognize the appropriate moment for intervention',[75] that counters the hylomorphic logic of production and its emphasis on logocentric emphasis on technical knowledge. An artisanal sensitivity demands an *attunement* with materiality and the dynamism of matter. Here, Deleuze and Guattari's notion of machinic assemblages is crucial. In their words, 'the *machinic phylum* is materiality, natural or artificial, and both simultaneously; it is matter in movement, in flux, in variation, matter as a conveyor of singularities and traits of expression ... this matter-flow can only be *followed*.'[76] But it may also be slightly coaxed. It is the artisan, the itinerant, the ambulant, and not the expert who according to Deleuze and Guattari is 'determined ... to follow a flow of matter ... To follow the flow of matter is to itinerate, to ambulate. It is intuition in action.'[77]

Following Deleuze and Guattari, John Protevi writes that this intuition (attunement) allows us to understand 'artisanal sensitivity [as] a "nomad science" of working with continuous variations rather than a "royal science" of establishing laws between constants'.[78] 'Nomad sciences' and the minor practices of the artisan – but also of the magician, the sorcerer – are not hylomorphic, and while they might produce artefacts that have the appearance of a stable, ordered object, this appearance is the result of linking, cutting, joining, weaving, forging; of negotiating with and following matter to bring about its implicit forms. Nomad and minor sciences thus challenge the assumptions that material systems are organicist or mechanist, 'nothing but a collection of parts', showing instead how it is the machinic, 'the total systematic interrelations' and 'self-ordering principles', and not the architectural, per se, 'that produce order'.[79]

In Deleuzian parlance, becoming-minor is intimately related to becoming-monster and ultimately to becoming-imperceptible.[80] The question at this junction is how we might tease out not the monster per se, but the *monstrous* within the aesthetic-artisanal sensitivity without losing touch with the architectural domain. For this we will have to invoke Daedalus's *daidala* one last time. As we have seen, *daidala* are more than assembled objects or parts of a transparent technological apparatus designed to (mechanically) make and remake straightforward 'things', or even to merely foster a relational, affective or machinic connection among these 'things'. They are the actualized product of particular assemblages through which run all sorts of symbiotic *and* dysfunctional, monstrous forces. As machinic assemblages they operate as an abstract machine, or 'war machine'.[81] One of the characteristics that would seem to make the *daidala* monstrous hinges on its operation, or more accurately, on the different forms of *manipulation*, which, as Hanafi writes, in relation to artifice and natural magic is relevant due to its connection with *manus*, the human hand. This would presuppose an apparently anthropocentric mode of thought that implies that, while 'nature can "operate" just as man and machines and impersonal forces can ... only human beings have the capacity to *manipulate* matter and form'.[82] However, upon closer inspection, what is interesting in this formulation is not the distinctions between nature and the human being but the reference to the hand as the 'organ' capable of manipulating matter and form. The hand is more than a passive, obedient 'mechanical' instrument (something like a prosthesis of the brain): it assumes an agential role in a 'machinic' exchange. In the process of artisanal or aesthetic production, the hand 'thinks' and participates on equal terms with other non-human agents. It enters a machinic assemblage of tools, fingers, materials, objects, ideas and technologies where the speed, forces and intensities of all the agents are simultaneously co-responsible in the process of morphogenesis. Within a plane of distributed non-hierarchical agency, the 'hand-tool-matter' assemblage produces a *poiētic* revealing; and what emerges is the product of co-creation, not of mastery.[83]

Although not much is revealed in the myth about the actual tools, materials and processes used in the making of the *daidala,* some of the 'things' within the myth would appear at first sight to be stable, elementary technical objects arranged within a set or collection of parts, an 'ensemble', that is, objects with instrumental, mechanical or functional value (the mechanical cow, the wings, the compass) within a delimited system (the myth, the labyrinth). Nevertheless, they are produced, preceded and surpassed by something that Gilbert Simondon refers to as technicity, or 'technology considered in its efficacy or operative functioning'.[84] As a machinic assemblage the *daidalon* processes the interactions of dynamic, non-complacent, vital material-forces,[85] and the dexterity of the human hand, mediated by technicity, understood very loosely as the capacity to manipulate tools. But how, we might ask, is this all related to the monstrous? Arguably – and many contemporary thinkers agree – it is in the articulation of technicity and the human, and in particular of the human hand, that we can locate a monstrous becoming: the hand as a sign of the monstrous, and the monstrous as a sign of humanity. When this hand is the hand of the architect, the question becomes all the more relevant.[86]

Coda

The problem with the monster is certainly not a poverty of scholarship but rather its overabundance.[87] It appears literally everywhere, polluting every single domain, from aesthetics to economic theory. It is used to serve all sorts of purposes and make all sorts of claims, yet it resists all attempts to determine a single line of signification:[88] a monster means everything, and nothing at the same time. There is, however, another approach to the monster that I find telling and which I believe may serve as a connection to architecture.

As most scholarly work on the monster reminds us, the English word 'monster' is etymologically related to the Greek words *teratos* and *teras* (prodigy, portent, ominous sign) and the Latin word *monstrum* (show, demonstrate, warn). From this derives its most common interpretation: the monster functions simultaneously as a messenger and as a message. It shows, (de)signs, signals, warns, demonstrates, signifies and so on. The communicative, demonstrative functions are also what give the monster its 'authority' and from where one could extract its power to command, to give directives and instructions and to confirm the rules and laws. Architecture, as Frascari suggests, is a 'theoretical discipline based on *auctoritas*, that is, the authority of architects, who obtain their authority by implementing acts of demonstration'.[89] As a practical discipline, it is often argued that architecture's duty is to produce non-trivial buildings, a duty that is embodied, according to Frascari, in the myth of Daedalus, the architect of the first labyrinth. He writes that 'the universe of architectural semiosis is and must be postulated as a labyrinth, a topological and a logical model for architectural production that is always an expression of an infinite process of interpretation',[90] and thus of demonstration. Elsewhere in his book Frascari pursues the notions of labyrinth, maze and meander. In a paragraph that deserves to be quoted at length, he writes,

> In a maze, Ariadne's thread is necessary, otherwise a life is spent in doing the same moves. No monsters are necessary in this kind of labyrinth. A maze is in itself the Minotaur; the Minotaur is the architect's trial-and-error process. On the other hand, a meander is a labyrinth that works like a net. In a net, every point is connected to every other point. These connections are not designed but are designable. Furthermore, meanders are full of monsters. These Minotaurs, monsters conceived by inconceivable unions, demonstrate the possibility of union between different kinds of realities. They are not abnormalities but rather they are extraordinary phenomena that indicate the way to how-to design for architecture.[91]

The monstrous, as I have been following it in this chapter, operates under the logic of the labyrinth as meander rather than that of the labyrinth as maze. The monstrous is what gives consistency to the different objects, materials, forces and vectors of a *daidalon*, which, as we have seen, includes the labyrinth and the agency of the architect, but only as two among many other unexpected, heterogeneous elements, vectors and forces that are continuously participating in non-hierarchical creative processes. We can never say with precision or certitude what these processes will produce. But we can follow the forces, speeds, vectors and movements that diagram their monstrous becoming.

Notes

1 The monster, however, has been decisive in the development of the natural sciences via early and especially modern teratology (study of monsters), teratogeny (embryology), medicine and evolutionary theory. See, for instance, the substantial work of Georges Canguilhem in this regard, in particular his *On the Normal and the Pathological*, trans. Carolyn R. Fawcett (Dordrecht: D. Reidel Publishing Company, [1966] 1978), reprinted.

2 With the exception of Marco Frascari's monograph, and *Perspecta*'s special issue *Monster*, the contribution of architectural discourse to contemporary monster studies has been relatively poor in the last three decades, peaking during the post-structuralist and deconstructivist period in architecture in the 1980s and 1990s, when the notions of the uncanny, for instance, became a trend. See Marco Frascari, *Monsters of Architecture: Anthropomorphism in Architectural Theory* (Lanham, MD: Rowman & Littlefield, 1991); and *Perspecta Yale Architectural Journal 40: Monster*, ed. Marc Guberman, Jacob Reidel and Frida Rosenberg (Cambridge, MA: MIT Press, 2008).

3 Herman Parret, 'On the Beautiful and the Ugly', *Trans/Form/Ação, Marília* 34 (2011): 29–30.

4 David J. Skal, 'Foreword: What We Talk about When We Talk about Monsters' in *Speaking of Monsters: A Teratological Anthology*, ed. Caroline Joan Picart and John E. Browning (New York: Palgrave Macmillan, 2012), xi.

5 Jeffrey Jerome Cohen, 'Monster Culture (Seven Theses)' in *Monster Theory, Reading Culture*, ed. Jeffrey J. Cohen (Minneapolis: University of Minnesota Press, 1996), 12.

6 See, for instance, the body of work of Michel Foucault, in particular his collected lectures *Abnormal: Lectures at the Collége de France, 1974–1975*, trans. Graham Burchell (New York: Verso, 2003) and his *The Order of Things* (originally published 1966, English translation 1970); or Georges Canguilhem's essay 'Monstrosity and the Monstrous' included in his *Knowledge of Life* (New York: Fordham University Press, 2008), 134–46.

7 Asa Simon Mittman, 'Introduction: The Impact of Monsters and Monster Studies' in *The Ashgate Research Companion to Monsters and the Monstrous*, ed. Asa Mittman and Peter Dendle (London: Routledge Ashgate, 2012), 8.

8 Alexa Wright, *Monstrosity: The Human Monster in Visual Culture* (London: I.B. Tauris, 2013), 3.

9 Ibid.

10 Patricia MacCormack, *Posthuman Ethics: Embodiment and Cultural Theory* (Burlington: Ashgate, 2012), 81.

11 Jeffrey Andrew Weinstock, 'Invisible Monsters: Vision, Horror and Contemporary Culture' in *The Ashgate Research Companion to Monsters and the Monstrous*, ed. Simon Mittman and Peter Dendle (Burlington: Ashgate, 2012), 287.

12 Denise Gigante, 'Facing the Ugly: The Case of Frankenstein', *English Literature History* 67, no. 2 (2000): 576.

13 Mark Dorrian, 'On the Monstrous and the Grotesque', *Word and Image* 16, no. 3 (2000): 310.
14 The experience of horror and the monstrous is described in many sources as 'vertiginous', a term that is reminiscent of religious experience and connotes a sensation of arrested, endless suspension between fear and desire, repulsion and attraction. See, for instance, Daniele Quinodoz, *Emotional Vertigo: Between Anxiety and Pleasure*, trans. Arnold Pomerans (New York: Routledge, 2004)
15 Jeffrey Jerome Cohen, 'Postscript: The Promises of Monsters' in *The Ashgate Research Companion to Monsters and the Monstrous*, ed. Simon Mittman and Peter Dendle (Burlington: Ashgate, 2012), 454.
16 Ibid.
17 According to Huet, (natural) monsters are sterile, unviable, not reproductive; thus, she argues, they are always created, not engendered. See Marie-Hélène Huet, *Monstrous Imagination* (Cambridge, MA: Harvard University Press, 1993), 237.
18 See, for instance, Rosi Braidotti, *Metamorphoses: Towards a Materialist Theory of Becoming* (Cambridge: Polity Press, 2002); Rosi Braidotti, *Nomadic Theory* (New York: Columbia University Press: 2011); Rosi Braidotti, 'The Ethics of Becoming-Imperceptible' in *Deleuze and Philosophy*, ed. Constantin Boundas (Edinburgh: Edinburgh University Press, 2006), 133–59.
19 Gigante, 'Facing the Ugly', 579.
20 Wright, *Monstrosity*, 4.
21 Gigante, 'Facing the Ugly', 568.
22 Parret, 'On the Beautiful', 30 (emphasis in original).
23 'We will not oppose the beautiful to the ugly, but will look for the uglier than ugly: the *monstrous*': Jean Baudrillard, *Fatal Strategies* (Los Angeles, CA: Semiotext(e), 2008), 25–6 (my emphasis).
24 Allen S. Weiss, 'Ten Theses on Monsters and Monstrosity', *The Drama Review* 48, no.1 (2004): 124 (my emphasis).
25 Eugene Thacker, 'Un-Nameable Thing', *Nyx, a Nocturnal: Monsters* 6 (2011): 13.
26 Stephen Zagala, 'Aesthetics: A Place I've Never Seen' in *Shock to Thought: Expression After Deleuze and Guattari*, ed. Brian Massumi (London: Routledge, 2002), 22.
27 Thacker, 'Un-Nameable Thing', 13.
28 Ibid., 12.
29 Eugene Thacker, *In the Dust of This Planet* (Alresford Hants: Zero Books, 2011), 194 (my emphasis).
30 Ibid.
31 Ibid.
32 Thacker, 'Un-Nameable Thing', 15.
33 Félix Guattari, *Chaosmosis: An Ethico Aesthetic Paradigm*, trans. Pail Bains and Julian Pefanis (Indianapolis: Indiana University Press, 1995), 92–3.

34 Michel Serres, *Genesis*, trans. Geneviève James and James Nielson (Ann Arbor: University of Michigan Press, 1995), quoted in Cohen, 'The Promises of Monsters', 453.
35 Rosi Braidotti, 'Interview: Univocity of Being and Single Matter' in *New Materialisms: Interviews & Cartographies*, ed. Rick Dolphijn and Iris van der Tuin (Ann Arbor, MI: University of Michigan Press Open Humanities Press, 2012), 29.
36 Charles T. Wolfe, 'Introduction' in *Monsters and Philosophy*, ed. Charles T. Wolfe (London: College Publications, 2005), xiii.
37 Cohen, 'Monster Culture', 10.
38 Braidotti, 'Interview: Univocity'.
39 Barbara Bolt, *Art Beyond Representation: The Performative Power of the Image* (London: Tauris, 2004), 82 (my emphasis).
40 Cohen, 'Monster Culture', 10.
41 Cohen, 'Promise of Monsters', 452.
42 Amit S. Rai, 'Ontology and Monstrosity' in *Monster Culture in the 21st Century: A Reader*, ed. Marina Levina and Diem-My T. Bui (New York: Bloomsbury, 2013), 17.
43 Ibid., 15.
44 Brian Massumi, *The Principle of Unrest: Activist Philosophy in the Expanded Field* (London: Open Humanities Press, 2017).
45 Gilles Deleuze and Félix Guattari developed their notion of the machinic assemblage (also referred to as 'desiring machine') in their books *Capitalisme et schizophrénie. L'anti-Œdipe* (1972) and *Mille Plateaux* (1980), first published in English as Gilles Deleuze and Félix Guattari, *Anti-Oedipus: Capitalism and Schizophrenia*, trans. Robert Hurley, Mark Seem and Helen R. Lane (London: Athlone, 1984), and Gilles Deleuze and Félix Guattari, *A Thousand Plateaus: Capitalism and Schizophrenia*, trans. Brian Massumi (Minneapolis: University of Minnesota Press, 1987).
46 Elizabeth Grosz, *Architecture from the Outside: Essays on Virtual and Real Space* (Cambridge: Massachusetts Institute of Technology, 2001), 110–12.
47 Elizabeth Grosz, *Volatile Bodies: Towards a Corporeal Feminism* (St Leonard: Allen & Unwin, 1994), 167.
48 Ibid., 168.
49 Brian Massumi, *A User's Guide to Capitalism and Schizophrenia* (Cambridge, MA: MIT Press, 1992), 15.
50 Ibid., 14.
51 Ibid.
52 Ibid., 94.
53 Ibid.
54 Ibid.
55 Marco Frascari, *Monsters of Architecture: Anthropomorphism in Architectural Theory* (Lanham, MD: Rowman & Littlefield, 1991), 8.

56 Homer, *Chapman's Homer: The Odyssey*, trans. Georges Chapman (Princeton, NJ: Princeton University Press, 2000).
57 See, for instance, Félix Guattari's chapters six and seven in *Chaosmosis* (99–135); and Bile's elaboration of Georges Bataille's approach to the labyrinth and crucifixion, in Jeremy Biles, *Ecce Monstrum: Bataille and the Sacrifice of Form* (New York: Fordham University Press, 2007), 100–3.
58 Indra Kagis McEwen, *Socrates' Ancestor: An Essay on Architectural Beginnings* (Boston: Massachusetts Institute of Technology, 1997), 57.
59 Mary Ellen Snodgrass, *Voyages in Classical Mythology* (Santa Barbara, CA: ABC-Clio, 1994), 142.
60 Lian Chang, 'On Fire and the Origins of Architecture' in *Chora, Volume Six: Intervals in the Philosophy of Architecture*, ed. Alberto Pérez-Gómez and Stephen Parcell (Montreal: McGill-Queen's University Press, 2011), 41.
61 Kagis McEwen, *Socrates' Ancestor*, 55.
62 Zakiya Hanafi, *The Monster in the Machine: Magic, Medicine and the Marvelous in the Time of Scientific Revolution* (Durham: Duke University Press, 2000), 175.
63 Chang, 'On Fire', 40.
64 Timothy Morton, 'All Objects Are Deviant: Feminism and Ecological Intimacy' in *Object-Oriented Feminism*, ed. Katherine Behar (Minneapolis: University of Minnesota Press, 2016), 66–81.
65 Ibid., 78.
66 Ibid., 79.
67 Hanafi, *Monster in the Machine*, 176.
68 John Wall, 'Space, Body, Expression' in *Meditations in Cultural Spaces: Structure, Sign, Body*, ed. John Wall (Newcastle: Cambridge Scholars Publishing, 2009), 30–1.
69 John Protevi, *Political Physics: Deleuze, Derrida and the Body Politic* (London: Athlone Press, 2001), 8.
70 See: Carl Kerényi, *Dionysius: Archetypical Image of Indestructible Life*, trans. Ralph Manheim (Princeton, NJ: Princeton University Press, 1978), 100.
71 Kagis McEwen, *Socrates' Ancestor*, 72.
72 Protevi discusses this at length in chapter five 'Master and Slave in the Platonic Body Politic' in his *Political Physics*, 115–48.
73 Morton, 'All Objects', 79.
74 Protevi, *Political Physics*, 7.
75 Protevi, in *Political Physics*, 121, paraphrases David Roochnik, *On Art and Wisdom: Plato's Understanding of Techne* (University Park: Pennsylvania State University Press, 1999), 52.
76 Deleuze and Guattari, *A Thousand Plateaus*, 409 (emphasis in original).
77 Ibid.
78 Deleuze and Guattari, *A Thousand Plateaus*, 446–64 and 361–74, cited in Protevi, *Political Physics*, 122.

79 Protevi, *Political Physics*, 124.
80 Deleuze and Guattari discuss this at length in the Tenth Plateau, 'Becoming-Intense, Becoming-Animal, Becoming-Imperceptible', in *A Thousand Plateaus*, 232–309.
81 See Gilles Deleuze and Félix Guattari, *Nomadology: The War Machine* (Seattle, WA: Wormwood Distribution, 2010).
82 Hanafi, *Monster in the Machine*, 40 (my emphasis).
83 Bolt, *Art Beyond Representation*, 9.
84 Aud Sissel Hoel and Iris van der Tuin, 'The Ontological Force of Technicity: Reading Simondon and Cassirer Diffractively', *Philosophy and Technology* 26, no. 2 (2013): 187.
85 Deleuze and Guattari, *A Thousand Plateaus*, 364.
86 For an interesting and original elaboration on technicity and architecture, see for instance: Stavros Kousoulas, 'The Undetermined Hand: Architectural Technicities' (Paper presented at the international conference *Tools of the Architect*, TU-Delft, November 2017), https://www.academia.edu/35397860/The_Undetermined_Hand_Architectural_Technicities [accessed May 2018].
87 Mittman, 'The Impact of Monsters', 3.
88 Fred Botting, *Making Monstrous: Frankenstein, Criticism, Theory* (Manchester: Manchester University Press, 1991).
89 Frascari, *Monsters of Architecture*, 2.
90 Ibid.
91 Ibid., 108.

CHAPTER FIVE

Traces of ugliness in Bofill's *Les espaces d'Abraxas*

Thomas Mical

This essay reconsiders the work of architecture in the age of postmodern media through the anti-aesthetic categorical lens of ugliness, or, more precisely, the slippages and distortions that form the wider bandwidth of ugliness which arises from a modern category of arbitrary beauty. It takes as its object of analysis the postmodern housing complex *Les espaces d'Abraxas* (1978–83) by Spanish architect Ricardo Bofill (Figure 5.1). In examining this well-known project through its composition (but also its media image), we will come to see how the tensioning of intentions and effects are oriented towards a faux monumentality of parts. The Abraxas complex delivers a vague typological and crafted scenographic solution for the problem of social housing, one curiously cloaked in the a phantasmal Brutalism, and this creates tension and dissonance when closely examined. Though seen as an exception or example of excess, this building complex is visually consistent, with a strong three-part parti, and much of the design work addresses human habitation, civic space and a desire for placemaking when Brutalism and minimalism in housing complexes were fading. It was part of a series of new large-scale social housing projects started under President Giscard and continued under Mitterrand that were intended to operate symbolically as well as serve the housing crisis.[1]

The Abraxas complex foregrounds this change in social housing, circulating in architectural media and reception, but also exemplifies a maturation of the aesthetic consideration of late-modern and postmodern architecture. The range of ugliness of much second-generation twentieth-century Modern architecture is narrower and significantly different from the aesthetic practices of postmodern surfacing, which we can identify as the tendency to

FIGURE 5.1 *Ricardo Bofill*, Les espaces d'Abraxas, *Paris, 1983. Photography by Fred Romero.*

hollow out meaning and deep structures in favour of surface effects. In Abraxas we detect a new type of default ugliness arising from focus upon desired monumentality-effects of the surface, a differentiated but continuous surface propped up around familiar pre-modern urban forms that conjure up appearances of permanence, but also troubling the psyche of the viewer/user with contradictory signals and layers of perceptible tensions and distortions.

How Abraxas slips

We can expect that the production of this work of architecture was driven by the contractual pressure to organize and compose the discrete housing units into a larger ensemble. In this necessary process of formation, Bofill has taken his cue from his populist overtures to neoclassical tendencies running throughout most European postmodernism – with Bofill's flamboyant playfulness marking one extreme and Aldo Rossi occupying the more austere end of the spectrum. Bofill addressed the problem of housing primarily as a problem of form, or, more precisely, the meaning of form, that was to be resolved within the constraints of the financial expediency of prefabricated components. He was obligated to produce a figural figure-ground massing of the part on the site but also took liberties with the materiality and formalism to produce effects – effects not originally linked to the conjured building types. This site strategy exploits the vagueness of type itself, as identified by De Quincy: 'All is precise and given when it comes to the model, while all is more or less vague when it comes to the "type."'[2] This site strategy also takes the vagueness of type literally. Here the three components of the project can be thought of as vague types of blocks that can be stacked or chained around imagined voids, with some degree of formal autonomy. In the Abraxas complex Bofill amplifies the vagueness to increase the ease of combination in the manner of compacting three major formal elements into a singular figure-ground ensemble that come to appear at mass scale: palace, theatre and the arch. The almost 600 units of housing are configured within these monumental forms, and the forms retain their distinct monumental geometry by encasing the units. The housing units are object-like, simple, grey, functional and efficient, like the insides of Warhol's Brillo boxes but scaled up to monumental stacks.

These strong forms are not as pure as they may first appear, especially if one closely examines their edges and scale elements, the locus of dissonance and simultaneously the quiet entry points of ugliness. For this reason we can take these disquieting spaces and constructed distortions as formative conditions, using analytic terms from Eco's *On Ugliness* as an exegetical tool. At least three formal compositional operations can be distinguished in the composition of Abraxas that each produce a mode of aesthetic dissonance: ugliness as a slippage (from the norm), ugliness as an omission (of key parts) and ugliness as the overgrown.

In the dissonant conditions of slippage, elements are changed, transformed or distorted beyond their typological or historical sources and parameters, and in these articulations they morph outwards from within the register of common usage and acceptance into something partially legible but also partially other.

In the tensing conditions of omissions, key elements, significant parts and expected components are absent, leaving literal or perceptual gaps. Missing matter and content produce a break in the expected optical or spatial field conditions. Within a clear field condition any gap takes on a particular significance and draws excess attention to breaks or seams which is amplified if the surround fields are neutral or generic.

The third dissonance noted is when some component or systems becomes overgrown. In the case of Abraxas this repeatedly appears as a hasty 'scaling up' of neoclassical forms and motifs to meet the expectations of monumentality but in such a heavy-handed manner that they begin to take on a menacing character. In some details these grow to properly monstrous sizes fully out of scale for the bodies and functional spaces that interact with them. This excess to the limit of aesthetic sensibility is a conscious and deliberate effort by the architect whose drawings are legal instruments of service defining the professional allocation of resources and labor.

Over scaling is part of monumentality, but also the epigenesis of the monstrous. We see aspects of monumental ugliness in the theories of Umberto Eco, and the recent figuration of monstrous/monster theory as the unexpected interest for everyday aesthetics.[3] This domestication of monster theory into the spectrum of disorder and the ugly is forecast in the early-twentieth-century surrealist fixation on the neo-Gothic and grotesque which persist as a latency still present in works of some arts-driven Modern architecture and urbanism. This tendency of upscaling monstrous hybridity can also be seen in much of today's parametric design strategies and the overall cultural big data bias.

Certainly Bofill stages the Abraxas complex as a monumental composition of block housing, intending the project to perform as a built polemic – indeed, much of the published texts detail the aesthetic decision-making process to produce wide social meaning and value.[4] In this and other housing projects he favours strong form, not weak form.[5] Thus, he eschews the informal and the formless, which are also tagged elsewhere as Surrealist tropes and eventually recognized in the aesthetic schema of Rosenkranz as ugly categories themselves.[6] There are three types of formless ugliness identified by Rosenkranz: 'in plain language as shapelessness, as non-form, and disunity' or more precisely defined as 'the opposite of form, amorphism; that of the rational ordering of differences, asymmetry, and that of living unity, disharmony'.[7] It is in this last category of disharmony that we can identify some portions of the strong form of the Abraxas ensemble as sliding to formless. Rosenkranz notes that

> disharmony is indeed in itself ugly, but one must distinguish right away between that which is necessary and thus beautiful and that which is accidental and thus ugly. Necessary disharmony is the conflict into which the so-to-speak esoteric differences within a unity can fall through their justified collision; the accidental is the as-it-were exoteric contradiction imposed on a unity. The necessary kind reveals the entire depth of a unity in the monstrous rip it tears open.[8]

In this aesthetic schema formless has some affinity with accidental carelessness, though the Venturi-era populism places ugliness as intentional.

Arbitrary beauty today

Beyond compositional slippage, there is a more categorical aesthetic slippage occurring in the Abraxas project, as this project explicitly draws upon concrete prefabricated elements supporting a grand neoclassical scenographic impulse urbanism. In these we see the mobilization of the arbitrary and the pastiche of stylistic fragments and distorted citations. These come to the surfaces of predetermined brand-forms whereby glass and concrete give the seamless continuity. If we accept the aesthetic reductions of modernism specified by intellectual classicizing seventeenth-century precedent in the architecture of Claude Perrault, beauty bifurcates into positive contra arbitrary, a distinction which holds into the late twentieth century. This legacy theorization sets two types of 'default settings' in industrializing architecture. It is worth recalling the schema, as well as the rhetorical formation of these two as a dissonance, in Perrault's sweeping articulation two types of beauty:

> Against the beauties I call positive and convincing, I set those I call arbitrary, because they are determined by our wish to give a definite proportion, shape, or form to things that might well have a different form without being misshapen and that appear agreeable not by reasons within everyone's grasp but merely by custom and the association the mind makes between two things of a different nature. By this association the esteem that inclines the mind to things whose worth it knows also inclines it to things whose worth it does not know and little by little induces it to value both equally.[9]

George Baird examined this closely in his 1969 essay 'La Dimension Amoureuse' where arbitrary beauty morphs over time from eclecticism in the early modern to camp in the postmodern.[10] More recently Matthew A. Cohen argues, based in part on a new interpretation of Claude Perrault's 1683 codification of the notion of positive beauty in which 'architects and others have always had access to two parallel strands of thought pertaining to proportional systems: a sceptical-pragmatic strand and a respectful-metaphysical strand' which allows us 'to separate aesthetic from historical considerations'.[11] But this analysis of tracks within positive beauty leaves unclear the potential hidden mechanisms in the more formless category of arbitrary beauty.

With the postmodern eclipse of Brutalism, it seems that positive beauty is once more valued above the beauty of the arbitrary. The prior Brutalism lets architects initiate ugliness into the abstract razor edge concrete aesthetics of Brutalism as a deformation of expectations for architectural ornament, and in this way the stark efficiency becomes code for institutions and control spaces, a negative process of value disappearing and seeping into the void. The postmodern moment could have staged a collective desire for reversal back to positive beauty, but the industrial mode of production still constrained its operations within the socius of modernity. So long as postmodernism was produced in the same industries as Brutalism, the arbitrary beauty of the industrial was not banished. Both eras sustain a bare technological ugliness, sometimes performative but never sublime, expansive or subliminal.

Umberto Eco identifies a light sequence of progression of the industrial to the decadent phases of (architectural) ugliness in his text *On Ugliness*, drawing upon a range of mostly Parisian sources and examples, which sets a dual context for understanding the Abraxas complex. The first industrial ugliness is the squalor of progress, evolving into Decadentism and the licentiousness of the ugly, with riches as accoutrements of the industrial era.[12] Eco's 'Industrial ugly' and Perrault's 'arbitrary beauty' still intertwine today in a second industrial phase of the late-modern Paris sprawl, and they seem to appear more often through omission than commission in more recent variants of industrialized architecture. The prefab concrete panels and concrete slabs in Abraxas are legible as industrial decisions and thus are bound into industrial-arbitrary ugliness, a complex pool of surface forms susceptible to discrete waves of dissonance, as if all hard forms are secretly pulled by the lunar body of industrialization.

Faux monumentality

Before the blank voids of ascetic Modern architecture, the prior reception and hunger for figural space was long established in pre-modern urbanism but becomes a recessive trait in Brutalism only to resurge in postmodern aesthetics. The strong forms of the Abraxas complex generate monumental impulses in the co-dependent forms of the shaped public space. This is where we can locate the resurrected bodies of figural spaces in the Abraxas complex – now neither as tragedy nor farce but more precisely a semiotic signification of the figural – where these nascent public spaces are tellingly empty. This mirrors the change of material from early modern honorific and monumental stone to the repetition of prefab concrete which tells us all we need to know about the new order of friction-free neoclassical tableaux. Here the signifier 'tableaux' is invoked ironically from the aesthetic imperative of Boullée for architecture to speak as a unified painting held together through mass. When mass is disbanded, we are often left with image and surface effects. Monumentality was more pronounced due to excess of scale in the early modern and loses this mass in the immediacy of mnemonic media (such as memory analogues in the emerging digital world). In the television-era writings and projects of Robert Venturi and Denise Scott Brown, the arbitrary beauty of the Brutalist era leads to the later postmodern emergence of a faux monumentality in much of the published works of Bofill and his contemporaries.

This media-scape from which that ersatz postmodern consumer culture arises colours the relation of monumentality and ugliness in generic postwar architecture. The postmodern seduction of monumentality is actually part of this longer process of architecture becoming realized in various media simulations. We can see the descent of monumentality and the rise of faux monumentality as a mechanism tied to media politics, in the writings of Jean Baudrillard who defined seduction as a sequence culminating in the weak postmodern:

> In this last phase the original of seduction, its ritual and aesthetic form, disappears in favour of an all-out ventilation whereby seduction becomes the informal form of politics, the scaled-down framework for an elusive politics devoted to the endless reproduction of a form without content. (This informal form is inseparable from its technical nature, which is that of networks – just as the political form of the object is inseparable from the techniques of serial reproduction.) As with the object, this 'political' form corresponds to seduction's maximum diffusion and minimum intensity.[13]

There are thus likely to be both weak forms of seduction and some stealthy operations in the quasi-panopticon, or more accurately the cycloptic-tinged open spaces of the Abraxas complex. The three formal components – palace, theatre, arch – are combinatory, discrete and separate, not completely fused like the sources in Boullée, Ledoux and other postmodern idols. Bofill here executes a shift of this prior technique – a sort of internal branding – whereby tectonics and unit planning are more similar and efficient across the complex while the scale-shifts of the three blocks, pediments, hollow columns and other final construction details undermine the perfectly formed monumentality of the past with a postmodern pastiche of slippages and omissions. We could read the Abraxas complex as a longing for a monumental past or a player in a desired Nietschean, postmodern monumental history. This could be an ironic return of the prior culture of architectural taste and classical vitalism rising to challenge the functionalism of Brutalism for automatically dispensing culture.

Critic Owen Hatherley in recent subtle reading instead sees in Bofill's Abraxas complex not a reactionary monumentality such as the expected 'stage set where the most important thing is not the experience of space, but communication ("this is a traditional building"), even if it's made of breeze blocks. There's a huge difference between this and how Bofill has employed his classical sources: "here you cannot forget for a moment that you're in a massive modern housing estate."[14] And this housing is also tensioned and distorted by the formalism.

Domestic trouble

The slow pulsations of work and days within the rigid containers of the brut architecture of Abraxas play out as everyday life and domestication of the monumental. The reversal of Palladian noble domesticity may be a strain of postmodern anti-aesthetics that are still latent in Bofill's project today. Before Abraxas there is the investigation of composition of the everyday in dispersed sources such as the literary formula of Georges Perec's *Species of Spaces*, Henri Lefebvre's *Critique of Everyday Life* and the sociologic of the disgorged tectonic detail prevalent in the social welfare projects of Parisian control. 'Daily life should not be banalized,' Bofill explains, 'but exalted to become rich and meaningful.'[15] Diane Ghirardo clarifies 'while claiming to celebrate everyday life, Bofill effectively holds it in low esteem'.[16]

In the series of housing complexes which recede and follow the Abraxas complex, the capability and promise of social architecture is to vary the routines of everyday life and amplify chance contingency. *Le espaces d'Abraxas* was described as 'a monument to everyday life, it is conceived and composed in space after the rules of classical art'.[17] Abraxas is a speculative satellite city, a fragmented utopian hedge on de-historicized soil that cloaks the human needs for shelter. With limited impulse control the architect's desire for architecture moves far beyond the lower threshold of providing shelter, taking a certain liberty to exceed the weakest standards of the welfare state through ambition of clearly defining the socius whereas the dwelling unit belongs to habitus. Bofill's project can be seen in this framing as a directed search for the reversal of industrial forms of alienation. In its media image but also through its composition, we see the tensioning of intentions and effects that are oriented towards a monumentality of parts.[18]

Bofill's works of architecture include their media presentation and attention as extensions of the architectural imagination, a consequence of the emergent media-architecture split in the postmodern era between plot and story. Architecture, like cinema, can create seduction through the pleasure of projection. In the Abraxas complex we see a clear and present need for attention, projection and media circulation. The popular images of these thrifty-cut material layers shaped into sledgehammer monumentality recall a histrionic legacy of architectural history, while also attending to the collapse of perspectival space and subject positioning in the then-dominant social media form of television (and to a lesser degree, cinema). Arbitrary ugliness is thus only partially concealed, held at a strange focal distance, a forced diminished perception of the ugly as localized within the persistence of objects and the cues of misdirection.

The Abraxas complex delivers a vague typological and crafted scenographic solution for the problem of social housing, one curiously in the after-image of a prior Brutalism. The turn from Brutalist form to neoclassical form while retaining the prefab brutalist concrete – here for symbolic purposes – is a double-game troubled by the traces of uglinesss. The column-body-cylinder tropes are not foregrounded as delicate or supportive filters and screens. They are not fingers transferring loads into the soil but just as much sentries and fences for the block formation of the housing canisters inside. The complex holds curious operations on the scenography of cutting and framing of privacy privacy is settled among the spectacle of the subtle otherness of the social-scenographic characterization of social housing as social class container.

Conclusion

In *Les Espaces d'Abraxas* the arrangement of the ordering systems and the arrangement of the housing units work as two discretely separate scaffolds, two scales, two arrays that interface in seams, joints and gaps – and these we know are the easiest locations for secrets, errors, distorions and traces of ugliness to emerge. Somehow the fine-scale connections of parts in the architecture are expected to register a similar cohesion in the socius of people in their everyday life. This near-equivocation of social and tectonic is perhaps most clear in the curious tectonic joints of the project we see, on the one hand, exaggerated proportions and disruptive friezes, slipped discs, fragmentary citations of classical theatrical baroque, almost everything performative and propagating (or propaganda) messages – as if the core of the project is producing dissonances. On the other hand, the overall forms of the Abraxas complex seek to legitimately overturn suburban sprawl and are a foil or repelling points for all sorts of eccentric or blank details manifest in the calm repetition of prefabrication techniques where assembly is not surprise but preconceived and predetermined before prefabrication. Abraxas draws from, but moves beyond, the early days of prefabrication, optimized in Brutalism, but seems to perform a focused arbitrary retro-Brutalism returning into the seams of neoclassical monumentality. Nigel Whiteley notes, 'Ricardo Bofill's massive neoclassical palace at the Abraxas housing scheme outside Paris is, arguably, appropriate because it expresses contemporary ideas about a socially and culturally mobile community. But Banham, while acknowledging that Bofill's work was "technically brilliant," dismissed it as "stylistically depraved" because it was revivalist.'[19]

The Abraxas complex is a mixed media and a mixed success – it can also be seen as habitable and generating of some values, as well as operating as a higher-order social housing experiment whose criteria for success dovetail with the emergence of a new social ugliness. This social ugliness is evident in the Reagan–Thatcher–Mitterrand embrace of neo-liberal ideology to support the state which has been shown to collapse social safety nets. Here monumentality is an aspiration executed through suspicious means, and here ugliness in the European postmodern manner works aggressively outside the Venturi-inspired creeping malaise to prop up other social illusions and fleeting televisual concepts/constructs, such as 'the public'.

To ascertain the function of ugliness, outside of the function of function, like other infiltrators of architectural production – it lies for the critic to track and diagnose its seepage. Only under certain conditions can we demonstrate that ugliness is a category or strong attribute. Increasingly it is a weak field condition within stronger field conditions, co-present as potential but tensioning our peripheral vision and suspension of disbelief in an era where the architectural image has superseded the function of architecture in determining our 'sense' of architecture. The apparent determinism of postmodern architecture is to stage and comport sense to the world, through the sensorium and experience of architecture. When ugliness in architecture is aligned with nonsense, it opens up possibilities becoming surreal or absurd. In this way we can see a wide range of effects possible through scales and degrees of ugliness in architecture, and in the traces of ugliness we unexpectedly can see a new type freedom as Umberto Eco under-states: 'Ugliness is unpredictable and offers an infinite range of possibilities.'[20]

Notes

1 For an interesting analysis of these social projects, see Annete Fierro, *The Glass State: The Technology of the Spectacle, 1981–1998* (Cambridge, MA: MIT Press, 2003).

2 Quatremere de Quincy, 'Type' (1825) in *The Oppositions Reader: Selected Essays 1973–1984*, trans. and ed. K. Michael Hays (New York: Princeton Architectural Press, 1998), 618.

3 Umberto Eco, *On Ugliness* (New York: Rizzoli, 2007).

4 See the range of architect-centred readings of the *Les espaces d'Abraxas* in Charles Jencks, *Post-Modernism: The New Classicism in Art and Architecture* (London: Academy Editions, 1987); Bartomeu Cruells, *Ricardo Bofill Architecture Workshop* (Barcelona: G. Gill, 1992); and the recently published Pablo Bofill, *Ricardo Bofill: Visions of Architecture* (Berlin: Die Gestalten Verlag, 2019).

5 Ignasi de Sola-Morales, 'Weak Architecture' in *Architecture Theory since 1968*, ed. K. Michael Hays (Cambridge, MA: MIT Press), 616–23.

6 Yve-Alain Bois and Rosalind Krauss, *Formless: A User's Guide* (New York: Zone Books, 1997).

7 Karl Rosenkranz, *Aesthetics of Ugliness: A Critical Edition*, ed. and trans. Andrei Pop and Mechtild Widrich (London: Bloomsbury, 2015), 63.

8 Ibid, 83.

9 Claude Perrault, *Ordonnance for the Five Kinds of Columns after the Method of the Ancients* (Santa Monica, CA: Getty Publications, 1996), 51.

10 George Baird, 'La Dimension Amoureuse' in *Architectural Theory since 1968*, ed. K. Michael Hays (Cambridge, MA: MIT Press), 50.

11 Matthew A. Cohen, 'Introduction: Two Kinds of Proportion,' *Architectural Histories* 2, no.1 (2014): 21.

12 Eco, *On Ugliness*, 333, 350.

13 Jean Baudrillard, *Seduction* (Basingstoke: Macmillan Education, 1990), 180.
14 Owen Hatherley, 'The Good, the Bad and the Ugly – Neoclassical Architecture in Modern Times', *Apollo Magazine* (3 January 2019).
15 Ricardo Bofill cited in *Places* 2, no. 3, 1985.
16 Diane Ghirardo, *Out of Site: A Social Criticism of Architecture* (Seattle, WA: Bay Press, 1991).
17 Yukio Futagawa, ed., *GA Architect: Ricardo Bofill and Taller de Arquitectura* (Tokyo: A.D.A. Edita, 1985), 120.
18 The project appears in Terry Gilliam's *Brazil* (1985) and Francis Lawrence's *Hunger Games* (2015).
19 Nigel Whitely, *Reyner Banham: Historian of the Immediate Future* (Cambridge, MA: MIT Press), 299.
20 Eco, *On Ugliness*, 315.

CHAPTER SIX

Post-communism and the monstrous: Skopje 2014 and other political tales

Mirjana Lozanovska

In February 2010, during an event at the Aleksandar Palace Hotel hosted by the municipality of Skopje, the capital city of the Republic of Macedonia, the national government hosted the screening of a video entitled *Visualization of the Skopje Centre in 2014*, an animation of a virtual architectural and urban model of the city in the future.[1] In it, hundreds of statues, both figures in history as well as metaphoric compositions, and an abundance of domes, bridges and fountains set against neoclassical facades reveal this new vision as urban scenography. The video employs two video techniques. The first magnifies and rotates one statue after another; the second shows a panorama of the city centre to convey the effect of new, inserted structures and facades, with an overall effect of a nineteenth-century aesthetic constructed as a twenty-first-century city. The mayor made clear the problem was indeed one of aesthetics: 'Skopje needs a new image. We will turn it from a city in a grey, socio-realistic style into one with an aesthetic nature.'[2] While clumsy in its virtual technology, the design concept was a new aesthetic approach driven by a post-capitalist, cultural tourism economy that would cast aside the ghost of socialist realism.[3]

The mayor's phrase 'grey, socio-realistic style' is not a description of the actual city, however, but a pejorative political reference to the urban reconstruction of Skopje following the earthquake of 1963, when Skopje and the Republic of Macedonia were part of Tito's socialist Yugoslavia. Its architecture was epitomized by Kenzo Tange's winning project for the city centre in the international competition organized by the United Nations and Yugoslavia in 1965.[4] Tange's architectural language may be grey in colour, as are many of the key structures that manifested its implementation, but it is hardly 'socio-realistic'. Tange's master plan promised not only a city reconstructed after an earthquake but also a whole new aspiration for Skopje as an international modern city, proposing to solve its transportation and housing problems and symbolically articulating its resilience, through scale and an aesthetic of mass and structure. The post-earthquake reconstruction of the city centre comprised major state institutional structures as well as infrastructure. They include the Telecommunications Building (1974/79), by Janko Konstantinov; the main campus of Ss. Cyril and Methodius University (1974), by Marko Mušič; the National Hydraulic Institute (1972), by Krsto Todorovski; and the Bank Complex (1970), by R. Lalovik and O. Papeš. These collectively produced a *béton brut* cityscape, inspiring twenty-first century writers to label Skopje the 'brutalist capital of the world'.[5]

Brutalist Skopje covered a broader area than Skopje 2014 and the major institutions noted above mapped a network of a new optimism and a gravitas about work still to be done. The architecture of this Skopje is characterized by bulk, large volumes, heavy walls and expressive concrete structures with ornament. While Tange's master plan was met with scepticism at the time and with negativity in the decades that followed, these raw concrete structures were embedded in the modernizing consciousness of this most southern Yugoslavian republic.[6] The mayor's terminology is political rhetoric, mimicking the popular critique of communist architectural aesthetic from the West, it ostensibly denounces the aesthetic of the city's Brutalist architecture but actually denounces all that it has come to represent: Yugoslavia, Yugoslavia's lead in the Non-Aligned Movement at the height of the Cold War and the country's alliance with the United Nations. The mayor's words align a perceived grey aesthetic with socialism and the Brutalist architecture that characterized Skopje from the mid-1960s to the late 1970s. The aesthetic tension within the city that results from the facadism of Skopje 2014 coexisting with the concrete masses of the post-earthquake reconstruction requires careful navigation of an entangled politics.

With Skopje 2014, the government set an agenda to erase, mask and conceal the grey concrete Brutalist architectural landscape under a new aesthetic veil of pastiche, ornamentation and historicism. From the outset, the promotional representation of Skopje 2014 evoked postmodern theories of the anti-aesthetic, recalling end-of-modernism essays and the architectural expression of historicist facades intended to resolve the problem of the sameness of internationalist architecture. However, the global spread of Brutalist architecture is distinct from corporate internationalism, and was instead a public-oriented program conveying stature and stability through scale and massing and a relative ease of construction, though also often erected in haste, out of expedience and with very little expertise. Brutalist architecture has been disparaged by the architectural and popular press, in Skopje and beyond, as ugly in its raw, overscaled and aggressive physical presence.

This aesthetic perception of Brutalism warranted the demolition of many Brutalist structures around the world. In response to this demolition, social media sites and recent publications, such as *Raw Concrete: The Beauty of Brutalism,* 'Tough Love: In Defense of Brutalism', *Beautiful Monster* and *SOS Brutalism*, have developed to defend the 'unusual beauty' and heritage value of such Brutalist architecture.[7]

Skopje's Brutalism is of a different kind than the one described in Reyner Banham's 1955 essay (Figure 6.1).[8] The dominant, almost infrastructural urban design elements of Tange's 1965 master plan, the City Wall and City Gate, emerged from Japanese Metabolism to frame and organize the city. The competition raised the international profile of this small marginal city, prompting Yugoslavian students to study at major US universities on United Nations fellowship, where many were influenced by the American Brutalism of Paul Rudolph at Yale University (including pioneering Macedonian architect Georgi Konsantinovski[9]). Following Tange's master plan of 1965, noted international and Yugoslavian architects contributed to the city's *béton brut* aesthetic, and architectural design in Skopje participated in an innovative and experimental in-situ concrete phase of Yugoslavian architecture in the 1960s and 1970s.[10] Despite its uniqueness, however, Skopje's Brutalist heritage tends to be treated as a single amorphous entity of greyness, the erasure of which was the goal of Skopje 2014.[11]

The post-communist aesthetic moment in Skopje

The Skopje 2014 project has been a spearhead of the political agenda of the Internal Macedonian Revolutionary Organisation (VMRO), who won the 2008 election in a coalition with the Democratic Party of Albanians.[12] Aiming to cement the transition from a pan-Yugoslavian communist ideology to a twenty-first-century global economy, both cultural and financial, hastened by the fall of its socialist system, the government, led by VMRO, mobilized an anti-aesthetic strategy.[13] Dominated by images and a new historicist scenography, Skopje 2014 conveys a sense of a historical déjà vu, recalling the postmodern moment as the Western cultural economy grappled with new forms of multinational capital in the late 1970s. Against this political spectrum the staged opposition between the hyperrealism of Skopje 2014 and the Brutalism of Skopje in 1965 is entangled with what Fredric Jameson calls the 'political unconscious' – a political monster that can appear, reappear and be cemented in various guises of the visual.[14] The implementation of the aesthetic upgrades exceeded the scope of spectacular presentation in the animation, as the programme was expanded and ever more sites were appropriated.[15] By 2014, four years after the work began, the transformation of the city centre was absolute.

FIGURE 6.1 *The Telecommunications Centre by Janko Konstantinov, 1974–79. Overlooking the Vardar River, its three components – a horizontal slab office building, a tower with concrete cylindrical services and the post office – present a raw, tough structural expressionism at a large scale, which characterizes Skopje Brutalism. The circular post office (shown) was damaged by a fire in 2013 that destroyed the interior, the cubist murals of acclaimed post-cubist painter Borko Lazevski and retro decor. Photograph by Mirjana Lozanovska, Skopje 2013.*

How has ugliness been politicized in the post-communist era? In his seminal essay 'Postmodernism, or the Cultural Logic of Late Capitalism' of 1984, Jameson argues that postmodernism had emerged out of a 'whole "degraded" landscape of schlock and kitsch, of TV series and Reader's Digest culture, of advertising and motels, of the late show and the grade-B Hollywood film'.[16] While much of the condition his essay was describing has passed, Jameson's analysis of the aesthetic logic of neoclassical postmodernism as it appeared in a new type of society – a consumer, media, information, electronic and high-tech society – provides a useful aesthetic perspective for explaining how this type of postmodern ugliness reappeared belatedly in Skopje. Jameson's aesthetic concepts of flatness and depthlessness, of pastiche and its erosion of parody, of the imitation of dead styles, and the effects of these in breaking down the chain of historical time can assist in interpreting the aesthetic agenda of Skopje 2014 and how it reconfigures Brutalist Skopje.

In that essay of 1984, Jameson observes a 'waning of *affect*' in postmodern culture, but the concept of 'affect' is also used in contemporary aesthetic theory to explain the 'experiential' dimension of post-capitalist environments – including the logic behind Skopje 2014 as it enacts a double kamikaze: a post-communist reaction to its architecture and a post-capitalist desire for 'experience'.[17] Affect theory addresses the increasing role of 'immersion' and 'experience' as central to the twenty-first-century perception of art.[18] While experience may have been theorized as partial, contingent and intersubjective, 'immersion' has become a condition somewhere between virtual and sensory realities. Affect theory goes beyond Jean Baudrillard's theory of simulacra, because a key tenet of affect theory is that simulacra are transposed onto experience in so-called augmented realities. What is of interest is not the overlay of the copy, or the textual, onto the real, but the real as a sensorial condition of virtual and signifying realities – in other words, the inverse of what Baudrillard understood as simulacra. The Skopje 2014 project created such an augmented reality when the inhabitants of Skopje and the Republic of Macedonia could not untangle the conflation of the experience of the publicity video in 2010, staged as community consultation, from the imagery that circulated on social media and, even more spectacularly, from the actual remodelling of their everyday spatial environment.

The animation of Skopje 2014 was broadcast on television in 2010 and then highlighted regularly in programmes to promote the government's agenda of transforming the republic. Its dissemination provoked numerous media debates over identity politics in Macedonia and the ugliness of the Skopje 2014 urban renewal plan. The anthropologist Goran Janev has written extensively denouncing the plan: 'The late explosion of nationalism, or rather the late demonstration of latent nationalism, is about to turn Skopje from an open city into a claustrophobic city with excluded spaces.'[19] With its focus on the renewal of a small area of the city centre, Skopje 2014, as shown in the 2010 video, omitted the spaces surrounding this centre, the districts and peripheral areas of Skopje.

Such earnestness of critique depends on a structuralist or pre-postmodernist division of truth from lie, history from fantasy, reality from fabrication, which formed the basis of many of the criticisms uttered against Skopje 2014 and, by extension, against the government for being inadequate and incompetent. The proposed beautification evoked a postmodern form of ugliness characterized by the hyperreal, an excess of surface and the materialization of the superficial. The pastiche that covers up Skopje belongs to this anti-aesthetic of postmodern culture, as described by Jameson, against the sobriety, seriousness and even stability of the Brutalist architecture and its societal network of institutions. In addition to this anti-aesthetic, Skopje 2014 has more fully morphed into a sensorial aesthetic of augmented immersion and affect. According to *The Economist*,

> This corner of the Balkans is suffering the shock of the new. For this is more than just a city rejuvenation project. Almost every structure and statue is part of a wider ideological scheme to recast Macedonia's identity. The heart is Skopje's central square, which for decades was a bleak and empty space. Now it has been crammed with statuary.[20]

In other words, Skopje's central square has always been perceived as ugly, not only by the mayor and the governing political party in 2010, but by a generation of Western sentiment, because it was 'bleak and empty' and thus too reminiscent not of socialist realism but of socialism. And after 2014, it is still ugly because it is now 'crammed with statuary', the result of the mechanisms set in motion by a contemporary political unconscious navigating a post-communist aesthetic economy.

Facadism

The main strategy of the beautification project that became known as 'Skopje 2014', by which the city centre was transformed (beyond 2014 to 2018), was re-facading. In the 2010 video, a virtual facade is applied to a digital model of the existing Pelister Building, a rectilinear, modern building on a site now read as one of the radial jigsaw pieces of Macedonia Square. Re-facading extended far beyond this projection. Historicist masks of modular panels resurfaced, one building at a time, one facade after another, piece by piece, gearing towards an aggressive methodical facadism that refashioned the entire city centre, transforming a rectilinear and modernist landscape into a new urban scenography.

The most shocking moment for Skopje's local architectural community was the wrapping of the Government Building in a historicist envelope. Petar Mulichkovski designed this building in 1970, as the Headquarters of the Communist Party of the Federal Republic of Macedonia. It was noted for its innovative suspended structural system comprising a series of cubic volumes that hovered over a raised platform, giving the building the appearance of overcoming gravity, its modernist lightness in a direct architectural dialectic with the medieval stone wall of the Kale Fortress. The new 2014 makeover, both facade and envelope, turned this light, suspended structure and its system of prefabricated metal panels into a heavy, neoclassical building, uncannily mimicking the White House in Washington, provoking a storm of protest from the architectural community. The most vocal objection came from the staff and students of the Faculty of Architecture at Ss. Cyril and Methodius University in Skopje. The mutilation of the building was such that nothing of the original could be identified. This architectural monster demonstrated what re-facading could do. The final result of the new makeover was an affront to structuralist modern views, according to which the facade was seen as subservient to volume, form and structure.

Facadism in Skopje extended beyond literal re-facading. Following a paradigm of masking and veiling, new buildings and numerous other structures, along with statues, sculptures, landscapes and bridges, were inserted into the city, into the voids of the 1965 master plan – both planned free spaces and unbuilt residual sites (Figure 6.2). New aesthetic registers of pastiche and hyper-historicism applied to Skopje's Brutalist and modernist architecture implemented a new political orientation, one that Jameson calls 'an implicitly or explicitly political stance on the nature of multinational capitalism today'.[21]

On the north bank of the Vardar River at the Stone Bridge, a series of thin, rectilinear slices of buildings were inserted. The neoclassical facade they present forms a linear and uniform curtain that effectively masks the structures and the hybrid urban fabric behind them. Alejandro Zaera-Polo argues against any historical distinction between the 'facade' as representational surface and the 'building envelope' as material skin mediating the climate of the interior. Instead, he proposes that both the facade and the building envelope are sites of architecture's interface with politics and power in the twenty-first century.[22] For Zaera-Polo, the building envelope, safely guarded by the paradigm of environmentalism, should be considered as being on the same level as the facade, both forming a dominant mode of commodification. The choice of a neoclassical architectural language for these facades has become a focus for criticism of the Skopje 2014 project, from Janev's arguments that this is an invented heritage, a 'production of selective tradition by the state system', to the numerous platforms that erupted on social media between 2010 and 2018, fusing into a convoluted hyper-critique.[23] Janev criticized what he saw as the nationalist government's oversight, calling it a failure to realize that only a handful of 'authentic instances' of neoclassical/neo-baroque existed in Skopje and that these belonged to the rule of the Serbian Kingdom.[24] But for all this concern, unlike the government's neoclassical projects, the corporate glazed envelopes – also defacing and more frequently demolishing existing structures – have escaped criticism.

Is the hyper-historicism of Skopje different from the ravenous eclecticism of the postmodernist consumption of space, whose mechanisms of imitation and replication, as described by Henri Lefebvre, produce a capitalist regime of 'images and signs of history, of authenticity, of style. ... Neo-this and neo-that, consumed as novelties'?[25] The situation in Skopje is similar

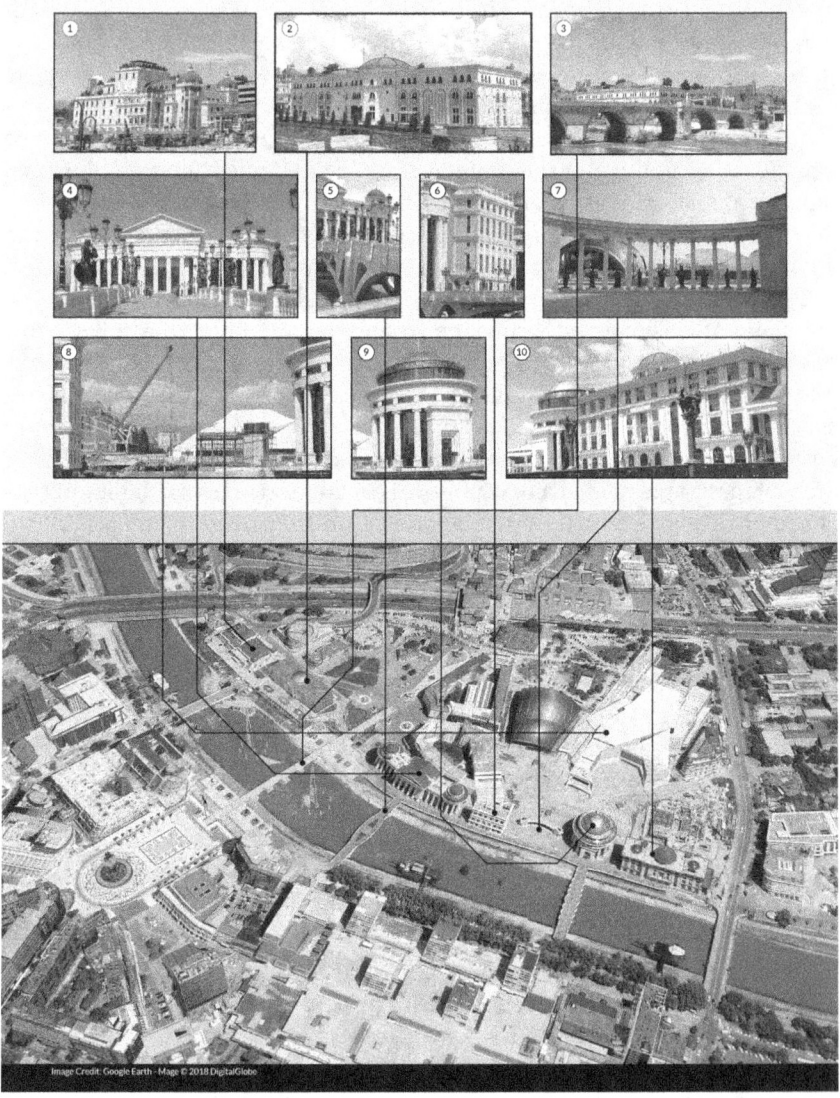

FIGURE 6.2 *Map of the implementation of Skopje 2014, illustrating the 'masking' strategy of thin architectural interventions on the north bank of the Vardar River. These numbered interventions are as follows: 1. Macedonian National Theatre, 2. Museum of the Macedonian Struggle, 3. Stone Bridge, 4. Archaeological Museum of Macedonia, 5. The Bridge of Civilizations, 6. Agency for Electronic Communications, 7. Colonnade of Mother Teresa Square, 8. Macedonian Opera & Ballet, 9. Public Prosecutor's Office of the Republic of Macedonia, 10. Ministry of Foreign Affairs. Image reconstruction by Ali Rahimi. Photographs by Mirjana Lozanovska. Google Earth – Mage © 2018 Digital Globe.*

to the aesthetic of post-communist urban renewal programmes in Eastern European nations that became integrated with transnational corporate global capital, but are these not in turn similar to the challenge faced in the West thirty years earlier, as outlined also in David Harvey's analysis of postmodernism?[26]

Hartmouth and Tolić argue that the re-facading of Skopje 'involves creating a wall of facades to hide the old part of the city (and the soaring minarets and numerous mosques)', effectively masking five centuries of Ottoman rule.[27] They and other critics extend this aesthetic argument to a concern about dividing Albanian and Macedonian citizens along ethnic lines.[28] While the buildings selected for re-facading and the positioning of the thin splice insertions affected the existing Ottoman architecture, the predominant impact was on the existing socialist-Brutalist architecture. In fact, anxiety about minority rights confuses and misrepresents the impact of Skopje 2014. The hybridity and heterogeneity of ethnic and cultural differences is a normative register promoted in postmodern aesthetics: 'modernist styles thereby become postmodernist codes: and ... the stupendous proliferation of social codes today into ... the badges of affirmation of ethnic, gender, race, religious, and class-fraction adhesion, is also a political phenomenon, the problem of micropolitics sufficiently demonstrates'.[29] Skopje 2014 has produced a kind of hybridity and ugliness, the aesthetics of which all too easily exceeds critiques on cultural hybridity or identity.

The National Archaeological Museum on the north bank appears as a two-dimensional cut-out of an enormous building. A preoccupation with what this architectural style should be called – neoclassical, baroque, faux-baroque or Imperialist – thwarts rigorous analysis of the drastic effect of this series of thin structures. In contrast to claims of context and history, the intention of postmodernist projects was not to coexist with the inherited modernist city but to displace or substitute it with something else. By reconfiguring entire buildings as facades, Skopje 2014 extends postmodernist facadism, retrieving 'dead styles, speech through all the masks and voices stored up in the imaginary museum of a new global culture'.[30] A landscape of overscaled columns, pilasters and domes displaces the modernist city and makes up the new postcard view of the city from across the river. Skopje now carries a mask that alludes to historical continuity by displacing historicity. It does not represent local historicism but rather the ghost of what it has covered, present only in its concealment.[31]

To the west of the Stone Bridge a renewed urban landscape that aspires to become a top destination in the global tourist economy obstructs the view of the Kale (pronounced 'kallé') Fortress – a site of real archaeological heritage value in Skopje. Another important structure in this area is the 'new Old Theatre', a reconstruction of the Old Theatre destroyed during the 1963 earthquake but now reconstructed in a 'not-quite' copy of the original. Like the adjacent Museum of the Macedonian Struggle, its historicist envelope is characterized by a postmodern flatness and superficiality, and further, it does not aspire to value 'culture' except in quotation marks.[32] The sheer size of the urban transformation entailed a conflation of any distinction of scale between architecture, urbanism, landscape design and the decorative arts. Whereas only the acclaimed Stone Bridge near the new Old Theatre once framed the view across the River Vardar, an additional four fanciful bridges now facilitate the view: the Bridge of the Arts, the Oko Bridge, the Bridge of Civilizations and the Freedom Bridge. These join a huge inventory of 'urban ornamentation': sculptures differentiated from hundreds of statues, including forty-seven sculpted statues and the giant 'figures of Macedonian history'; street lamps, balustrades, benches; and neoclassical rotundas and colonnades. This new scenography, along with the textual and signifying veil of advertising, keep brutal materiality out of the public eye. Construction cranes, tourists, lights and fountains absorbed the entire central area, turning it into a theatrical 'carnivalesque' of public enjoyment.

Aesthetic obligation to perform

This spectacular compression of time and space induces both 'euphoria and self-annihilation', but the resulting fragmentation of the subject is not of the type described in Jameson's essay on postmodern culture; rather, it consists of a slippery and fluid immersion of the subject into an atmospheric anytime of the future-past.[33] New aesthetic concepts of atmosphere emphasize the intersubjective mood as characterizing the 'aesthetic scene' often linked to the picturesque and the English garden. Beyond the desire to experience and immerse oneself in a particular atmosphere, Gernot Böhme argues there is an obligation to 'perform' the commodity that is fabricating it, not just to view or purchase it.[34] The speedy re-facading and the new insertions mean the slow death of many structures central to the 1965 reconstruction programme. Neglect, disrepair and lack of maintenance of modernist and Brutalist structures – their ruinous decay – are absorbed within the new, clean and shiny, stylistically hyper-historicist insertions, bringing about a random postmodern mixing of times, histories and memory. The emotional obligation of the viewer towards the immersive atmosphere has added a new totalitarian aesthetic beyond the postmodern pastiche that eclipses parody. The augmented reality of Skopje, as Frode Nyeng observes, 'imposes something on us', as if we are not 'able to be disconnected emotionally, but always thinking, judging and acting in the light of a prevalent mood'.[35]

This has been the fate of the white prismatic structure of the Macedonian Opera and Ballet (Figure 6.3). Built in 1979, it was one of four components in the winning master plan of the cultural precinct designed by the acclaimed Slovenian firm headed by Štefan Kacin, Jurij Princes, Bogdan Spindler and Marijan Uršič. With no regard for this master plan, additions,

FIGURE 6.3 *The Macedonian Opera and Ballet, 1979, architects Štefan Kacin, Jurij Princes, Bogdan Spindler and Marijan Uršič. The building, photographed in 2007, is in a neglected state; the new Skopje 2014 ornamental insertions mask it from view. Photograph by Mirjana Lozanovska, Skopje 2007.*

as part of the Skopje 2014 project – a colonnade arc, a strip of neoclassical structures and dispersed urban ornamentation – join the bulbous, glazed envelope of the new Philharmonic Orchestral Hall, surrounding the original building (Figure 6.2). The remarkable architecture of the Macedonian Opera and Ballet is at risk of demolition as it belongs to the post-earthquake reconstruction programme and no longer suits the atmosphere and mood of Skopje 2014. This sense of displacement is also evident in a renewed logic of Skopje 2014: the masking of its own structures, surpassing the original renewal programme. By 2017, the spectacular view of the Archaeological Museum from across the river, one of the thin-facade, narrow-in-depth buildings erected in 2014, was screened by the four new ornamental bridges, and these were in turn veiled by the decorative intent of the massive ship-like structures, along with fountains sprouting in the River Vardar itself. All this can be inhabited and experienced, including the restaurant interior of the ships. As Nyeng argues, a constant renewal of the architectural scenography also 'imposes' on the subject an obligation to perform and participate in that relentless renewal. The developments of Skopje 2014 have attracted much interest in recent times, becoming a popular backdrop for on-site selfies.

Balkanology and monstrosity

Considered in the context of the Balkan question, the ugliness resulting from Skopje 2014 could be interpreted as monstrous. Aesthetic criticisms of Skopje 2014 invoke political criticisms of the Macedonian government, such as, 'It is a Disneyland. They consider Macedonia to be the ancient cradle of civilisation and not a normal, small, modern European country. That would be below their standards.'[36] Such criticisms are neither analytical nor explanatory but rather charged with a vocabulary typically related to the Balkan question. Balkanology is a questionable and derogatory term. It preserves a structural divide between Europe and the Balkans, Europe 'as the cradle of civilization' and the Balkans (Macedonia included) as a synonym for the backward, tribal and uncivilized. In *Imagining the Balkans*, Maria Todorova dismantles this divide by examining the problem with the Balkans, not in contrast with Europe but as an 'imputed ambiguity', an overlapping and entangled history of modernity.[37] Europe projects its own political monstrosity onto the Balkans.

This projection, as well as the risk of such an approach, is illustrated in *Balkan Baroque* (1997), a performance by artist Marina Abramović. Sitting on top of 1,500 cow bones in a white overcoat, Abramović spent four days, six hours a day, washing the blood off bones, making the experience 'visceral due to the unbearable heat of the basement room and [the] fetid smell'.[38] Abramović's *Balkan Baroque* performance, which followed the disintegration of Yugoslavia in 1992 but came before Skopje 2014, provides a way to frame the 'neo-baroque' aesthetic of the renewal project: as a nationalist spectacle and political monstrosity, comparable to the monstrous in art. Charging mundane domestic labour – cleaning – with a universal burden of killing, war, death, murder and shame, Abramović simultaneously highlights how Europe projects its own monstrosity onto the Balkans, which she then redirects to each individual and to human society as a collective. Persevering carefully, but hopelessly, Abramović also touches the fragile realities of the inhabitants of the former Yugoslavia and Skopje, bringing the aesthetic accusation of *Balkan Baroque* back to the question of historical truth.

In contrast, two examples illustrate how political bias structures aesthetic critiques of Balkan architectural histories. Hartmouth and Tolić criticized the Skopje 2014 renewal programme for its neglect of the historic Ottoman urban fabric, and linked it to the government's treatment of Muslim ethnic minorities.[39] Such criticisms are historically fallacious since the Ottoman fabric was first demolished by the 1963 earthquake and then reconstructed as part of the modernist 1965 post-earthquake master plan. The Ottoman Bazaar in Skopje, messy and hybrid, preserves its urban tradition, adapting informally rather than via the aesthetic of cultural tourism. Adopting a negative bias towards the Balkans, Hartmouth and Tolić do not analyse the history of Ottoman architecture in Macedonia and assume it to be identified with the contemporary Muslim population.

The second example is related to a research project and exhibition on the architecture of the former Yugoslavia, *Balkanology*, developed by the Swiss Federal Institute of Technology (ETH) together with the Swiss Architecture Museum (SAM) in Zurich.[40] Both the negative connotations of the title and the projects selected appear to respond to a question about European modernity and how a wider European architectural history of Brutalism can be enriched. As such, the ETH/SAM project overlooked examining the Balkan's hybrid history of late modernism.

These approaches to Balkan architectural histories exemplify the politics of aesthetics that operate within multinational capitalism. Žižek's observation that architectural forms and compositions may appear playful but may also elicit a 'return of the repressed' that is literally written in the aesthetic codes over the surface of the building reiterates Zaera-Polo's political analysis of facades and envelopes.[41] Žižek's label of 'neo-Stalinist postmodernism' describes the aesthetic combination of a random recollection from the past and a 'hyper-capitalist present' but argues that a monstrosity connected to the new capitalist elite of the post-political is evident in 'a (no less vulgar) pan-aestheticism of the neo-liberal order', seen in the hyper-urbanism of advanced economies in the West.[42]

Criticism of and protest against Skopje 2014 reveal the Balkans as a mirror, reflecting how a global post-political monster is colonizing the Balkans. The gradual erosion of both Ottoman and Brutalist architecture is an example of the current political indifference to architecture or its history. Perceiving Skopje 2014 and its post-communist and hyper real capitalist fabrication of nationalism focuses on ahistorical ideologies produced in parallel with a destruction of the 'open city' of Kenzo Tange's 1965 master plan.[43] With this focus on the destructive operation only of Skopje 2014, history is conveniently forgotten: since 1965, Skopje has been continually subjected to aggressive urban renewal. Implementation, negation, revision, abandonment and resistance to Tange's master plan occurred from 1965 onwards and displaced its 'utopia' long before 2014.

Skopje 2014 not only makes the city 'ugly' but also raises the issue of security. When expedience of design and an accelerated construction schedule are the reaction to an anxiety about post-Yugoslavian identity, the safety of the nation is at risk. While excessive forms of security in the global spaces of airports and tourism clash with the twenty-first-century architectural aesthetic of those spaces, Janev's statement that 'we are under threat'[44] points to more precarious realities, and underscores Žižek's warning that '"playful indifference" conceals the reality of the ruthless exercise of power: what they stage as an aesthetic spectacle is reality for the masses of ordinary people'.[45] Skopje has witnessed a series of tragedies, such as the destruction of real heritage, and the illegal export of precious archaeological artefacts, which, like the looting of the Baghdad museum, involves transnational criminal markets and the corruption of internal personnel, both fuelled by insatiable Western economies. Added to this risk are the real, constant and continuing military attacks, including the 2001 attack in the Aračinovo mountains and the suspicious death of President Trajkovski.

The latest protest against the defunct historicism of Skopje 2014 came from an action group called the 'colour revolution'.[46] A well-informed group of young radicals blasted many of the Skopje 2014 surfaces with paint, literally splashing numerous colours on the newly applied historicist facades and newly erected urban ornamentation. Their main target was the Porta Macedonia, one of the larger new artefacts on the edge of the central square. The intent of the 'colour revolution' was to oppose the agenda of Skopje 2014 and its destruction of the architectural aspirations of the Tange legacy. However, while levelled against the ugliness of Skopje 2014, the paint and colour became absorbed into the very aesthetic of the city's image (rather than its programme, infrastructure or mass) and exposed an incapacity to change the urban agenda. While celebrated as 'revolution', this colourful application merged, one could argue, with the resurfacing logic of Skopje 2014, enhancing, assisting and accentuating the anti-aesthetic further, indeed bringing it level with the recent endorsement by public and art institutions of the graffiti and street art that were once considered subversive. The colour revolution gives rise to a new version of the 'cultural pathology of existence' as a pathology of protest.[47] The performative aesthetic of the colour revolution was readily absorbed in Skopje's pastiche, adding a patina, and a political radicalism, it was lacking. In contrast, in veiling the grey built environment of socialism, Skopje 2014 both effaced its visual aesthetics *and* displaced its politics.

Notes

1 Macedonian Informative Agency (MIA), 'Prezentiran Proektot Skopje 2014 (Skopje 2014 Project Is Presented)', http://www.mia.mk (2013) [accessed July 2013].

2 Ibid.

3 Michal Mádr and Luděk Kouba, 'Diversity of Capitalism in the European Post-Socialist Economies: The Balkan States at a Crossroads', *Scientific Papers of the University of Pardubice* 36 (2016).

4 Mirjana Lozanovska, 'Brutalism, Metabolism and Its American Parallel: Encounters in Skopje and in the Architecture of Georgi Konstantinovski', *Fabrications* 25, no. 2 (2015): 152–75.

5 Nate Robert, 'Communist Architecture of Skopje, Macedonia', http://www.yomadic.com/communist-architecture-skopje-kenzo-tange/ [accessed 10 December 2013].

6 Leonora Grcheva, 'Reshaping the Skopje City Centre as a National Agenda: Skopje 1965 vs. Skopje 2014' (MA dissertation, Katholieke Universiteit, 2011).

7 Barnabas Calder, *Raw Concrete: The Beauty of Brutalism* (London: William Heinemann, 2016); Michael Kubo, Mark Pasnik and Chris Grimley, 'Tough Love: In Defense of Brutalism', *Architect* 99, no. 4 (2010): 46–8; Michal Korta, *Beautiful Monster: Skopje Brutalist Architecture* (Bochnia: Korta Studio, 2016); *SOS Brutalism* (crowdsourced online database), http://www.sosbrutalism.org/cms/15802395#home [accessed June 2017].

8 Reyner Banham, 'The New Brutalism', *Architectural Review* 118, no. 708 (December 1955): 354–61.

9 See Mirjana Lozanovska, 'Brutalism, Metabolism and Its American Parallel: Encounters in Skopje and in the Architecture of Georgi Konstantinovski', *Fabrications* 25, no. 2 (2015): 152–75.

10 Dubravka Djurić and Miško Šuvaković, eds, *Impossible Histories: Historic Avant-Gardes, Neo-Avant-Gardes, and Post-Avant-Gardes in Yugoslavia, 1918–1991* (Cambridge, MA: MIT Press, 2003).

11 Maroš Krivý, 'Greyness and Colour Desires: The Chromatic Politics of the Panelák in Late-Socialist and Post-Socialist Czechoslovakia', *Journal of Architecture* 20, no. 5 (2015): 765–802.

12 The perception of VMRO as a nationalist and singular ethnic party is too simplistic, especially since it formed a government with the ethnic Albanian party.

13 Carmen Popescu, 'Being Specific: Limits of Contextualising (Architectural) History', *Journal of Architecture* 16, no. 6 (2011): 821–53.

14 Fredric Jameson, 'Postmodernism, or the Cultural Logic of Late Capitalism', *New Left Review* 1, no. 146 (1984): 15; Fredric Jameson, *Postmodernism, or the Cultural Logic of Late Capitalism* (Durham: Duke University Press, 1991), 406; Fredric Jameson, *The Political Unconscious: Narrative as a Socially Symbolic Act* (Ithaca, NY: Cornell University Press, 1981).

15 Ljubica Dimishkovska, 'A New Ancient City', *Transitions Online* (2010): 1–3; 'Revamping Skopje, Stones of Contention: Macedonia Writes a New Story for Its Capital', *The Economist* (2013), https://www.economist.com/books-and-arts/2013/01/05/stones-of-contention [accessed 13 June 2016]; Maximilian Hartmuth and Ines Tolić, 'Turkish Coffee and Béton Brut: An Architectural Portrait of Skopje', *EAHN Newsletter* 4, no. 10 (2010): 22–36; Vesna Stanković Pejnović, 'The Project Skopje 2014 from the Perspective of Mass Culture Criticism of F. Nietzsche', *Creativity Studies* 8, no. 1 (2015): 58–71; Jasna Stefanovska and Janez Koželj, 'Urban Planning and Transitional Development Issues: The Case of Skopje, Macedonia', *Urbani izziv* 23, no. 1 (2012): 91–100; Leonora Grcheva, 'Reshaping the Skopje City Centre as a National Agenda' in *Unfinished Modernisations: Between Utopia and Pragmatism*, ed. Maroje Mrduljaš and Vladimir Kulić (Zagreb: Udruženje hrtvatskih arhitekata / Croatian Architects' Association, 2012); Milan Mijalkovic and Katharina Urbanek, *Skopje, the World's Bastard: Architecture of the Divided City* (Klagenfurt/Celovec: Wieser Verlag, 2011).

16 Jameson, 'Postmodernism', 55.
17 Ibid., 61 (my emphasis); Gernot Böhme, 'The Theory of Atmospheres and Its Applications', *Interstices* 15 (2014): 92–9.
18 See Böhme, 'The Theory of Atmospheres'; and Henning S. Olesen and Kirsten Weber, 'Socialization, Language, and Scenic Understanding: Alfred Lorenzer's Contribution to Psycho-Societal Methodology', *Historical Social Research* 38, no. 2 (2013): 26–55.
19 Goran Janev and Blaz Kriznik, 'From Open City towards Grand National Capital: Mapping the Symbolic Reconstruction of Skopje', *Western Balkans Policy Review* 2, no. 1 (2012): 78–99.
20 Anonymous, 'Revamping Skopje, Stones of Contention'.
21 Jameson, 'Postmodernism', 15.
22 Alejandro Zaera-Polo, 'The Politics of the Envelope: A Political Critique of Materialism', *Volume,* no. 17 (2008): 76–105.
23 S. Herold, B. Langer and J. Lechler, *Reading the City: Urban Space and Memory in Skopje* (Berlin: Verlag der Technischen Universität, 2010); Stefan Bouzarovski, 'Skopje', *Cities* 28, no. 3 (2011); Fabio Mattioli, 'Unchanging Boundaries: The Reconstruction of Skopje and the Politics of Heritage', *International Journal of Heritage Studies* 20, no. 6 (2014).
24 Goran Janev, 'Skopje 2014: Instrumentalising Heritage for Unexpected Results' in *European Quarterly of Political Attitudes and Mentalities*, ed. Camelia Florela Voinea (Bucharest: University of Bucharest, 2008).
25 Henri Lefebvre, *The Production of Space*, trans. Donald Nichlson-Smith (Oxford: Blackwell, 1991), 389.
26 David Harvey, *The Condition of Postmodernity: An Enquiry into the Origins of Cultural Change* (Oxford: Basil Blackwell, 1989).
27 Hartmuth and Tolić, 'Turkish Coffee and Béton Brut', 6.
28 Janev, 'Skopje 2014: Instrumentalising Heritage for Unexpected Results'; Goran Janev, 'What Happened to the Macedonian Salad: Ethnocracy in Macedonia', special issue Southeast European (Post)Modernities, *Ethnologia Balkanica* 15 (2011): 33–44.
29 Jameson, 'Postmodernism', 65.
30 Ibid.
31 Mark Cousins, 'The Ugly', [part 3] *AA Files* 30 (Autumn 1995): 29.
32 Slavoj Žižek, 'Architectural Parallax: Spandrels and Other Phenomena of Class Struggle', *Lacanian Ink*, 1–18, http://www.lacan.com/essays/?page_id=218 (2009) [accessed 14 February 2018].
33 Jameson, 'Postmodernism', 62.
34 Böhme, 'The Theory of Atmospheres'.
35 Frode Nyeng, *Følelser i filosofi, vitenskap og dagligliv* (Oslo: Abstrakt forlag, 2006), 125; cited in Ib Imland and Leroy Tonning, 'The Wooden Gown of Stavanger', *Journal of Urban Design* 15, no. 3 (2010): 423–41.

36 Anonymous, 'Revamping Skopje, Stones of Contention'; Dimishkovska, 'A New Ancient City'.
37 Maria Todorova, *Imagining the Balkans* (Oxford: Oxford University Press, 1997), 4–20.
38 Marina Abramović, 'Balkan Baroque' (1997), https://www.theartstory.org/artist-abramovic-marina-artworks.html [accessed April 2017].
39 Hartmuth and Tolić, 'Turkish Coffee and Béton Brut'.
40 Swiss Architecture Museum, 'Sam Balkanology Series of Conferences & Exhibitions' (2011), http://www.sam-basel.org/home.html [accessed June 2016].
41 Žižek, 'Architectural Parallax'.
42 Ibid.
43 Jurica Pavičić, 'Postkomunizam u dvorani zrcala, Skopje = Post-Communism in the Hall of Mirrors', *Oris* 15, no. 85 (2014): 206–23.
44 Goran Janev, 'Narrating the City, Narrating the Nation', special issue Narrative Spaces in a Multicultural City, *Cultural Analysis: An Interdisciplinary Forum on Folklore and Popular Culture* 10 (2011): 3–21.
45 Žižek, 'Architectural Parallax'.
46 Srdjan Jovanovic Weiss, 'Skopje Scomparirà', *Abitare* 504 (July–August 2010): 82–95.
47 Jameson, 'Postmodernism', 63.

CHAPTER SEVEN

Here be monsters
Andrew Leach

To cast architecture as ugly is both an aesthetic and a moral judgement, as Bart Verschaffel explains in Chapter Two. Neither perfect nor cute, a truly 'ugly' building suggests a lack of correctness at the core (an aberration, a monstrosity) that has found its way to the surface, where it is judged not for what it is but for what it evidences. This judgement, naturally, has a history, wherein the correct way to build, and in which to have built, is underpinned by the relationship of architectural works to a notion of propriety that owes as much to the utilitarian origins of the orders as to architecture's standing as a form of idealized nature. Of course, something once thought ugly can find redemption through a change in values or an injection of irony; just as something apparently innocuous (normal) can be rendered ugly by figuring violence, injustice or oppression into its fabric. Works of the Middle Ages, the modern movement entire, the architectural baroque, and neoclassicism have each been parsed by their critics and historians as egregious or correct, redeemable or otherwise. As Verschaffel makes clear, to call architecture ugly is to make a neutralizing judgement of the zone between appearance and core that masks the (truly) disturbing. It inhabits the gap between the seen and the thought.[1]

Of the subjects taken up by historians and critics of architecture over the last two centuries, few have to the same degree forced authors to grapple with ugliness as the turn in the history of the so-called Renaissance towards nature, myth and the murky past of the medieval world that was variously declared anti-classical, anti-Renaissance (*late*-Renaissance) and mannerist. Threatening to undermine order and equilibrium – a modern inheritance from the ancient world – the experimentation of the mid-sixteenth century quickly invited moral judgement couched as historical criticism. Comparatively benign, the interwar historiography of this period

FIGURE 7.1 *Antonio Fantuzzi, after Rosso Fiorentino, The Enlightenment of Francis I, c. 1542 Etching, 30.9 × 42.6 cm. © Trustees of the British Museum.*

nonetheless sits comfortably alongside the reflections on 'kitsch' penned by Gillo Dorfles in relation to Nazism, pornography and Catholic iconography; or the reassessment of proto-reactionary architectures in Germany of the 1920s and 1930s; or the grappling with the embodied racism of nineteenth- and twentieth-century town planning in colonized Africa, Asia and Australia.[2] But the premises of these judgements – that architecture might serve to express something unnatural or monstrous within, thus trumping what would, in other circumstances, be an objective assessment of a building as a work of fine art – rest on assumptions that extend deep into the historiography of art.

Even at the level of criticism based on appearance, only postmodernism today seriously contends with mannerism for the mantle of most ugly, doing so on terms that are tested early and overtly on the painting, sculpture and architecture of the *cincequento*. It is perhaps the last architectural 'style' in which the moral and aesthetic judgement of ugliness are made explicitly to meet. It is not that both of these moments are extraordinarily subject to universal aesthetic responses. Instead, they explicitly and conspicuously work *with* the inherent instability of rules and hence with the threat of the dissolution of all forms of order. It is this shared threat that leads to this shared judgement. Umberto Eco put it well in conflating mannerism and postmodernism (and, hence, their status for criticism and history) in his observation that 'you might say that mannerism is born whenever it

FIGURE 7.2 *Proteus-Glaucus, Sacro Bosco, Bomarzo. Gardens designed by Pirro Ligorio, c. 1551–2. Photograph by Andrew Leach.*

is discovered that the world has no fixed center, that I have to find my way through the world inventing my own points of reference'.[3] This loss of centre equates, in one sense, with the loss of the sense of what was proper (natural) in any given moment, and was seen to have been manifested in, for instance, the 'grotesque' *portone* and window frames on Federico Zuccari's *palazzetto* on Rome's Via Gregoriana, or his red and black illustrations, made at the Escorial in 1586, of Dante's *Divina commedia*, or indeed of the grotto forms, on which they draw, in Pirro Ligorio's monsters in the Sacro Bosco of Bomarzo (Figure 7.2).[4]

In his survey of the architecture of sixteenth-century Italy, Wolfgang Lotz concludes with two 'monstrous' examples as evidence not only of a bizarre anti-classicism, but also of an absence of conscience: 'From ancient times the architect was regarded as the image of God; as God created the order of the world, the architect creates the order of his building. In the world created by God, Hell is the opposite of "right being"; in the world of the architect, the "bizzarrie" are the opposite of rule and order.'[5] The reminder offered by Andrea Palladio's Villa Capra (la Rotonda) or by Pirro's own Villa d'Este rendered more violent for the historian of architecture these apparent repudiations of the *concinnitas*, wherein beauty had, by the end of the fifteenth century, come to reside. For a certain Italian architecture of the sixteenth century, mannerism's ugliness rested in its manifest loss of 'right being' – a judgement, that is, of expression, style, technique, subject matter and morality.

Naming this architecture mannerist is an extension of judgements levelled within history of painting and painters and hence of the evolution of art historiography. In his book-length essay *Mannerism and Maniera* (1963), Craig Hugh Smyth recalls the pride with which Vasari wrote of the efficiencies introduced by *la maniera*, through which artists systematized the techniques of painting (privileging this over the mediation of nature through painting) to realize in mere weeks or months what had once taken years. Vasari added this detail to the second edition of his *Vite* (1568, orig. 1550), in which he not only seized the opportunity to write (or conclude) those biographies omitted in his first edition (completing, e.g. the life of Michelangelo, which had only drawn to a close in 1564) but also to reflect on what we can (now) defensibly call the mannerist decades, shaped as they were by the uptake of ideas fomented by Michelangelo and Raphael, who as geniuses cast their shadow over a generation of imitators.[6] When Vasari writes (as Smyth quotes) that painting had become 'so perfect and easy for anyone having *disegno*, invention, and coloring', he might as readily be invoking the possibility – after the treatises of Leon Battista Alberti, Il Filarete, Francesco di Giorgio Martini and (perhaps most importantly) Sebastiano Serlio – of building according to the distilled rules of the *quattrocento* and *cinquecento* treatises.[7]

This sequence of books (not to mention their ancient Vitruvian model and the various editions, translated and commentated upon) gradually distilled a concept of beauty informed by proportion, propriety, economy, balance and so forth into operating procedures that played out, in Palladio's case, in his own villas and churches. Vasari himself celebrated the need for licence and invention within rules, and James Ackerman has noted Palladio's inclination, including at the Villa Capra, to eschew the perfect symmetry upon which his manifold and yet imperfect imitators (including those who completed the Villa Capra itself) insisted in their Palladianism – and which might have been inferred from the drawings of his *Quattro libri*.[8] Nonetheless, it remains difficult, on these terms, to ignore the shared roots in licence, tradition and *il concetto*, of at once the most faithful extensions of the 'high Renaissance' and its most troubling rejections – where the architect's embrace of a certain monstrosity, an alignment with an anti-mathematical nature, a lack of faith in the ordered world, would open their work up to judgement.

Vasari was hardly so vulgar (or anachronistic) as to make *la maniera* all about productivity, but he noted its implications in this respect even as he celebrated the artistic achievements of his most illustrious contemporaries and their predecessors. It offered freedom to realize art beyond the constraints of genius or fidelity to nature, aided by, and informed by, knowledge of artistic technique and an imitation of art rather than art's subject. The 'game' of art was no longer the deception of man, as it was with Zeuxis' grapes and the drapery of Parrhasius, but of working *with* art's deceptions, openly, knowingly. The painter had made his or her way to court and had followed a path from tradesman to genius, through which the work itself had acquired status. Smyth tempered the general impression of mannerist painting on such terms with a degree of judgement: some things are properly mannerist and can be tested against the (historically legitimate) theory of *maniera*; but not everything called mannerism is realized under this theory. Walter Friedlaender, he suggests, had the right idea in naming some art of the period anti-classical: a rejection of the rules with all they allow rather than an extension of those rules through informed manipulation.[9] The anti-classical, it follows, fits elsewhere, and to call its exemplars mannerist demands that we agree to set aside any real meaning for the term as a critical category in the history of art. Moreover, to invoke mannerism is to endorse Bellori's seventeenth-century dismissal of the values advanced by Vasari in his use of *maniera*, and to conflate (as many would go on to do) the judgement of artworks with judgement of the path of art as a whole. The art of the mid-sixteenth century is a fall from grace and beauty and purity and nature in no small way because Bellori taught us to see it that way – taught us, that is, to regard the surface as evidence of something irredeemably corrupted. As he put it: 'Hence those who do everything on the basis of practice, without knowing the truth, depict spectres instead of figures; and those others are not dissimilar, who borrow talent and copy the ideas of others, creating works that are not daughters but bastards of nature, and who appear to have sworn allegiance to the brushstrokes of their masters.'[10]

Smyth's essay on *maniera* fits within a generational project, barely articulated as such, to test the veracity of the interwar historiography of sixteenth-century art against the image of a disturbed and disturbing mannerism as had been tabled by historians like Max Dvořák and Nikolaus Pevsner. This project was about historicizing the analytical choices of those historians who had been caught up in the expressionistic, post-war historiography of an age (a mannerist age, its centre lost, its values adrift) that seemed to many writers to be as subject to crises beyond art, undermining culture across its many and varied departments, as its own.[11] Dvořák's mannerism expressed an interior, psychological unease; Pevsner's crisis of faith being held together with institutional scaffolding. Their mannerism was not at odds with Bellori's (though Bellori never called it mannerism as such) but functioned to make the apparent eruption of disorder from a moment of artistic perfection (or indeed the concurrent insistence on a now artificial order) a response to a general state of unease to which all departments of culture were necessarily subject, and which painting was above all suited to express. Just as the arts could express the anxieties of a world racked by global war and epidemic, confronting economic instability and dramatically recast borders, both geopolitical and cultural. Its diagnostic value resided in its expression of a world come undone – its ugliness resided in the resonances of that world to the world of the critics. This (too) obvious parallelism was, in many respects, the proper subject of writers from the start of the 1940s to the end of the 1960s, who understood the liberties that had been taken by a generation of historians connecting culture's artefacts with a deep cultural substrate.

It came to a head in such events as those for which Smyth first wrote his essay. Among these number the session at the International Congress of Art History in New York, 1961, as well as the conference staged at the Palazzo Strozzi to commemorate the quatercentenary of Vasari's *Vite* (*Studi vasariani*, 1950), the meeting at the Accademia dei Lincei in Rome to test the vocabulary of contemporary art history (*Manierismo, barocco, rococo*, 1960) and the events marking the quatercentenary of Michelangelo's death (1964), including the major exhibition *Michelangiolo architetto*, curated by Paolo Portoghesi and Bruno Zevi (in which mannerism and late/postmodernism comfortably met on Rome's Via Nazionale). The critical attention directed towards this work served to undermine the nomenclature that had long been used to keep it in its place, distinct from the classical (to invoke Heinrich Wölfflin) and the Renaissance (and their various forms of perfection) and from the baroque (with its rhetorically direct line from art to the aspiring spirit). Even in a situation like that fostered by Portoghesi and Zevi, the term's elasticity is shown to be limited by their own 'pyrotechnic' uses of it.[12]

These are, arguably, three of the four key phases in the modern criticism and historiography of mannerism – in painting, initially, but beyond that across the fine arts (including architecture) and thence to culture more broadly. Each recalls the problem of critics identifying with their subjects, all bound up in a presumption that the so-called Renaissance (and the so-called High Renaissance of Raphael and Bramante, in particular) was something of a cultural apex towards which artists crept across the second half of the fifteenth century, and from which they descended after (variously) the death of Raphael and Bramante, the papacy of Julius II, the defensive crises of Rome in 1527 and Florence in 1530, the course of the Lutheran Reformation and the economic upheaval of American gold arriving into Europe. Wölfflin suggested at the outset of his 1888 *Renaissance und Barock* that the historian's task in addressing the Renaissance after its most perfect form is primarily diagnostic: What happened? And in what way? The explanation never runs, in this book, to context (although Evonne Levy has admirably explored the underpinnings of Wölfflin's assumptions), but the diagnosis of art (and, for him, architecture) is a diagnosis of a decline in culture, society and their institutions – registered against artful buildings as their expression.[13] Wölfflin's most widely read books on this problem, *Renaissance und Barock* and *Kunstgeschichtliche Grundbegriffe* (the latter, 1915), do not address mannerism, either as such or through the content that had begun to accrue to the term, but they problematize the baroque as an endpoint of a descent in which what was later more commonly called mannerism (the work of the *manieristi*) inevitably participated.[14]

Wölfflin could easily have done so, however, since his own teacher had gone some way to cast this as decline over dispersal. Writers from the end of the eighteenth century (like Luigi Lanzi) to Jacob Burckhardt himself (in *Der Cicerone*) gradually translating a process through which the lessons of Raphael and Michelangelo made their way north, sustaining the interference of visual cultures less securely moored to Rome and Florence, into one of deformation, deterioration, degradation, et cetera (to use the critical language of the expressionist 1920s): mannerism as entropy over diffusion, to be diagnosed, but never admired. In this, the *manieristi* were artists who deployed the tool of *la maniera* but failed collectively to appreciate the distance this fomented between their art and that of the Renaissance masters, between the accomplishments of art's 'greatest generation' and the way they were squandered by their children and grandchildren.

Burckhardt's major consideration of the Renaissance (*Die Cultur der Renaissance in Italien*, 1860) sets aside the question of the mannerists entirely. Consider, though, the slights with which *Der Cicerone* is peppered. He writes of various mannerisms (in a general sense) but that 'Lomazzo and Figino belong to *the mannerists* proper'. The term then reoccurs across the following pages: Michelangelo 'we shall meet again among the mannerists'; Bronzino 'must, as a historical painter, be placed among the mannerists' (but not as a portrait painter, since in this 'he is inferior to none of his contemporaries'). Raphael, in his Entombment at the Borghese Gallery, begins to approach a mannerism 'from which [he] was again able to work himself free'. Having been called to Rome in 1508, Raphael 'displayed the inconceivably rich productiveness which stands alone as a moral marvel. It is not,' Burckhardt continues, 'the height of genius, but the power of will, which is the grandest: the first would not have kept him from mannerism; it is the last which never suffered him to rest on his laurels, but always urged him to higher modes of expression … And, further, in art no one can linger behind with impunity; mannerism lies in wait to take possession of the inactive artist.' More: 'The Genoese pupils of Perin belong altogether to the mannerists'; Benvenuto Tisio, too conscientious, 'is not a mannerist'; Bomarzo's nephew, Allessandro Allori, is 'still half a mannerist'; Giovanni Battista Piazzetta is a 'sometimes very tolerable mannerist'. Casting mannerism as a form of conquest, he writes (in relation to Tintoretto): 'The forced adoption of the mannerisms of the Roman school was at least spared to the good town of Venice.' Burckhardt is full of praise for those *quadri* of Ridolfo Ghirlandajo to be found at the Uffizzi, but 'Other things [of his] are pure mannerism.'[15].

To be called a mannerist is to sustain a Burckhardtian insult – and to face the dangers of mannerism and avoid them, as Raphael did through the sheer force of his genius, is commendable. Faced with a moral plight, one can work to avoid mannerism, or succumb. To be a mannerist is to have a fl awed character; to be less than accomplished. In her own guide to the public galleries of London, published more than a decade before Burckhardt's tome, Anna Jameson wondered aloud: 'I am not sure that critics will go with me in considering *manner*, even in this sense, as part of the *morale* of painting; but I think, if I understand myself, that I am right.'[16] Burckhardt would indeed go with Jameson on this point: to be a mannerist (even a 'very tolerable mannerist,' or 'half a mannerist') is to suffer a character failing (the deep-seated embrace of an error), and express it in art. A conscientious painter can be spared the appellation, as can an entire city, just as it can be rendered subject to this fault and have the art of its painters coloured as a result. At the heart of this assessment, explicit for Burckhardt (at least in *Der Cicerone*) and skipped over by Wölfflin, is a strong sense that something has gone wrong.

This sense persisted in scholarship through to the Second World War, after which it coalesced around a notion of mannerist art as something deformed within limits. By the end of the 1960s, two things had happened to the concept of mannerism. On one hand, historians of art had to some extent come to agree that the epithet functioned at best in a limited way, so that when used precisely, rigorously, it pertained to a family of works constrained chronologically, geographically and conceptually – and hence to a thoroughly localized artistic phenomenon that could be studied as a body of conceptually consistent paintings. On the other hand, this concept proliferated on the back of an appreciation that the creative historiography of the interwar period, with its diagnoses of crises both interior and exterior, with its sense of art expressing the anxieties of religious, economic, geopolitical and cultural instability, could manifest not just in painting but also in architecture, music, science and philosophy. This world, forced to invent its own points of reference looking to a past similarly adrift, tested the judgement bound up in the term mannerism – in part determining to maintain its expressive (aesthetic) force; in part neutralizing this judgement, rendering it available, as strategies, to the culture of this moment.

The category of 'mannerist architecture' was in part responsible for this wider cultural proliferation, since to call sixteenth-century architecture mannerist demanded that the strictures allowing the aforementioned coherence across paintings manifesting the Vasarian *maniera*, made by a generation of painters, had to be relaxed in a way that allowed for the operation of those abstractions that could permit the translation of ideas in the criticism of painting into the criticism of architecture. The principal abstraction that persisted into the 1960s was one that had been explored in the interwar years by the so-called expressionist historians of mannerism, who had been alert to the relationship between art and its time, the artist and his or her world – in other words, to the interaction of artistic worldviews and the limits that shaped their edges. When Pevsner later wrote of the shrill dissonance inflecting Giulio Romano's Palazzo Te, he invoked a language, supplementing technical breakdowns of his observations, located unequivocally in the architecture, that enabled one to move from the particular to the general (from building to culture).[17]

Over the 1950s and 1960s, such books as *Die Welt als Labyrinth*, published by Gustav Hocke in 1957, and *Der Manierismus*, published by

Arnold Hauser in 1964, with its telling subtitle *Die Krise der Renaissance und der Ursprng der modernen Kunst*, both spoke to an enduring suspicion of a mannerist art responding to a broken world – and hence maintaining the sense of its ugliness even as the world of that moment appeared more and more clearly to itself be broken.[18] Even Frederick Hartt, the scholar of Giulio and Michelangelo, spoke in 1961 of the fundamental relationship between art and its time, the artist and his or her age, and hence of art's diagnostic value in history. The High Renaissance, to use his terminology, gives way to a less certain epoch (as Julius II gives way to the ill-prepared Leo X) and 'tormented compositions', superhuman beings (Michelangelo's David and the like), form the images that document the experience of that epoch.[19] The image of mannerism as a crisis in the style *all'antica*, or of mannerism as the inevitable expression of a world in trouble, persisted despite the scholarly referenda that cast this approach to the history of art as a facile parallelism.

By the end of the 1970s, then, it was possible for three kinds of books to be published on the art and architecture of the sixteenth century. The first of these was the serious study of art independent of the restraints of stylistic nomenclature, able to reflect without the burden of this device on the appearance, meaning, circumstances of production and reception of an artist's (or architect's work). This, in other words, was an art and architectural history preoccupied with questions other than style, and with change beyond judgement (or beyond explicit judgement). The second possibility lay with the formalization of the historiographic form as a preoccupation in and of itself, responding to the historicity of history's nineteenth- and twentieth-century literature as a partisan force. Amedeo Quodnam's *Problemi del manierismo* (1975) is exemplary of this, tracking as it does the rise and fall of post-war attitudes towards mannerism through the writing that first sought to historicize the art, architecture and (more broadly) culture of the Italian sixteenth century.[20] It describes the manoeuvres made by critics and historians to locate mannerism in (its) history and hence admitting (in the form of actions if not by way of explicit intentions) mannerism's specificity as a twentieth-century reconstruction of the artistic culture and its context in the sixteenth-century world, playing with layers of conceits that work with mannerism's artifice and the judgements levelled at it.

The third kind of study is well represented by Achille Bonito Oliva's *L'ideologia del traditore* (1976, The Ideology of the Traitor), in which the relation between the proper and improper, art and artifice, are explored in a series of thematic groupings in which the values that accrued to a modern mannerism, rather than the works themselves, are explored historically.[21] Here the leitmotif of sneaky distortion reigns supreme, and mannerism once more aligns with the faults assigned to it by Bellori. All that one sees in those cultural acts with a mannerist bent are rendered ugly by that which they attempt – inevitably without success – to conceal. The path followed by mannerism to this point – from judgement to history; from an inevitable ugliness to conscious tactic – is thus made plural by the differing speeds of the discourses of art, architecture and culture. But the generation that looked with distaste to the paintings and buildings of their forebears, seeing manner and artifice obscure a rejection of (a certain kind of) nature and order (for nature and order of another kind), had sown seeds of distrust that persist in a discourse circumscribed by the morality of appearance and distinct from an interior, impossible truth.

The architecture of Giulio Romano, Buontalenti, Salviati or Vasari himself is not, objectively, hard to look at. One can cast an eye without compromise over the surfaces of the Palazzo Farnese at Caprarola. Or the interrupted phrasing of the Biblioteca Laurenziana. Even that most mannerist of postmodern gestures, Robert Venturi's Ironic Column, does not turn the stomach of any but the most sensitive aesthetes – even as it winks at its sincere dismissal of sincerity. But the persistence of Bellori's historiographical premise, rendered 'scientific' by Wölfflin, ensures that the conceit remains and that historical analysis can identify the moments when culture fails. Dvořák's suspicion remains, and inflects the criticism of later mannerisms: in this overwrought, troubled moment lives the distinction between what one sees and what one could know, wherein lies the real worth of the work, as art.

Notes

1 This essay reflects on themes I explored as a Wallace Fellow at the Harvard Center for Italian Renaissance Studies, Villa I Tatti. Thanks to Katie Anania, Elizabeth Petcu, Maria Loh, Alexander Nagel, Alina Payne and Caspar Pearson for their conversations on the historiography of mannerism in architecture in the 1950s and 1960s – the larger project on which this draws.
2 Gillo Dorfles, *Kitsch: The World of Bad Taste* (New York: Universe Books, 1969).
3 Stefano Rosso and Umberto Eco, 'A Correspondence with Umberto Eco, Geneva-Bologna-Binghamton-Bloomington, August-September 1982, March-April 1983', trans. Carolyn Springer, *boundary 2* 12, no. 1 (August 1983): 3.
4 Zuccari's drawings are reproduced in Corrado Gizzi, ed., *Federico Zuccari e Dante* (Milan: Electa, 1993). On Bomarzo, see Sabine Frommel, ed., *Bomarzo: Il Sacro bosco* (Milan: Electa, 2009).
5 Wolfgang Lotz, *Architecture in Italy 1500–1600* (New Haven, CT: Yale University Press, 1994), 172; originally published as *Architecture in Italy 1400–1600*, by Ludwig Heydenreich and Wolfgang Lotz (London: Penguin, 1974).
6 In full English translation: Giorgio Vasari, *Lives of the Painters, Sculptors and Architects*, 2 vols, trans. Gaston du C. de Vere (London: Macamillan, 1912–15).
7 Quoted in Craig Hugh Smyth, *Mannerism and Maniera* (Locust Valley, NY: J. J. Augustin, 1963), 9. See also Manfredo Tafuri, *L'architettura del Manierismo nel Cinquecento europeo* (Rome: Officina, 1966), 125–85.

8   James Ackerman, *Palladio* (Harmondsworth: Penguin, 1966), 164.
9   Walter Friedlaender, 'Die Entstehung des antiklassischen Stils in der italianischen Maleri um 1520', *Repertorium für Kunsgeschichte* 46 (1925): 49–86.
10   Giovan Pietro Bellori, *The Lives of the Modern Painters, Sculptors and Architects*, trans. Alice Sedgwick Wohl (Cambridge: Cambridge University Press, 2005), 61.
11   Max Dvořák, 'On El Greco and Mannerism' (based on a lecture delivered in 1914) in *The History of Art as the History of Ideas*, trans. John Hardy (London: Routledge & Keegan Paul, 1984), 97–108; Nikolaus Pevsner, 'Gegenreformation und Manierismus', *Repertorium für Kunstgeschichte* 46 (1925): 243–62.
12   See *Manierismo, barocco, rococo: concetti e termini*, special issue based on a conference held in 1960, *Problemi attuali di scienza e di cultura* 52 (1962); *The Renaissance and Mannerism*, vol. 2, *Studies in Western Art: Acts of the Twentieth International Congress of the History of Art* (Princeton, NJ: Princeton University Press, 1963); Paolo Portoghesi and Bruno Zevi, *Michelangiolo architetto* (Turin: Einaudi, 1964); and *Mostra critica delle opera michelangiolesche*, exhib. cat. (Rome: Comitato nazionale per le onoranze a Michelangeliolo nel IV centenario della morte, 1964). The criticism is from Manfredo Tafuri, 'Il "progetto" storico' (1977), *La sfera e il labirinto. Avanguardie da Piranesi agli anni '70* (Turin: Einaudi, 1980), 21.
13   Evonne Levy, *Baroque and the Political Language of Formalism (1845–1945): Burckhardt, Wölfflin, Gurlitt, Brinckmann, Sedlmayr* (Basel: Schwabe, 2015).
14   Heinrich Wölfflin, *Renaissance und Barock: Eine Untersuchung über wesen und entstehung des Barockstils in Italien* (Munich: Theodor Ackerman, 1888); Heinrich Wölfflin, *Kunstgeschichtliche Grundbegriffe. Das Problem der Stilentwicklung in der neueren Kunst* (Munich: Bruckmann, 1915).
15   Jacob Burckardt, *The Cicerone: An Art Guide to Painting in Italy* (New York: Charles Scribner's Sons, 1908) (my emphasis). Reference to Lomazzo and Figino is on page 121; Michelangelo, 128; Bronzino, 134; Raphael, 140, 141, 146; the pupils of Perin, 166; Tisio, 169; Tintoretto, 206; Allori, 222; Piazzatta, 249; Ghirlandajo, 135. I also make reference, in this paragraph to Burckhardt's *Die Cultur der Renaissance in Italien* (Basel: Schweighauser, 1860).
16   Anna Jameson, *A Handbook to the Public Galleries of Art in and Near London* (London: John Murray, 1842), xx.
17   Nikolaus Pevsner, 'The Architecture of Mannerism' in *The Mint: A Miscellany of Literature, Art and Criticism*, vol. 1, ed. Geoffrey Grigson (London: Routledge, 1946), 121.
18   Gustav René Hocke, *Die Welt als Labyrinth: Manier und Manie in der europäischen Kunst* (Hamburg: Rowohlt, 1957); Arnold Hauser, *Manierismus: Die Krise der Renaissance und der Ursprung der modernen Kunst* (Munich: Beck, 1964).

19 Frederick Hartt, 'Power and the Individual in Mannerist Art' in *The Renaissance and Mannerism: Studies in Western Art*, vol. 2, 222–38, esp. 223.

20 Amedo Quodnam, *Problemi dei manierismo* (Naples: Guida Editori, 1975). The book, published in Italian, contains writing by Georg Weiss, Erwin Panofsky, Arnold Hauser, Riccardo Scrivano and Eugenio Battisti: all regularly cited in as key late-modern commentators on the history of the concept of mannerism.

21 Achille Bonito Oliva, *L'ideologia del traditore. Arte, maniera, manierismo* (Milan: Feltrinelli, 1976).

CHAPTER EIGHT

To make monsters
Caroline O'Donnell

Questions of ugliness and monstrosity motivate a body of work in the experimental design practice, CODA, underpinned by a series of essays arguing for a 'contextually responsive' architecture.[1] The book *Niche Tactics: Generative Relationships between Architecture and Site* (2015) envisions a rethinking of the traditional meaning of context, to include not only the static adjacent buildings that contextualism proposed but also the dynamic forces of the weather and the energies surrounding a building. Such thinking is nothing new: in fact, it can be traced back to the commonly accepted origins of architecture; to Vitruvius, who, in 'On Climate as Determining the Style of the House', writes that 'it is obvious that designs for houses ought ... to conform to the nature of the country and to the diversities of climate'. Yet, the domination of aesthetic concerns over climatic response follows quickly, when in the following chapter Vitruvius writes that 'symmetry and order are *primary*, and only *after* these considerations have been made, should one consider the nature of the site (as well as use and beauty)'.[2] *Niche Tactics* challenges the order of the hierarchy here and asks: What if we truly value response as a primary concern? What then of symmetry, order, and aesthetics? If a building is responding to a series of dynamic systems, surely the response will be a lop-sided, ill-formed monstrosity?

While making ugly architecture is not the goal of CODA, we accept that ugliness and monstrosity can be an unsurprising side effect of responsive architecture. Our practice simply tries to adhere to the following mantra: If architecture is to be malleable to the dynamic forces of its environment – an environment in constant flux and asymmetry – we must free ourselves from the preconceptions of that fixed standard of beauty that have pervaded our discipline and our society. If we deviate from these norms, we must accept that we might *make monsters*.

Mutations and monsters

While on the one hand monstrosity might be considered an extreme case of ugliness, this essay will differentiate the two terms by considering ugliness as existing within a species and monsters as being mutated beyond the limits of a species in order to (potentially) create new and as yet unrecognized typologies. This differentiation follows Francis Bacon, who, in his 'Aphorisms on the Composition of the Primary History' (1620), separates nature into three parts: Species, Monsters, and Artificial Nature. The first and last are described plainly enough: as free and developing ordinarily, and as constrained and moulded by human intervention, respectively. The monster, however, is seen as an aberration from each of these two categories, as having been 'forced out of her proper state by the perverseness and insubordination of matter and the violence of impediments'.[3]

In a particular strand of evolution theory, this definition holds true: mutations beyond normal limits have at times been considered to be monsters.[4] For example, a genetic malfunction can occur in Antennapedic *Drosophila* (fruit flies) which confuses antenna and leg/foot (pedia) production. This can occur such that the antennae are replaced by an additional pair of legs. Such a mutation might lead to the creature's demise due to the lack of antennae; on the other hand, it is conceivable that an extra leg or two could, in some contexts, be beneficial.

If a creature's mutation proves to adapt successfully in its environment – if it *fits*, in Darwinian terms – such a mutant has been called a 'hopeful monster'. The term was coined by Richard Goldschmidt in 1933 who believed that monstrous mutations contributed more significantly to macroevolution than previously thought[5] Goldschmidt proposed numerous examples in which successful mutations may have caused a split in the evolutionary trajectory: the archaeopteryx's mutant tail feathers that may have jump-started the mechanics of flying; or, in controlled breeding, achondroplastic bow-legs of the dog is monstrous, but once it is used to chase badgers (dachs) into their dens, it is evolutionarily beneficial to the dachshund.[6]

For Goldschmidt, such leaps were the foundations of evolution. Gradual variation existed, he believed, but accounted only for variation *within* a species. Monsters represented great evolutionary leaps and the origins of *new* species. While they may have begun as erroneous whether heterogeneous, geometrically operative, or both – and as deviations from the norm, those that happened to fit into a niche were the hopeful monsters that would later become species and enter a newly created normal territory under that heading. They would, conceptually, have a new Platonic form created for them, as they moved from the realm of the monster to that of the species.

Such ideas, Goldschmidt points out, were nothing new. Darwin originally believed that mutations (then known innocuously as 'sports') played a major evolutionary role but later changed his mind. In support of his argument, Goldschmidt provides examples of new traits that cannot possibly have arisen through gradual microevolutionary stages: hair on mammals, feathers in birds, segmentation of anthropods and vertebrates, teeth, shells of mollusks, ectoskeletons, compound eyes, blood circulation, poison apparatus of snake and so on. Like Bateson, he believed that these phenomena cannot have appeared gradually.[7]

At the end of the 1930s, however, Goldschmidt's views were largely disparaged among his peers, due mainly to his opposition to the more commonly accepted Darwinian theories. Only recently there is unexpectedly a renewed interest in his theories. Biologist Stephen Jay Gould believed that hidden beneath the distraction of Goldschmidt's more radical ideas were important concepts that reintroduced the notion of hierarchical models into evolutionary theory. Goldschmidt's vision, Gould writes in his introduction to the republication of *The Material Basis of Evolution* (1940), 'supplied (or rather re-supplied) an essential ingredient that strict Darwinism had expunged from evolutionary theory: the idea that evolution works through a hierarchy of distinct levels with important independent properties'.[8] In the Goldschmidtian interpretation, the monstrous mutation is considered a positive and generative phenomenon, and it is in relation to its context that the 'hopeful' evolution occurs.

Monsters and architecture

Vitruvius's analogy of the human body with architecture became animalistic via Leon Battista Alberti who, in *De Re Aedificatoria*, saw the animal as analogous to architecture. Like the human, the animal could be compared to architecture as a structure which embodied the natural principles of order in its part-to-whole relationships as well as its adaptation to an environment.[9] Alberti wrote, for example, that 'the supports of ancient buildings were generally even in number, as animals support themselves on an even number of feet; but the apertures were generally odd in number, in the same way that the mouth is a single opening in the face'.[10] Here we see a model of symmetry and order as the elements of beauty that must be aspired to in the production of the architectural artifice.

The slip from architecture-as-animal to architecture-as-monster is perhaps inevitable, as disorder in the natural is inevitably seen as a degeneration towards monstrosity. Alberti warns the architect of all possible 'errors of excess,' which would push architecture to the limits of its species and produce a 'monster with limbs disproportionate'.[11] This early warning begs a fundamental question: How far can such practices of mutation go before passing the boundaries of the architectural species and into architectural monstrosity?

In his *Monsters of Architecture*, Marco Frascari describes, among other buildings, James Stirling's addition to the Neue Staatsgalerie in Stuttgart

(Figure 8.1) as an architectural monster. He cites John Summerson, who refers to Stirling's 'monstrously ingenious "Queen Anne' play"'[12] and Susan Doubilet, who calls it a '"faceless" monster, a grotesque exotic animal'.[13] Frascari investigates the motivations for such monstrous language and concludes that, at Stuttgart, 'impossible things have been unified in a whole ... classical stone stereonomy has been combined with Pop elements, and with brutalistic concrete mushroom columns ... a summa of typological and iconographical references'.[14]

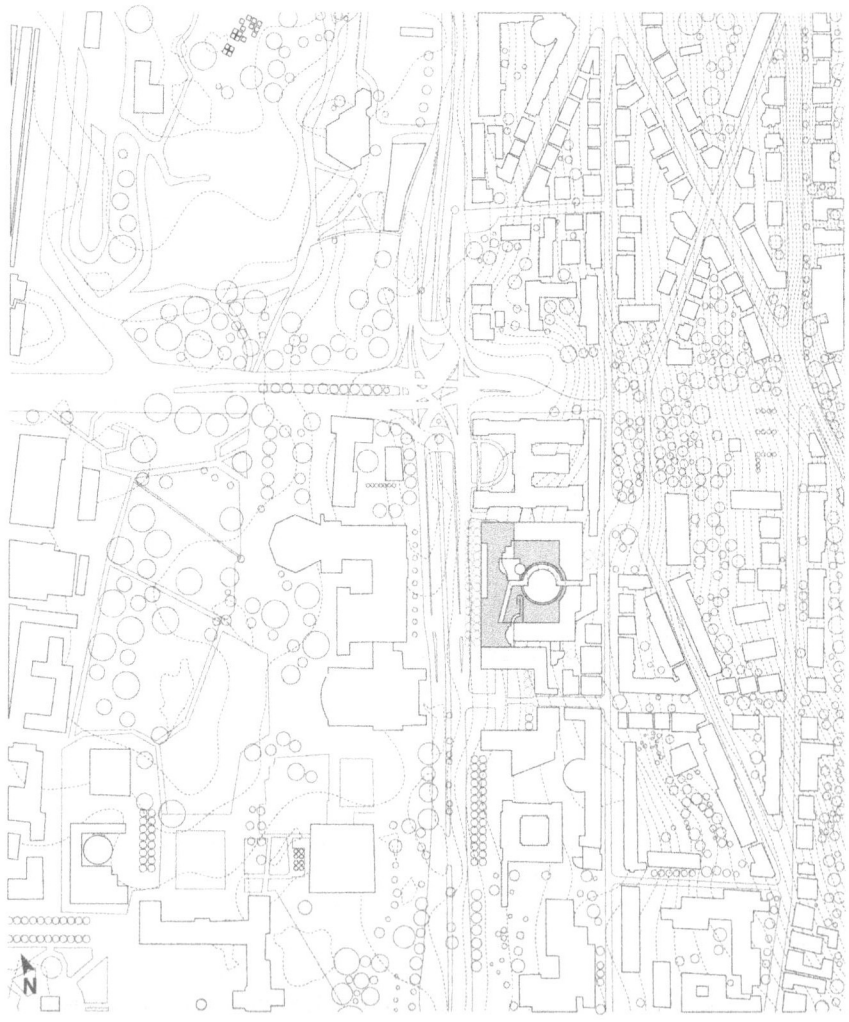

FIGURE 8.1 *James Stirling, Michael Wilford and Associates, Neue Staatsgalerie, Stuttgart, 1977–84. Redrawn with site by CODA.*

Considered by Frascari a child of many illicit fathers, the Neue Staatsgalerie is the quintessential romanticist monster because, according to Frascari's criteria, it is an organism created out of parts of diverse and unrelated species. Had it come from more analogous origins, it may have been a novel and interesting variation within a species, but its sources were too wildly divergent. As with the oft-cited Berlin Sphinx, which is a combination of lion, human and goddess – which Erwin Panofsky calls 'monstrous' due to its combinatory nature[15] – it is ejected from the world of species and thrust into the world of monsters.

For Goldschmidt, a monster requires a thorough examination of its surroundings in order to understand if this radical mutant might be considered a *hopeful* monster, the very hopefulness of which depends on the positivity of this relationship. Frascari's lengthy analysis of the Neue Staatsgalerie, however, barely mentions the context of the museum. Considering it as an isolated object of multiple parentages leads inevitably to a monstrous conclusion, while zooming out allows perceiving its fitness to its context, and thus its hopefulness.

The site is compressed between a busy multi-lane road and a steep topographical shift, and between the city and an adjacent neighbourhood. The museum's circular drum and public circulation that run through the building operate at an urban level to connect the two sides of the city. The heterogeneous nature of the fragments allows the building to act as a series of smaller urban parts, a neighbourhood in itself that can be conceptually passed through or alternatively as a piece of infrastructure that can be passed along and on. Seen as a system, rather than a collection of style-samplings into one discreet object, the Neue Staatsgalerie appears, like Goldschmidt's archaeopteryx-monstrosity become flying-bird, hopeful indeed. It *affords* a use-value, in the Gibsonian sense:[16] it offers something new in relation to its site. Precisely because of this particular mutation, it has advantages over its neighbouring like-types that form a barrier between the districts.

The notion of the hopeful monster introduces an alternative, more positive approach to typological (or species) thinking, one which involves taking the geometry of the organism as a strong indicator of the organism's environmental setting. For example, when the eye of the flatfish migrates to meet the other eye on one side of its skull, it provokes the question of what in nature, below or above the fish, has conferred an advantage on the fish that it survived and reproduced better than those without the mutation. This thinking is geared towards temporality and a dynamic future of possibilities in relation to a changing environment. The successful mutation points to something outside itself in order to make sense of itself.

In its comparable monstrosity, Le Corbusier's Carpenter Center for the Visual Arts (1962) in Cambridge, Massachusetts, ties in with the work of Stirling. In a critique of the Carpenter Center, Stan Allen asks, like Stirling's earlier critique of Ronchamp and like a mutation beyond the bounds of its species, if this work can be judged in the terms of the modern movement or if it is itself 'a new kind of movement'.[17] Allen goes on to explain the building in monstrous terms, through the subversion of expectations, and, as one of a series of late-Corbusian projects that are 'hopeful' and 'complex paradoxes' which, 'rather than looking backward, making incremental adjustments to know solutions ... look forward... propose new projects, and ... hold out the possibility of as yet unrealized solutions'.

Described by Fred Koetter as a 'contextual grotesque',[18] the Carpenter Center's main volume is rotated and penetrated by an S-shaped ramp, pulling lobes from the cube along its trajectory. This slicing of the public trajectory through rectilinear mass and the resultant fragmentation are descendants of Le Corbusier's early paintings and his *promenade architecturale*. But now they have escaped the confines of the box and have become dominant and exteriorized. In the genetic sense, a genotypic mutation has become phenotypic, meaning it has become perceptible rather than simply existing as part of the code. This gesture of pulling the public path through the building, re-composed in Stirling's museum, is the mutation that allows the Neue Staatsgalerie to function 'hopefully', that is, to be a monster in successful interaction with its site. In both projects, the trajectory is not forced but knitted into the fabric of the city. The cut has the effect of shaking the other parts, so that each side, and each corner, is different. They point not only to their adjacencies but also to the cut itself.

In the above cases, it is impossible to capture from one point of view a whole image of the building, as each image loses its definition against the backdrop of the world. It becomes amorphous, monstrous: less object and more object–environment system. This lack of definition reinforces Bakhtin's statement that 'the image of the grotesque body is unfinished and open and it is not separated from its surroundings by clearly defined boundaries'.[19] Similarly, this accidental or unformed composition that lacks an overall identifiable figure or gestalt is what John Macarthur has described as 'unideal' and 'weak form'.[20] Macarthur's correlation between weakened form and heightened phenomenal experience overlaps partially with Eisenman's definition of weak form, as 'arbitrary, undecidable, excessive', but differs where Eisenman defines it as having 'no strong relationship to narrative space or time'.[21] These terms suggest contingent and deformative external and internal forces acting on the form, as well as the legibility of those forces. Here, the monstrous is insecurely conditioned by its context. The monster becomes less a definable object and more an unnameable, unintelligible and unfinished systematic non-thing.

Hopeful architectural monsters can exist in many forms. But this particular lineage, like the antennapedic fly, is an example of one normal part of architecture (the path/street) being relocated to a more dominant position, creating new possibilities of how this deformed 'part' might be used and how it might affect newly adjacent parts. The architecture then, points to its other, a partially consumed and endlessly extending network of adaptability, and to its dynamic relationship with it.

Architecture unfinished, open and not separated from its surroundings

The practice of the design studio CODA sets as its goal the production of architecture that cannot be conceived of without its environment; that means that it is unfinished, open and not separated from its surroundings in the same way that Bakhtin defined the grotesque (see earlier). Such a practice inevitably grapples with conditions such as ugliness, roughness or monstrosity.

Bloodline (Figure 8.2), for example, analyses the parent–child relationship of a pair of umbilically connected baroque palaces outside Stuttgart, Germany, and proposes a third in the lineage. The 'descendent' not only exposes the barely concealed monstrosity of the second 'badly behaved baroque' but also foregrounds the idea of evolution through the new form itself. The intervention, a *self-consuming grill pavilion*, begins, as its 'grandparent' does, as a perfect form: in its contemporary situation, a cube, clad with local barbecue wood whose colour is a perfect match for the existing palaces. As the grill is used, the cladding is removed and consumed, revealing an interior volume, grotesque and programmatically derived (as is the case in the poché spaces of its parent, in which the poché had provided access to stoke the fires from behind).

The shedding and consumption of skin in *Bloodline*, which continues to evolve during its lifetime, is an exploration of architecture's potential transformation from animal to monster. As a perfect cube it represents CODA's preconception of ideal form, in a material seemingly connected to the comparably pure (if baroque) form of the adjacent palace. As it transforms, the de-purification of the form and material corresponds to the revelation of the potential reinterpretation of cladding as 'fuel'. Wood affords appropriate enclosure from one perspective, but it affords burning – and grilling – from another. In itself the cladding activates the cube's program to shift from pavilion to barbecue. The grill window's alignment with the forest axis (which is missing its 'castle'), or the chimney's alignment with the prevailing wind, point to factors outside itself, while the folds of the exterior point to internal functional needs, such as fire safety equipment, grilling tools, food storage and ash storage. Use, interaction and consumption cause the form and its reading to evolve in response to its environment or, more accurately, its niche.

This approach is situated in a territory somewhere between indexical formal theory (as promoted by Peter Eisenman with reference to Rosalind Krauss and Charles Sanders Peirce[22]) – in which dynamic diagrams result in a static but legible form – and a material practice, in which change over time is fundamental. As James Lowder has described it, 'the processes behind the formal erosion of the skin are not conceptual in nature and occurring in a virtual space, but rather are the actual physical and material processes based on the forces of program in a *literal* temporal field'.[23] As an ecdysic

FIGURE 8.2 *Bloodline, CODA, 2010. Above: 1:10 model and 1:1 mock-up presented in 'Self-Consuming' an exhibition at Tjaden Experimental Gallery, Cornell, supported by the CCA and the College of Architecture, Art, and Planning, as well as by Akademie Schloss Solitude and Elise Jaffe + Jeffrey Brown. Photographs by CODA.*

spider periodically sheds its skin, or a chameleon adapts to unpredictability changing backgrounds while preserving its integrity as an organism, CODA engages this active, open and tactical – if indeterminate – model both in principle and in practice.

FIGURE 8.3 *Party Wall*, MoMA/PS1 Young Architects' Program, CODA, 2013. View from dance floor. Photograph by Brent Solomon.

The concept of the ecdysis was also key to *Party Wall* (Figure 8.3), a temporary pavilion constructed as the winner of PS1/MoMA's 2013 Young Architects' Program. Originally, two contradictory briefs were presented to shortlisted competitors, requesting both the maximization of floor area and, at the same time, large areas of seating for various events. The proposal to use the pavilion's facade simultaneously as a storage device for seating, shedding and re-skinning was explored during the first experiment in real-time behaviour. The facade being removable, usable and returnable, turned the architecture into an animal/monster whose skin is, for a time, consumable.

In an Uexküllian sense, *Party Wall* resulted from extracting elements of the environment necessary to create its niche. This niche is defined by projecting needs: movement of the sun (because we need shade), minimal footing possibilities (because we need space to dance), maximum sitting possibilities (because we need to be an audience) – and by observing local opportunities – the proliferation of steel signage, graphic text and graffiti with which it may enter into dialogue, a walled-in irregular site with multiple sub-sites. In the end, *Party Wall*'s monstrous achievement is not its size but its engagement with its extracted environment and its self-demonstration as a sign.

Crucially, the pavilion does not communicate as a literal, architectural sign but relies on its context to reveal its meaning. Under sunny lighting conditions, around 1.00 pm to 2.00 pm in late summer, the concept at work is spelled out as a shadow in text on the ground. Read: WALL. A continuous linear element, *Party Wall* is all-wall at the top, but at the bottom, it stands only on four splayed feet, and allows passage through the space it encloses. Being syntactical with its environment, the object becomes more sign than wall, like the billboards that proliferate like grazing beasts around the site. In its condensation and elision, *Party Wall* evades categorization as the semantic Duck and the syntactic Domino. Like the joke, it plays with the manipulation of expectation and transformation on a number of levels.

At the finer scale, a similar tension is set up between the Comet Skateboard's longboard off-cuts and the pattern reminiscent of the recent wave of digital architecture. The original expectation, one of a digitally designed surface, is overthrown as the voided longboard shape becomes apparent. Mounted on the facade under the woven boards, the solid boards afford enclosure and architectural baseline. When removed, they afford sitting (with legs, we

FIGURE 8.4 *Urchin, CODA, 2016. Photograph by Joe Wilensky.*

call them benches) or play (with soft Trucks they revert to a strange kind of skateboard). Working backward, in fact, the bench reveals its other affordances by its underside print, which in turn hints at the facade pattern as a functional series of longboard-shaped voids and a chain of events which potentially conjures up the origins of the material and its many transformations and affordances throughout its own diverse life cycle.

Urchin (Figure 8.4), a pavilion made using 360 white plastic chairs, further explores the phenomenon of adjusted affordances. From a distance the pavilion appears to be a bristly torus, but upon closer inspection, the viewer understands the fabric as a series of familiar chairs, upended and aggregated. When the chair is in its normal state – singular, right-side up, legs on the ground, awaiting the human body – the response it demands is clear: 'sit down'! Reconfigured in this way, the chairs collectively refuse to 'speak' to an interior audience who will be denied their expectation to sit, and exclaim to an exterior environment other, more ambiguous thoughts and sentiments ('go away,' perhaps?).

Beyond responsiveness: Deposed expectation

Beyond any simplified notion of ugliness as an antonym for beauty, much theory on ugliness has revolved around the Baudelairean notion of affect, wherein the subject has more engagement, arousal or interest in the ugly than the beautiful. While CODA's work does indeed aspire to an increased affect, it is the deeper structure that causes the affective response that is at the core of the work. This underlying structure is one that might be summarized as *deposed expectation*.

Monsters have long been considered ugly because they exist outside existing norms of the species. In 1561, Pierre Boaistuau described them as 'the works of nature inverted, mutilated, and truncated'.[24] This same notion of failed expectation underlies Karl Rosenkranz's nineteenth-century definition of ugliness.[25] Overriding his detailed categorization of ugliness as formlessness, deformation and non-unity is a definition of ugliness as something fundamentally unplanned, unexpected, not supposed to be, in a given context. Rosenkranz's amorphousness, for example, has conditions: the amorphous is ugly only when it is intended to have a form, yet does not. The asymmetrical is ugly when it has been symmetrical and the symmetry has been destroyed or if the realization of its potential symmetry has been stilted. If decay occurs as it is supposed to, as a mountain range disappears behind clouds, it can be beautiful. It is unexpected decay that is ugly: the withered arm of a cripple, the gothic cathedral with one unbuilt tower, an amputation. Similarly, Umberto Eco, in his book *On Ugliness*, describes the reaction to a toothless stranger as a deviation from the expected: 'What disturbs us is not the form of the lips or the few remaining teeth, but the fact that the few survivors are not accompanied by the others that *should be* in that mouth

…Faced with the inconsistently or incompleteness of that whole – we feel compelled to say dispassionately that this face is ugly.'[26] This incompleteness has the potential for a new functional basis for ugliness.

The above-mentioned CODA projects play with notions of the expected, and, unexpectedly, ugliness here approaches comedy, as both rely often on a certain set up that is overthrown. Take, for example, the joke:

Two Goldfish are in their tank.

One turns to the other and says, 'You man the guns, I'll drive.'[27]

Here the second sentence forces a recontextualization that produces the comedy.

Conclusion

CODA understands the production of ugliness and monstrosity to have the following qualities:

1. Geometric and material logic in relation to site (rather than in relation to itself, as traditional notions of beauty would require)
2. Affect: having a more visceral response than a beautiful object, as described by Baudelaire
3. Openness/unfinishedness, as described by Bakhtin
4. Unexpectedness (and potentially the funny) as described by Rosenkranz

While all of the projects mentioned have site responsiveness as a fundamental generator, it is their unfinishedness, their existing in two states, in constant transformation, that is perhaps key to the production of both the unexpected (for it is to a large extent the very unfinishedness that is unexpected) and to the consequent affect. The 'aha' effect produced in these projects belongs to the world of the ugly and the joke and is key to the body of work. The projects aim to straddle these worlds, using the tools of contextual and functional expectation set-up and recontextualization of that expectation. In the end, the projects push beyond any formal understanding of ugliness and towards producing an effect, whether a laugh or a grimace: either way, a baring of the teeth, something beautiful architecture may be loath to do.

Notes

1 Caroline O'Donnell, *Niche Tactics: Generative Relationships between Architecture and Site* (New York: Routledge, 2015).

2   Vitruvius, *The Ten Books on Architecture*, trans. Morris Hicky Morgan (New York: Dover, 1960), 174.
3   Francis Bacon, 'Aphorisms on the Composition of the Primary History, Aphorism 1' in *The Works of Francis Bacon: Volume 4*, ed. William Rawley (London: Longmans, 1858), 253.
4   Richard Goldschmidt, *The Material Basis of Evolution*, Silliman Milestones in Science (New Haven: Yale University Press, 1982), 390.
5   Ibid.
6   Ibid., 391.
7   Ibid., 7.
8   Stephen Jay Gould, in his introduction to Goldschmidt, *The Material Basis of Evolution*, Xl.
9   Manfredo Tafuri, *Interpreting the Renaissance: Princes, Cities, Architects* (New Haven, CT: Yale University Press, 2006). From Catherine Ingraham, *Architecture, Animal, Human: The Asymmetrical Condition* (New York: Routledge, 2006), 19.
10 Ingraham, *Architecture, Animal, Human*, 183.
11 Leon Battista Alberti, *The Ten Books of Architecture*, trans. James Leoni (New York: Dover Publications, 1986), 13–14.
12 John Summerson, 'Vitruvius Ludens', *Architectural Review* no. 173 (March 1983): 19.
13 Susan Doubilet, 'The Talk of the Town', *Progressive Architecture* 65, no. 10 (1984): 74.
14 Marco Frascari, *Monsters of Architecture: Anthropocentrism in Architectural Theory* (Lanham, MD: Rowman & Littlefield, 1991), 78.
15 Erwin Panowsky, 'The History of the Theory of the Proportions as a reflection of the History of Styles' quoted from Greg Lynn, 'Body Matters' in *Folds, Bodies and Blobs* (Brussels: La Lettre Volée, 2004), 141.
16 James J. Gibson, *The Ecological Approach to Visual Perception* (Mahwah, NJ: Lawrence Erlbaum Associates, 1986), 8.
17 Stan Allen, *Practice: Architecture, Technique and Representation* (New York: Routledge, 2000), 121.
18 Fred Koetter, quoted in Allen, 'Le Corbusier and Modernist Movement', 121.
19 Mikhail Bakhtin, *Rabelais and His World* (Bloomington: Indiana University Press, 1984), 26.
20 John Macarthur, *The Picturesque: Architecture, Disgust and Other Irregularities* (New York: Routledge, 2007), 111, 157.
21 Peter Eisenman, 'Strong Form, Weak Form' in *Architecture in Transition: Between Deconstruction and New Modernism*, ed. Peter Noever (Munich: Prestel, 1997), 43.
22 Peter Eisenman, 'Digital Scrambler: From Index to Codex', *Perspecta* 35, Building Codes (2004): 40–53.

23 James Lowder, 'Skin Problems' in *The Expanding Periphery and the Migrating Center: Proceedings of the 103rd ACSA Conference*, ed. Lola Sheppard David Ruy (Miami, FL: ACSA, 2015), 603–9.

24 Pierre Boaistuau, *Histoires Prodigieuses* (1561) quoted by Mark Dorian, 'On the Monstrous and the Grotesque', *Word and Image* 16, no. 3 (2000): 310–17.

25 Karl Rosenkranz, *Ästhetik des Häßlichen* (Stuttgart: Reclam Taschenbuchen, 1990), 57. Translated for the author by Sarah Haubner.

26 Umberto Eco, *On Ugliness*, trans. Alastair McEwen (New York: Rizzoli, 2007), 19 (my emphasis).

27 Matthew Hurley, Daniel Dennett and Reginald Adams, *Inside Jokes* (Cambridge, MA: MIT Press, 2013), 42.

PART TWO

Ugly and ordinary

CHAPTER NINE

'Ugly': The architecture of Robert Venturi and Denise Scott Brown
Deborah Fausch

Critiquing Venturi and Rauch's 1967 competition entry for a housing project in Brighton Beach, New York, Philip Johnson dismissed the proposal as 'ugly and ordinary'. Robert Venturi and Denise Scott Brown took Johnson's remark for their motto, adopting the ugly as a lens for investigating the condition of American architecture and urbanism in the second half of the twentieth century, as a device for conveying their discoveries and as a means for displaying their incorporation of the visual forms, construction systems and communication structures of post-war America into their work. An evolving exploration of two modes of the ugly – the banal and the grotesque – characterizes both their theory and their designs.

Two forms of ugliness

In her essay on ugliness, art historian Nina Athanassoglou-Kallmyer describes the traditional relationship of beauty to its ugly opposite:

> Beauty was construed as the 'center' and the 'canon.' It stood for the ideal, reason, truth, goodness, perfection, clarity, order, harmony, civilization: for humanity's higher aspirations. ... On the flip side of beauty, ugliness served as the all-purpose repository for everything that did not quite fit this centered and elevated norm: mundane reality, the irrational, evil, disorder, dissonance, irregularity, excess, deformity, the marginal: in short, the Other.[1]

Contingent rather than unconditionally valid, the ugly represents the empirically real. Particular rather than universal, the ugly serves as the source or carrier of the new. 'Low' rather than 'high', ugliness challenges established standards of taste and, with them, standards for living. Disruptive of formal order, the monstrously ugly foregrounds that order and those forms while its disorder throws them into doubt.

The ugly occupied a prominent position in Modernism art and architecture, as both aesthetic and ethical/political agent of shock, display and revolutionary action. But in post-war America, Modernism had succeeded at the price of ceding these revolutionary aims to a realized formalism – whether in ideal, quietistic order (Mies van der Rohe), return to the columnar symmetry of Modernism's precursors (Edward Durrell Stone, early Johnson himself), expressionistic exaggeration of structure (Le Corbusier, Eero Saarinen) or 'contextual' evocation of vernacular forms (Walter Gropius, Marcel Breuer). In labelling the Brighton Beach proposal ugly, Johnson was thus reacting from a neo-traditional aesthetic to the project's typical Modernist move of incorporating vernacular or 'low' building forms into high art architecture. That year, an identical accusation came from the opposite aesthetic direction. Gordon Bunshaft, the chief designer for the High Modernist firm Skidmore Owings Merrill, charged the firm's proposal for Transportation Square in Washington, DC, with the same offense of ordinary ugliness, judging it not to be a design at all. Their redesigned proposal he pronounced a 'nonentity of architecture', again calling it ugly.[2] To understand why Venturi and Scott Brown's work was so provocative and so disliked, we must examine their uses of the ugly. And to do so, we must tease apart the different forms of ugliness they employed.

The category of the ugly has at least two subdivisions. Everyday, banal ugliness may have inelegant proportions, awkward shapes or shoddy materials; it can be unthought or undesigned, ad hoc or post hoc. It can be jumbled, garish, sentimental, a mishmash, or simply banal and boring. This form of the ugly stands for realism; it is the representation of low forms of art and society, found in comedy and the novel, as contrasted with the 'noble' strata of society and its representation in the 'high' forms of tragedy and epic. But if the empirical, contingent, quotidian ugliness of much of the post-war built environment qualified for Johnson's and Bunshaft's label of 'ugly and ordinary', there is another, more shocking form of ugliness that represents a direct attack on norms of beauty. As fascinating as it is repellent, this grotesque ugliness is unbalanced, unruly, disorderly, distorted, disproportionate, particular. Paradoxically, the grotesque's aberrant forms, which could be termed 'ugly and extraordinary', recall by their negation the order they call into question.

These two forms of ugliness are closely related to the 'indifferent in intuition' (sensible experience) and the 'loathsome' or 'disgusting' in Immanuel Kant's Third Critique. In the *Lectures on Metaphysics*, Kant elaborates:

That which pleases through mere intuition is *beautiful*, that which leaves me indifferent in intuition, although it can please or displease, is *non-beautiful*; that which displeases me in intuition is ugly. Now on this pleasure rests the *concept of taste*.[3]

Whereas the loathsome or disgusting, which 'displeases in intuition', evokes a physiological revulsion, the 'non-beautiful' may either please or displease but cannot, according to Paul Guyer, do so *aesthetically*. Indeed, neither of these forms of the ugly provides a purely aesthetic, reflective evaluation of 'disinterested interest'; instead such experiences bleed over into the practical, the moral or the visceral. Neither, therefore, according to Kant, constitutes art.[4]

When the grotesque, loathsome ugly strains against an ideal order, its energy may be increased and its power enhanced. Represented in architecture by Saarinen's structural extravagances and Louis Kahn's deliberately awkward solids, this form of ugliness was little theorized during the post-war period. On the other hand, while the indifferently ugly or 'non-beautiful' was not considered art (or architecture) at all, it interested architects seeking, in the Modernist tradition, to understand architecture's relationship to its larger cultural context. Opinions about the nature and value of the ordinary, undesigned built environment varied from deep engagement with the vernacular and 'popular' arts to dismay about the effects of advertising and the automobile. In the 1950s, *Perspecta* highlighted vernacular and 'anonymous' architecture and *Architectural Review* featured a monthly entry on 'Townscape,' while critics such as Peter Blake, J. M. Richards and Geörgy Kepes decried the despoliation of the post-war urban and suburban landscape.

The ugly in *Complexity and Contradiction*: Between 'the everyday' as a source of valid vitality and 'the grotesque' as a technique of Mannerism

Venturi's *Complexity and Contradiction in Architecture* (1966) explores the implications of both kinds of ugliness for a late modernism grown too preciously exceptional or too beautifully stale. In turning to existing forms of vernacular and mass-market construction and design for inspiration, its reconsideration of architecture's non-architectural, ordinarily ugly context follows Modernism's realist lead. It also proposes grotesque form as a means adequate to express the complications of post-war American culture.[5]

Complexity and Contradiction's sections on context and convention, on Main Street and on the highway draw on the contemporary discussions of the ordinary environment, but its approach is neither nostalgic nor apocalyptic. Venturi had published a short analysis from his master's thesis in *Architectural Review* detailing the damaging effects of changing context on Rome's Campidoglio. But his view of context, based on the Gestalt principle that forms take their meaning from their context and conversely create the context for other forms, is not revivalist.[6] And although he analyses the visual effects of moving towards and around buildings in an urban environment, Venturi does not strive for a picturesque unity of urban experience as did the Townscape theorists. Rather, he is drawn to the disorderly energy of the undesigned auto-generated environment of post-war America. Prefiguring the later distinction between the 'is' and the 'ought' in *Learning from Las Vegas*, Venturi declares that 'the old clichés involving both banality and mess will still be the context of our new architecture, and our new architecture significantly will be the context for them. ... As an art [architecture] will acknowledge what is and what ought to be, the immediate and the speculative.'[7] He rejects any ambition to create the 'total work of art' and instead advocates accepting the role of a 'combiner of significant old clichés – valid banalities – in new contexts'.[8] The idea that architecture can not only draw on the forms of everyday building but consist of deliberate and conventional banality will furnish the theoretical basis for the Brighton Beach project.

What Venturi means by the conventional elements of architecture is 'the vast accumulation of standard, anonymously designed products connected with architecture and construction, and also ... commercial display elements which are positively banal or vulgar in themselves'. Venturi adduces the example of Pop artists Robert Rauschenberg and Jasper Johns to demonstrate that, despite their banality and vulgarity, 'commonplace elements are often the main source of the occasional variety and vitality of our cities'.[9] But his architecture does not aim to 'transfigure the commonplace', as Arthur Danto characterized Andy Warhol's 'Brillo Boxes'.[10] Rather, the transfusion of the commonplace into a moribund Modernism reduced to stultifying stylistic conformity has the power to transfigure architecture. Epitomized in Venturi's plea, 'Is not Main Street almost all right? Indeed, is not the commercial strip of a Route 66 almost all right?' is the conviction that the banal, often ugly realism of these environments will be the source of renewal for late modernism, as the industrial buildings of the early part of the twentieth century were for Modernists.

Venturi also discerns aspects of the grotesque in the circumstantial realism of the American urban environment, commenting that 'the vivid lessons of Pop Art, involving contradictions of scale and context, should have awakened architects from prim dreams of pure order'.[11] Unlike Aldo Rossi's roughly concurrent study *The Architecture of the City*, which proposes as an alternative to Modernism's revolutionary functionalism a city composed of traditional typological fabric and unique monuments, *Complexity and Contradiction* celebrates the undesigned, even chaotic newness of the

American post-war landscape – the 'violent juxtapositions' of superhighway and suburban subdivision and the overscaled strip signage of the national cross-country roads.[12] Venturi sees these examples of American urbanism's 'messy vitality' as a way out of the enervated charm of post-war architecture and the artificially picturesque order of Townscape-inspired New Towns.

'Violent juxtapositions' are, according to Frances Connelly, characteristic of grotesque forms, which 'combine unlike things in order to challenge established realities or construct new ones'.[13] Similarly, Peter Stallybrass and Allon White describe the grotesque as 'formed through a process of hybridization or inmixing of binary opposites, particularly of high and low, … a heterodox merging of elements usually perceived as incompatible'.[14] Geoffrey Galt Harpham observes that the grotesque possesses an 'atrocious and inappropriate vitality'.[15] These characterizations are echoed in Venturi's evocation of the post-war urban environment: 'The seemingly chaotic juxtapositions of honky-tonk elements express an intriguing kind of vitality and validity, and they produce an unexpected approach to unity as well.'[16]

In viewing grotesque art, we are 'caught off guard, we are surprised and shaken, we have a sense of being played with. It evokes a range of feelings – uneasiness, fear, repulsion, delight, amusement, often horror and dread'.[17] Despite or perhaps because of the uneasiness, fear, repulsion, horror, and dread evinced by Blake, Richards and Kepes, Venturi praises Times Square's 'messy vitality', a term evocative of the grotesque's 'atrocious and inappropriate vitality', seeing in the ungovernable liveliness of the grotesquely paradoxical, chaotic, unseemly post-war city the energy for a new approach to architecture.[18]

Integral to Venturi's interest in Mannerism is his attraction to grotesque form. Stimulated by his reading of Rudolf Wittkower's *Architectural Principles in the Age of Humanism* (1949) and Wylie Sypher's *Four Stages in Renaissance Style* (1955) as well as by his study of Italian Mannerism during his stay in Rome, this fascination gives *Complexity and Contradiction* some of its greatest significance for its late-modern architectural audience.[19] Examples of the grotesque in works by Francesco Borromini, Edwin Lutyens, Frank Furness and others trace 'complex and contradictory' Mannerism through the history of Western architecture, demonstrating the way grotesque techniques call into question – stretching, but without breaking – established canons of form. Venturi describes Frank Furness's demolished Philadelphia Clearing House (1883–4) as a forceful collision of two disparate halves, containing

> an array of violent pressures within a rigid frame. The half-segmental arch, blocked by the submerged tower which, in turn, bisects the façade into a near duality, and the violent adjacencies of rectangles, squares, lunettes, and diagonals of contrasting sizes, compose a building seemingly held up by the buildings next door: it is an almost insane short story of a castle on a city street. All these relationships of structure and pattern

contradict the severe limitations associated with a façade, a street line, and contiguous row houses.[20]

Much in this description – violent pressures, blockage, violent adjacencies of unlike things – recalls depictions of the grotesque. Indeed, the chapter title for which this building serves as an example, 'Contradiction Juxtaposed', is also a grotesque attribute. Other chapter headings ('Ambiguity', 'Contradictory Levels', 'Both-And', 'Contradiction Adapted'), descriptive adjectives ('perverse', 'incomplete', 'wrong', 'fragmented', 'distorted'), Venturi's memorable phrases and slogans ('heterogeneous ideas yoked together by violence', 'ambiguity and tension', 'oscillating relationships', 'vivid tension', 'violent superimpositions', 'the difficult whole') and the book title itself also delineate characteristics of the grotesque.

In contrast to the 'expressionistic' use of extravagant form by some late-modern architects, Venturi claims these grotesque techniques are appropriate when they correspond to complex sociocultural conditions and contribute to an architecture adequate to its circumstances: 'abstruse architecture is valid when it reflects the complexities and contradictions of content and meaning. Simultaneous perception of a multiplicity of levels involves struggles and hesitations for the observer, and makes his perception more vivid.'[21] Challenges to an order ought not to be capricious, but ought to arise out of structural or functional necessity or the accommodation of a form to its context. For example, the gambrel roof is an alteration to a pre-existing order which it stretches but does not destroy:

> In the typical gambrel roof the need to accommodate living space within a roof angle essentially determined by drainage and structural functions results in an eloquent distortion of the original gable, … distinguishable from the expressionistic distortions of Rococo or of German Expressionism where the distorted is not contrasted with the undistorted.[22]

The lack of reference to an order is for Venturi a hallmark of unmotivated expressionism, the opposite of a valid grotesque which points beyond itself to a larger encompassing system. Thus the forms of the grotesque allow Venturi to aim towards what he calls 'the difficult whole', a way of expressing the complexity of the social world that his architecture both houses and inhabits. Compositionally and culturally the difficult whole is 'a taut composition which contains contrapuntal relationships, equal combinations, inflected fragments, and acknowledged dualities. It is the unity which "maintains, but only just maintains, a control over the clashing elements which compose it. Chaos is very near; its nearness, but its avoidance, gives … force"' – an apt description of the grotesque's property of straining, but not quite breaking, an existing order.[23]

Grotesque form in Venturi's early architecture

Early projects make use of many of these grotesque techniques to call into question Modernist tropes and to display the ironic deployment of traditional forms for communicating shifts in building practices and cultural purposes.[24] One such example must suffice: Venturi and Short's North Penn Visiting Nurse Association Headquarters in Ambler, Pennsylvania (1961). This small structure employs outsized scale, 'improper' placement and 'incorrect' shape to locate the building within a traditional classical idiom while simultaneously pointing out that this idiom has lost its constructional referent in modern lightweight, standardized building practices.

The plan of the Visiting Nurse Association Headquarters, which Venturi calls a 'distorted box' with an 'awkward' interior, is shaped by the needs of its siting. The car courtyard next to the building is of equal size, the other half of a duality of 'full' and 'empty', so that the project threatens to split into two, held together by the acute-angled 'prow' of the building forming one half of a containing neck for the car court. The trapezoidal shape of the building, derived from using the entire lot to accommodate the building's needs, distorts the ideal form of the rectangular box that would most economically accommodate the program.

The small building gathers together its openings to create a sense of monumentality that is of indeterminate scale. These openings slide along the facade, their regular rhythm distorted by the programmatic needs of the interior. In contrast to the precedent Venturi cites – Michelangelo's small windows in the Basilica of St. Peter in Rome, wider than they are tall, with an enormous lunette on top – it is no longer possible for the basement windows of the Visiting Nurse Association Headquarters to act as an amusing, unsettling play on customary ways of spanning an opening. Here the message of the oversized windows with their too-thin ornament decouples referential meaning and embodied construction – one of the most important problematics in Venturi and Scott Brown's architectural work (Figure 9.1).

Venturi is emphatic that grotesque formal moves not be deployed for merely 'expressionistic' reasons: 'These, I think, are the two justifications for breaking order: the recognition of variety and confusion inside and outside, in program and environment, indeed, at all levels of experience; and the ultimate limitation of all orders composed by man. When circumstances defy order, order should bend or break: anomalies and uncertainties give validity to architecture.'[25] Thus, although he later opined that *Complexity and Contradiction in Architecture* should have been called *Complexity and Contradiction in Architectural Form*, it is clear that for Venturi form and function ought, in Modernist fashion, to relate to if not directly reflect each other.[26] Here the grotesque is a means for correlating building plan with the needs of the urban context, and the facade, the meeting point between inside and outside, is the locus of this adjudication. This surface can also affect the

FIGURE 9.1 *Venturi and Short, North Penn Visiting Nurse Association Headquarters, 1961, Ambler, Pennsylvania. Photograph by George Pohl, provided by Venturi, Scott Brown and Associates, Inc.*

plan; thus the grotesque records a story of the alteration of ideal form by internal and external necessity. The project both establishes an order and bends it almost beyond recognition, using grotesque form to make Venturi's point that the complexities of the culture of what would come to be called the postmodern era require equal complexities of built form.

From the grotesque of *Complexity and Contradiction* to the banal of Brighton Beach

If *Complexity and Contradiction* makes use of grotesque aesthetic principles to argue for a complex, historically connected, culturally adequate architecture, Venturi and Scott Brown soon discovered the limits of their ability to apply these principles to their building designs. They commented at the beginning of 'Theory of Ugly and Ordinary' in *Learning from Las Vegas* (1972):

> After the appearance of *Complexity and Contradiction in Architecture*, we began to realize that few of our firm's buildings were complex and contradictory, at least not in their purely architectural qualities of space and structure as opposed to their symbolic content. ... Most of the complexities and contradictions we relished thinking about we did not use,

because we did not have the opportunity. ... Therefore our Brighton Beach entry ... turned out 'ugly and ordinary', as two such divergent critics as Philip Johnson and Gordon Bunshaft have described our work.[27]

Venturi and Rauch's submission to the Brighton Beach Housing project (Brooklyn, New York, 1967) was a competition for middle-income housing for the City of New York's Housing and Development Authority. It is a response to what Stuart Cohen calls the cultural, rather than the immediate environmental, setting.[28] The structure of their third-place entry is modern, the Aalto-esque building layouts affording good views of the ocean to all but two apartments while respecting the scale of street. But their project is distinguished from the other premiated submissions by its more contextual massing, construction and plans. The imagery is similar to that of 1930s New York apartment buildings, emulating an empirically, regionally and historically specific building type. Charles Moore's partner Donlyn Lyndon, a competition juror, called the project 'a thoughtful use of existing possibilities' that did not detract from or demean the surrounding neighbourhood but benefitted it with simple, well-built construction that would contribute to the personal dignity of the inhabitants (Figure 9.2).[29]

What makes this project, which does not literally copy its context, seem 'ugly and ordinary'? While evoking, in its fenestration and concern for views, Alvar Aalto's Neue Vahr high-rise housing project (Bremen, 1962) rather than the megastructural idiom favoured by the winning scheme, it also adopts the brick facing, 'punched' windows and circumstantial floor plans of the prewar apartments in its immediate neighbourhood and the larger New York region. Rather than using Modernist materials of steel, glass and concrete, the project associates itself to these local precedents, displaying

FIGURE 9.2 *Venturi and Rauch, Brighton Beach Housing Competition, 1967, Brooklyn, New York, site model. Photograph provided by Venturi, Scott Brown and Associates, Inc.*

in a deadpan way conditions of customary planning and construction. It thus communicates an acceptance of – and seemingly a positive valuation of – these models.

An important precedent for Venturi and Scott Brown's work was the deadpan art of the Pop artist Edward Ruscha. His photographs of Los Angeles's apartments, parking lots and the Sunset Strip, observed with an even, fascinated gaze, would become a model for their non-judgemental approach to building and urban form. Benjamin Buchloh notes of Ruscha's *26 Gas Stations* that it was

> a particularly laconic type of photography, … one that explicitly situated itself as much outside of all conventions of art photography as outside of those of the venerable tradition of documentary photography, least of all that of 'concerned' photography. This devotion to a deadpan, anonymous, amateurish approach to photographic form corresponds exactly to Ruscha's iconographic choice of the architectural banal.[30]

The undecidable valuation of Ruscha's subject matter was an essential part of his photographs' message. Starting with Marcel Duchamp's ready-mades, deadpan art had been used to call into question traditional categories of art/non-art and to display for aesthetic appreciation the banal objects of everyday life – to problematize, in other words, Kant's categorization of the non-beautiful as non-art. But as the reaction to Venturi and Scott Brown's competition entry showed, this approach had its limitations in architecture. Unlike Duchamp's urinal or Ruscha's photographs of Los Angeles, their buildings were not located in a setting that already designated them as art. An essential difference between architecture and the visual arts is that, lacking this situational designation, architecture not only portrays but also enacts. And the problem with this project, as far as most of the competition jury was concerned, was that it was so contextual in its portrayal and enaction of the customary that there was no way to tell that it was architecture.

Research into the 'is' versus the 'ought': *Learning from Las Vegas*

Venturi, Scott Brown and Steven Izenour's *Learning from Las Vegas* assays the post-war built environment for principles of architectural design that can meet mass culture on its own terms. Understanding this environment as a primary generator of building form, the book argues that architecture is necessarily and essentially symbolic; thus, it adds communication to structure and function as another determinant of architecture.

The work is organized centrally around Scott Brown's researches into post-war America's emerging urban structures and imagery. At the

Architectural Association, Scott Brown was influenced by the Smithsons's and the Independent Group's interest in the 'as-found' – modern unadulterated concrete and steel construction and the off-the-shelf components of industrial design – and their captivation by American advertising and commercial products. Her early fascination with the 'as-found', 'agonized beauty' of buildings and signage that gave her an 'aesthetic shiver' provided object lessons in the undecidable emotions of the grotesque. This schooling in 'learning to love what you hate' also represented another challenge to Kant's dichotomy between art and ugliness.

Echoing the Smithsons, *Learning from Las Vegas* puts forward a program of 'withholding judgment … as a tool to make later judgment more sensitive', and as 'a way of learning from everything'.[31] This 'interested yet disinterested' approach – which Kant connected with the aesthetic sense – to the ordinarily ugly – which Kant did not include in the aesthetic – funded Venturi and Scott Brown's investigations of post-war urban and suburban environments. These explorations took form in their Yale research studios on Las Vegas in 1968 and Levittown's mass-market housing in 1970. In the process, 'loving what you hate' evolved into an exploration of the 'is' versus the 'ought', and the use of deadpan presentation techniques to convey their findings in their architectural works.

Scott Brown invited Venturi to visit Las Vegas in the mid-1960s. The two were, as she related, 'jolted out of their aesthetic skins' by the brilliant desert light and the gigantic, ever-in-motion neon. After this 'eyeball-to-eyeball encounter with the real' they set about trying to understand the Strip's underlying order.[32] Treating Las Vegas as a hypertrophied example of 'the automobile-oriented commercial architecture of urban sprawl', they studied not only the extravagant signage but also the less dramatic structural regularities of the Strip.[33] Their novel mapping techniques delineated the visual and spatial organization, arising from use and communication, that underlay the seemingly chaotic jumble of gas stations, wedding chapels, convenience stores and light poles.

This urban organization also gave rise to a characteristic, although not entirely new, building type, the 'Decorated Shed'. In contrast to the pseudo-grotesque 'expressionism' of some Late-Modern works that Venturi and Scott Brown labelled 'Ducks', the Decorated Shed was a banal, 'mute' structure with applied, communicative ornament. This separation of structure and envelope was common to many post-war buildings – cinemas, sports stadia, speculative office buildings and 'big box' shopping outlets. Once communication was admitted as a function of buildings, this building type, in which 'systems of space and structure are directly at the service of program, and ornament is applied independently of them', could be seen as a Modernist response to contemporary cultural conditions.[34] Its apotheosis, and the most complete exemplar of its constructional, functional, aesthetic and communicative principles, was that middle-class mirage of opulence in the desert, the Las Vegas strip casino-hotel.

Scott Brown's planning training at the University of Pennsylvania, with its focus on the emerging forms of West Coast urbanism, furnished her with analytic tools for understanding the order and structures of these new, decentralized urban spaces dominated by Decorated Sheds and in particular the new forms of 'communication channels' that had evolved to meet the needs of the automobile.[35] The flamboyant signage found on the Las Vegas strip in the mid-sixties functioned as such a communication channel; Venturi and Scott Brown's physiognomic diagram of a typical Las Vegas sign delineates the Decorated Shed as the emblem of this emergent semio-spatial order.[36]

But the energy and exuberance of the signs themselves exceeded the logic of this order. The exaggerated sign-as-ornament offered both a fantasy and a factual description about what might be inside. In order to communicate quickly across great distances to a person in a moving vehicle, the ornamental, 'come-on' elements needed to be overscaled and high above the roadway, whereas the advertisements of entertainment on offer needed to be at eye level and smaller scale, to be taken in close up. Thus, the typical Las Vegas sign had a heraldic 'high reader' and an informational 'low reader', a hybrid, unorthodox organization of two unrelated parts incongruously yoked together but consumed as separate parts. According to Rémi Astruc, the grotesque manner is characterized by doubleness, hybridity and metamorphosis, making use of stretched and contorted forms, extravagant and excessive shape and scale, offering ambivalent and ambiguous identities and relationships that communicate its essentially improper nature.[37] Because of its categorical uncertainty, grotesque form, as Harpham observes, has to be perceived 'in bits', by 'breaking down the strange into the recognizable', and unified form falls apart into its components.[38] These descriptions aptly characterize the casino signs, whose forms made free use of grotesque techniques as rhetorical come-ons, separately conveying in more sober fashion the details of what was on show. The requirements of the Strip, experienced by automobile, dictated this mutation of Main Street signage by means of grotesque hybridity, doubleness, exaggeration, distortion – and, in keeping with the fantastical atmosphere of Las Vegas, humorous, playful, even cartooned forms.

Venturi and Scott Brown drew on the grotesque techniques of Pop Art not only for their understanding of Las Vegas but also for inspiration in their architecture.[39] To illustrate how these strategies applied to their designs, they used the windows in their elderly housing project Guild House (Philadelphia, 1961) as examples of the way 'pop distortion', change in scale, and changes of context communicated the nature of the window as a cultural element, understood by means of association to 'all the windows you know':[40]

> The windows [of Guild House] look familiar; they *look like*, as well as *are*, windows, and in this respect their use is explicitly symbolic. But like all effective symbolic images, they are intended to look familiar and

unfamiliar. They are the conventional element used slightly unconventionally. Like the subject matter of Pop Art, they are commonplace elements made uncommon through distortion in shape (slight), change in scale (they are much bigger than normal double-hung windows), and change in context (double-hung windows in a perhaps high-fashion building). ... The double-hung window in Guild House is familiar in form but unusually large in size and horizontal in proportion, like the big, distorted Campbell Soup can in Andy Warhol's painting.[41]

Alterations to a figurative, conventionally understood element – one that is part of an architectural 'language' – by means of techniques such as 'familiar and unfamiliar', 'conventional element used slightly unconventionally', 'distortion in shape', 'change in scale', 'change in context' – all are hallmarks of the grotesque in architecture. As this quotation shows, Venturi and Scott Brown used the grotesque techniques of Las Vegas signage, as well as those of Pop Art, to highlight aspects of their building design that related it to convention and tradition ('all the windows you know') while also taking an ironic stance towards those traditions.

Venturi and Scott Brown's later grotesquery: Wu Hall

Venturi and Scott Brown's investigations of post-war urban and suburban form eventuated in an exhibition entitled *Signs of Life: Symbols in the American City* (Washington, DC, 1976) at the Smithsonian Institution's Renwick Gallery. Attended by thousands of visitors who wrote enthusiastic reviews, the exhibition elicited puzzled or disapproving comments from most architectural critics, who mistook the even-handed presentation of Main Streets, commercial strips and highway signage, urban row houses and suburban subdivision housing for approval of these forms.[42] Likewise, their projects during this period – the Thousand Oaks Civic Center (1969), a sensitively sited, systems-built low-rise strip building off the California 101 Freeway with an overscaled entry sign; the Best Products Catalog Showroom (Langhorne, Pennsylvania, 1978) and BASCO Showroom (Philadelphia, Pennsylvania, 1976), big box 'sheds' which featured gigantic applied ornament visible at highway speed; and the City Edges project (Philadelphia, 1975), a signage 'gateway' into the city for motorists – were too close to their mass-culture prototypes for most architects, or for that matter the public, to appreciate. In later work the architects often returned to the grotesque as a communicative strategy to convey the nature of the post-war context as well as to highlight the detachability of ornamental/communicative elements from their underlying structures.

FIGURE 9.3 *Venturi, Rauch and Scott Brown, Gordon Wu Hall, 1982, Princeton University, Princeton, New Jersey. Photograph by Tom Bernard, provided by Venturi, Scott Brown and Associates, Inc.*

One of the best examples of Venturi and Scott Brown's use of the grotesque is Gordon Wu Hall at Princeton University (Princeton, New Jersey, 1982), a social and dining center for Butler College, a new group of dormitories (Figure 9.3). The building accommodates its program in the leftover space between the north–south passageway of Butler Walk and the neighbouring college. It is skinned with a highly mannered envelope sporting enormous keystones above a long window opening and an enigmatic marble blazon over the main entry.[43] Wu Hall's materials, proportions and ornamental/signifying elements establish a relationship to Princeton's neo-Gothic and neo-Renaissance architectural idiom while simultaneously asserting the building's 'conditions of production'. Making use of grotesque techniques, they communicate a complex message about the relationship of ornament to construction and of contemporary building practices to traditional forms.

The west wall adjoining Butler Walk, containing the main entry as well as the long picture window along the dining hall, constitutes the main facade of the building. Alan Chimacoff and Alan Plattus describe it as 'a register of particularized responses to the intricacies of local context, … [an] episodic

FIGURE 9.4 *Wu Hall, entry and keystones. Photograph by Tom Bernard, provided by Venturi, Scott Brown and Associates, Inc.*

articulation of that volume as part of the ... exercise in sustained ambiguity'.[44] And indeed, the building threatens to fall apart into a congeries of disparate materials, proportions, and ornamental/signifying elements, each addressed to a different aspect of Princeton's architecture and its larger social context. The marble panel over the entry (Figure 9.4) is modelled after the chimneypieces and entries of Renaissance and Baroque architecture, but its abstraction detaches it from these precedents. The juxtaposition of the small scale of the doors below and the gigantic face above causes it to assume a looming, monstrous character altogether at variance with the first impression of a puzzling but banal ornamental form. What seems to act as the nose in the composition is in fact the jamb of the windows set into the marble surface, introducing a 'real', three-dimensional component into the flat yet vaguely representational forms. This oscillation between representation and reality contributes to the grotesque 'undecidability' of the panel—is it ornament, message or functional element? The ambiguity and plurality of reference incorporates an entire sociocultural, disciplinary and technological world in its commentary.

Over the picture window sit several keystones – flat, hugely overscaled, distorted representations of a structural element associated with openings in brick bearing-wall construction. Here, keystones are structurally unnecessary because the brick above the long opening is carried by a steel lintel; an expansion joint cutting through one of the keystones emphasizes their structural otiosity. Their cartoonlike forms call ironic attention to the discrepancy between the nonstructural use of the brick in a curtain wall and the social and constructional references embodied in the masonry buildings around the Princeton campus. The irony embodied in the keystones foregrounds the complex cultural problem of meaning in post-industrial mass society, at once granting and taking away the reference points of familiar forms. The 'message' of the cut-through keystone thus extends beyond a particular witty, ironic, even regretful structural reference to call into question the role of architecture in this complex postmodern cultural situation.

Reception of Venturi and Scott Brown's work: The problem of taste

Paulette Singley observes that 'the oscillation between lack and surplus that structures the paradox of representing the ugly' is part and parcel of the difficulty of encountering grotesque form.[45] The ornamental panel above the entry to Wu Hall is at once a desiccated remnant of former plasticity and a monstrous overgrowth; the keystones are at once too grotesquely large and too lacking in tangible, plastic presence, too significant a communication and not significant enough a structure. This oscillation explains some of the negative reaction Venturi and Scott Brown's buildings still receive. Indeed, both their strategies of design and display – deadpan and grotesque – garner similar reactions. Grotesque form induces repulsion because it breaks categories; for many observers, as Kant pointed out, the undecidable quickly transfigures into the loathsome and from there rapidly descends into the immoral. Correspondingly, deadpan presentation with its suspension of judgement caused many of their critics to mistake Venturi and Scott Brown's efforts to research and portray the condition of postmodern architecture and urbanism for uncritical acceptance – and worse, bad taste. For as Kant states, the beautiful and the ugly are matters of the judgement of *taste*. In complaining about the ugliness of their Brighton Beach proposal, Johnson was expressing such a judgement; and taste, with its inherent mixture of absolute conviction and empirical relativism, moralism and aesthetic discernment, is at the heart of the difficulty architects and the public alike still have with Venturi and Scott Brown's work.

As Tom Wolfe observed, in the mid-twentieth century, for the first time in Western history the lower-middle class had – collectively at least – the financial power to exert its taste: 'Suddenly classes of people whose styles of life had been practically invisible had the money to build monuments to their own styles'.[46] Wolfe saw in Las Vegas a monument to what Herbert Gans, in his contemporaneous study of six American sociocultural fractions, or 'taste cultures,' labelled 'lower-middle' taste culture.[47] Numerically dominant and newly prosperous – a higher percentage of American households owned their own dwellings than ever before – lower-middle taste culture had what architectural critics considered bad taste.[48] But the feeling was mutual. Gans discovered that each of the taste cultures that made up American society in the post-war period was self-contained. Each fraction formed an organically intact, self-reinforcing sociocultural whole in which all facets – ethics, aesthetics, politics, culture and taste – interpenetrated and reinforced each other.[49] Morality and taste, in other words, were interwoven, and this was as true of the 'creator-high' culture to which most architects and critics belonged as it was of lower-middle culture.

Thus it was one thing to abstract formal elements from vernacular building practices, as Modernists had done; to seem to advocate mass-market building forms wholesale was to abandon the aesthetic and, therefore, also the moral, values of Venturi and Scott Brown's own creator-high culture tribe. Their practice of 'loving what you hate' represented a crucial shift from emphasizing the shock value of contemporary urban forms to learning to see them, if not as beautiful, at least as necessary. Even more significant was their shift in the use of this ugly imagery, from employing it to destabilize a too-complacent bourgeoisie to an open-minded investigation and display of its characteristics. By explaining one taste culture to another, Venturi and Scott Brown appeared to be either 'slumming' or capitulating, and in either case, to be abandoning the values and mores of their own cultural fraction. While the Smithsons were influenced not only by their own working-class upbringing but also by Michael Young's and Peter Willmott's studies of working-class life in London's East End, their emphasis on existing 'forms of life' did not extend to reproducing the visual preferences or living arrangements of those whom they studied; instead they designed 'streets in the air' emulating Le Corbusier's *Unité d'habitation* in Marseilles (1952).[50] Venturi and Scott Brown, on the other hand, had the 'bad taste' to propose that suburban mass housing, like Main Street, was 'almost all right'. Calibrating this imagery with Modernist values of 'truth to structure and function', their work sought to inoculate architecture against mass culture by incorporating its excesses while finding a 'style for the times' that could appeal to lower-middle consumers as well as high-culture creators. But critics like Kenneth Frampton reacted vehemently, contending that their work flirted not only with kitsch but with what Ada Louise Huxtable, in the *New York Times*, described as the 'cult of the "dumb and ordinary". Frampton wrote of their work: '[t]he cavalier attitude to material, the monumental gesture that dissolves into historicism, ... the overt use of out-sized Pop imagery ... all testify to a "popular" wit that is ultimately conservative.'[51] Their position was accused of not being ideological enough, of selling out to corporate capitalism, of amelioration.[52] Yet amelioration was what their lower-middle clients felt mocked for their desire to have. Ironically, the aspects of Venturi and Scott Brown's work most criticized by architects were precisely the qualities that alienated the lower-middle taste culture whose values had produced so much of the post-war architectural and urban environment the architects sought to represent. And despite their appeal to the deadpan techniques of Pop Art for justification of their forms and methods, the question whether architecture could 'pander' to lower-middle-class taste and still constitute art was repeatedly raised by Venturi and Scott Brown's critics. This was, however, a question that could only be asked, and answered, within the ethical and aesthetic terms of the creator-high taste culture to which they and their architectural critics belonged.[53]

A still-contentious discussion of the nature, purpose and significance of ugliness in Venturi and Scott Brown's work has marked both its popular and critical reception. Their work overturns a Modernist canon premised on the incorporation of the ordinary ugliness of industrial culture by means of a deadpan presentation of the ordinary ugliness of mass culture. Its other ugly face is a grotesque architecture whose techniques strain the high-art traditions of convention and beauty to convey the contradictions of the postmodern everyday. The controversy is an extension of the originally difficult reception of Modern architecture, with the additional complication that Venturi and Scott Brown's work can be read as mocking the lower-middle-class aspirations and popular modes of building it attempts to display and to address. Unsettling both to cultural elites and to the lower-middle taste culture from which it draws its forms, Venturi and Scott Brown's 'ugly' architecture continues to challenge and disturb all its intended audiences.

Notes

1 Nina Athanassoglou-Kallmyer, 'Ugliness' in *Critical Terms for Art History*, 2nd edn, ed. Robert S. Nelson and Richard Shiff (Chicago, IL: University of Chicago Press, 2003), 281.

2 Robert Venturi, Denise Scott Brown and Steven Izenour, *Learning from Las Vegas*, 1st edn (Cambridge, MA: MIT, 1972), 138–41.

3 Immanuel Kant, *Lectures on Metaphysics*, trans. Karl Ameriks and Steve Naragon (Cambridge: Cambridge University Press, 1997), 480 (29:1010).

4 Paul Guyer, 'Kant and the Purity of the Ugly', *Values of Beauty: Historical Essays in Aesthetics* (New York: Cambridge University Press, 2005), 161, and Immanuel Kant, *Critique of the Power of Judgment*, trans. Paul Guyer and Eric Mathews (New York: Cambridge University Press, 2000), §48.

5 Robert Venturi, *Complexity and Contradiction in Architecture*, 2nd edn (New York: Museum of Modern Art, 1977); references are to the second edition.

6 Robert Venturi, 'The Campidoglio: A Case Study,' *Architectural Review* 113, no. 677 (May 1953): 333–4.

7 Venturi, *Complexity and Contradiction*, 42–3.

8 Ibid., 44.

9 Ibid.

10 Arthur Danto, 'The Transfiguration of the Commonplace', *The Journal of Aesthetics and Art Criticism* 33, no. 2 (Winter, 1974): 139–48.
11 Venturi, *Complexity and Contradiction*, 104.
12 Ibid., 54, 68. Aldo Rossi, *The Architecture of the City* (Cambridge: MIT, 1982). See also Esin Komez Daglioglu, 'The Context Debate: An Archeology', *Architectural Theory Review* 20, no. 2 (2015): 266–79.
13 Frances S. Connelly, 'Introduction' in *Modern Art and the Grotesque*, ed. Frances S. Connelly (Cambridge: Cambridge University Press, 2003), 2.
14 Peter Stallybrass and Allon White, *The Poetics and Politics of Transgression* (Ithaca, NY: Cornell University Press, 1986), 43–4.
15 Geoffrey Galt Harpham, *On the Grotesque: Studies in Contradiction in Art and Literature* (Aurora, CO: The Davies Group, 1982), 6.
16 Venturi, *Complexity and Contradiction*, 104.
17 Wilson Yates, 'Introduction to the Grotesque: Theoretical and Theological Considerations' in *The Grotesque in Art and Literature: Theological Reflections*, ed. James Luther Adams and Wilson Yates (Grand Rapids, MI: Wm. B. Eerdmans, 1997), 2.
18 Venturi, *Complexity and Contradiction*, 104.
19 See Philippe Barrière and Sylvia Lavin, 'Interview with Denise Scott Brown and Robert Venturi,' *Perspecta* 28 (1997): 127; Maarten Delbeke,' Mannerism and Meaning in Complexity and Contradiction in Architecture', *Journal of Architecture* 15, no. 3 (2010): 267–82.
20 Venturi, *Complexity and Contradiction*, 57.
21 Ibid, 25.
22 Ibid, 46.
23 Ibid, 104; quoting August Heckscher, the former Special Consultant on the Arts to President Kennedy and New York City Parks Commissioner, in *The Public Happiness* (New York: Atheneum, 1962), 289 (ellipses in original).
24 On Venturi's ironic stance, see Deborah Fausch, 'Towards "An Architecture of our Times" – Scaffold and Drapery in the Work of Venturi, Scott Brown and Associates' in *Architecture: In Fashion*, ed. Deborah Fausch et al. (New York: Princeton Architectural Press, 1994).
25 Venturi, *Complexity and Contradiction*, 41, 46.
26 Robert Venturi, 'Donald Drew Egbert – A Tribute' in Donald Drew Egbert, *The Beaux-Arts Tradition in French Architecture* (Princeton, NJ: Princeton University Press, 1980), xiii–xiv.
27 Robert Venturi, Denise Scott Brown and Steven Izenour, *Learning from Las Vegas: The Forgotten Symbolism of Architectural Form*, 2nd edn (Cambridge: MIT, 1977), 128; unless otherwise noted, references are to the second edition.
28 Stuart Cohen, 'Physical Context/Cultural Context: Including It All', *Oppositions* 2 (January 1974): 1–40.
29 Donlyn Lyndon, quoted in *Learning from Las Vegas*, 1st edn, 134–7.

30 Benjamin H. D. Buchloh, 'Conceptual Art 1962–1969' in *October, The Second Decade, 1986–1996*, ed. Rosalind E. Krauss et al. (Cambridge: MIT, 1998).
31 Venturi, Brown and Izenour, *Learning from Las Vegas*, 3. C.f. Peter and Alison Smithson, 'But Today We Collect Ads', *Ark* no. 18 (November 1956).
32 The phrase is Terry Eagleton's in 'Capitalism, Modernism, and Postmodernism', *New Left Review* 1/152 (July–August 1985): 69.
33 Quoted in Denise Scott Brown, 'Denise Scott Brown' in *Particular Passions: Talks with Women Who Have Shaped Our Times*, ed. Lynn Gilbert and Gaylen Moore (New York: Clarkson N. Potter, 1981), 316; Venturi, Brown and Izenour, *Learning from Las Vegas*, 89. Venturi and Scott Brown's and their students' street photography is highlighted in Hilar Stadler and Martino Stierli, eds., *Las Vegas Studio: Images from the Archives of Robert Venturi and Denise Scott Brown* (Kriens and Zürich: Museum im Bellpark/ Verlag Scheidegger & Speiss AG, 2008). Aron Vinegar has characterized the position Venturi and Scott Brown took toward Las Vegas as one of wonder, connecting it to scepticism. Aron Vinegar, *I Am a Monument: On* Learning from Las Vegas (Cambridge: MIT, 2008).
34 Venturi, Brown and Izenour, *Learning from Las Vegas*, 88.
35 Denise Scott Brown, *Urban Concepts* (London: Academy Editions, 1990).
36 Venturi, Brown and Izenour, *Learning from Las Vegas*, 66–7.
37 Rémi Astruc, *Le Renouveau du grotesque dans le roman du XXe siècle* (Paris: Classiques Garnier, 2010).
38 Harpham, *On the Grotesque*, 5.
39 Venturi, Brown and Izenour, *Learning from Las Vegas*, 63, 72. As Martino Stierli notes, Venturi and Scott Brown highlight the aspects of Pop Art that suit their own purposes and fail to mention some of its other salient characteristics. Martino Stierli, *Las Vegas in the Rearview Mirror* (Los Angeles: Getty Research Institute, 2013), 251–3.
40 Venturi, Brown and Izenour, *Learning from Las Vegas*, 129.
41 Ibid, 91, 132; emphasis in original.
42 See Deborah Fausch, 'Ugly and Ordinary: The Representation of the Everyday' in *Architecture of the Everyday*, ed. Steven Harris and Deborah Berke (New York: Princeton Architectural Press, 1997).
43 Alan Chimacoff and Alan Plattus, 'Learning from Venturi,' *Architectural Record* 171 (September 1983): 86–97.
44 Ibid., 90.
45 Paulette Singley, 'Devouring Architecture: Ruskin's Insatiable Grotesque,' *Assemblage* 32 (April 1997): 115.
46 Tom Wolfe, 'Introduction' in *The Kandy-Kolored Tangerine-Flake Streamline Baby* (New York: Farrar, Strauss, and Giroux, 1965), xiv–xv; see also, in the same volume, 'The Kandy-Kolored Tangerine-Flake Streamline Baby', 77.
47 The six classes are creator-high, upper-middle, middle, lower-middle, lower and quasi-folk culture. Herbert J. Gans, 'Popular Culture in America: Social Problem in a Mass Society or Social Asset in a Pluralist Society?' in *Social*

Problems: A Modern Approach, ed. Howard S. Becker (New York: John Wiley, 1966). See also Herbert J. Gans, *Popular Culture and High Culture: An Analysis and Evaluation of Taste* (New York: Basic Books, 1974); Herbert J. Gans, *The Levittowners: Ways of Life and Politics in a New Suburban Community* (New York: Pantheon Books, 1967).

48 Chester Rapkin, personal communication, 1989. Implicit in this point of view is another one, that capitalism is working well for 'ordinary' people, much more true in the America of the late sixties and early seventies than it is today.

49 A condition that has only been exacerbated by the media that were supposed to unify and homogenize American culture.

50 Michael Young and Peter Willmott's *Family and Kinship in East London* (London: Routledge and Kegan Paul, 1957) inspired Nigel Henderson's street photography and influenced the Smithsons's reformulation of the CIAM functional grid developed by Le Corbusier in terms of 'patterns of association': house, street, district, city.

51 Kenneth Frampton, quoting Huxtable, in 'America 1960–1970: Notes on Urban Images and Theory', *Casabella* 35, nos. 359–60 (December 1971): 33.

52 See Tomas Maldonado, 'Las Vegas and the Semiological Abuse', *Design, Nature and Revolution: Toward a Critical Ecology*, trans. Mario Domandi (New York: Harper and Row, 1972); Manfredo Tafuri, *Theories and History of Architecture*, trans. Giorgio Verrecchia (New York: Harper and Row, 1980); and Mary McLeod, 'Architecture and Politics in the Reagan Era: From Postmodernism to Deconstructivism', *Assemblage* 8 (February 1989): 22–59. Hal Foster articulated a similar critique in 'Image Building', *Artforum International* 43, no. 2 (October 2004): 270–3.

53 See the debates between Kenneth Frampton and Scott Brown in *Casabella* 35, nos. 359–60 (December 1971): Denise Scott Brown, 'Learning from Pop,' 15; Kenneth Frampton, 'America 1960–1970: Notes on Urban Imagery', 31–3; Denise Scott Brown, 'Pop Off: Reply to Kenneth Frampton', 41–5. For a discussion of the issues involved, see Deborah Fausch, 'She Said, He Said: Denise Scott Brown and Kenneth Frampton on Popular Taste,' *Footprint* 8 (Spring 2011): 77–90.

CHAPTER TEN

Camp ugliness: The case of Charles W. Moore
Patricia A. Morton

The first duty in life is to be as artificial as possible. What the second duty is no one has yet found out.
—Oscar Wilde, Phrases and Philosophies for the Use of the Young

The ugliness of camp resides in its excessiveness, its lack of wholeness, its valorization of bad taste, its deployment of incongruity and its recuperation of past images, objects and products that have lost their value. Through artifice, theatricality, spectacle, parody and humour, camp mimics pre-existing cultural forms and performs their transformation. In a reversal of aesthetic judgement, the ugly object out of place becomes the camp object recontextualized by a passion for the awful. Incongruity is a basic technique through which camp overturns definitions of taste (and normalcy) and produces self-conscious pleasure in the excessive and the vulgar.

If good taste can be determined by adherence to Kantian aesthetics, in which judgement is disinterested, universal, purposive and intersubjective, bad taste fails to make judgements that are sufficient to these criteria and valorizes the vulgar or disgusting.[1] For Pierre Bourdieu, the pure aesthetic is rooted in an ethic or ethos of elective distance from the necessities of the natural and social world, whereas popular taste 'performs a systematic reduction of things of art to the things of life'.[2] Bourdieu characterized Kant's aesthetics as a negative relation to that which provokes our interest: 'Thus, Kant's principle of pure taste is nothing other than a refusal, a disgust – a disgust for objects which impose enjoyment and a disgust for the crude, vulgar taste which revels in this imposed enjoyment.'[3] In the twentieth century, bad taste was often equated with mass culture and popular taste; critic Dwight Macdonald, for example, argued that the bad taste of the masses was produced by the degraded mass culture, or 'Masscult', they consumed.[4] In the 1960s, camp dissolved such taste conventions, making bad taste acceptable, consumable and mainstream.[5]

Charles W. Moore's work in the 1960s provides a case study of how camp ugliness manifested in American architecture at the moment when it emerged into mainstream culture. Moore was a leading theoretician and practitioner of early postmodern architecture, which drew on popular culture, vernacular environments, found objects and historical referents. As director and faculty member of architecture at Yale University from 1965 to 1975, he was a leading figure in the debates around postmodernism, in which Robert Venturi, Denise Scott Brown, Robert A. M. Stern, James Stirling, Philip Johnson and Vincent Scully participated, among others.[6] Moore's work demonstrates how camp allowed architects to challenge the constraints of good taste and create work of spatial complexity and unexpected juxtapositions through subversion of norms, parody, pastiche and exaggeration.

Notes on 'Camp'

Susan Sontag's Notes on 'Camp' (1964) codified the definition and history of camp and brought camp subculture to a wider audience.[7] In a series of sometimes-contradictory notes, Sontag detailed the logic of camp sensibility and taste. According to Sontag, camp is the third of the great creative sensibilities, after high-culture and avant-garde art. It is the sensibility of 'failed seriousness, of the theatricalization of experience' whose point is to dethrone the serious. It is a 'certain mode of aestheticism ... a way of seeing the world as an aesthetic phenomenon' through artifice and stylization.[8] For Sontag, camp 'turns its back on the good-bad axis of ordinary aesthetic judgement', but it does not argue that the good is bad or the bad is good. 'What it does is to offer for art (and life) a different – and supplementary – set of standards.'[9] Camp overturns the opposition of good and bad taste and produces what Sontag called 'the good taste of bad taste', an inversion of high- and low-taste categories. Camp emphasizes fantasy and extravagance over seriousness and control. 'It is a vision of the world in terms of style – but a particular kind of style. It is the love of the exaggerated, the "off," of things-being-what-they-are-not.'[10] As 'failed seriousness', style in camp is always a surface phenomenon that lacks moral or tragic content.[11] Like early-eighteenth-century art and architecture, camp is characterized by 'a feeling for artifice, for surface, for symmetry; its taste for the picturesque and the thrilling, its elegant conventions for representing instant feeling and the total presence of character'.[12] Referring to the rococo churches of Munich, among other examples, she noted that camp taste privileged visual décor that emphasizes texture, surface and form over content. Art Nouveau's expressive artificiality exemplifies camp style because Art Nouveau objects convert one thing into another, as do Hector Guimard's Paris Metro entrances that take the shape of cast-iron flowers.[13]

In emphasizing style, Sontag believed camp slighted content and was, therefore, disengaged, depoliciziated or at least apolitical. The camp sensibility blocks out content in favour of pure artifice and the wholly aesthetic, grounded in a consistently aesthetic experience of the world. Sontag made a distinction between naïve and deliberate camp, privileging the naïve: 'Pure Camp is almost always naïve. Camp which knows itself to be camp ("camping") is usually less satisfying.'[14] She referred to camp as a 'private code' among urban cliques – a sidelong allusion to its origins in homosexual subculture – but averred that it was 'much more than homosexual taste'. Nevertheless, she posited a 'peculiar relation between Camp taste and homosexuality' by dubbing homosexuals the 'vanguard – and most articulate audience – of Camp'.[15] According to Sontag, the camp connoisseur, the modern dandy, has no need for refined or rare sensations or things but finds amusement in the coarsest, most common pleasures, in the arts of the masses. Making no distinction between the unique object and the mass-produced object: 'Camp taste transcends the nausea of the replica.'[16]

Camp, therefore, embraces the revulsion produced by the ugly. As Sontag observes, the new-style dandy, the lover of Camp, finds delight in vulgarity. Whereas the old-style dandy was offended or bored by the vulgar, likely to swoon while holding a perfumed handkerchief to his nose, 'the connoisseur of Camp sniffs the stink and prides himself on his nerves'.[17] The amusement and pleasure that camp elicits in its amateurs can only be produced by the tastemaker; it cannot inhere in an object. It can be measured by the extent of its artifice and exaggeration.

Umberto Eco notes that Sontag saw the extreme manifestation of camp in the expression 'it's beautiful because it's awful', which he signals as an important point for the history of ugliness.[18] According to Eco, camp is a form of recognition by an intellectual elite that is so sure of its refined taste that it could 'proclaim the redemption of the bad taste of the past, on the basis of a love for the unnatural and the excessive'.[19] Not so much a style as a capacity to interpret the style of others, camp is a manifestation of aristocratic taste and snobbery linked with a predilection for the vulgar. Those who would be the aristocrats of taste created what Andrew Ross refers to as the 'pseudoaristocratic patrilineage of camp'.[20]

As Fabio Cleto's meticulous anthology on camp documents, Sontag's essay helped disseminate camp into contemporary culture as a refined – and apolitical – aesthetic taste for the vulgar, such that it captured the attention of the mass media and became a popular fad.[21] In 1966, *Time* called camp 'a sort of tongue-in-cheek philosophy of pop culture' the result of which is that 'there is ... every expectation that grown men will be showing up at Andy Warhol's next party dressed like the Batman'.[22] In 'Girl of the Year', Tom Wolfe described Andy Warhol's socialite protégé Baby Jane Holzer in 'the world of High Camp – a world of thin young men in an environment, a décor, an atmosphere so – how can one say it? – so indefinably Yellow Book... so Beyond Pop Art, if you comprehend'.[23] Time asserted that 'vulgarity is no longer a nasty word but good taste is'.[24] Bad taste became a new norm, associated with the abandonment of elite taste standards and the 'sacrilegious reuniting of tastes which taste dictates shall be separated'.[25]

Despite Sontag's insistence that camp is apolitical and not just homosexual taste, its connection to pre-Stonewall homosexual subculture was fundamental to its popular reception and its subsequent embrace by contemporary queer theorists. Fabio Cleto links camp's history before 1964 to a 'homosexual lingo', a way to communicate with those in the know without revealing one's homosexuality.[26] By the time Sontag wrote her essay in 1964, camp had a wider resonance, encompassing the Teds' and Mods' taste for forgotten cultural forms (especially Victoriana, with links to Oscar Wilde and the dandy), androgynous figures of pop music like the Rolling Stones' Mick Jagger and David Bowie, Andy Warhol's Pop Art and a generalized, snobbish appreciation for low culture. According to Eco, 'camp transforms what was ugly yesterday into today's object of aesthetic pleasure'.[27] Camp's recuperation of products from the past, the leftovers that Andy Warhol famously preferred to work with, allowed their redefinition by contemporary codes of taste.[28]

The failed seriousness of camp links it with theories of ugliness, such as Karl Rosenkranz's *Aesthetic of Ugliness*, introduced by Caroline O'Donnell. O'Donnell describes ugliness in Rosenkranz's theory as failed expectation, 'something unplanned, not supposed to be'.[29] The expectation of wholeness, symmetry and harmony is disappointed by the ugly, such that the perception of the ugly is always informed by what is anticipated. Mark Cousins defines the ugly as 'that which prevents a work's completion or deforms a totality – whatever resists the whole', a further connection between the ugly and the camp.[30] As Cleto notes, 'representational excess, heterogeneity, and *gratuitousness* of reference, in constituting a major *raison d'être* of camp's fun and exclusiveness, both signal and contribute to an overall resistance to definition, drawing the contours of an *aesthetic of (critical) failure*'.[31] Cleto points to an essential aspect of camp ugliness: that it defeats expectation with excess, mixture and an unwarranted proliferation of allusions that break down the possibility of unity and harmony in favour of incompleteness. This failure, moreover, formed the basis for the deliberate deployment of camp for critical purposes. In 1970, George Melly, the English jazz musician and Pop intellectual, declared that camp was 'central to almost every difficult transitional moment in the evolution of pop culture ... [it] helped pop make a forced march around good taste'.[32] The new taste elite appeared from the margins of society and culture; Sontag recognized the loss of 'authentic aristocrats in the old sense' and identified the bearers of the new taste as 'an improvised self-educated class, mainly homosexuals, who constitute themselves as aristocrats of taste'.[33]

Camp ugliness and architecture

In 1949, Russell Lynes, an editor at *Harper's* magazine, schematized a new American hierarchy of everyday tastes consisting of Highbrow, Middlebrow and Lowbrow.[34] Lynes's categories codified a new social stratification based on taste and what he called 'high thinking', rather than traditional divisions by class, family or wealth. According to Lynes, intellectuals – atomic scientists, cultural historians, writers, commentators – were the new heroes and trendsetters of taste. Clothes, furniture, useful objects, entertainment, salads, drinks, reading, sculpture, records, games and causes revealed a person's taste on this spectrum. A chart in his article showed that Highbrow taste tended to modern design and art (illustrated by an Eames chair, a Kurt Verson lamp and an Alexander Calder sculpture), while Lowbrow taste preferred an unnamed mail order overstuffed chair and fringed lamp.[35] Lynes demonstrated that taste has a history and that artworks once considered Highbrow could descend to Lowbrow in a matter of decades; for example, the Highbrow painting, Whistler's 'Arrangement in Gray and Black No. 1' (1871), was transformed into the Lowbrow 'Whistler's Mother'. By the 1960s, however, Lynes's analysis appeared increasingly irrelevant to a relativist culture in which distinctions of 'low' and 'high' taste were increasingly blurred.

A decade after Lynes's article appeared, Douglas Haskell, then editor of *Architectural Forum*, wrote an essay on 'adapting design to an era of popular mass culture'. In 'Architecture and Popular Taste', Haskell asked how architecture should respond to popular taste when 'a free people never before had such a wealth and range of choice … but what the American people have chosen is ugliness'.[36] He equated ugliness with mass culture, a formulation echoing Clement Greenberg's theory of kitsch, which characterized urban popular culture as 'ersatz' or kitsch.[37] Yet Haskell saw the potential for architecture to engage the ugly. He pointed to work by Edward Durrell Stone, Vernon DeMars and Minoru Yamasaki that employed 'drama, fairy tale, allusion and symbol' to create a 'new baroque' based on schmaltz, googie and honky-tonk sources.[38] He speculated that this *rapprochement* between popular taste and Modern architecture might produce a similar revolution, based on mass culture, as had the confrontation with the machine thirty years earlier.

Haskell later considered the degree to which architecture could positively connect with the 'ugly' American landscape. In a 1965 essay in *Landscape*, he noted that Americans had adopted the harsh judgement of their popular taste, exemplified when Mary Mix Foley, in *Architectural Forum* of February 1957, declared in the broadest terms that 'never in the history of the human race has a culture equaled ours in the dreariness and corrupted fantasy of its popular taste'.[39] Haskell pondered the hostility among architects towards cars, billboards and single-family houses, and their effect on the landscape, but noted that they were hardly likely to disappear or become better as a result of 'anti-ugly' campaigns. He ended by posing the provocative case of junkyards, an evident reference to Peter Blake's *God's Own Junkyard* diatribe against the disfigurement of America's landscape by highways, billboards and other blight. 'In sorting out whether our objections to new popular activity arise out of real ugliness, or out of our own perversity combined with blindness, let's make a test case of junkyards. They are obviously the pariah manifestation of our society, visually speaking, the ne plus ultra of degradation, the sign of degeneracy, the final blight – but are they?'[40] He argued that junkyards have their own logic and beauty based on an order that can become discernable to the unprejudiced observer. In conclusion, he urged that class prejudice and snobbery be put aside in the search for beauty appropriate to the new American landscape. 'Professionals and public must sort out what is good taste, what is bad taste, and what is bad simply because it is unaided or helpless waste.'[41] In recuperating the ordinary, ugly environment for architectural beauty, Haskell attempted to maintain taste standards that were subsequently inverted by the rise of camp and its valorization of bad taste.

During the historical moment of camp's ascendancy, architects deployed Pop and camp design strategies as part of the reaction against institutionalized modernism and the search for a more populist and popular architecture inspired by a countercultural fascination with the everyday. The reception of camp in architecture culture could be highly negative. Resistance to camp focused on its faddishness, bad taste and tawdry qualities. C. Ray Smith, an editor of architectural journal *Progressive Architecture*, quoted criticisms characterizing the 'new idiom' as a shallow style that 'substitutes wit for intelligence, queerness for charm, and adroitness for skill' and 'flamboyant, meretricious, and ingenious … novelty for novelty's sake'.[42]

In *Modern Movements in Architecture* (1973), critic Charles Jencks used the term 'camp' as a sweeping, pejorative category to encompass a broad spectrum of buildings influenced by popular culture. His chapter, 'Camp-Non Camp', defined camp as 'failed seriousness', which he saw manifested in formalism, aestheticism, classicism, pragmatism and 'chaoticism.'[43] Jencks equated camp's rejection of Modernist dogma and revival of historical reference with bad taste, kitsch and the return of Fascist traditionalism. For Jencks, camp is 'morally cool, pretty, the product of overheated urban society, whereas non-camp is morally hot, a flower with odor, rather than a pretty object, and is the product of an underheated rural or academic place'.[44] The camp object, in Jencks's view, must be univalent, the work of the intellect and fancy, and is amoral and destructive of the public realm. Philip

Johnson's work, for example, is 'entirely camp'; it displays an 'impeccably perverse taste, motivated by historicist allusions'.[45] The willful reversals of Johnson's campiness were ambiguous in a manner that Jencks associated with fascism and degeneration, likening Johnson's New York State Theater at Lincoln Center with Albert Speer's Zeppelinfeld in Nurnberg.[46]

C. Ray Smith considered camp essential to the new architecture of the mid-twentieth century. He defined camp as 'the witty recognition and ... ironic acceptance of the visual environment of our ordinary daily life – the popular culture that motivated Pop art'.[47] In his account, camp was a reaction to the philistinism and squalor that pervaded the American landscape in the 1950s and early 1960s, and was the product of a determination by artists to make fun of 'our undesigned, uncouth, philistine, everyday culture'.[48] The wit and whimsy of the new attitude manifested architecturally in spatial puns and visual jokes, the humorous use of connotative materials and colours, and surprise juxtapositions, resulting in what he called 'Campopop'.[49] His formulation of camp saw it as a detached aesthetic vision focused on surface and style that allows reversals of judgement: 'Bad to good, from bad to fun, from serious to humorous ... Perverseness with a goal of humor is its core.'[50] Its self-consciousness and detachment from content and context equally indicated that camp appealed to the intellect rather than the emotions. It was interesting without being interested.[51]

Eco notes that the canon of camp changes over time and can 'enhance the standing of things that repel us today because they are too close to us'.[52] Camp ugliness induces displacement of expected meaning to arouse our interest. In camp, this interest reverses the sense of revulsion into aesthetic pleasure. The transformation of history's detritus into camp objects of desire operates, as Eco points out, 'in an ambiguous play in which it is not clear whether ugliness is redeemed as beauty or whether beauty (as the "interesting") is reduced to ugliness'.[53] In camp, the 'interesting' is not what Schopenhauer condemned as an appeal to the senses but is closer to the fascination that Rosenkranz attributed to disharmony, which is ugly as such but can be resolved into beauty: 'The disharmonic can in fact arouse our interest without being beautiful; this we call interesting.' The complicated, contradictory, uncertain, unnatural, strange and lunatic are exemplary of disharmony that is interesting.[54] Camp, however, cannot produce unity. It cannot become true disharmony, which acts as 'the redemptive gateway of unity' according to Rosenkranz, therefore, it remains ugly.

Charles Moore's camp

In 1964, the same year that Sontag published *Notes on 'Camp'*, Charles Moore and his partners designed archetypal sea resort buildings at The Sea Ranch, north of San Francisco. Sea Ranch Condominium #1 (1964–5) by Moore

Lyndon Turnbull Whitaker (MLTW) combined vernacular and camp in a vastly influential synthesis of California farm buildings, Bay Area Regionalism and Pop graphic art. Moore's own condominium at The Sea Ranch, unit #9, exhibited a camp mixture of objects, materials and spaces: heavy gilt mirrors, pony skin, supergraphics, folk art and exposed wood. The mixture of connotative objects, materials and colours in Condo #9 produced a camp incongruity that evoked the hodgepodge of the flea market.

MLTW's Swim Club #1 at Sea Ranch (1966) juxtaposed a supergraphic-intensive interior with a quietly picturesque exterior, an example of camp techniques for generating double meaning and contradiction (Figure 10.1).

FIGURE 10.1 *Moore Lyndon Turnbull Whitaker/Moore–Turnbull, Sea Ranch Athletic Club #1, Sea Ranch, California, 1966, interior of locker room with supergraphics by Barbara Stauffacher Solomon. Courtesy author.*

The exterior is composed of the same weathered, vertical boards as the Condominium, organized around a spine wall from which the locker rooms and service spaces hang. On the inside, supergraphics by Barbara Stauffacher Solomon, ordinary heat lamps in plain porcelain holders and mailboxes for lockers created an interior equivalent of camp juxtaposition and Pop recycling of everyday materials. Moore believed these Pop graphics should be ephemeral, easily changed: 'I think the danger in pop art is that if it's taken seriously, it becomes automatically expensive. I think the importance is that the decoration should really be cosmetic – it should be very cheap and able to be redone, changed by the people, and reconsidered by the people who live there.'[55] The Swim Club's chaos of forms, ambiguity of space, discordant colours and ornament accorded with camp, that which is self-consciously 'off'. It employed the detritus of industrial capitalism recycled to take advantage of pre-existing meanings that could be decontextualized outside their 'proper' context.

In 1965, when Moore became director of architecture at Yale, he transformed a small house in New Haven into a wildly eclectic space, 'a grand knick-knack shelf', as he called it.[56] Moore left the exterior of the eighteenth-century wood structure untouched, but its interior was fragmented into complex, disjunctive spaces filled with found objects and camp interventions (Figure 10.2). Into the house, Moore inserted three two-story towers or tubes of space – named Howard, Berengaria and Ethel – made of double-layered plywood walls with large, often incomplete geometric cutouts to suggest larger geometric orders, reminiscent of the Dome in John Soane's House. *House and Garden* referred to his New Haven house as 'a constantly changing, probably never-to-be-finished workshop for himself and his students, a crucible where ideas are born, theories tested, and form given to whimsy'.[57]

'The glimpses of other spaces and other colors and patterns that you get through these cutouts,' Moore pointed out, 'tease the eye so that it registers like a movie camera rather than taking a simple static picture. You can see that space extends, but you don't know how far, so you unconsciously assume it extends to infinity.'[58] The many varied shapes of varied scale made it hard to distinguish the elements. 'By contradicting preconceived ideas about the relative size of one object to another, these tricks of scale make you look at space in a new way.'[59] The cacophony of shapes, scale and colour reflects what Rosenkranz identified as undetermined difference and excess conflict that result in ugliness: 'If multiple colors are flaunted in a painting but the decidedness of one color contrast is lacking, the eye will soon be blunted by mere chaos.'[60]

The disparate objects found in Moore's house form a camp inventory: stained-glass panels, Turkish carpets, Mexican pottery and nineteenth-century family portraits mingled with industrial lighting equipment, exposed plumbing, a Wurlitzer jukebox, neon sculpture, negative-positive design motifs, mirror tricks, silver mylar and op art objects. One stair

FIGURE 10.2 *Moore Lyndon Turnbull Whitaker/Moore–Turnbull, Charles Moore House, New Haven, Connecticut, 1966, rear facade*. House and Garden, 133, no. 1 [January 1968]: 110. Courtesy John T. Hill.

featured a figure from a Volkswagen ad, while a cutout of Shirley Temple could be moved around the house as a silent reminder of the past film age. The classical columns in the kitchen evoked defunct conditions of production repurposed for a new taste culture (Figure 10.3). They were excessive objects out their proper place in a deliberately cultivated incongruity. The *New York Times Magazine* noted that modern purists did not like Moore's work, but a younger generation 'who believe in shiny vinyl, the old-clothes fad and op art, think of his house as revolutionary and a victory for their point of view'.[61] The juxtaposition of borrowed elements told inside jokes to the cognoscenti: the absurdity of St Peter's dome painted on the inside of the aedicule over the bed, the mix of humble and aristocratic names for the tubes, family portraits mounted below a Pop cutout, an Op Art fence using

FIGURE 10.3 *Moore Lyndon Turnbull Whitaker/Moore–Turnbull, Charles Moore House, New Haven, Connecticut, 1966, 'Ethel' at the kitchen.* House and Garden, *133, no. 1 [January 1968]: 115. Courtesy John T. Hill.*

optical illusions. Droll and jumbled, these references required a camp eye to see them as other than simply discordant or ugly.

His work was an unembarrassed mix of high and low, combing camp sensibility and postmodern parody.[62] In an interview, he summarized his method of borrowing everyday elements: 'My particular interest is in familiar pieces, mostly cheap pieces, putting them together in ways that have never been before, so as to get something that's strange and revolutionary and mind-boggling and often uncomfortable, but only using the ordinary pieces.'[63] His method of using objects out of order, in awkward disunity, resisted totality and resulted in camp bricolage. His challenge to 'good taste' was plainly stated in *The Place of Houses* (1972):

> Good taste, we are told, is a singularly important factor in the design of a house. We are usually told this by someone who is assumed to possess it, and who generally makes a considerable point of the rest of the assumption: that there are people who don't have it, that that includes you, and that you will have to pay dearly to be suitably worked over. ... good taste seeks to intimidate us with rules and limitations that stifle personal choice.[64]

Moore's critique of the strictures of good taste resonated with a contemporaneous polemic offered by Robert Venturi and Denise Scott Brown in *Learning from Las Vegas*.[65] In a later essay, 'Architectural Taste in a Pluralistic Society', Denise Scott Brown cited sociologist Herbert Gans's theories of 'taste cultures' and urged architects to address the needs and wants of various architectural audiences and produce an architecture of greater social awareness and meaning.[66]

As a corrective to the stultifying dogma of good taste, Moore championed the 'bad taste' of the Madonna Inn in San Luis Obispo, California, a motel opened in 1958 by a family of road contractors that featured 110 themed rooms and a famous rock waterfall urinal in the restaurant restroom.[67] Moore pointed to the Inn's rock grotto entry into a purple velvet upholstered dining room as one of the 'most surprising and surprisingly full experiences to be found along an American highway'.[68] Umberto Eco, by contrast, characterized the Madonna Inn as a signal example of kitsch ugliness, declaring that words were inadequate to describe it: 'Let's say that Albert Speer, while leafing through a book on Gaudi, swallowed an overgenerous dose of LSD and began to build a nuptial catacomb for Liza Minelli. But that doesn't give you an idea.'[69] In an exercise of camp connoisseurship, Moore reversed the camp ugliness of the Madonna Inn and celebrated its excesses as 'everything instead of nothing'.[70]

In this period, Moore's work was camp in its theatricality, its humour, its daring mixture of styles and objects of heterogeneous origin, its strategic exaggeration and its salvaging of what Andrew Ross calls 'history's waste', the neglected and forgotten symbols of the past.[71] David Littlejohn foregrounded the camp aspects of Moore's work when he described the reception of his house at Orinda, California (1962):

> What excited the architectural community ... about this and similar houses were a number of unorthodox and novel ideas. Out of either perversity or deep personal conviction, the designer of this curious sport appeared to defy the modernist creed and to reintroduce into serious

architecture a number of formal, emotional, sensual, historically recollective, and just plain comical elements and pleasures that had long been banished or forgotten.[72]

Moore exhibited a fascination with 'history's waste', a taste for the unconventional, neglected or marginal and for transgressing the dominant aesthetic, a camp sensibility that he perfected in this early work.

Conclusion

Camp gave architects access to multiple codes of representation and allowed them to re-introject taboo elements associated with bad taste, especially ornament, into their work. Moore and his contemporaries looked to ordinary environments and things that were not beautiful, a method summarized by an aphorism that C. Ray Smith attributed to Robert Venturi: 'Learn from what you don't like.'[73] Rather than substituting a 'true' or 'real' aesthetic for modernism's symbolic order, however, Moore instigated a self conscious campiness. Its double-coded borrowings gathered motifs eclectically, fragmenting the cohesion and continuity of high architecture taste, and re-presented them in a loose fit of witty and parodic allusions resulting in a camp ugliness.

The camp ugliness of Moore's New Haven house operates through the excessive object out of place, discordant and abnormal, linking it to the 'interesting' as disharmony. A schematic shell filled with camp objects from history's leftovers, the house defies completeness with a proliferation of popular and high-culture references and a confusion of spaces. Its campiness recuperates the vulgar and displaces expected meanings, becoming interesting, but defeats our interest by never achieving unity or beauty. In this way, the camp object transforms disgust into aesthetic pleasure while it resists the whole and remains incongruous, that is, ugly.

Notes

1 John Macarthur and Naomi Stead, 'Introduction: Architecture and Aesthetics', *The SAGE Handbook of Architectural Theory*, ed. C. Greig Crysler, Stephen Cairns and Hilde Heynen (London: SAGE, 2012), 125–6. See Immanuel Kant, *Critique of the Power of Judgment*, trans. Paul Guyer and Eric Mathews (Cambridge: Cambridge University Press, 2000).

2 Pierre Bourdieu, *Distinction: A Social Critique of the Judgment of Taste*, trans. Richard Nice (Cambridge, MA: Havard University Press, 1984), 5.

3 Ibid., 488.

4 Dwight Macdonald, 'A Theory of Mass Culture' in *Mass Culture*, ed. B. Rosenberg and D. M. White (Glencoe, IL: Free Press, 1957), 59–79.

5 Ken Feil argues that discussions of bad taste pervaded mainstream culture in the mid-1960s and was not only confined to marginal subcultures. Ken Feil, '"Talk About Bad Taste": Camp, Cult, and the Reception of *What's New Pussycat?*' in *Convergence Media History*, ed. Janet Staiger and Sabine Hake (New York: Routledge, 2009), 139–50.

6 On Moore's writing in this period, see my chapter, 'Charles Moore's *Perspecta* Essays: Toward Postmodern Eclecticism' in *Mediated Messages: Periodicals, Exhibitions, and the Shaping of Postmodern Architecture*, ed. Véronique Patteeuw and Léa-Catherine Szacka (London: Bloomsbury, 2018), 159–74.

7 Susan Sontag, 'Notes on 'Camp', *Partisan Review* 31, no. 4 (Fall 1964): 515–30. Reprinted in *Against Interpretation* (New York: Picador, 1966), 263–74. and *A Susan Sontag Reader* (New York: Farrar Strauss Giroux, 1982), 105–19. Citations refer to page numbers in *A Susan Sontag Reader*.

8 Sontag, 'Notes on 'Camp', 106.

9 Ibid., 114.

10 Ibid., 108.

11 See Sontag's essay, 'On Style', for an extended exegesis of style and the split between content and form in modern art and criticism. Susan Sontag, 'On Style' in *Against Interpretation, and Other Essays* (New York: Farrar, Straus & Giroux, 1966).

12 Sontag, 'Notes on 'Camp', 109.

13 Ibid., 107–8.

14 Ibid., 110.

15 Ibid., 117–18.

16 Ibid., 116.

17 Ibid., 117. In his book, *Disgust*, Winfried Menninghaus analyses the connections between modern aesthetics and the prohibition of what is disgusting. *Disgust: The Theory and History of a Strong Sensation*, trans. Howard Eiland and Joel Golb (Albany: State University of New York Press, 2003).

18 Umberto Eco, *On Ugliness*, trans. Alastair McEwen (New York: Rizzoli, 2007), 417.

19 Eco, *On Ugliness*, 408.

20 Andrew Ross, 'Uses of Camp' in *No Respect: Intellectuals and Popular Culture* (New York: Routledge, 1989), 145.

21 Fabio Cleto, *Camp: Queer Aesthetics and the Performing Subject: A Reader* (Ann Arbor: University of Michigan Press, 1999).

22 Anon, 'Holy Flypaper!' *Time* 87: 4 (28 January 1966): 61.

23 Tom Wolfe, 'The Girl of the Year' in *The Kandy-Kolored, Tangerine-Flake Streamline Baby* (New York: Farrar, Straus and Giroux, 1965), 209.

24 Anon., 'Holy Flypaper!', 61.

25 Pierre Bourdieu, 'The Aristocracy of Culture' in *Media, Culture and Society: A Critical Reader,* ed. Richard Collins, et al. (London: Sage, 1996), 192.

26 Cleto, *Camp*, 9.

27 Eco, *On Ugliness*, 417.

28 'I always like to work with leftovers, doing the leftover things. Things that were discarded, that everybody thought were no good.' Andy Warhol, *The Philosophy of Andy Warhol* (1975), quoted in Eco, *On Ugliness*, 388.

29 Caroline O'Donnell, 'Fugly', *Log* 22 (Spring/Summer 2011): 96.

30 Mark Cousins, 'The Ugly', *AA Files* 28 (Autumn 1994): 61.

31 Cleto, *Camp*, 3 (emphasis in original).

32 George Melly, quoted in Ross, 'Uses of Camp', 136.

33 Sontag, 'Notes on 'Camp'', 117.

34 Russell Lynes, 'Highbrow, Lowbrow, Middlebrow', *Harper's Magazine* (February 1949): 19–28.

35 Lynes's article was republished in the 11 April 1949 issue of *Life* magazine with a chart that expanded the categories to Highbrow, Upper Middlebrow, Lower Middlebrow and Lowbrow.

36 Douglas Haskell, 'Architecture and Popular Taste', *Architecture Forum* 109 (August 1958): 104.

37 'Losing their taste for folk culture, discovering a new capacity for boredom, the new urban masses set up a pressure on society to provide them with a new kind of culture fit for their own consumption …: ersatz culture, kitsch.' Clement Greenberg, 'Avant-Garde and Kitsch', *Partisan Review* 6, no. 5 (Fall 1939): 34–49.

38 Haskell, 'Architecture and Popular Taste', 106.

39 Douglas Haskell, 'The Drive for Beauty and the Popular Taste', *Landscape* 15, no. 1 (Autumn 1965): 3.

40 Haskell, 'Architecture and Popular Taste', 5. See Peter Blake, *God's Own Junkyard: The Planned Deterioration of America's Landscape* (New York: Hold Rinehart and Winston, 1964).

41 Ibid.

42 C. Ray Smith, *Supermannerism: New Attitudes in Post-Modern Architecture* (New York: Dutton, 1977), 324.

43 Charles Jencks, *Modern Movements in Architecture* (Garden City, NY: Anchor/Doubleday, 1973), 185–237.

44 Jencks, *Modern Movements in Architecture*, 218.

45 Ibid., 207–8.

46 Ibid., 184–5. On Johnson's own fascist history, see Mark Lamster, *The Man in the Glass House: Philip Johnson, Architect of the Modern Century* (New York: Little, Brown, 2018).

47 Smith, *Supermannerism*, 160.

48 Ibid., 161.

49 Ibid., 160.

50 Ibid.
51 According to Sianne Ngai, the interesting indexes late capitalism's economic processes of circulation and gives insight into problems in aesthetic theory that are amplified by the postmodern condition. In her account, the interesting marks the tension between the unknown and the already known. Sianne Ngai, *Our Aesthetic Categories: Zany, Cute, Interesting* (Cambridge, MA: Harvard University Press, 2012), 1–2. Mark Dorrian draws on Ngai's work to think about the interesting as connected to situations in which there is a flaw or problem that makes it visible without finality. Mark Dorrian, 'What's Interesting? On the Ascendancy of an Evaluative Term', *Architecture and Culture* 4, no. 2 (July 2016): 178–9.
52 Eco, *On Ugliness*, 417.
53 Ibid.
54 Karl Rosenkranz, 'Aesthetic of Ugliness', *Log* 22 (Spring/Summer 2011): 108–9.
55 Kevin Keim, *An Architectural Life: Memoirs and Memories of Charles W. Moore* (Boston, MA: Little, Brown, 1996), 77.
56 'More Than Modern – Hip Baroque', *New York Times Magazine* (February 26, 1967): 79.
57 'A Noted Architect Plays Games', *House and Garden* 133, no. 1 (January 1968): 111.
58 Ibid., 112.
59 Ibid.
60 Rosenkranz, 'Aesthetic of Ugliness', 106.
61 'More Than Modern – Hip Baroque', 79.
62 Linda Hutcheon defines postmodern parody as a 'repetition with critical distance that allows ironic signaling of difference at the very heart of similarity'. Linda Hutcheon, 'The Politics of Postmodernism: Parody and History', *Cultural Critique* no. 5 (Winter, 1986–7): 185.
63 Keim, 190.
64 Charles Moore, Gerald Allen and Donlyn Lyndon, *The Place of Houses* (New York: Holt, Rinehard and Winston, 1974), vii.
65 Robert Venturi, Denise Scott Brown and Steven Izenour, *Learning from Las Vegas: The Forgotten Symbolism of Architectural Form* (Cambridge, MA: MIT Press, 1972).
66 Denise Scott Brown, 'Architectural Taste in a Pluralistic Society', *Harvard Design Review* 1 (Spring 1980): 40–51. See Herbert J. Gans, *Popular Culture and High Culture: An Analysis and Evaluation of Taste* (New York: Basic Books, 1999).
67 See Phyllis Madonna, *Madonna Inn: My Point of View* (San Luis Obispo, CA: Pick & Shovel, 2002), and https://www.madonnainn.com/ [accessed 29 December 2018].
68 Charles W. Moore, 'Plug It in, Rameses, and See if It Lights up. Because We Aren't Going to Keep It Unless It Works', *Perspecta* 11 (1967): 43.

69 Umbert Eco, 'The Madonna Inn' in *Faith in Fakes: Travels in Hyperreality*, quoted in *On Ugliness*, 396.
70 Moore, 'Plug It in, Ramses', 43.
71 'Camp irreverently retrieves not only that which had been excluded from the serious high-cultural "tradition", but also the more unsalvageable material that has been picked over and found wanting by purveyors of the "antique."' Ross, 'Uses of Camp', 320.
72 David Littlejohn, *Architect: The Life and Work of Charles W. Moore* (New York: Holt, Rinehart and Winston, 1984), 62.
73 Smith, *Supermodernism*, 162.

CHAPTER ELEVEN

Architecture in El Alto: The politics of excess

Elisabetta Andreoli

> *Fair is foul and foul is fair.*
> —William Shakespeare, Macbeth

Anyone who walks around the streets of El Alto, in the Andes of Bolivia, will be surprised by the colourful buildings that have been popping up all over the city since the late 1990s. Their facades present a range of bizarre motives and decorative elements, surprising us not only by how playful and colourful they are but also by their excess and unashamed lack of unity. Until recently, this architectural phenomenon had received only sporadic coverage in the local press and was largely ignored by Bolivian architects, architectural bodies and universities, their silence betraying dismay and even annoyance at this unusual exuberance. Some dismiss these buildings as little more than facades, and facades alone do not constitute architecture; others consider them a mere display of the owners' wealth. And some strongly object to the claim that this architecture is 'neo-Andean', inspired by pre-Colombian cultures, and instead criticize it for opening the door to all sorts of extravagances, such as buildings that look like characters from the *Transformers* game.

Ignored by the architectural milieu and the media in general, the indigenous engineer Freddy Mamani Silvestre, who designed most of these buildings, decided to take matters into his own hands by commissioning a book documenting the sixty odd buildings he has completed since the late 1990s.[1] Since the publication of his book in 2014, Mamani has gained national and international attention. His work has featured in international newspapers

FIGURE 11.1 *Freddy Mamani Silvestre, El Tren Diamante, El Alto, Bolivia.*
Photo by Alfredo Zeballos.

and architectural magazines such as *Icon Magazine* and *The Architectural Review*, as well as in TV programmes around the world, and Mamani himself was invited to speak at conferences abroad. While his buildings are far removed from the tradition of Western architecture, they found their way into the international press mostly because of their extravagant appearance: extraordinary, flamboyant, psychedelic, odd and kitsch are some of the terms used to describe this new architecture. In the Andean region, meanwhile, they struck a different chord. Once news and images of Mamani's work began to circulate in the mainstream press, support poured in from

Bolivia and neighbouring Andean countries via social media. Certain sectors of these populations have been praising Mamani's work precisely for its peculiar and coloured facades, which are deemed to somehow express a local Andean identity. In Bolivia, however, the acceptance of the flamboyance and the claim that it represents the region seems to have inflamed the animosity among architects and students of architecture against Mamani's work:

> Leaving aside the issue of aesthetic likes or dislikes; or if this constitutes architecture or not, the questions are: Will we tolerate architectural 'delirium' and exacerbated urban behaviours of all sorts in this century? Will this exultant architectural carnality be the one that represents us in the XXI century?[2]

Although colourful buildings and unusual facades have been present in the built environment of El Alto and La Paz for a while, produced by various unidentified builders, the work of Freddy Mamani is unique in that it articulates elements in a consistent style and programme. This articulation is not accidental. Coming from a humble background, a member of the Aymara indigenous population and living in what was a poor, nondescript city, Mamani has a precise and deliberate agenda: 'I want to give an identity to my city, El Alto.'[3] Not one to mince words, Mamani considers that academic architectural models inspired by Western canons have little or nothing to do with local customs or culture and thus have little to offer El Alto, a largely self-built city populated almost exclusively by indigenous Aymara people.

Having studied engineering at Universidad Mayor de San Andrés in La Paz and later getting a degree in architecture at a technical university in El Alto, Mamani points to racial and class bias: 'At university we felt discriminated against because of our indigenous culture.'[4] To those who question the validity of the definition he gives to his work – neo-Andean architecture – Mamani replies that Bolivian culture is hybrid, that everything is 'mixed-up'. In other words, he brushes away philological questions as far as architecture is concerned but also any 'essentialist' views of indigenous culture as being 'frozen' in time, as if indigenous people cannot be 'contemporary'. The reality is that indigenous Bolivians carry vernacular culture from their rural origins but live a fully urban life, with its mass culture, industrial artefacts and technological products and networks. Mamani's work and its extraordinary, controversial aesthetics intersect with questions of class and ethnicity but also of modernity, postmodernity and the contemporary indigenous identity.

Chicha, chola, huachafa

In Ecuador, Peru, Chile, as well as in Central American countries such as Honduras, Guatemala and El Salvador, scholars have been discussing the autonomous constructions that have appeared in the fast-growing peripheries over the past twenty years and which sometimes can constitute entire new boroughs in the face of rapidly increasing urban populations. The odd combination of vernacular and modern elements, local and foreign materials, forms and colours, is characteristic of these emergent single houses and low-rise buildings.

Some scholars question how the discipline of architecture should relate to this architectural phenomenon of a 'contemporary vernacular' and whether architecture schools should take it into account at all. Cristina Dreifuss Serrano presents the question as follows:

> Nowadays a series of situations make it derisory to pretend that architecture as a discipline can carry on ignoring the production of the informal city. For a start, time has transformed the small precarious huts into four-storey buildings of more noble materials; at the same time slums have become lively neighbourhoods and are part of the modern city; finally, many descendants of the first generations of migrants have been able to substantially improve their families' economic conditions and moved to more traditional neighbourhoods, taking with them their formal preferences. To all this one must add the proliferation of architectural schools and economic conditions that have made architecture cease to be a profession for elites. Students and young teachers frequently come from such informal environments and live in *huachafas* houses.[5]

The ubiquity of such 'informal architecture' is problematic, and the very terms used to discuss it express such difficulty.

Depending on the location and conceptual references of these buildings, they are referred to as *chicha*, *chola* or *huachafa* architecture.[6] The etymology of the terms that feature in this debate is bizarre. *Chicha* refers to a maize-based drink, popular in the Andean countries and by extension to popular indigenous culture. *Chola* is a loosely defined term originally indicating a person of mixed European and indigenous descent but often used in a derogatory way. Like *chicha*, *huachafa* refers to anything of indigenous popular culture. Its origin is uncertain, but the most creditable explanation deems it to be the Peruvian phonetic version of 'whitechaps' (referring to the London's borough of Whitechapel) used in the late nineteenth century by English engineers working in the railway company in Peru; allegedly, in Britain the term was a disrespectful reference to the nouveau riche of Whitechapel, who were considered to be overdressed and to have bad taste. To these, one has to add 'remittance' architecture that refers specifically to constructions built with funds (remittances) from numerous Latin American citizens who emigrated to Europe or North America in the 1980s and 1990s. Scholars consider 'remittance architecture' as having its own peculiar logic relating less to vernacular and identitary motifs and more to an imagery built from foreign elements.[7]

The oddness of these terms testifies to the difficulty of dealing with forms – whether in music, graphic street art (such as posters and homemade advert billboards, which abound in the urban peripheries) or architecture – that are expressions of a local, urban, hybrid and contemporary indigenous culture. In contemporary Peru, for example, the anthropologist José Matos Mar regards the omnipresent *chicha* culture in Lima as a sign of successful democratization and the emancipatory construction of a national identity.[8] Other scholars, however, despise it for its excess, chaos and *baroquism* – all features that part of the population equates with bad taste, kitsch and ugliness. Thus, while the terms *huachafa*, *chicha* and *chola* ostensibly describe the cultural expression of an urban population with indigenous origins, their often negative connotations point to class conflict and ethnic tensions.[9]

Given the presence of so many indigenous cultures – thirty-six ethnic groups, each with their own language, although the Aymara and Quechua are by far the largest – it is not surprising that in Bolivia, studies about identity issues and paradigms of cultural expression abound. This wealth of research does not extend into the field of architecture. A notable exception is the work of Carlos Villagomez, an architect, lecturer and critic who in 2003 set up the Foundation for Andean Aesthetics, whose Spanish acronym, FEA, translates into English as 'ugly'. With FEA, he went straight for the jugular, as it were, taking at face value the disseminated aesthetic of kitsch and addressing head-on the contradictions and complexities of modernity in a peripheral country with strong colonial and indigenous legacies. The role of Villagomez's foundation was to record and promote, through a website, the multiple expressive forms of Bolivia's cultural landscape, particularly in the urban contexts of La Paz and El Alto. It encouraged a wider view on what constitutes aesthetic experience. Villagomez suggested that photography was to be used to document traces of graphic street art and architecture; videos and audio recordings would capture sounds and movements, the latter being so much part of the contemporary urban environment. The aim of FEA was to create a sort of index, a collective work that could help redefine the aesthetic field and its practices, given the unavoidable coexistence of social groups with 'inalterable permanence of habits that are not synchronized to those values imposed by modernity and globalization'.[10] To put it another way, instead of discussing how to 'deal with' *chicha, chola or huachafa* culture, Villagomez suggests nothing less than reframing what constitutes aesthetics and aesthetics experience in the context of Bolivia's social and political contemporary realities, with the goal of formulating a composite aesthetic that will have to be inscribed in 'multiple modernities'.[11] This discussion hits Bolivia just when it is in the midst of substantial social change. After the economic crises of the 1980s and 1990s, and the intense political and grass-roots movements which followed that were partly organized around questions of ethnicity and identity, the twenty-first century has witnessed the economic and political establishment of the so-called Aymara bourgeoisie – a class that is taking hold of the state apparatus and is becoming overtly present in Bolivia's cultural expression.

Unfortunately, but perhaps significantly, FEA does not seem to have had an impact in the face of the overwhelming social and political dynamics of Bolivia's intense urban life. Villagomez's own attempts to design a few projects with FEA aspirations in El Alto failed to catch the attention of the locals, as he explains: 'I cannot keep up. While I am about to finish a couple of works, next door they are already building even more delirious things ... Really, one has to re-educate oneself about what one understands as architecture.'[12] FEA as a project still exists, but it is dormant.

'Anonymity' is a term often associated with peripheries. In El Alto, for all its precarious infrastructure and self-built character, there is a sense of consistency and identity, both in the built environment and in its industrious population: boroughs are organized politically and administratively; informal policing is carried out by locals to compensate for the poor presence of the State police; enormous numbers of small and medium enterprises and local markets animate the streets. In this context, architecture with a strong and more definite character like Mamani's is multiplying quickly, a phenomenon which finds no parallel in neighbouring countries. What is it about El Alto and La Paz that produces something so striking and so consistent when compared with the wide variety of *huachafa* architecture one finds in the urban peripheries of Peru, Ecuador and other countries in the region?

El Alto, locus of a national identity?

Of all South American countries, Bolivia has long ranked among the poorest. Situated between the Andes and the vast Amazon basin, it has remained fairly isolated and with a strong predominance of indigenous population. Bolivia's colonial heritage is evident both socially and politically, and attempts to alter colonial relations through the 1952 National Revolution fell short of producing significant lasting changes. During the 1980s and 1990s, the societal consequences, in Bolivia as in other South American countries, of the abrupt implementation of privatization policies designed by the so-called Chicago Boys became evident. The combination of social unrest due to economic crisis, and the widespread grass-roots movements mobilized around questions of identity and ethnicity, culminated in 2003 in the Black October uprising in El Alto. The specific trigger was the government's 'gas trade' agreement with Chile, which was perceived as being against Bolivian interests. During the confrontations between citizens and government, around eighty Alteños (inhabitants of El Alto) lost their lives. The violent government response and the Alteños' fierce resistance eventually forced Bolivia's president, Sanchez de Lozada, to flee to the United States, which opened the way for Evo Morales's election in 2006. Morales, the leader of the Movement towards Socialism (Movimiento al Socialismo) and of Aymara origins, called for a constituent assembly, and a new constitution was adopted in 2009, amid strong political tensions. The new constitution established the country as the 'Plurinational State of Bolivia'. Since then, the state apparatus has slowly but steadily been taken over by militants of indigenous groups, syndicates and associations.

El Alto had previously been seen as a suburban dormitory town serving the capital of La Paz, but following the Black October uprising, it gained political relevance and prestige for having been instrumental in changing the course of Bolivia's history. Black October also helped its inhabitants reclaim their own class and ethnic roots: 'El Alto de pie nunca de rodillas' (El Alto on its feet, never on its knees) was the main slogan in 2003, chanted in the streets and written on walls and posters. Meanwhile, El Alto's economy also improved. In the age of global commerce and internet communication, its strategic location at the crossroads linking La Paz to the rest of the country as well as to Chile, Peru and the Pacific coast proved advantageous. Today it effectively operates as a 'hub': huge quantities of imported merchandise, especially from Asia, arrive at Peruvian and Chilean ports and are then transported up the steep slopes of the Andes to El Alto; from El Alto, they are distributed throughout Bolivia and to neighbouring areas such as Paraguay and Brazil's Amazonian region. In El Alto, the intense trade of globalization takes place within a tight social and cultural fabric formed by a well-established population of second- and third-generation internal migrants. In the last two decades, a new Aymara middle class has emerged that trades with Asia as well as throughout the country. It has adopted Freddy Mamani's architecture as a way of marking its own identity and improved social status. In just two decades, over sixty buildings designed by Mamani, each commissioned by individual owners, have sprung up across the city, rising high over much poorer and duller dwellings.

Mamani's architectural formula is analogous to the postmodern 'shed and façade' model: an extraordinary iconic façade covers an ordinary structure built in concrete and brick, four or five storeys high. In the facades, regular and functional fenestrations give way to large, round, oblique, irregular coloured windows. Zigzag motifs are common translations of the indigenous Andean cross or *chakana* – a stepped cross indicating the cardinal points of the compass over which is superimposed a square; it is considered to be the most enduring symbol of the old cultures of the Andes. Similar flamboyant elements decorate internal walls, doors and floors. Mamani claims that his architecture 'seeks to give my city an identity by taking up elements of our indigenous culture'.[13] Although there are no direct references to what remains of the local pre-Hispanic Tiwanaco buildings, it is possible to argue that Mamani's motifs echo native geometric traditions as seen in Andean textiles and ceramics. Artefacts from pre-Colombian cultures from the Altiplano, for example, often contain figurative elements reduced to their essential geometric form and organized in diagonal compositions or juxtapositions. Locals easily recognize these references: 'This is our kind of stuff', said one of the owners, interviewed in 2010 for a field study, led by architect Randolph Cárdenas, on El Alto's new architecture.[14]

In his study, Cárdenas describes one of the mechanisms that may have helped set in motion this new aesthetic, which I suggest can be called an 'aesthetic of excess'. Cárdenas recorded the peculiarly close relationship between the client, the builder and the architect (or structural engineer) as well as the fluid nature of the design process. For example, if new money becomes available to the client during the building process, they ask for more 'stuff' to be added, regardless of the stage the construction or how the 'stuff' fits with the architect's original design. Keen on showing off, the client asks for more: 'like my neighbour, but better'. The addition may consist of additional volume, extra material or more colour.[15] The architect or structural engineer then has the task of coming up with something 'of that sort', different but at least equally impressive and flamboyant. As Cárdenas noted, the client's desire for 'showing off' has a very strong visual impact on the surroundings – a backdrop of undifferentiated monochromatic constructions, often left unfinished, characteristic of El Alto when it was a less affluent dormitory city, regarded with contempt by La Paz's bourgeoisie.

As for the abundant use of colour in the facade, the recent introduction of industrial materials such as aluminium and large coloured glass panels meant that windows could take different dimensions and shapes, and the proximity of diverse shiny colours could create remarkable effects. If down in La Paz other architects use such materials to create plain, monochrome facades that give buildings a traditional 'modern' look, in El Alto Mamani and his colleagues take full advantage of the chromatic possibilities of these same materials.

The appreciation of strident colours (*colores chillones*), visible everywhere in Bolivia, is often overtly claimed to be part of Bolivian culture. It is evident in the *aguayos*, the Andean shawls commonly used to carry things or babies on one's shoulders; in the costumes worn during the popular *fiestas* that abound in the country; as well as in the everyday *pollera* skirts worn by the *cholitas* (women dressed in traditional costumes) – particularly now that traditional, naturally dyed fabrics have been replaced by cheaper synthetic products made in Asia that are significantly shinier and feature more saturated colours. The appreciation of strong colours may also be a result of intersecting cultures, or West meets East, so to speak; the bias for exaggerated colours could be retro-fed by images and artefacts from Asian countries with which Andean countries trade profusely, particularly people from El Alto.

The internal decoration of Mamani's buildings matches the excessiveness of the facades, particularly in the *salon de eventos*, or 'events hall'. This double-height space, comprising the first and second floors of the building, is rented out for parties and weddings. The extravagance of the facade translates internally as an array of mirrors, decorated columns, elaborate chandeliers and hundreds of LED lights imported from Asia. Most weekends these *salones*, or halls, are fully booked by families, unions, congregations and other local groups. The cost of fitting out such a *salon* in this exuberant style accounts for a significant share of the $300,000 to $600,000 budget for the whole building, an investment that is easily recouped within a few years through events bookings. Andean communities have a long tradition of organizing celebratory gatherings in informal spaces such as internal patios or halls, as well as in public streets and piazzas. In this sense, Mamani did not invent the *salon de eventos* as such; people used a variety of spaces for their numerous celebrations. The significance of his contribution lies in codifying the *salon* with its peculiar internal distribution of volume and decoration as the main focus of the whole building. He created a specific typology, so much so that nowadays people refer to these buildings as *salones* (party hall).

Externally, the extraordinary facades turn these salon buildings into palaces, enhancing their private/public function. Thus, what could strike the observer as being an excessive and eccentric use of colour and unusual forms – an aesthetic which, from a Western perspective, could be associated with fun fairs – is in reality a commercial operation built around recognizable codes that come from both vernacular and modern urban cultures, the latter including products and images acquired via the internet and global trade. The upper floors consist of flats that are often reserved for the owner's children or rented out, while the owner lives in a sort of private villa on the roof. This additional roof structure oddly departs in style and shape from the rest of the building, and is often capped by a gabled roof with a multi-tiered chimney. The incongruous chalet is perhaps the feature which most shocks *paceños* (La Paz's inhabitants) and architects alike, for different reasons: as well as breaking the architectural unity of the building, the chalet, as a type of construction common in the Alps, is not only an element that belongs to Western architecture, but it is one on which the mansions of La Paz's elites were modelled in the nineteenth and early twentieth centuries. As a result, much to the dislike of Mamani, people refer to the *salon* typology he helped to establish, as *cholets* – a combination of the word *chalet* with *cholo*.

Another feature of this *salon* typology is the mini shopping arcade at street level, with small shops arranged along a central corridor, occasionally with a public toilet at the rear. By renting out parts of the building, the owner makes a significant income. In a sort of native version of 'money makes the world go round', Mamani says, 'In Andean culture everything is alive. This applies to money as well; it has to move on, to work; it has to produce more money.'[16] Here Mamani refers to the way Aymara and other indigenous cultures understand the Pachamama, or Mother Earth, as an all-encompassing entity in which everything is alive and of equal value: humans, mountains, rivers, plants, rocks, animals. Everything is part of an *unicum* with no precedence given to human beings. Hence the central tenet of the Andean world view or philosophy of life is the Buen Vivir, Sumak Kawsay (in Quechua) or Suma Qamaña (in Aymara), meaning life in plenitude, in harmony and balance with nature and the community. However, nowadays urban Aymaras are caught between tradition and modernity, communal habits and harsh self-imposed labour conditions, commitments to Pachamama and consumerism and its inherent toll on the environment.

These tensions unfold in a particular way in El Alto. As researchers have shown, migrants from the Andean regions retain a stronger link to their original land and culture compared to migrants from other regions.[17] Many residents of El Alto have kept their rights to land in their rural communities (*ayllus*) and return there during planting and harvest seasons and for festivals to fulfil their community duties. The relationship between the countryside and the city is thus maintained and contributes to keeping alive, even in the city, the communal cultural traditions of rural communities. The way in which El Alto emerged as a city is another important characteristic. Several of the oldest neighbourhoods were established following the arrival of entire communities of rural people, including miners, who had to find another place to live and work as a result of the devastating drought of 1983 and the closure of the mines in the 1980s and 1990s. Because they moved as a group, they did not lose their communal and cultural ties but quickly re-established them in the new location. These ties also provided the basis for the establishment of remarkable and diverse networks, which helped creating and accessing much-needed basic urban services. El Alto FEJUVE, the federation of local associations, is made up of hundreds of organizations: neighbourhood committees, the federation of parents' committees, women's clubs and all sorts of trade unions and guilds. It commands respect for its organizational capacity, which translates into remarkable political strength. This rich network means tight social relations, celebrated in numerous fiestas; hence the abundance of *salon de eventos*.

El Alto's tight social and cultural network and the strong relationship its people have maintained with rural communities and habits, along with the creativity of an indigenous population well versed in local and now transnational trade, are all features that could help explain perceived differences in the urban built environment of El Alto and of cities in neighbouring countries. Much to the dismay of Bolivia's conservative elite, whose political and economic power has been shrinking, Mamani's buildings and their 'excessive aesthetics' symbolize the success of an entrepreneurial indigenous culture transposed from the countryside to the city. It is a culture that refuses to be contained by the cliché of the 'essential' indigenous being – unchanging, nostalgic, archaic, naive, an outsider to modernity – which is how the bourgeoisie traditionally characterize the indigenous population.

Architecture and the economy of excess

The Bolivian sociologist Silvia Rivera Cusicanqui has produced a wealth of theoretical, historical and political research on Bolivia. In the 1980s she was one of the founders of the seminal Taller de Historia Oral Andina (THOA), an interdisciplinary workshop of Andean oral history. In Spanish, Quechua and Aymara, students and researchers of this workshop carried out extensive fieldwork in rural communities, visiting *ayullos* (indigenous communities) in the Andes. As they learned more about the network of indigenous leaders, THOA members were able to identify the common struggle underlying a series of uprisings that official historiography traditionally identifies as isolated rebellions.[18] THOA participants went on to set up radio programmes and publications in both Spanish and indigenous languages that had a significant role in supporting the reconstruction of a strong political network of indigenous communities and organizations, a network that later became a protagonist in Bolivia's subsequent political upheaval.

At a certain point in her long career, Rivera, a militant and also a distinguished scholar of cultural and subaltern studies, claimed that colonialism and its dynamics of domination are sometimes reproduced by certain academics, primarily from northern/western countries. These academics, she argues, appropriate the terms – and ideas – of local scholars without fully grappling with the relationship of power inscribed in them, thus decontextualizing and depoliticizing these concepts as well as marginalizing indigenous scholars from their own debates. Considering that words, that is, the naming of things, is not a neutral operation but creates meaning in itself, Rivera also criticized fellow Bolivian colleagues, whether scholars or militants, who speak of – and for – the indigenous population without actually speaking their language. It is from this position that Rivera introduced Aymara words to academic discourse, such as the concept of *ch'ixi*.[19] In subaltern studies the term *mestizo*, which had been largely used in Latin American culture since the 1920s to describe a mixed ethnicity and culture that was neither fully Spanish nor fully indigenous, was substituted by the concept of a hybrid. A hybrid implies a certain fusion of different cultural models to create a new one. The concept of *ch'ixi* that Rivera eagerly promotes retains a certain difference between the elements. Rivera describes *ch'ixi* as something that both is and is not. It might describe the colour grey: from the distance we perceive grey as a single colour, but when we look closely the original black and white particles are still there. The concept *ch'ixi* represents how different cultures with different temporalities happen to coexist both in complementary and antagonizing ways. Beyond and below layers of coexistence and complementarity, this residual difference harbours a conflict. It is in this residual difference where the political – a crucial dimension for Rivera – is located.

Rivera identifies the excessive spending by the Aymara bourgeoisie during numerous festivities that take place everywhere in Bolivia as being an expression of *ch'ixi*.[20] The Fiesta del Gran Poder in La Paz and the Fiesta de la Virgen del Carmen in El Alto are very similar and equally extraordinary.[21] In each of these celebrations, tens of thousands of dancers, organized in more than sixty 'brotherhoods' (*fraternidades*), perform in a long procession through the streets of the city, from dusk till dawn, to the non-stop music of countless bands. Each brotherhood contains hundreds of people, usually from the same trade or profession. Overseen by a board of directors and following an elaborate and tightly hierarchical scheme, preparations last from December to June. They include the design and production of elaborate costumes – carefully kept secret until the day of the *fiesta* – lyrics, decorated invitations cards and gadgets as well as weekly rehearsals and commercial deals, especially with beer producers; abundant beer consumption is an integral part of the *fiesta* and the offerings. The *prestes* – one or several couples responsible for looking after the statues of the saints throughout the year – invest enormous sums of money as custodians and *padrinos* of the *fiesta*. Participants are also expected to contribute to the expenses and to pay for their own costumes, usually between one and two thousand dollars. El Alto's affluent entrepreneurs are among the most important sponsors of such processions. They thus perform a communal duty to their neighbourhood, their trade or other communal entity. Brotherhoods act as a crucial locus for exchange and social life for the *chola* elite. As Cárdenas has observed, often the *cholets* have the colours and colour combinations of the owner's brotherhood.

The economic logic of the *fiesta* and the way in which Aymara traders and entrepreneurs organize their successful trade cannot be understood only through the lens of traditional Western capitalist mechanisms. Its dynamics also follow the logic of an 'ethnic economy', as discussed by Olivia Harris in *Ethnicity, Markets, and Migration in the Andes*.[22] To overcome economic crises and marginalization from mainstream capitalist channels, such as access to bank credit, this indigenous sector of the population developed heterodox and creative strategies by reactivating traditional structures and institutions. These included using traditional networks, such as confraternities and extended family networks, as well as communal habits such as the *ayni* and *pasanaco*. *Ayni* is Quechua for 'sacred reciprocity', when someone asks for help and will repay by doing a similar work, while *pasanaco* or *rotación de ahorro colectivo* describes an informal rotation of savings and credit associations, derived from the Spanish *pasa* (to pass on) and Quechua *naku*, a suffix that indicates reciprocity. The economic success of such unusual strategies is such that Bolivia's vice president himself has commissioned a research study on the topic with a view to seeing whether it could be taken as a national or Andean economic model. The social anthropologist Nico Tassi, among others, has carried out extensive research to understand the success of the *cholo* economies. He analyzed the successful indigenous entrepreneurship in the markets of La Paz and El Alto by investigating the relationship between economic practice and religious beliefs, indigenous organizations and globalization.[23] In his study significantly titled 'The Postulate of Abundance: Cholo Market and Religion', Tassi highlights two specific features of such an economic model: it is transnational and ostentatious. This is to say, the demonstration of abundance and excessive spending in clothing, goods or religious parades is a constituent part of it.[24] In other words, the feature of *excessiveness* constitutes part of the peculiar dynamics that involve capitalist exchanges but also the pre-capitalist relationships and institutions that are still alive in Bolivia, particularly in El Alto and La Paz, given the tight social and cultural fabric described earlier.

In an analogous way, Cárdenas's study on the emergent architecture of El Alto, mentioned earlier, also stressed the underlying range of vernacular social practices that are active in conceiving and building the extraordinary constructions of El Alto. This aspect is often overlooked by architects and critics who focus solely on the flamboyant aesthetics and rely on orthodox architectural canons to explain or critique these buildings. Cárdenas suggests that the architectural phenomenon of extraordinary constructions that Mamani calls neo-Andean architecture and its underlying social practices might actually constitute the beginning of a real process of urban integration for a population with historical, rural roots that has been living at the margins because of the country's colonial divides. Gáston Gallardo, speaking from his position as the dean of the Faculty of Architecture at Universidad Mayor de San Andrés in La Paz, and one of the rare institutional voices to engage with Mamani's work, echoes this view: 'I consider this model as an identity *in the making*. In a society like ours, so deeply bound to colonial models, the only way to break away from it is through such a strong stance. And they did it! I think it shows a brilliant popular intuition. It is a break from all models imitating western architecture.'[25]

The *politics of excess* of the new Andean architecture is captured by the notion of *ch'ixi* – an unsettled difference, residual separateness, indigestible dissonance. It exposes the coexistence of social groups with different 'temporalities'. Ultimately, it defeats even the most open-minded attitude towards the Bolivian version of *huachafa* culture and architecture, as represented by the Foundation for Andean Aesthetics (FEA) mentioned earlier.

Meanwhile, Freddy Mamani is receiving more and more attention on the international stage. Initially, the foreign press was drawn by the boldness and colour of his buildings, which make for spectacular magazine covers and illustrated spreads. In October 2018, the exhibition *Southern Geometries, from Mexico to Patagonia* at the Cartier Foundation for Contemporary Art in Paris has provided a more sophisticated framework for Mamani's work. Blurring temporal boundaries, the exhibition presented pieces dating from 5000 BC to modern and contemporary art, aligning Mamani's work to the practice of geometric design in indigenous and contemporary Latin American art.

Whether, at an international level, the work of Freddy Mamani constitutes an element of a new aesthetic paradigm in the making, or whether it will simply be inscribed into the well-worn tropes of exoticism remains to be seen. But what is certain is that if, as foreigners, we see only the extravagance of Mamani's design without acknowledging the dynamics and tensions beneath the glossy surface, we miss the point – or rather, the *ch'xi*.

Notes

1. Elisabetta Andreoli and Ligiad'Andrea, *The Work of Freddy Mamani Silvestre* (La Paz: Freddy Mamani, 2014).
2. Carlos Villagomez Paredes, 'Arquitectura y Delirio', 26 August 2017, http://carlosvillagomez.blogspot.com/2017/08/ [accessed 22 February 2019].
3. Freddy Mamani, interview by Elisabetta Andreoli, La Paz, February 2014.
4. Ibid.
5. Cristina Dreifuss Serrano, '¿Qué es lo huachafo en la arquitectura?' *Archdaily*, 3 May 2016, https://www.plataformaarquitectura.cl/cl/786643/que-es-lo-huachafo-en-la-arquitectura [accessed 22 February 2019].
6. To these must be added 'remittance' architecture, which refers specifically to constructions built with funds (remittances) from Latin American citizens who emigrated to Europe or North America in the 1980s and 1990s. Scholars consider 'remittance architecture' as having its own peculiar logic relating less to vernacular motifs and more to an imagery built from foreign elements. See, for example, Sarah Lynn Lopez, *The Remittance Landscape: Spaces of Migration in Rural Mexico and Urban USA* (Chicago, IL: University of Chicago Press, 2015).
7. See, for example: Ibid.
8. José Matos Mar, *Desborde popular y crisis del Estado. Veinte años después* (Lima: Fondo Editorial del Congreso del Peru, 2004).
9. See, for example, Annelou Ypeij, 'Cholos, incas y fusionistas: El nuevo Perú y la globalización de lo andino', *European Review of Latin American and Caribbean Studies / Revista Europea de Estudios Latinoamericanos y del Caribe* 94 (2013): 67–82.
10. Carlos Villagomez Paredes, interview by Gemma Candela, La Razón, Bolivia, 27 May 2012.
11. Ibid.
12. Carlos Villagomez Paredes, interview by Gemma Candela, La Razón, 27 May 2012.
13. Mamani, interview by E. Andreoli, El Alto, Boliva, 2013.
14. Randolph Cárdenas, ed., *Arquitecturas Emergentes en El Alto. El fenómeno estético como integración cultural* (La Paz: PIEB, 2010), 105.
15. Mamani, interview by E. Andreoli.
16. Ibid.
17. Franck Poupeau, 'El Alto: una ficción política', *Bulletin de l'Institut français d'études andines* 39, no. 2 (2010): 427–49.
18. Silvia Rivera Cusicanqui, *Oprimidos pero no vencidos. Luchas del campesinado aymara y quechua de Bolivia, 1900–1980* (La Paz: Ed. Hisbol, 1986).
19. Ibid.

20 Rossana Barragán and Cleverth Cárdenas, *Gran Poder: la Morenada* (La Paz: IEB Instituto de Estudios Bolivianos, 2009).

21 Silvia Rivera Cusicanqui, *Principio Potosi Reverso* (Madrid: Museo Nacional Centro de Arte Reina Sofía, 2010).

22 Brooke Larson, Olivia Harris and Enrique Tandeter, eds, *Ethnicity, Markets, and Migration in the Andes: At the Crossroads of History and Anthropology* (Durham: Duke University Press, 1995).

23 Nico Tassi, Carmen Medeiros, Antonio Rodríguez-Carmona and Giovana Ferrufino, '*Hacer plata sin plata*'. *El desborde de los comerciantes populares en Bolivia* (La Paz: PIEB, 2013).

24 Nico Tassi, 'The 'Postulate of Abundance': Cholo Market and Religion in La Paz, Bolivia', *Social Anthropology* 18, no. 2 (2010): 191–209.

25 Gáston Gallardo, interview by Elisabetta Andreoli, in Elisabetta Andreoli, *New Andean: A New Indigenous Architecture*, published by *The Architectural Review*, 13 July 2015, https://www.architectural-review.com/films/new-andean-a-new-indigenous-architecture/8686133.article [accessed 22 February 2019].

CHAPTER TWELVE

The critical kitsch of Alchimia and Memphis: Design by media

AnnMarie Brennan

The experimental, postmodern group Alchimia was formed in 1976 by Italian designers formerly associated with Radical Design – an interdisciplinary avant-garde movement that questioned the established Modernist ethos and searched for unique yet critical solutions that responded to the age-old question of form and function. Inspired by Pop Art, the designers studied new expressive ways of designing which evolved into values imbued with precise political meaning and radical philosophical positions (Figure 12.1).[1]

The dismissal of Alessandro Mendini as editor of *Casabella* in 1975 signalled the end of Radical Design and the creation of Alchimia. There was a growing sentiment among Radical Designers that the movement had failed to revolutionize the field of design, and the arrival of Alchimia intimated a retreat by its members from the movement's resolute ideological positioning.

Mendini, co-founder of Alchimia, provides telling insights into the aesthetic and creative impetus that led to the creation of the group. Its design approach entailed an ironic appreciation of popular culture and tastes combined with a purposeful, acknowledged appropriation of kitsch colours, patterns, and shapes, best represented in the design of plastic laminate surfaces.[2] When explaining the design intentions of Alchimia, Mendini declared, 'Why should one not exploit the natural, intimate and mythical relationship that exists in every mass society between human beings and the so-called "ugly" object?'[3] It is with this question in mind that Alchimia members called for an exaltation of kitsch and the overturning of good taste.

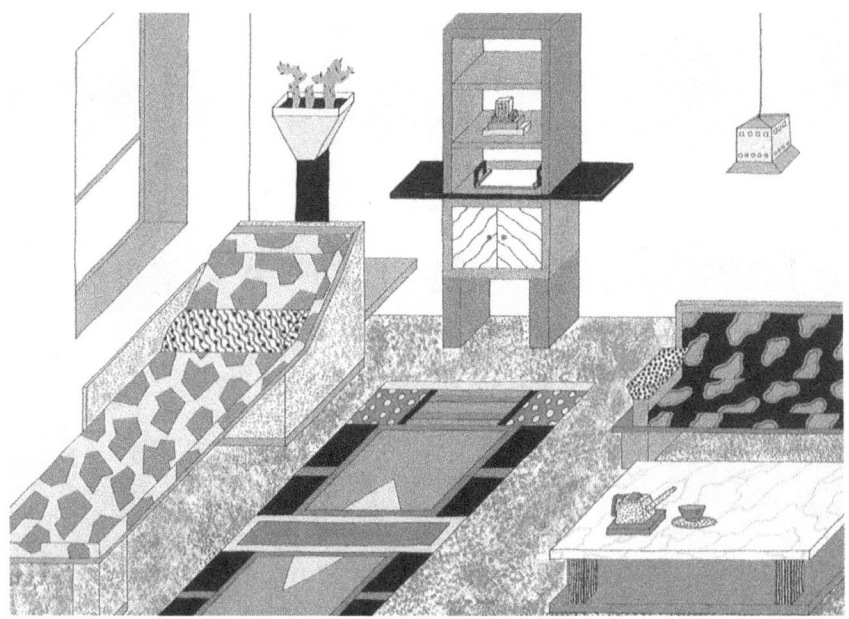

FIGURE 12.1 *Nathalie Du Pasquier, 'Interior', Drawing, 1982–3.*

This intent to embrace a more popular, consumer-driven culture appeared to contradict the forces which drove the Italian Radical Design. Yet the Alchimia manifesto hints at some of the original dogma of the Radical Movement, proclaiming that it was a response to the tumultuous state of Italian society where traditional values were being challenged. 'Alchimia', he writes, 'works on the values based on difference and transgression ... This is Alchimia's "new morality."'[4]

As a movement intellectually driven by deeper ideological concerns and values, Alchimia developed into a further iteration known as Memphis; a style portrayed as a commercial remodelling of Alchimia's avant-garde ideals.[5] Joseph Grima, in an interview with Mendini, sums up the relationship between the two groups, stating that Alchimia served as the 'hinge' between Memphis and Radical Design.[6] Memphis's aesthetic style can be categorized as the product of a self-formed group surrendering to the attention of a globalized mass culture and corresponding market demands after years of overly critical yet non-productive radicalness.

This essay claims that rather than abandoning the ideals of Radical Design, the work of Alchimia and Memphis attempted to radicalize by other means – to continue the battle over cultural and aesthetic values through the design of ugly, kitsch and ironic products for the marketplace. It examines the theoretical underpinnings of Alchimia through the concepts of ugliness and kitsch set out by French communication theorist Abraham Moles

(1920–1992). Mendini's essay 'Per un'architettura banale' served as the foreword to the 1979 Italian edition of Moles's book *Il Kitsch: L'Arte della Felicità*. This essay revisits these texts and the previous debates in Italian design culture on kitsch in order to question the role of media in formulating the characteristic kitsch aesthetic of Alchimia and Memphis.

The New International Style

The founders of Alchimia and Memphis originated from Italian Radical Design groups such as Superstudio, Archizoom, Global Tools, UFO and 9999. These counter-design factions, which were formed amidst the students' protests of 1968 and active into the early 1970s, constituted an alternative outlet for an architectural discipline in crisis. Its members were not interested in engaging with architectural practice so much as attempting to overturn the disciplinary discourse of the modernist functional aesthetic of 'good design' through provocative neo-avant-garde work. However, after years of attempting to subvert the status quo, Radical Design had lost its momentum when its members came to realize that despite their creative efforts, design by and for the working class would never coalesce; instead the market was dominated by the petty bourgeois designer working for bourgeois consumers.

After some theoretical reconfigurations, Alchimia started work when the graphic designer Alessandro Guerriero invited Mendini to collaborate. These two men, along with Alessia Guerriero, founded the movement in Milan in 1976. The group would often be referred to by different labels such as Critical Design, Nuovo Design, Neo-Modern, Banal Design, Memphis and The New International Style.

The contradiction and irony of dubbing Memphis as the New International Style was not lost on Charles Jencks. While Sottsass described Memphis as part 'mid-American city of Elvis, half the ancient capital of Egypt', the movement still maintained, Jencks deciphered, a lingering aspiration from the Sixties Underground combined with a celebration of 'provincial kitsch,' which is everything that the International Style battled against.[7] Similar to his definition of Postmodern architecture Memphis defined itself in opposition to utopian Modern design while 'detecting the conscious intention of parodying the old I.S. and at the same time, stealing its remaining magic'.[8] Memphis presumed to 'inherit the previous generations wealth', pointing out that all attempts to break away from the hegemony of Modernism and the International Style, could not deny, even when opposing, its irrefutable presence.

According to the assigned promoter, chronicler and theorist of Memphis, journalist Barbara Radice, Sottsass wanted to distance himself from Alchimia, in particular Mendini and Guerriero's pessimistic and ideological approach to design, and therefore created a more inclusive movement based on the iconography of mass culture and Indian spirituality along with fellow designers Nathalie Du Pasquier, Michele De Lucchi, George J. Snowden and Peter Shire, among others.[9] Nevertheless, throughout the years, Mendini would be associated with both Alchimia and Memphis.

Design and mass media

The issue of kitsch design and its relationship to mass media was not a new topic when Alchimia arrived on the scene in 1976. More than a decade earlier, in 1964, Italian art and design historians began to debate the emergence of two new types of post-war Modern Art: Gestalt Art and Pop Art, and their effect on industrial design.[10] During these debates, the question regarding these two new art movements took place within an emerging political environment in Italy which saw a shift to the left with a coalition government led by the Socialist Party (Partito Socialista Italiana, PSI) and the Christian Democrats. These conditions instigated the possibility of imagining a political role for art and design, one of that created a proletarian art.

The art historian Filiberto Menna published the 1964 article 'Design, comunicazione estetica e mass media' in the architectural journal *Edilizia Moderna*, where he discusses the origins of styling in industrial design, the problematic relationship between aesthetic quality of a product and the quantity demands required by the market, and how, in the post-war era, a dichotomy between production and consumption emerged within the design field. The stylizing of products by designers such as Raymond Lowy and Richard Dreyfuss, according to Menna, was a means to psychologically condition the public's taste while at the same time interpret its moods and aspirations with the assistance of advertising and marketing. Styling became a tool for designers and advertisers in the re-semantisation of the object, yet reflected the desires of consumers which were integrated to create an aesthetic requalification of the object.[11]

By the early 1960s, this approach diverged into two different strains which first appeared in the realm of art but ultimately played out in design and became the topic of a debate later that year at a round table held at Il Centro gallery in Naples titled 'Design and Mass Media'. The discussion included the art historian Giulio Carlo Argan, Italian philosopher Rosario Assunto, designer Bruno Munari and Menna. Argan noted the influence of Pop and Gestalt Art, or Arte Programmata, on contemporary art and its audience: 'The art of today no longer wants to be an art of the elite, art no longer wants to be an object of capitalism or an asset that is set aside [and appreciated] at a later time, or forever.'[12] Calling for an art for the masses, Argan asks, 'We would be very interested to know what it is or is to be the art of the proletariat.' He continues to respond to this question, describing a proletarian art as having 'the possibility of resolving the relationship between an art that takes into account the aspects of the world and an art that instead proposes itself as a hypothesis of reform in the abstract'.[13] Menna notes how the Gestalt group, represented in the design field by Tomàs Maldonado, the Ulm School and their scientific design methods, was aligned with industrial production and advanced technology, whereas Pop Art and its design equivalent of kitsch and stylized objects were driven by mass consumption.[14]

Missing from this round-table discussion in Naples was the art critic Gillo Dorfles, who in 1963 devoted his first book to theories of aesthetics and their application to the field of industrial design.[15] In the chapter on 'Industrial Design and "Mass Media"', Dorfles notes the effects of mass printing and publication on industrial design.[16] If designed objects are to serve the majority of society, they need to consider and respond to the aesthetics and taste of the largest amount of people, he argued, so that the products are enjoyed and appreciated by everyone. In doing this, the designer needs to put aside any aspirations of exceptionality and sophistication. It is this practice of searching for an average taste, satisfying an average sensitivity, that design shares with mass media.[17] Therefore, for Dorfles, the industrialization of expressive means of communication, and of art in general, portends that the triumphal and ubiquitous norm of art becomes kitsch (non-art).[18] Years later Dorfles would present the aesthetic of Alchimia as an embodiment of this new norm. Alchimia, he said, is 'seiz[ing] some characteristics of "bad taste" in order to give life to avant-garde objects'.[19]

'Per un'architettura banale' (Towards a banal architecture)

The 1978 exhibition *Bau-Haus* was the first occasion of early Alchimia participants to showcase the collection in their studio in Foro Bonoparte, Milan.[20] The exhibition, aiming to position the group within the industrial design world of domestic objects, showcased the work of Sottsass, Mendini, Andrea Branzi, Trix and Robert Haussmann, UFO, Michele De Lucchi and Paolo Navone.[21] For this occasion Mendini wrote the seminal essay 'Per una architettura banale' (Towards a banal architecture) which clarified the conceptual thinking of the Alchimia group. It was republished a year later as the foreword to Abraham Moles's Italian edition, *Il Kitsch. L'Arte della Felicità* (1979) with the Italian version published by Officina Edizioni as part of a series curated by Menna.[22]

At the time Moles was a leading theoretical figure at the Ulm School of Design writing on cybernetics, computers and visual research which inspired many Italian designers and artists.[23] Mendini would have been familiar with

Moles's theories as the author published two articles in *Casabella* while Mendini served as part of the editorial staff starting in 1965.[24] In his foreword Mendini dissects Moles's thesis while incorporating text from some of his previous articles published in *Casabella* and *MODO*. He uses the words ugly, banal and kitsch interchangeably and does not make a distinction between these terms, nor did the Italian design critics of the time. Arturo C. Quintavalle, reviewing 'The Banal Object' exhibition held at the inaugural Venice Biennale at the Corderie dell'Arsenale in 1980 for *Domus*, unpacks the term 'banal', claiming that its meaning is defined by a bourgeois culture that recognizes banality as valuable and worthy of attention after an adequate 'awakening of critical awareness'.[25] He writes,

> Let's have a good look at this banality, let's put it on pedestals, mark it off with phosphorescent flags in all its worn and torn ordinariness. We can draw attention to the iron's volute, the faceting of the false cut-glass, the unconvincing base to the food mixer; then we can add a 'banal' decorated room, the kind with false mahogany veneered table, the bar cupboard open to show its mirrored rectangles, the permanently-on television perhaps and the imitation leather chair.[26]

The banal in this context performs a socio-aesthetic transgression, both as a style that stands out, and an aesthetic of domestic interior design that emphasizes the normalization of the ugly for everyday life. Kitsch, as a significant component of mass culture, is part of an 'aesthetic system of mass communication' which is formed according to a set of principles set out by Moles. Many of them are quite familiar to the definition of kitsch: exaggeration, overstatement, lack of style, excess, mediocrity and comfort. Yet, two other principles of kitsch – synaesthesia (a simultaneous attack on various modes of sensory perception) and the provision of intense sensation – are directly related to the means by which kitsch is disseminated within mass consumer culture.[27] Perhaps the strongest connection that Moles makes between kitsch and the world of design is his claim that kitsch exists within a systemic milieu of objects, which, on a quotidian basis, maintains a reciprocal relationship between a series of communicative kitsch objects and the built environment.[28]

Moles formulated a 'needs theory', distinguishing his work from other writings on kitsch and design by authors such as Dorfles, Vittorio Gregotti and Umberto Eco, which was premised upon an imaginary, global market consisting of a plethora of excessive and ostentatious objects, with plentiful choices becoming a product of human civilization. This theory of needs is divided into four different points: functionalism, manipulation, lack of conflict and the creation of consensus, and, most importantly, the realization that a revolutionary proletariat does not exist anymore. Moles's first point, a 'crisis of functionalism', was the culmination of the emergence of the Bauhaus 'good design' doctrine, forged with an ever-expanding global capital marketplace that demanded the accelerated production of products for a consumer society. A poignant example provided by Moles is the creation of such unnecessary yet functional objects such as the 'grapefruit knife, the electric toothbrush, the pile knife, the egg holder for egg *à la coque*'. The design and production of these excessive products designed for a bourgeois lifestyle signal for Moles and Mendini a point in which the doctrine of modern functionality degenerates into 'kitsch frenzy'.[29]

The second point, needs and manipulation, discusses the cyclical relationship between a powerful elite and their ability to manipulate the needs of the masses. Kitsch, understood as a lifestyle that accommodates new needs, is conciliatory, accepting the banal and refuting the avant-garde. The spatial realm of the 'man-kitsch' is the apartment; a conflict-free zone organized for the purpose of consensus and harmony. Moreover, this assignment of kitsch to the domestic realm is based on the idea that the 'privileged domain' of kitsch is the individualized, quotidian space where the 'relationship with things is exercised constructively'.[30]

Moles's final point in the theory of needs explains how a revolutionary proletariat cannot exist within advanced capitalist countries, as the goal of that class within a capitalist society is to find contentment, which usually aligns with the values of man-kitsch. He asserts that the remaining revolutionary proletariat is either associated with the drug scene, militant groups or those who opt to choose the most difficult path, which is to refute the attainment of happiness and instead accept the 'critical and cynical acceptance of everyday banality'.[31]

In his foreword, Mendini synthesizes Moles's work and translates his claims from the 'socio-psychological terrain to the design one, with the big consequences and the serious risks that this may entail: from overturning the methods to the annulment of values'.[32] By transferring and applying Moles's sociological view of kitsch to design, Mendini formulates kitsch as more than just a methodological approach, but as a 'design conscience'.[33]

In a section subtitled 'The Amoral Project', Mendini proposes a model of banal architecture that critically positions itself vis-à-vis petty-bourgeois taste and confronts the problems created by modernism and capitalism. The absurd goal of designing an amoral project, in this case, a house, is to make it contain the 'maximum amount possible of bad taste'. It is an anti-heroic goal which can be achieved by applying a sort of amoral, reversal of what is understood as quality through a series of critical techniques and methods. A set of kitsch rules are formulated, which regulate the design and include,

> The use of false materials (typical of marble), the romantic use of natural materials (tree bark), dimensional aberration (miniature windows), the rattling of colors, materials and shapes (pink next to brown, iron next to the fabric, visibly wrong geometric shapes), rhetoric of tradition and dynamism (base of stone house, fireplace, Aerodynamic), the omission of

meanings (hotels that look like taverns), redundancy of quantities (excess balconies), and so on.[34]

A banal architectural style, Mendini explains, rejects all of the institutional and academic norms handed down from a classical architectural background and the values, such as the notion of 'good design' and methods such as 'compositional research, typological morphogenesis, and the prioritising of functionalism'. The product of this 'bad taste' design method culminates into a style of the banal house, within an aesthetic style of a 'happy conscience'. This can only be achieved once the designer realizes that they cannot uphold the proletarian myth of the late 1960s and early 1970s (Figure 12.2).

Mendini notes that when Radical Design was first conceived, the political and cultural enemy was clearly identified and known, however by 1979, the culturally progressive liberals and intellectuals were suffering from a crisis, as they had successfully emerged as the political majority and the ideological opposition was now a minority. Mendini defined this moment as being symbolized as a pendulum, with proletarian designers on one side and bourgeois designers on the other. In 1979, with the Socialists as the hegemonic governing power in Italy, this view conflicted with the emerging *anni di edonismo* (the age of hedonism). The pendulum then swung towards bourgeois designers, who attempted to alleviate their guilt by following

FIGURE 12.2 *Alessandro Mendini, 'Kandissi' sofa, Alchimia 1979. ©Atelier Mendini.*

a proletarian style, while proletarian designers naturally tended towards appeasing bourgeois taste. The only way, according to Mendini, to avoid designers (who at this time are now all considered bourgeois) 'consciously design[ing] the progressive death of the bourgeois project' would be to seek the negative development of the project, thereby leading to the formulation of a utopian idea of a banal architecture, or anaesthetic. 'In this way,' Mendini claims, 'banal design and stylistic amorality can be understood as revolutionary thought.'[35]

Design by media/design as media

Alchimia and Memphis were established in Milan – the centre of Italian design and home to the Triennale design exhibition and the Salone dei Mobili. It is where the headquarters of periodicals such as *Domus*, *Casabella*, *Abitare*, *Stile Industria*, *Ottagono*, *MODO*, *Casa Vogue*, *Stile Industria* and *Interni* were located. These journals served as the support system for Alchimia and Memphis during this time and the movement was dependent upon them.[36]

As editor-in-chief for *Casabella* from 1970, Mendini served as the handmaiden of Radical Design by providing a platform for the publication of its utopian and counter-design schemes. After his tenure as editor of *Casabella*, Mendini, along with Valerio Castelli and Giovanni Cutolo, established the magazine *MODO*; a 'journal of design culture' in 1977.[37] The magazine was funded by a group of industrialists headed by Giulio Castelli, founder of the Italian furniture manufacturer Kartell. It published advertisements of these companies, yet pursued the stance of being a controversial, critical voice on all design; attempting to equivocate all design disciplines; promoting an interdisciplinary project of fashion, visual art and kitsch, where the 'shoemaker is equal to the architect, the baker, the photographer, and the theater actor'.[38] In 1980, Mendini became editor of *Domus*, a magazine that would become a major purveyor of Postmodern Design, which featured Alchimia and Memphis projects.

While Mendini provided a platform for Radical Design, Alchimia, and Memphis over a period of fifteen years in three different magazines, their counter-designs were very much shaped by an awareness of how it was mediated through magazines, with the prospect that the work would, for the most readers, remain as an image on a magazine page. There is a reciprocal relationship between the ugly, kitsch aesthetics of Alchimia and Memphis and the mass media it was featured in. As debated by Dorfles, Menna and others, the main purpose of both media and kitsch is to emotionally move us, to reproduce a certain *effect*, to evoke real sensory experiences and emotions. Kitsch attempts to accomplish this task through its elaborate, ironic and overly expressive imagery in order to set off a preset, unreflective, emotional response.[39] It presents the most emotive effects of a carefully curated selection of an average, shared, collective experience. And therefore with its concentration on the mimicking and reproduction of effects, the kitsch and banal work of Memphis and Alchimia share the same objectives of media, while exploiting media's effective nature.

Marshall McLuhan, in formulating his concept of 'the medium is the message', explained the nature of media and how it serves to create effects at the expense of communicating a truth or information. In his 1967 text *The Medium Is the Massage: An Inventory of Effects*, McLuhan claimed that, as an extension of the human senses, media expands or 'extends' the abilities of the nervous system by massaging the aural and tactile capacities of the human sensorium. His definition of media corresponds to the purpose of kitsch to reflect and contort reality in order to evoke a certain emotion. Like the banal object, media is formed by us, mirroring our own cultural and social environment, and as McLuhan asserts, 'All media work us over completely. They are so pervasive in their personal, political, economic, aesthetic, psychological, moral, ethical, and social consequences that they leave no part of us untouched, unaffected, unaltered.'[40] Kitsch works on the emotions just as media works on the senses.

It is well established that the emergence of Modern architecture necessitated its reproduction in vehicles of mass media to distribute and transport the images of industrial architecture in order to create an International Style.[41] Alchimia and Memphis designers were acutely aware of the movement's dependence on media for the circulation of their ideas; indeed, they understood that media underpinned the movement's entire ideological reasoning and aesthetic style. As American Memphis designer Peter Shire noted, 'Memphis was *of* the media'.[42] This was evidenced in the preparation of images for publication. 'There was never any problem with colour separations, it always reproduced true, because we were using synthetic colours in the first place. The priority was to go for the image. The difference was between its existing and not existing.'[43] Franco Raggi, who succeeded Mendini as the editor of *MODO* wrote in one of his 'parable' editorials about the magazine in the third person: 'In search of a reassuring definition [of Neo-Modernism], he consulted some publications but realized that, as cinema does not define cinema, magazines did not define design, and in some cases they "were" design. Magnificent and enviable interiors.'[44] This sentiment reinforces Menna's earlier claim when he stated that the designed object performs as a type of mass media, concluding that design is not only in constant contact with mass media, but as a means of mass communication it is media.[45]

The most ironic aspect of Alchimia and Memphis is not the aesthetic but the manner in which these movements were able to thrive. The main goal was to gather the most notable, avant-garde designers, commission them furniture collections and then have the designers adhere to a style that called for a contradictory aesthetic that would appeal to the largest possible group of consumers. In order for the transgressive style to succeed, it needed to collude with industrial partners such as Abet Laminate, Kartell and others. These design objects were initially intended to appeal to a non-existent proletariat consumer but eventually became avant-garde pieces, status symbols for the wealthy and museum objects, which even the petit bourgeois consumer could not afford. Despite the radical, revolutionary underpinnings, the products of Alchimia and Memphis were dependent on a global, capitalist industrial production and distribution structure for their realization.

When Alchimia's 'mobile infinito' collection first appeared in 1981, Dorfles, who appreciated the social goals of the project, had already noted the contradictory conundrum that would follow the group throughout its years of success. He understood the 'mobile infinito' as a work of conceptual art and that to remain true to the intentions of its creators, the project would need to remain a conjectural project and not be manufactured into products to be sold to satisfy bourgeois fetishes, as the use value of the furniture would then be surrendered for an exorbitant exchange value. Despite their aspirations to the status of avant-garde kitsch, Alchimia and Memphis capitulated to forfeit those ideals once the works achieved commercial success.

Notes

1 Maria Cristina Didero, 'Radical Design Never Existed' in *Radical Utopias*, ed. Pino Brugellis, Gianni Pettena and Alberto Salvadori (Florence: Quodlibet, 2018), 62.

2 See Chiara Lecce, 'Abet Laminati: il design delle superfici', *AIS/Design Storia e Richerche* no. 4 (2014), http://www.aisdesign.org/aisd/abet-laminati-il-design-delle-superfici [accessed 11 December 2015]; and Catherine Rossi, 'Making Memphis: "Glue Culture" and Postmodern Production Strategies' in *Postmodernism. Style and Subversion, 1970–1990*, ed. Glenn Adamson and Jane Pavitt (London: V & A Publishing, 2011), 160–5.

3 Alessandro Mendini, 'Per un'architettura banale', 1979. See http://www.ateliermendini.it/index.php?mact=News,cntnt01,detail,0&cntnt01articleid=251&cntnt01detailtemplate=AnniDett&cntnt01lang=en_US&cntnt01returnid=191 [accessed 25 October 2017]; Alessandro Mendini, 'Fur ein Banales Design' in *Design aus Italien* (Hanover: Deutsche Werkbund, 1982), 279.

4 Alessandro Mendini, 'The Alchimia Manifesto' in *Alchimia. Contemporary Italian Design*, ed. Kazuko Sato (Berlin: TACO, 1988), 7. Although the manifesto lists Mendini as the sole author, the document was in reality the result of a collaboration.

5 All of the members of these two groups are too many to name here. A comprehensive list including over 200 names of Alchimia members can be found in Giacomo D. Ghidelli, *Alessandro Guerriero Senza Titoli nella storia del design* (Milan: Libraccio, 2017), fn 1, 39.

6 Joseph Grima, Alessandro Mendini and Vera Sacchetti, 'Interview with Alessandro Mendini: The Role of Radical Magazines' in *The Italian Avant-Garde, 1968–1976*, ed. Alex Coles and Catherine Rossi (Berlin: Sternberg Press, 2013), 11.
7 Charles Jencks, 'The…New…International…Style… e altra etichette', *Domus* no. 623 (1981): 41.
8 Ibid.
9 Penny Sparke, 'Ettore Sottsass and Critical Design in Italy, 1965–1985' in *Made in Italy: Rethinking a Century of Italian Design*, ed. Grace Lees-Maffei and Kjetil Fallan (London: Bloomsbury, 2013), Kindle Cloud Reader e-book, chap. 2.
10 Giulio Carlo Argan, Rosario Assunto, Bruno Munari and Filiberto Menna, 'Design e Mass Media: A Roundtable Discussion', *Op. Cit* 2 (1965). See http://www.opcit.it/cms/?p=14 [accessed 7 July 2017].
11 Filiberto Menna, 'Design, comunicazione estetica e mass media', *Edilizia Moderna* 85 (1964): 32–7.
12 Ibid.
13 Ibid.
14 Ibid., 36.
15 Gillo Dorfles, *Il Disegno Industriale e la sua estetica* (Bologna: Cappelli, 1963).
16 Ibid., 51–3.
17 Ibid.
18 Dorfles tackles the problem of kitsch in *Le Oscillazioni del Gusto* (Milan: Lerici, 1958); and in the article 'Kitsche e cultura', *Aut Aut* no. 73 (1963); and later in the edited anthology, *Kitsch: The World of Bad Taste* (New York: Bell, 1968).
19 Gillo Dorfles in Giacomo D. Ghidelli, *Alessandro Guerriero Senza Titoli nella storia del design* (Milan: Libraccio, 2017), 166.
20 Ibid., 90–1. The *Bau-haus* exhibition, which opened at the same time as the Salone del Mobile, was held off-location, initiating the practice of *Fuorisalone*, which showcases new work outside of the Salone grounds, opening up a multitude of showrooms and offices throughout the entire city of Milan during the Salone.
21 Kazuko Sato interview with Alessandro Guerriero, 'Bau • haus I.II', in *Alchimia. Contemporary Italian Design*, ed. Kazuko Sato (Berlin: TACO, 1988), 17.
22 Abraham Moles, *Il Kitsch. L'Arte della Felicità* (Rome: Officina Edizioni, 1979). The Italian edition was based upon the French editions, *Le Kitsch, L'art du bonheur* (Paris: Maison Mame, 1971) and *Psychologie des Kitsches* (Munich: Carl Hanser Verlag, 1972).
23 G. Anceschi and P. G. Tanca, 'Ulm and Italy: Rodolfo Bonetto, Enzo Fratelli, Pio Mazu, Andries van Onck, Hans von Klier, and Willy Ramstein', *Rassagna: Legacy of the School of Ulm* no. 19/3 (1984): 25–33.

24 Abraham Moles, 'Cibernetica e opera d'arte', *Casabella* no. 323 (February 1968): 46–51; Carlo Guenzi and Abraham Moles, 'Invenzione nella Macchina', *Casabella* no. 323 (February 1968): 4–11.
25 Arturo C. Quintavalle, 'Banal Design', *Domus* 612 (1980): 44–5.
26 Ibid.
27 Moles, *Il Kitsch*, 76–81.
28 Ibid., 11.
29 Ibid.
30 Mendini, 'Per un'architettura banale'. This is the same text as Mendini, 'Foreword' in Moles, *L'Arte della Felicità*.
31 Ibid.
32 Ibid.
33 Ibid.
34 Ibid.
35 Ibid.
36 Sparke, *Made in Italy*, chap. 2.
37 In Italian, the subtitle of *MODO*, chosen by Mendini is 'Rivista di cultura del progetto'.
38 Grima, et al., 'Interview with Alessandro Mendini: The Role of Radical Magazines', 8.
39 Robert Solomon, 'On Kitsch and Sentimentality', *Journal of Aesthetic and Art Criticism* 49 (Winter 1991): 454.
40 Marshall McLuhan and Quentin Fiore, *The Medium Is the Massage* (New York: Random House, 1967), 26.
41 Beatriz Colomina, *Privacy and Publicity. Modern Architecture as Mass Media*. (Cambridge, MA: MIT Press, 1996).
42 Glenn Adamson and Jane Pavitt, 'Postmodernism: Style in Subversion' in *Postmodernism. Style and Subversion 1979-1990*, ed. Glenn Adamson and Jane Pavitt (London: V & A Publishing, 2011), 47.
43 Ibid.
44 Franco Raggi, 'Design Neo-Moderno', *MODO* no. 39 (1981), republished in *20 Racconto di Architettura. Editoriali pubblicati su MODO dall'aprile 1981 al Maggio 1983* (London: Granger Press 2014) Apple e-book, page 8. (translation by author)
45 Menna, 'Design, comunicazione estetica e mass media', 37.

CHAPTER THIRTEEN

The immediacy of urban reality in post-war Italy: Between neorealism's and Tendenza's instrumentalization of ugliness

Marianna Charitonidou

Ugliness was used as a productive category in post-war Italian architecture. This chapter unfolds the debate among protagonists of Tendenza (Ernesto Nathan Rogers and Aldo Rossi) and neorealist architecture (Ludovico Quaroni and Mario Ridolfi) about the notion of ugliness in Italian cities after the Second World War, aesthetic views informed by the post-war urban reality. Rogers, Rossi, Ridolfi and Quaroni believed that post-war (sub)urbanization contributed to the 'uglification' of cities. An analysis of the design of the Torre Velasca project (1950–8) by Ludovico Belgiojoso, Enrico Peressutti and Ernesto Nathan Rogers (BBPR), and the development of the Tiburtino district (1949–54) by Ludovico Quaroni and Mario Ridolfi, in collaboration with certain young Roman architects, such as Carlo Aymonino, reveals how the anti-aesthetic and anti-elitist stance of Tendenza and neorealist architects was applied. The essay thus sheds light on the shared intention of Tendenza and neorealist architects to reformulate the ways in which we judge architecture. They theorized and built new models for urban expansion, and with these models established new criteria for evaluating urban aesthetics that took into consideration the struggle for social reconstruction characteristic of post-war Italian cities. The emergence of such new models by which to evaluate the aesthetics of a city is interpreted as a symptom of the debate regarding the reconstruction of the city's identity after 1945.

'Tendenza' architecture and the interpretation of forms as autonomous constructions

Aldo Rossi first employed the term 'Tendenza' to refer to rationalist architecture in 1969, in the introduction to the second Italian edition of *L'architettura della città*, and again in 'L'architettura della ragione come architettura di Tendenza', an essay in the catalogue of the exhibition *Illuminismo e architettura del '700 veneto*.[1] He used it as a category of architecture to help visualize a connection with realist architecture while remaining close to the intentions of rationalism. It allowed him to both challenge the concept of the avant-garde and reject utopianism. In addition, the desire for style accompanies the concept of Tendenza, which allowed an interpretation of forms as autonomous constructions. Rossi's main intention was to grasp the interrelation between pure speculation on figuration – modernism's 'utopian minimalism' – and the research on existing forms of architecture, or the 'sprawling "reality" of history'.

While Rossi's definition most clearly expresses what Tendenza architecture meant, he was not the first to use the term, and others before him and after used the term in slightly different ways. In 1946, Ernesto Nathan Rogers first employed the term in his essay 'Elogio della tendenza',[2] again in 1957 in the essay 'Ortodossia dell'eterodossia' and in 1958 in *Esperienza dell'architettura*. In 'Ortodossia dell'eterodossia', he, unlike Rossi, distinguishes the concept of Tendenza from style and coherence, defining it as 'an act of modesty that integrates the activity of each individual into the culture of their own epoch, inviting them to consider themselves as part of society before anything else'.[3]

Massimo Scolari, in his text for the catalogue of the XV Triennale di Milano *Architettura razionale* (1973), writes that for Tendenza (by this stage not just a theory but a movement),

> architecture is a cognitive process that in and of itself is today necessitating a re-founding of the discipline in the acknowledgement of its own autonomy. This means architecture refuses interdisciplinary solutions to its own crisis; that it does not pursue and immerse itself in political, economic, social, and technological events only to mask its own creative and formal sterility, but rather desires to understand them so as to be able to intervene in them with lucidity.[4]

The central point where Tendenza theory diverges from modernism, according to Scolari, is the attraction of the former to history as a series of events that he called a 'pile of simulacra'.[5] Meanwhile, Guido Canella, in 'Relazioni tra morfologia, tipologia dell'organismo architettonico e ambiente fisico', talks about the attention Tendenza architects paid to the pedagogical potential of a 'utopia of reality'. Despite the heterogeneity of the different protagonists of Tendenza, they all shared an understanding of 'architecture as a cognitive problem, whether specifically as the "conscious call to the city on the part of the most recent modern architecture" (Canella) or as an autobiographical or personal matter (Rossi)'.[6]

Rogers's temporally driven aesthetic approach relied on the concepts of continuity, of 'sensing history', drawing on his encounter with Enzo Paci's phenomenological approach. Paci, meanwhile, believed society should not be 'theorized or ideologized or structured beforehand according to the perspectives of a given sociology'; instead, architects should 'make alive and real the social relationships of … [their] country, with its needs and miseries, with its illusions and hard sense of reality, of the limits and conditions of life'. Paci was convinced that, to achieve an engaged view, it is indispensable to 'see the things the way they are'.[7] In his *Diario fenomenologico*, he defines phenomenon as something that appears and can then be faithfully described without judgement, even though we may not see it for exactly what it is.[8] In turn, Rogers's view in 'The Image: The Architect's Inalienable Vision'[9] was that architects should balance utility with beauty.

Neorealist ugliness and the recuperation of reality

One of the aims of this essay is to explore the differences between the conception of ugliness in neorationalist architecture and that in neorealist architecture. The term 'neo-realism' is associated, on the one hand, with the project of reformulating Italy's identity in the period immediately after the Second World War and, on the other hand, with the recuperation of the immediacy of reality. Gilles Deleuze, in *Cinema 2: The Time-Image*, relates the emergence of the action-image in post-war cinema to a historical caesura, caused by war, that rendered reality unpresentable.[10] In a similar way, the tendency of post-war Italian architects to respond to a city's ugliness, liberated from aesthetical preconceptions, could be interpreted as attempts to incorporate, in architectural epistemology, the 'unpresentability' of post-war urban reality within the context of an uncontrolled expansion of the urban fabric.

The adjective 'neorealist' connotes an anti-abstract attitude. Scolari, in 'Avanguardia e nuova architettura', describes neorealism as anti-avant-garde, implying that the avant-garde tends towards abstraction rather than attempts to convey life as it really is. Given that crudeness is on the same end of the spectrum as ugliness, the distinction between crudeness and aesthetic refinement that André Bazin, a major theorist of neorealism in cinema, makes could help us better understand the 'instant effectiveness of a realism which is satisfied to only present reality'.[11] The encounter of spectators with this unresolved opposition, he says, pushes their perception to embrace the enlightening power of the post-war situation. Bruno Reichlin finds that neo-realism has a 'propensity for an aesthetic of the ugly'.[12] According to Bazin, 'the originality of Italian Neorealism as compared with the chief schools of realism that preceded it and with the Soviet cinema, lies in never making reality the servant of some *a priori* point of view'.[13] Neorealist architecture, as a 'collective and timeless mode to building',[14] was related to Antonio Gramsci's invitation to formulate 'a new way of feeling and of seeing reality'.[15] The tension between Gramsci's call to shape new ways of conceiving reality and Paci's call to 'see the things the way they are'[16] is symptomatic of the schism between two opposed ways of understanding neorealism: one puts forward its social content and one is focused on formal aesthetic criteria. Bazin, who was an exponent of the second tendency, was convinced that neorealism 'was a matter of a new form of reality'. Paci, an exponent of the 'Milan phenomenological school' founded by Antonio Banfi, shared with Gramsci the insistence on the 'subjective' and 'humanistic' character of historical materialism.

Neorealist architecture was a product of the 'Roman school', with protagonists Mario Ridolfi and Ludovico Quaroni, both participants of the Associazione per l'architettura organica (APAO), founded by Bruno Zevi in 1944. Zevi believed that Modern architecture's liberation from rigid functionalism would permit humanism and democracy to serve as liberating forces in post-war Italian society; politics plays a role in architecture and is thus a feature of neorealist architecture. This concern about architecture's political connotations was shared by proponents of organic architecture, whose impetus was 'social, technical and artistic activity directed towards creating the climate for a new democratic civilisation'.[17]

The neorealist approach should be understood within the context of urban reconstruction in a new Italy after the Second World War. Maristella Casciato identifies that 'it was in the south that the new national architectural language of Neorealism found its concrete expression'. The contrast between southern and northern Italy is important for grasping the differences between neorealist and Tendenza architecture. The context par excellence of neorealist architecture is Rome, while for Tendenza it is Milan. Casciato explains that 'Milanese architectural culture had maintained a sense of the continuity of the modern movement and the rationalist European experience'.[18] This can explain Rogers's choice to give *Casabella,* which he directed beginning in 1953, the subtitle 'Continuità'.

Between neorealist and Tendenza architecture

Neorealist and Tendenza architecture are both characterized by an anti-aesthetic and anti-elitist stance. Their points of convergence and of divergence are insightful for recognizing what was at stake in post-war debates around the notion of ugliness in relation to the question of morality in architecture. The practitioners of both shared an interest in increasing architects' responsibility, in re-establishing the relationship between reality and utopia and in critiquing the homogenized and impersonal functionalism of modernism. Manfredo Tafuri, in *Progetto e utopia*, finds an 'inherent opposition within all modern art ... [between] those who search the very bowels of reality in order to know and assimilate its values and wretchedness; and those who desire to go beyond reality, who want to construct *ex novo* new realities, new values, and new public symbols'.[19] In 'Architettura e Realismo' he poses the following questions regarding the relationship of Italian post-war architectural culture with reality: How far did the architect's ambition extend within the actual conditions so as to change reality through the architectural project? Under what conditions did architecture become relevant to post-war conditions? What formal aesthetic criteria and tools did the intelligentsia invent to inscribe its practice in the process of reconstruction in Italy of the mid-1940s?[20] While Tendenza architecture and neorealist architecture shared the interpretation of the architectural project as the very device of the architect-citizen by which to transform actual conditions, neorealist architecture went further and developed an architectural language based on a set of mimetic devices. Neorealism's paradox lies in this double vocation to imitate and also reinvent points of reference of Italy's cultural identity.

Torre Velasca and *La torre di Babele*

The Torre Velasca in Milan, completed in 1958 by the Tendenza studio BBPR (founded in 1932 by Gian Luigi Banfi, Lodovico Barbiano di Belgiojoso, Enrico Peressutti, and Ernesto Nathan Rogers), is a case study for reflecting on Tendenza's aesthetic theory (Figures 13.1a and 13.1b). Given that it provoked several negative reactions and has been often characterized as ugly, its examination illuminates Tendenza's stance towards ugliness. Its height of ninety-nine metres and its embodiment of certain forms found in medieval architecture provoked a great deal of criticism. The year it was completed, the French journal *L'Architecture d'aujourd'hui* regarded it as an effect of the Italian appreciation for 'ugliness, baroque inflammation, exaggeration, false originality, the strange, and the bizarre'.[21] *Casabella* responded to this critique's ironic title, 'Casabella ... casus belli?', with a text prefaced by the equally caustic title 'Si vis pacem demain ... para bellum ... aujourd'hui'.[22] Reyner Banham, who had enthusiastically defended the Smithsons' aesthetic view in 1959, further attacked Rogers's approach, labelling it 'Neoliberty'.[23]

Rogers presented the Torre Velasca project at the Congrès Internationaux d'Architecture Moderne or International Congresses of Modern Architecture (CIAM) in Otterlo in 1959, where he explained how the 'preesistenze

FIGURE 13.1a

FIGURE 13.1b *a and b* Torre Velasca (1950–8) by Ludovico Belgiojoso, Enrico Peressutti and Ernesto Nathan Rogers (BBPR). Photo by Marianna Charitonidou, 13 June 2018.

ambientali' was central for this project. Embodying cultural values without literally imitating past forms was BBPR's goal. Rogers said that Torre Velasca's design strategy was 'to epitomize, culturally speaking – while avoiding repetition of the expressive language used in any of its buildings – the atmosphere of the city of Milan, its ineffable yet perceptible character'.[24] He maintained that the objective was to convey 'the essence of history' and to 'breathe the atmosphere of the place and even intensify it',[25] and to oppose the *tabula rasa* logic of modernism by using contemporary technology – reinforced concrete – and assimilating urban history.

Despite the affinity of Rogers's views with the attention that Team X paid to significance of the moral aspect of architecture,[26] two Team X members, Peter Smithson and Jaap Bakema, sharply criticized the Torre Velasca when it was presented at the Otterlo conference. They perceived a contradiction between its indisputable contrast with the urban fabric and Rogers's conviction that it was a paradigmatic expression of urban coherence and the continuity of certain emblematic architectural forms in Milan, such as the Duomo. Smithson argued that the project was aesthetically and ethically misguided and could have dangerous consequences; it was 'a bad model to give because there are things that can be so easily distorted and become not only ethically wrong but aesthetically wrong'.[27] He accused Rogers of not being aware of his position in the society.

Ironically, Rogers, an emblematic Tendenza theorist and architect, specifically invited architects to understand their 'responsibilities towards tradition';[28] they were shaping an aesthetic view based on the understanding of tradition as 'life-world', as he wrote in 1954. The notion of responsibility was also central for Quaroni, who, as a representative architect and urban planner of the so-called neorealist architecture, believed that the architects should embrace the task of urban design. In 1956, he explored how architects could play a role in the formation of society in his keynote lecture 'The Architect and Town Planning' at the CIAM International Summer School, held at the Istituto universitario di architettura di Venezia (IUAV). In 1979, he expanded further on the topic, bemoaning how 'today, skilful architects console themselves by designing "their" architecture, and leave others the responsibility for a city'. He maintained instead that it is the architect's responsibility to reflect on the city's future and shape it. Cities had become 'too anonymous, too ugly, too inefficient', he said, because architects were doing nothing to change this situation, and left 'political friends ... [and] city planning cousins'[29] to decide both their own future and those of architects and the rest of society. When architects lose their sense of responsibility for urban transformation, he said, the result is an ugly city.

The Torre Velasca project embodied BBPR's intent to transcribe through architectural composition a given culture's characteristics without imitating an existing visual language. This intent recalls the neorealist approach, which also aimed to invent an architectural language, based on cultural points of reference; Quaroni and Rogers were thus prompted to reinvent the relationship between utopia and reality. Quaroni's approach is characterized by a belief in the potential of imaginary reality to revitalize urban design. In *La torre di Babele*, he expressed his belief 'in the creative value of utopia – of an imaginary reality ... which ... holds the seeds for revitalizing a process like urban planning that has lost its capacity for energetic response'.[30] Quaroni's conception of utopia's creative force as imaginary reality, capable of revitalizing urban planning processes, brings to mind Rogers's understanding of the 'utopia of reality' as a 'teleological charge that projects the present into the possible future'. For Rogers, the very potential of the 'utopia of reality' lay in the fact that 'its forms are still unrealizable'. Rogers believed that utopia had the capacity 'to transform reality in its deepest essence, in the moral and political, as well as in the didactic and pedagogical fields'.[31] The existential aspects of his perception of architecture's 'experience' draw on Paci's phenomenological perspective, who associated the problem of 'the heart of the city', the main theme of 1951 CIAM's congress, with the necessity of a 'synthesis of permanence and emergence'.[32] The 'città meravigliosa' of Quaroni, the neorealist, and the 'città analoga' of Rossi, the Tendenza theorist and architect, share the intent to transform the unrealized forms of the 'utopia of reality' into tangible and vital expressions of urban reality, where architecture is liberated from the conventional dichotomies of ugly/beautiful, ordered/diffused, rational/irrational. The means to realize this is to embrace a close understanding of reality as it is, without preconceptions about a city's vitality. To both Quaroni and Rossi, it is the grasp of this reality in its immediacy on which architectural praxis should be based, in particular the existing conditions of the urban fabric. Quaroni's intention to take as the starting point of his architectural design strategies the existing conditions was conceptualized through the notion of 'qualità diffusa', an expression of his rejection of the grand gestures of design and planning.

The critique of modernist functionalism and the reformulation of the models for judging the aesthetics of architecture and cities can be interpreted here as expressions of an epistemological shift in which the modernist universal user is replaced by the post-war hybrid, or pluralist, engaged user, an activator of change. For instance, both Quaroni and Rossi criticized modernist functionalism for being reductive, naive and homogenizing. To Quaroni, 'function cannot be determined by means of mere square or cubic meters, since it is a compound of physical, special, psychological, moral factors'.[33]

In *La torre di Babele*, Quaroni argues that 'the modern city is really ugly' and that the neglected lesson of historic cities is the well-integrated synthesis of function, technology and aesthetics. The quality of architectural and urban artefacts depends on the extent to which this synthesis is based on 'an immediate, direct, good-natured relationship'. Quaroni focuses on the tension between the historic and the modern city, ascribing the historic city's beauty to its 'clear design ... and structure' and claiming that the modern city was ugly because it was 'chaotic', a term he employs frequently in *La torre di Babele*, which opens as follows: 'The architect tends by its nature, and by professional deformation, to the total control of the city, as if it were a single building. But the mythical Tower of Babel, you know, never came to fruition.'[34] Quaroni adopts Henry Miller's definition of confusion – 'an order that you do not understand'[35] – to explain that the impossibility of modern urban control was due to the incapacity of architects to understand the order of post-war cities and their transformation and expansion.

The ugly and the poetics of non-fabulation

In contrast with Karl Rosenkranz's thesis that ugliness is the active negation of beauty,[36] Mark Cousins maintains that the ugly cannot be thought of as the opposite of the beautiful and defines ugly 'as a matter of place' and the ugly object as 'an object which is experienced both as being there and as something that should not be there'.[37] This sense of not belonging to one's place is similar to Deleuze's interpretation of neo-realism for cinema, as a profound stage of confusion that had led to the loss of belief in this world. The Second World War led to a post-war era characterized by 'situations we no longer know how to react to, in spaces we no longer know how to describe'.[38] This state of confusion, according to Deleuze, is not negative but constitutes an opportunity to invent new signs in cinema, as in the case of Federico Fellini's 'deliberate confusion of the real and the spectacle'.[39] This is valuable for architecture too. Deleuze's understanding of confusion can be compared to Quaroni's conception of the confusion of post-war Italian cities and the need to invent architectural and urban strategies that can respond to this confusion. Tafuri described Quaroni's compositional method as a 'poetic of non-fabulation'.[40] This distinction between a poetic of fabulation and a poetic of non-fabulation could help us grasp the perceptual mechanisms of Quaroni's design process.

Quaroni believed that the ugliness of modern cities could be avoided if architects could find ways to preserve and reinforce their role in the way cities expand. The inability to comprehend the order of the contemporary urban fabric is related to the perception that the modern city is ugly. He considered that architects should not understand ugliness as a product of forces that are external to their agency. Rather, they should try to reshape their epistemological tools and their conceptual edifice so that they can see how to transform the pressures of economics and politics into parameters that can be treated by architects and urban planners. He also thought that the distinction between the agency of architects and that of urban planners had to be dissolved, and that these different spheres of action and different realms of responsibility had to be articulated, as the only means to formulate an engine for a new societal order. In Rossi's introduction to *La torre di Babele*, he writes that 'Quaroni's theory ... revolves around ... the fundamental question: What does it mean for us architects if the modern city is ugly?' Rossi claims, however, that Quaroni failed to recognize the modern city's potential beauty because he blamed modern architecture itself instead of speculation and ignorance, the result of 'an absurd mechanism which operates on several different levels'.[41]

Any mutation of the way ugliness is conceived implies a transformation of the status of the relationship between object and subject.[42] In the case of the beautiful, the relationship between object and subject is of a different order than in the case of the ugly, in the sense that the spectator of beautiful objects is disinterested while the spectator of ugly objects is engaged.[43] This distinction could shed light on how Quaroni replaced the bipolar relationship beautiful/ugly with that of vital/non-vital. Engagement and civic responsibility were the means of upgrading the city's ugliness to its very vitality. At stake is not the flâneur's attitude of disinterest as an antidote to the vitality of the urban dynamic, not the opposition between a hyper-alert attitude and a disinterested one; rather, it is the suspension between engagement and disinterest. The flâneur, as conceived by both Charles Baudelaire and Walter Benjamin, views urban reality through a 'dissecting vision'.[44] In neorealism, 'there are always awareness and involvement'.[45] The kind of engagement that neorealism seeks to activate is related to 'social polemic', but not to propaganda.

To describe the viewer's state of suspension caused by his understanding of an object as part of both reality and ideality, Adam Fure employs the concept of 'in-between-ness "ugly"'.[46] According to Gretchen Henderson, a characteristic of ugliness, which is useful for grasping the nature of the relationship between the observer and the architectural artefacts in both Tendenza and neorealist architecture, is that it pushes and pulls 'a viewer towards alternative readings or connections of disparate parts'.[47] Because of this simultaneous attraction and repulsion, the viewer cannot stay disinterested. The viewer's imagination is activated in a different way when confronted with the suspension of the synthesis of architectural forms, which provokes an instantaneous immediacy in the perception of reality. Deleuze explains how a specific genre of cinematographic images provokes a fundamental disturbance of the visible and a suspension of one's perception of the world.[48]

The effect of suspension caused by the sense of simultaneous attraction and repulsion that an encounter with the city's 'ugliness' can produce could also be interpreted as the result of defamiliarization. According to Umberto Eco, Bertolt Brecht's works can function as 'open' because of the defamiliarization, or estrangement ('verfremdung'), of the work from the beholder, an estrangement caused by 'the specific concreteness of an ambiguity' and 'the conflict of unresolved problems'.[49] The way the aesthetics of the concrete is transformed into an instrument to access the immediacy of post-war reality, in the case of neorealism, is also an effect of defamiliarization, in the sense described by Eco. The subject is pushed to enter into a state in which it is no longer possible to be disinterested. Such an interpretation can help explain the engagement of post-war Italian architects in the reinvention of conceptual tools that would reshape the ugly aspects of urban and suburban formations. Immanuel Kant understands the impact of ugliness on the subject as part of an act of liberation from the search for order, the capacity of ugly artefacts to push 'the freedom of the imagination almost to the point of the grotesque'.[50]

The ethics of *aischros*

A common preoccupation of both Tendenza and neorealism was the concern for architecture's moral dimension. In neorealism, what was at stake was the moral dimension of ugliness. I would claim that the ambition to counter the city's ugliness is associated with overcoming an understanding of ugliness in mere visual terms. That the problem of urban expansion should be part of the architect's task became a common demand of different post-war Italian approaches. The exigency to reshape the architect's practice in order to embrace and reinforce the architect's responsibility for controlling urbanization and suburbanization is the core of Quaroni's point of view. This comprehension of ugliness as an ethical and cultural question brings to the fore Henderson's question: 'Is ugliness a cultural quest?'[51]

The neorealists believed that ugliness was a way to present the reality of the post-war Italian city. They wanted to recuperate the immediacy of reality, to instrumentalize and aestheticize urban ugliness, to transform ugly features of the urban landscape into architectural instruments of social and moral engagement, devices of reflection about how aesthetic criteria interfere with the meaning one gives to reality. The very basis of neorealism was the post-war identification of the aesthetics of the concrete with antifascist ideology through the act of grasping that immediacy of reality. The intention to respond to a context dominated by the raw material of '[d]estroyed cities, poverty, and a disintegrating social fabric'[52] was neorealism's point of departure. Such an understanding of the connection between ugliness and reality is apparent in post-war Italian neorealist cinema, such as Roberto Rossellini's *Roma città aperta* (1945) and Vittorio de Sica's *Ladri di biciclette* (1948).

That the connection of ugliness to morality was central for neorealist architects becomes evident in the case of the Tiburtino district, designed by Quaroni and Ridolfi and built between 1949 and 1954, which is often interpreted as a neorealist expression in architecture. For Quaroni and Ridolfi, building social housing in a suburban neighbourhood of post-war Rome contributed to citizens' moral engagement in the public sphere of urban life. Aesthetic criteria had shifted to political, ethical, moral, social and civic criteria. The morality inherent in aesthetic evaluation is apparent in Aristotle's *Poetics,* where the identification of something as *aischros* (ugly) has moral

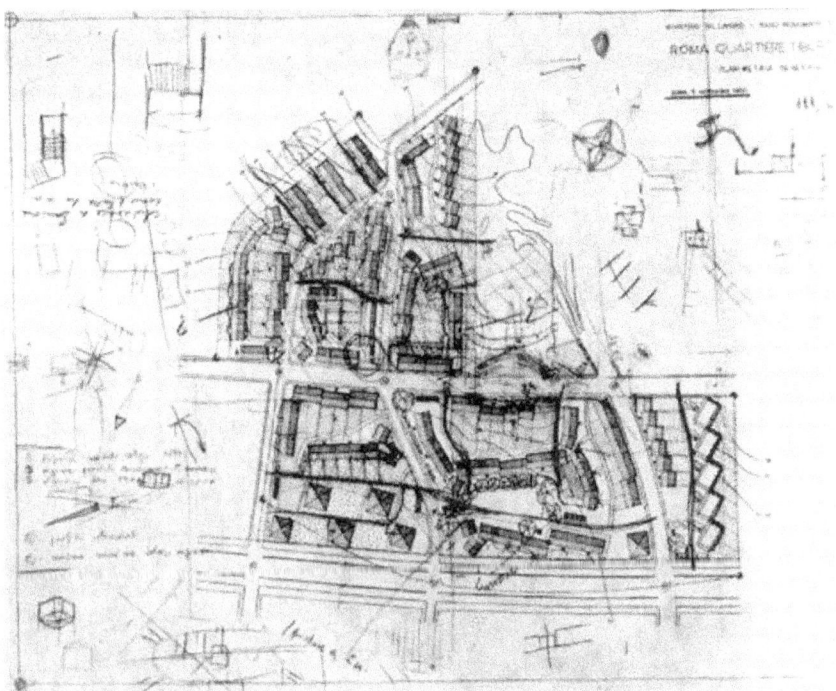

FIGURE 13.2 *Plan of the Tiburtino district, Rome, 1949–54. The main architects of the project were Ludovico Quaroni and Mario Ridolfi. Other architects who worked on this project were Carlo Aymonino, Mario Fiorentino, Federico Gorio, Maurizio Lanza, Piero Maria Lugli, Giulio Rinaldi, Michele Valori, Carlo Aymonino, Carlo Chiarini, Sergio Lenci, Carlo Melograni, Gian Carlo Menichetti and Volfango Frankl. Credit: Associazione archivio storico Olivetti, Fondo Quaroni Ludovico, Serie Progetti e corrispondenza, fasc. 130.*

as well as aesthetic implications.[53] Such a moral engagement is at the core of Tafuri's description of the Tiburtino district as a 'manifesto of a state of mind, of an impelling need to communicate, to build a reality together with society and not simply for society'.[54]

The project in the Tiburtino district, located along the Via Tiburtina that in the late 1940s was part of the expanding periphery of the city, is typical of the formal expression of neorealist architecture: no pre-established concept of compositional unity here, but rather one obtained through the aggregation of successive elements and the obsessive fragmentation of walls and fences (Figure 13.2). The project is characterized by the elaboration of formal discontinuities, the rediscovery of the value of streets where people walk and the surgical examination of the singularities of the visible world and everyday life. Quaroni and Ridolfi treated the housing unit form as a canvas on which to express the quotidian life of citizens. This treatment is evident

FIGURE 13.3 *Mario Ridolfi and others, Quartiere Ina-Casa Tiburtino a Roma. Lotto B, case con ballatoio, riproduzione fotografica. Courtesy Accademia Nazionale di San Luca, Roma. Archivio del Moderno e del Contemporaneo, Fondo Ridolfi-Frankl-Malagricci, www.fondoridolfi.org.*

in the photographs taken in the 1950s, where the movement of people on the streets recalls the quotidian aspect of the urban context (Figure 13.3).

The Tiburtino district was built within the framework of a program of the Italian state to build public housing throughout the Italian territory during the post-war years using funds managed by a special organization at the Istituto Nazionale delle Assicurazion, the Gestione INA-Casa. This context is important for understanding the urban ideology behind the project. The housing units were conceived as devices that would help the post-war citizens feel familiar with the new urban identity after the traumas of the war. Their forms, although they do not imitate the vernacular, are based on an intent to respect the human scale, places that invite their inhabitants to become familiar with a new urban identity. The housing units are not closed but rather are considered *non finito* objects that could be adjusted according to the future needs of the inhabitants.

The intention of the architects of the Tiburtino district project, to grasp the vitality of Rome, illustrates neorealism's wider intention: the transformation of the city's ugly features, its disorder, into architectural instruments of social and moral engagement. In 1954, Quaroni wrote that 'the baroque spirit is the spirit of Rome. It is a spontaneous generation, a creature of the site: autochthonous. It uses, even in the order of architecture, the vital disorder of the life of Rome.'[55] The aesthetic project of neorealist architecture lies in the double vocation to render architectural composition mundane and to renounce the artificiality of the new. In 1957, several years after the completion of the project, Quaroni said that vitality was evident in the Tiburtino district, and ugliness had become aestheticized: 'There was life, in any case, in the neighbourhood. Beautiful or ugly, it lived as best it could.'[56] This vitality was more important than anything else, and so replaced the opposition of beautiful/ugly with vital/non-vital.

This search for a method to respond to the post-war crisis was shared by Tendenza architects. Cristiana Mazzoni, in *La Tendenza: Une avant-garde architecturale italienne, 1950–1980*, reminds us that 'the word Tendenza designates the movement of these architects who, with Rossi, offer through their intellectual work an alternative and operational critique to the crisis of the European architecture, its professional structures and its system of education'.[57] In 1977, Rossi saw typology as an instrument for measuring reality and resisting the confusion of contemporary architecture, as he explains in the introduction to the Portuguese edition of *Architettura della città*: 'Topography, typology, and history come to be measures of the mutations of reality, together defining a system of architecture wherein gratuitous invention is impossible. Thus, they are opposed theoretically to the disorder of contemporary architecture.'[58] Because he believed that typology was both an antidote for disorder and a means to evaluate, he also thought that the choosing of the correct typology before the design process began was a way to avoid ugliness. A 'lot of architecture is ugly', he wrote, 'because it cannot be traced to a clear choice; without one, it is left deprived of meaning'.[59] This meant identifying 'the individuality of the urban artifact', because that 'moment of decision' was the one 'in which typological principles were applied to the real city'.[60] Rossi asserted in 1974 that 'if the modern city is ugly, as Quaroni says, it means that the models of reference have gradually worn out ... [and that the] rationalism that arose from the Haussmannian solutions has been lost; the capitalist modern city has, in its instability, the inability to give itself a face'.[61] A year earlier, however, in his introduction to *Architettura razionale*, the catalogue of the XV Triennale di Milano, which he curated, Rossi declared that 'there is no longer any ideological shield for ugly architecture',[62] an assertion that, coupled with the title he chose for the catalogue, creates an apparent paradox with his later idea that the very notion of rational architecture is ineffective.

For Rossi, ugly architecture was architecture that is not characterized by a clearly defined individuality and has not emerged through a clear typological choice. Pivotal for understanding what Rossi understood as clearly defined individuality is the notion of 'locus', which should not be equated with the notion of context. It concerns a 'relationship between a certain specific location and the buildings that are in it' that is at the same time 'singular and universal'.[63] Rossi conceives the city as the 'locus of the collective memory'. The defining parameters of an architectural artefact, then, are 'the autonomous principles according to which it is founded and transmitted';[64] architectural artefacts are both individual and social works. Rossi's view towards common architecture is therefore a positive one; his research was 'focused on the whole city, and not just on authored architecture'.[65]

However, Rossi's aesthetic view on ugliness in *Architettura della città* is different from that in *A Scientific Autobiography*. In *Architettura della città*, published in 1966, he identifies ugly architecture as one that does not derive from a definitive choice of typology. His criterion for judging if architecture is ugly or not is the extent to which its form-making was based on a clear choice of typology. His approach to disorder is negative but gradually changes to a selective affirmation of disorder. In his memoir *A Scientific Autobiography*, published in 1981, he writes that what he was trying to do was to understand the space of encounter between order and disorder: 'I felt that the disorder of things, if limited and somehow honest might best correspond to our state of mind. But I detested the arbitrary disorder that is an indifference to order, a kind of moral absurdness, complacent well-being forgetfulness.'[66]

He thus distinguished two types of disorder: the non-arbitrary that derives from honesty, which is appropriate, and the arbitrary that derives from indifference and moral absurdness, which is not. This attraction for 'the boundary between order and disorder' arises from his interest in 'the union of different techniques' that result in 'a sort of realization-confusion'. That boundary is a wall, 'a fact of mathematics and masonry', and so 'the boundary or wall between city and non-city establishes two different orders'.[67] To Rossi, the schism of order versus disorder parallels the distinction of urban and non-urban, unlike Zevi, for whom finding a building beautiful or ugly is the same distinction as architecture and non-architecture, distinctions that, along with city/non-city, are at the centre of the debate around ugliness within the post-war Italian context.

Rossi relates the notion of ugliness to a defamiliarization process of thought. He employs the term 'analogy' to describe the 'unforeseen results' of the encounter with architectural artefacts that intensify semantic ambiguity. In 'An Analogical Architecture', he adopts Carl Jung's definition of analogical thought as 'sensed yet unreal, ... archaic, unexpressed, and practically inexpressible in words'.[68] In 'The Analogous City', he explores the dialectics of the concrete, in particular the 'capacity of the imagination born from the concrete'.[69] If we adopt the view that the spectator of beautiful objects is disinterested, while the spectator of ugly objects is engaged, we could assume that ugly objects activate imagination. Such a hypothesis shows that Rossi's dialectics of the concrete is close to the aestheticization of the ugliness of post-war Italian cities. Rossi's belief in the creative force of concrete disorder reflects Kant's idea that 'ugliness is constituted by the free imagination being unrestrained by the understanding's need for order' and that 'ugliness pushes the freedom of the imagination to a high degree'.[70] Both positions interpret ugliness as a powerful source of creativity. In *A Scientific Autobiography*, Rossi employs the concepts of 'deformation' and 'bewilderment'[71] to describe the effect of confusion that is provoked when one looks in a specific way at urban artefacts such as the ruins of the city. He argues that his architecture was based on a desire to transform this sense of 'bewilderment' into projects.

Beauty is not the property of objects, says Kant, but rather emerges from the subject's experience of pleasure or displeasure. He notes, 'Fine art shows its superiority precisely in this, that it describes things beautifully that in nature we would dislike or find ugly.'[72] Architecture too has that 'capacity to be transmitted and to give pleasure', as Rossi says, but this capacity is part of technics – the 'means and principles' of architecture.[73] Rossi intends to discern the parameters on which architecture's capacity to transmit pleasure depends, a search for specifics of the sort that Zevi describes, in his *Saper Vedere l'Architettura* of 1948, when making a distinction between beautiful and ugly architecture: 'Beautiful architecture [is] ... architecture in which the interior space attracts us, elevates us and dominates us spiritually ... [while] ugly architecture would be that in which the interior space disgusts and repels us.'[74]

In 'The Analogous City', Rossi refers to the special 1976 issue of *Nuova società* dedicated to the question of 'how beautiful the city is', where beauty is identified with that which is useful.[75] In this issue, Carlo Aymonino's paradoxical assertion that 'the beauty of the city is that it was always ugly'[76] was a response to 'how ugly the city is'. Zevi had earlier advocated usefulness as the primary value for judging a space as either 'beautiful' or 'ugly',[77] rather than according to purely aesthetic criteria, which prompted him to ask some critical questions:

> What, then, is architecture? And, perhaps equally important, what is non-architecture? Is it proper to identify architecture with a beautiful building

and non-architecture with an ugly building? Is the distinction between architecture and non-architecture based on purely aesthetic criteria?[78]

Zevi believed that 'the content of architecture is its social content' and gave primacy to the experience of interior space, defining architecture as 'the way space is organized into meaningful form'.[79] Both Zevi and Rossi questioned the adoption of purely aesthetic or purely functional criteria and searched for the junction between use and aesthetic fulfilment. While Zevi proposed a conception of use, replacing impersonal functionalism with an organic architecture at the service of democracy, Rossi disapproved any ex nihilo aesthetic or functional models applied to new cities, and believed only in concrete opportunities, which could only be tested *hic et nunc* and emerge through analysis and comparison.

The paradoxical effect of both estrangement and familiarization at Torre Velasca creates a tension between 'continuità' and 'preesistenze ambientali' that Rogers espoused in Tendenza architecture.[80] Paci's view of the relationship between past and present helps us to see how both could exist at the same time: 'It is while questioning the past (but not by becoming the past) that I understand the present and the interest of the present for its own transformation.'[81] Similarly, what is at stake in Rossi's concept of analogy is a process of defamiliarization, which intensifies the semantic ambiguity Quaroni explored in his response to complexity of the modern city. The transformation of the status of the architect and his architecture has the potential to bring about the 'città meravigliosa', a term from his *La torre di Babele*,[82] where he insists on the capacity of the ancient city to express what he called 'qualità diffusa'.[83] Quaroni's quest for a diffuse or widespread quality is founded on his intention to conceive 'new forms of developed fabric', like his Tiburtino district, that responded 'to current housing needs, and to the requirements of ready-made and quantitative multiplication'.[84] In replacing beautiful/ugly with vital/non-vital, Quaroni demonstrates that the concepts of 'città meravigliosa' and 'qualità diffusa' cannot be understood without untying their existential load, which, as in Rogers' and Rossi's cases, moralizes ugliness. This appropriation of estrangement and defamiliarization and their existential implications justifies neorealism's and Tendenza's aestheticization of the ugliness of post-war Italian cities.

Notes

1. Aldo Rossi, 'Prefazione alla seconda edizione' in *L'architettura della città* (Padova: Marsilio, 1969), 3–7; 'L'architettura della ragione come architettura di Tendenza' in *Illuminismo e architettura del '700 veneto*. Exh. cat, ed. Manlio Brusatin (Resina, Treviso: Grafiche Giorgio Paroni, 1969).
2. Ernesto Nathan Rogers, 'Elogio della tendenza', *Domus* no. 216 (1946): 47.

3 Ernesto Nathan Rogers, 'Ortodossia dell'eterodossia', *Casabella Continuità* no. 216 (1957): 4; Ernesto Nathan Rogers, 'Elogio della tendenza' in *Esperienza dell'architettura* (Turin: Einaudi, 1958), 90.

4 Massimo Scolari, 'Avanguardia e Nuova Arhitettura' in Ezio Bonfanti et al., *Architettura Razionale: XV Triennale di Milano Sezione Internazionale di Architettura* (Milan: Franco Angeli, 1973), 153–87. Reprinted in English in *Architecture Theory since 1968*, ed. K. Michael Hays (Cambridge, MA: MIT Press, 1998), 131–2.

5 Ibid., 132; Francesco Tentori, 'D'où venons-nous? Qui sommes-nous? Où allons-nous?' in *Aspetti dell'arte contemporanea*, catalogue of the exhibition at L'Aquila, July 28–October 6, 1963, ed. Antonio Bandera, Enrico Crispolti, Sandro Benedetti and Paolo Portoghesi (Rome: Edizioni dell'Ateneo, 1963), 264–5.

6 Ibid., 137.

7 Enzo Paci, 'L'architettura e il mondo della vita', *Casabella Continuità* no. 217 (1957): 53–5.

8 Paci, *Diario fenomenologico*, 5th edn (Milano: Il Saggiatore, 1961),

9 Ernesto Nathan Rogers, 'The Image: The Architect's Inalienable Vision' in *Sign, Image, Symbol*, ed. György Kepes (New York: George Braziller, 1966), 242–51.

10 Gilles Deleuze, *Cinema 2: The Time-Image*, trans. Hugh Tomlinson and Robert Galeta (Minneapolis: University of Minnesota Press, 1989).

11 André Bazin, *What Is Cinema?*, vol. 2, ed. Hugh Gray (Berkeley: University of California Press, 1971), 25.

12 Bruno Reichlin, 'Figures of Neorealism in Italian Architecture (Part 1)', *Grey Room* no. 5 (2001): 83.

13 Bazin, *What Is Cinema?*, 64.

14 Maristella Casciato, 'Neorealism in Italian Architecture' in *Anxious Modernisms: Experimentation in Postwar Architectural Culture*, ed. Sarah Williams and Rejean Legault Goldhagen (Montreal: Canadian Centre for Architecture, 2000), 48.

15 Antonio Gramsci cited in Williams and Goldhagen, eds., *Anxious Modernisms*, 25.

16 Paci, *Diario fenomenologico*, n.p.

17 L'Associazione per l'architettura organica, 'La costituzione dell'Associazione per l'architettura organica a Roma', *Metron* no. 2 (1945): 75–6.

18 Casciato, 'Neorealism in Italian Architecture', 29, 31.

19 Manfredo Tafuri, *Progetto e Utopia: Architettura e Sviluppo Capitalistico* (Bari: Laterza, 1973).

20 Tafuri, 'Architettura e realismo' in *Architettura moderna. L'aventura delle idee nell'architettura 1750–1980*, ed. Magnago Lampugnani (Milan: Electa 1981), 123–45.

21 'Casabella … casus belli?' *L'Architecture d'aujourd'hui* no. 77 (1958): 55.

22 'Si vis pacem demain … para bellum … aujourd'hui', *Casabella Continuità* no. 220 (1958): 53.
23 Reyner Banham, 'Neoliberty: The Italian Retreat from Modern Architecture', *The Architectural Review* 125, no. 747 (1959): 231–5.
24 Ernesto Nathan Rogers, *Esperienza dell'architettura*, ed. Luca Molinari (Milan: Skira, 1997).
25 Ernesto Nathan Rogers, cited in Oscar Newman, *New Frontiers in Architecture: CIAM '59 in Otterlo* (New York: Universe Books, 1961), 93.
26 On Team X, see Luca Molinari, 'Constructing New Continuities in a Post-War World: The Relationship between Jaap Bakema and Ernesto Nathan Rogers' in *Un palazzo in forma di parole. Scritti in onore di Paolo Carpeggiani*, ed. Carlo Togliani (Milan: Franco Angeli 2016), 487–95.
27 Peter Smithson cited in Oscar Newman, *New Frontiers in Architecture: CIAM '59 in Otterlo* (New York: Universe Books, 1961), 94–7.
28 Ernesto Nathan Rogers, 'Le responsabilità verso la tradizione', *Casabella Continuità* no. 202 (1954): 1–3.
29 Ludovico Quaroni, 'Il ratto della città', *Spazio e Società* no. 8 (1979): 28.
30 Ludovico Quaroni, *La Torre di Babele* (Padova: Marsilio Editore, 1967).
31 Ernesto Nathan Rogers, 'Utopia della realtà', *Casabella-Continuità* no. 259 (1962): 1; Ernesto Nathan Rogers, *Utopia della realtà* (Bari: Laterza, 1965).
32 Rogers, *Esperienza dell'architettura*; Enzo Paci, *Esistenza ed immagine* (Milan: Tarantola, 1947); Enzo Paci, 'The Heart of the City', *Casabella Continuità* no. 202 (1954): viii.
33 Quaroni cited in Herman van Bergeijk, 'CIAM Summer School 1956', *Over Holland* 9 (2010): 123.
34 'L'architetto tende per sua natura, e per deformazione professionale, al controllo totale della città come fosse un'unico edificio. Ma la mitica Torre di Babele, si sa, non arrivò mai a compimento', from the epigraph in Quaroni, *La Torre di Babele* (my translation), cited in Antonino Terranova, *Dalle figure del reale: Risignificazioni e progetti* (Rome: Gangemi Editore spa), 22.
35 Henry Miller, *Tropic of Capricorn* (London: Penguin, 2015), 176.
36 Karl Rosenkranz, *Aesthetics of Ugliness: A Critical Edition*, trans. Andrei Pop and Mechtild Widrich (London; New York: Bloomsbury Academic, 2015).
37 Mark Cousins, 'The Ugly', *AA Files* no. 28 (1994): 61–4.
38 Deleuze, *Cinema 2*, xi.
39 Deleuze, *Cinema 2*, 5.
40 Manfredo Tafuri, 'Les "muses inquiétantes" ou le destin d'une génération de "Maîtres"', *L'Architecture d'aujourd'hui* no. 181 (1975): 17.
41 Rossi, 'Introduzione', in Quaroni, *La torre di Babele*, published in English as Aldo Rossi, 'The Tower of Babel' in *Aldo Rossi: Selected Writings and Projects*, ed. John O'Regan (London: Architectural Design, 1983), 36.
42 Kassandra Nakas, 'Putrefied, Deliquescent, Amorphous: The 'Liquefying' Rhetoric of Ugliness' in *Ugliness: The Non-Beautiful in Art and Theory*, ed. Andrei Pop and Mechtild Widrich (London: I.B. Tauris, 2014), 176.

43 Nicola Cotton. 'Norms and Violations: Ugliness and Abnormality in Caricatures of Monsieur Mayeux' in *Histories of the Normal and the Abnormal: Social and Cultural Histories of Norms and Normativity*, ed. Waltraud Ernst (London: Routledge, 2006), 122.

44 Kevin Hetherington, *Capitalism's Eye: Cultural Spaces of the Commodity* (London: Routledge, 2007).

45 Jim Hillier, ed., 'Part Three Italian Cinema' in *Cahiers du Cinéma. The 1950s: Neo-Realism, Hollywood, New Wave* (Cambridge, MA: Harvard University Press, 1985), 177.

46 Adam Fure, 'Glittering Ugly Objects' in *The Expanding Periphery and the Migrating Center*, ed. Lola Sheppard and David Ruy, 103rd ACSA Annual Meeting Proceedings (Toronto, 2015), 549, http://www.acsa-arch.org/forms/store/ProductFormPublic/103rd-annual-meeting-paper-proceedings-the-expanding-periphery-and-the-migrating-center [accessed 3 March 2019].

47 Gretchen E. Henderson, *Ugliness: A Cultural History* (London: Reaktion Books, 2015).

48 Deleuze, *Cinema 2*, 201.

49 Umberto Eco, 'The Poetics of the Open Work' in *The Role of the Reader: Explorations in the Semiotics of Texts* (Bloomington: Indiana University Press, 1979), 55.

50 Immanuel Kant, *Critique of the Power of Judgment*, trans. Paul Guyer and Eric Matthews (New York: Cambridge University Press, 2000), 126.

51 Henderson, *Ugliness: A Cultural History*.

52 Scolari, 'Avanguardia e Nuova Architettura'.

53 Aristotle, *Poetics*, ed. John Baxter and Patrick Atherton, trans. George Whalley (Montreal: McGill-Queen's University Press, 1997), 62.

54 Manfredo Tafuri, *Ludovico Quaroni e lo sviluppo dell'architettura moderna in Italia* (Milan: Comunità, 1964), 94.

55 Quaroni cited in Tafuri, *Ludovico Quaroni e lo sviluppo dell'architettura moderna in Italia*, 190.

56 Quaroni, 'Il paese dei barocchi', *Casabella continuità* no. 215 (1957): 24.

57 Cristana Mazzoni, *La Tendenza: une avant-garde architecturale italienne, 1950–1980* (Marseille : Éditions Parenthèses, 2013), 32.

58 Aldo Rossi, 'Introduction' in *Arquitetura da Cidade* (Lisbon: Edições Cosmos, 1977).

59 Rossi cited in Terry Kirk, *The Architecture of Modern Italy, Volume II: Visions of Utopia, 1900-Present* (New York: Princeton Architectural Press, 2005).

60 Pier Vittorio Aureli, 'Rossi's Concept of the Locus as a Political Category of the City', *OverHolland* 8 (2009): 59.

61 Aldo Rossi, *L'Analisi urbana e la progettazione architettonica: contributi al dibattito e al lavoro di gruppo nell'anno accademico 1968/69* (Milano: Clup, 1974), 61.

62　Rossi, 'Introduzione' in *Architettura Razionale: XV Triennale di Milano Sezione Internazionale di Architettura*, ed. Ezio Bonfanti et al. (Milan: Angeli 1973), 13.
63　Rossi, *The Architecture of the City*, 103.
64　Ibid., 127, 130.
65　Pier Vittorio Aureli, 'The Common and the Production of Architecture: Early Hypotheses' in *Common Ground: A Critical Reader*, ed. David Chipperfield, Kieran Long and Shumi Bose (Venice: Marsilio Editori, 2012).
66　Aldo Rossi, *A Scientific Autobiography*, trans. Lawrence Venuti, Oppositions Books (Cambridge, MA: MIT Press, 1981), 83.
67　Ibid., 50.
68　Aldo Rossi, 'An Analogical Architecture', *Architecture and Urbanism* 56 (1976).
69　Aldo Rossi, 'The Analogous City', *Lotus International* no. 13 (1976): 6.
70　Mojca Kuplen, 'The Aesthetic of Ugliness: A Kantian Perspective', *Proceedings of the European Society for Aesthetics* 5 (2013): 275.
71　Rossi, *A Scientific Autobiography*, 23.
72　Immanuel Kant, *The Critique of Judgment* (Indianapolis, IN: Hackett, 1987), 180.
73　Aldo Rossi, *The Architecture of the City*, trans. Diane Ghirardo and Joan Ockman (Cambridge, MA: MIT Press, [1966] 1982), 127. First published as *L'architettura della città* (Padova: Marsilio, 1966).
74　Bruno Zevi, *Architecture as Space: How to Look at Architecture* (New York: Horizon Press, [1948] 1957). First published as *Saper Vedere l'Architettura* (Turin: Einaudi, 1948).
75　Saverio Vertone, 'Com'è bella la citta', *Nuova Società* no. 67 (1976): 18.
76　Carlo Aymonino, 'Com'è brutta la citta', *Nuova Società* no. 159 (1979): 25.
77　Henri Lefebvre, *The Production of Space* (Oxford: Basil Blackwell, 1991), 128.
78　Zevi, *Architecture as Space*, 24.
79　Ibid., 49.
80　Ernesto Nathan Rogers, 'Continuità', *Casabella-Continuità* no. 199 (1953–54): 2–3.
81　Enzo Paci, *The Function of the Sciences and the Meaning of Man* (Evaston: Northwestern University Press, 1972), 24.
82　Antonino Terranova, *Dalle figure del reale: Risignificazioni e progetti* (Rome: Gangemi Editore spa, 2009), 28.
83　Antonio Riondino, *Ludovico Quaroni e la didattica dell'architettura nella Facoltà di Roma tra gli anni '60 e '70: Il progetto della Città e l'ampliamento dei confini disciplinari* (Rome: Gangemi Editore spa), 162.
84　Manuel de Solà-Morales, 'Quaroni, la distante lucidez', *Urbanismo revista* 7 (1989): 43.

CHAPTER FOURTEEN

Ugliness as aesthetic friction: Renewing architecture against the grain

Lara Schrijver

The growing discourse around the 'ugly' provides depth to a category of aesthetic experience and judgement that has been notably underrepresented.[1] To some extent, this growth is a response to an increasingly loaded discourse on beauty, in which, some have noted, speaking of beauty as such is no longer allowed.[2] While the notion of the 'ugly' has been similarly absent from architectural discourse, the field of aesthetic approaches in architecture has expanded, including a notable interest in architecture that is not deemed 'beautiful' but rather 'kitsch', 'ordinary', 'as-found' and other categories that preclude the type of aesthetic delight typically attached to the category of 'beauty'. The paradox of these categories is that they require their counterfoil (in the case of beauty, ugliness) yet simultaneously need to exclude the threat provided to the cultural order, as first coherently argued by Mary Douglas in 1966.[3] This implicit threat also shows the strength of the counterpart: ugliness not only contrasts beauty but also questions its rules and categories and thereby potentially recalibrates them. While this precarious condition is present throughout the history of architecture, it becomes a particularly salient point of discussion in the second half of the twentieth century, when the early detractors of modernism, such as the members of Team X, began to incorporate expressions of popular culture. Taking a cue from examples such as Marcel Duchamp's *Fountain* (1917) or Andy Warhol's Brillo boxes (1964), the Smithsons in particular began to include advertising imagery and the 'as-found' in their designs and their writings.[4] Marked by self-consciousness and self-reflection, the delineation of aesthetic quality thus was transferred from qualities intrinsic to beauty to a process of critical selection that substantiated an intellectual discourse on the role of the artist. This expanded field of what was considered art in the late twentieth century, most notably addressed by Rosalind Krauss in her 1979 article 'Sculpture in the Expanded Field', also complicated the debates on aesthetics in postmodern architecture.[5] In the post-war era, traditional architectural guidelines such as proportion, regularity or symmetry thus became increasingly guided by a variety of focal points: popular reception, engaging with the banal, or understanding the logic of spaces not typically included in architecture studies, such as Las Vegas, the developer's architecture of John Portman or the generic condition of airports and shopping malls.

In other words, the advent of postmodernism in architecture expanded the horizon of aesthetic possibility to include not just classical notions of beauty but also other interpretations and mechanisms, such as irony and pastiche. A key figure in this expansion is Charles Jencks, whose publication of *The Language of Postmodernism* introduced an explicitly inclusive approach that sought to position unconventional forms within a system of signs and coding that allowed aesthetic judgement to be suspended.[6] Jencks also reintroduced the value of historical forms and conventions that had been largely suppressed in favour of the clean lines of late modernism. Nevertheless, the horizon of postmodernism is neither the first nor the only place where aberrations of beauty have found a solid place to dwell; throughout history there are moments where these aberrations (briefly) gained their share of the footlights, such as the recurring interest in the grotesque.

Until the second half of the twentieth century, expressions of ugliness served primarily to show and reinforce the standards of beauty, and perhaps to provoke a moment of intellectual delight in knowing better. Postmodernism has been extensively discussed for the way it added symbolically meaningful elements and reintroduced ornamentation to the highly abstracted language of modern architecture. However, the implications of inhibiting the classical mechanism of aesthetic judgement, I will argue, underpin the aesthetically inclusive approach of postmodernism, which incorporates the ordinary, the explicitly symbolic and the banal in the interest of providing freedom from existing standards.[7] It is this mechanism that may indeed provide a form of friction that questions not just a particular convention but puts the entire framework of judgement to the test. As such, we must explore the role of ugliness as a form of renewal in the discipline.

Since the 1960s, when the very notion of beauty became less clear cut, the general notion of the 'ugly' gained various new connotations beyond its position as the 'antithesis of beauty', a position that is one of the driving forces behind Eco's and Mark Cousins's desire to study ugliness as a condition in its own right.[8] Eco states that in the first comprehensive study of the ugly, written by Karl Rosenkrantz in 1853, the author presents a spectrum of contorted forms and disproportionate beings to demonstrate that the ugly is itself more than merely the counterform to the beautiful – that it has its own spiritual, formal, social and moral dimensions that go far beyond purely aesthetic categories.[9] This independent approach to the ugly has become more and more relevant to the arts in general and to architecture in particular. If we focus on understanding the cultural function of what we typically denote as 'ugly' in any given time, or that which does not adhere to standards of beauty, it may also become more apparent which changes have been prompted by approaches that provided clear opposition to 'good taste' or to 'pleasing' architecture, such as camp, kitsch or pop culture.[10] What is perceived as 'ugly' may thus introduce a radically alternate aesthetic or attribute value to existing cultural expressions within everyday culture. Here, Boris Groys's identification of the continuously shifting line that separates the valuable from the worthless, and culture from profanity, is helpful in understanding what constitutes artistic innovation and which processes underpin its recognition and appropriation.[11] Thus, rather than focusing on the theoretical understanding of what constitutes the 'ugly', we focus on its role in transforming standards of beauty. To examine this role of aesthetic conventions in architecture requires first an exploration of the theoretical framework of the subjective experience of beauty that accompanies these conventions.

Beauty in architecture: Convention, natural order or social agency?

Notwithstanding notable departures throughout history in the direction of mannerism and the grotesque, architecture treatises and projects have repeatedly returned to the Vitruvian identification of *venustas* (beauty) as one of the three central functions of architecture: *firmitas*, *utilitas* and *venustas*. While definitions of what constitute this 'beauty' have changed over time, *venustas* remained a central and often unquestioned requirement within architecture and its theoretical foundations until the early twentieth century. Architecture is found to possess *venustas*, beauty, 'when the appearance of the work is pleasing and in good taste'.[12] This pleasing character is defined by eurhythmy, proportion and symmetry, among others. The 'ugly' is therefore defined by such perturbations of beauty as irregularities, discord and asymmetry, which in turn are dependent on a thorough understanding of aesthetic conventions. In his own treatise on architecture, Leon Battista Alberti shows an awareness of the central role of convention by adding the notion *concinnitas*, which implies 'propriety'. This notion of appropriateness furthermore suggests a moral undercurrent that resonates with the analysis of Mary Douglas: if what is 'out of place' (in her study, dirt) is threatening to the social order, it is the reinforcement of convention (in Alberti's work, through beauty) that strengthens it.[13]

Even when architecture was guided by generally accepted conventions, however, a contrary aesthetic existed that broke the rules yet did not diminish the stability and continuity of conventions. The clearly legible violations in mannerism, for example, of the sense of harmony and delight so admired in these treatises simultaneously reinforce the stability of their overall framework. At most, this provides an intellectual pleasure to the discriminating observer: the experience of seeing the principles being distorted is coupled with an intellectual pleasure of knowledge reserved for those initiated in the language of architecture. For example, Fil Hearn calls attention to the work of Horace, a contemporary of Vitruvius, who distinguishes licentiousness from poetic license, which both stabilizes the frame of aesthetic judgement and provides an intellectually satisfying experience:

> if the delectation of an aesthetic based on rules – rules like those controlling the orders – is satisfied by recognizing how the rules have been followed, then an aesthetic based on violation of the rules raises knowledgeable delectation to a more rarefied plane. The viewer attuned to such a work enjoys simultaneously both a knowledge of the rules and an awareness of how they have been broken, a more sophisticated cognition than the straightforward appreciation of regularity.[14]

The alternative aesthetic that violates expectation and consciously makes use of aberrations thus serves to demonstrate both aesthetic sensibility and intellectual capability. Such acts of disrupting beauty as a signal of aesthetic knowledge and prowess were strengthened with the rise of romanticism. Its sustained embrace of ugliness in the form of the grotesque is aligned with the subconscious and the sublime, introducing a darker undercurrent to aesthetic perception.

While adaptations of the Vitruvian triad recur, such as when Jean-Nicolas-Louis Durand favours the objective categories *économie* and *convenance*, the most rigorous changes in the assumed requirement of beauty took place in the early twentieth century. Various avant-garde movements such as dadaism, futurism and Soviet constructivism turned to jarring aesthetic experiences to heighten awareness of social and aesthetic conventions, or even to fundamentally transform perception. This became visible within many forms of artistic production, from the theatrical 'shock' of Bertolt Brecht, to atonal experiments in music by Arnold Schoenberg, to the futurists' appeal to destruction as a creative force and the dadaists' search for a rhythmic and primal tone of syllables.

The main precursor to these critical reinterpretations of art and culture, or what later was referred to as 'anti-aesthetics', must be sought in the late nineteenth century and the advent of romanticism, when the interest in inner logic and a natural order put these formal rule-based ideas of beauty into question.[15] In this period, classical notions of harmony, proportion and symmetry were put to the test by other forms of aesthetic appreciation, such as the fear and awe that determine the sublime. Although romanticism's dark and expressive experiments in literature, art and architecture did not necessarily seek out the 'ugly' as an aesthetic experience, the interest in decay and ruin as components of aesthetic reflection prefigured some later changes in aesthetic appreciation. Additionally, it was in the nineteenth century that Eugène Emmanuel Viollet-le-Duc called attention to the experience and perception of architecture as eminently distinct from the other arts:

> But, if everybody can detect bad grammar or an ill-made verse, if all ears are offended at a discord or a false note, it is unhappily not the same with architecture. A very few recognize a fault of proportion or scale, an error of construction, or a disregard of even the most vulgar rules of practice.[16]

The suggestion here is that although people are continually exposed to architecture, its complexity makes identifying particular flaws in and arriving at a discriminating judgement about it more difficult than in the other arts. From the classical period through the nineteenth century, this claim not only set architecture apart from (and above) the other arts but also revealed the emancipatory potential of architecture due to its particular social function, as can be seen, for example, in the writings of Augustus Pugin, John Ruskin and also Robert Owen, which relate aesthetic standards to moral, social and political considerations.[17]

The relationship between architecture's social role and its assumed aesthetic autonomy became increasingly complicated in the face of industrialization. Aesthetic principles were applied in societal critiques, technological progress and the (formerly) autonomous domain of artistic judgement and discrimination. While these areas often remain implicitly linked or even conflated, the alignment of 'beauty' with the 'good' is important to bear in mind.

Elaine Scarry demonstrates that this alignment has remained present within the traditional aesthetic vocabulary, as 'fair' may equally denote beauty or morality.[18] This close relationship remains appealing even as irony and scepticism have become more present in architecture and art theory. Yet even while the demonstration of the good and the just is a recurring pursuit in architecture, there are also moments in history when the opposite holds true: when dissonance is seen as a sign of authenticity or of elevated moral standing. In a review article on the role of ugliness in art, David Beech describes Scarry's understanding of beauty as the first 'training ground' for ethical living and argues for understanding the monstrous and the ugly in artistic production as an eminently political act, showing society the dark underbelly of the overly rigorous categories of artistic production.[19]

As architecture has historically set itself both 'apart' from the arts and at times 'above' the arts, architecture's continued use of aesthetics resides in the social dimension in a particular way. The distinction of architecture from the arts lies in its functional properties – the fact that alongside being aesthetically pleasing, it must also address a specific purpose – even while maintaining its artistic roots in the projective dimensions of conceiving a building, as captured by the Renaissance notion of *disegno*.[20] Yet the key to this discussion lies in two elements. First, the sense of social engagement is frequently conflated with the artistic form, beginning with the early writings of Pugin and Ruskin, through the Arts and Crafts, to the Werkbund and the Bauhaus and all the way through to the post-war avant-gardes, expressed by those who preferred a vernacular language that may at times have seemed 'ugly' or at least 'not beautiful', but also expressed by those who chose the cheerfully abrasive language of pop culture. In many cases, these forms of architecture appealed to a sense of beauty considered 'not beautiful' at that time, transforming what was conventionally accepted – the well-known grain silos of Le Corbusier that showed a functional aesthetic, the gaudy customized cars described by Tom Wolfe or the science fiction and pop culture gadgets applauded by Reyner Banham.[21] The second key element of the discussion is the actual transformation of aesthetic criteria, which may take place with or without a notion of social agency. All in all, these two elements intimated a shift in emphasis from the aesthetic considerations that formed a key feature to classical treatises, to a sense of social engagement expressed in alternative aesthetic approaches in the twentieth century.

From the nineteenth century onwards, the idea of social emancipation became increasingly prominent, leading also to the assumption that aesthetic invention could enhance social reform. The explicit goal of the futurists, for example, was to transform aesthetic principles through forms at odds with dominant standards of beauty, to run directly against the grain of what was deemed aesthetically pleasing, in order to awaken their viewers to other modes of perception and thereby prepare them for a modern life determined by power, speed and technology. Referring to Eco's chapter on 'The Avant-Garde and the Triumph of Ugliness', one reviewer notes that 'jarring forms, as exemplified by those of Picasso, became central to an artistic creed that would have baffled the ancients, just as it did many gallerygoers of the day'.[22] With the advent of the twentieth century, this implied ability of aesthetics to contribute to social reform began to create its own logic, with programmes from the Werkbund to the Bauhaus and many other avant-garde movements whose aim was to fundamentally transform the visual and spatial sensibilities of their viewers.

Against the grain of beauty: Mid-century transitions from ugly to ordinary

As Jencks notes in an early essay on 'pop' culture, postmodernism redefines and essentially expands the field of what is aesthetically acceptable.[23] Where the avant-garde made use of aesthetic experimentation to step outside the bounds of conventional beauty, introducing machines, cars and industrial production to the domain of artistic production, postmodernism introduced 'accepted' conventions that fell outside the realm of 'art' and elevated their status to the realm of artistic production. One of the early examples in architecture of this open approach was the 1957 exhibition *This Is To-Morrow*, held at the Whitechapel Gallery in London. In the small collage by Richard Hamilton that became the symbol for the event, the language of advertising is incorporated into the rendition of a home. More importantly for this discussion, the entrance to the exhibition was demarcated by a life-sized cardboard Robbie the Robot character from the movie *Forbidden Planet*. According to a review, this 'low-culture' sign at the door rendered the white space of the gallery more accessible, encouraging the children playing football in the streets to enter, while 'critics loosened their aesthetic criteria'.[24]

In both cases, the sense of friction that arises from the 'ugly' or the 'not beautiful', such as low-culture elements of advertising and science fiction, draws attention to what is not adequate, what runs against our sense of pleasure, contentment or harmony. The ugly is, in that sense, a more powerful experience than the ordinary, which, in contrast, can hide by virtue of its being a habitual part of the scenery.[25] It is not distinct, nor does it contribute anything of note to the surroundings; it rather fades into the background. At the same time, there was a moment when the ordinary was brought into focus, into the consciousness of architecture. While one may identify the ugly as a *negation* of beauty, if we take on the ugly instead as the type of critical interpretation signalled by Hal Foster, something that instigates a moment of reflection and awareness through its jarring effect, then the ordinary fulfilled a similar role for a brief period in the architecture of the 1960s.

Particularly prominent in the work of Alison and Peter Smithson, the ordinary played its part in the post-war transformation of architectural styles, which one might see as a precursor to the language of postmodern architecture. The post-war visual language of social realism in Great Britain (or 'kitchen-sink' realism, as many called it) drew a new attention to the scenery of everyday life. In the article 'To-day We Collect Ads', Alison Smithson refers to the 'magical power' of advertising and to the typical distinction between a liveliness of pop culture and the respectability of traditional arts.[26] The 'ordinary' became of interest to the Smithsons not only because it demonstrated how the majority of the European population lived but also because it contained within it an energy they did not find in classical works of architecture. These everyday items contained hidden hints about dwelling habits and aesthetic preferences and were continually rejuvenated by their very use. For the Smithsons, both the ordinary and the 'as-found', another notion they used to draw attention to what is already there, injected a sense of poetry into everyday life.[27]

Around the same time, Robert Venturi and Denise Scott Brown ventured to Las Vegas to understand what drew so many of their fellow Americans to the city.[28] Rather than follow the accepted judgement on Las Vegas as 'kitsch', Venturi and Scott Brown had their students examine the mechanisms of signage, expression, composition and traffic flows. In essence, they followed the principles of Scott Brown's erstwhile teacher and mentor Herbert Gans, who had reflected on the work of art as a 'social agent', in the sense that it demarcated symbolic capital (drawing on the ideas of Bourdieu) and offered a network of associations that situated its owner socially.[29] Gans also explored such everyday environments as Levittown, built to provide affordable yet distinctive housing for soldiers returning from the fronts of the Second World War.

The post-war turn to the ordinary and the everyday as an environment of *vitality* escapes the stultifying rules of aesthetic appreciation and the constraints of modern abstraction. From here, it is but a small step to distinguishing between 'kitsch', 'culture' and 'camp'. Susan Sontag, in the domain of art criticism, introduced a reflection on camp as a crucial and rejuvenating idea in art, one that performs precisely this social distinction between low culture and the ironic, high-culture appropriation of the vitality of pop expressions.[30] Charles Jencks also offers a notable position on 'kitsch' in architecture, acting as apologist for postmodern architecture while acknowledging its increasingly commercial character.[31] Following along the lines of his earlier essay on 'pop' and 'non-pop', he argues that the boundaries of aesthetic appreciation are in dire need of expansion. At the same time, he concedes that the practice of architecture is in regular danger of simply 'entertaining' or following the lines (and money) of those in power. In other words, his hopes for the vitality of pop culture and the friction produced by postmodern architecture were belied by its easy appropriation in general culture, with the headquarters of the Disney Corporation by Michael Graves as an example.

Ugliness and the Instagram era: The continued vitality of the anti-aesthetic?

The nod Jencks makes to the 'entertainment value' of architecture is an important one for today's culture. Ugliness may trigger renewal or transformation, yet once the 'not yet beautiful' has become an accepted expression, it can quietly leave the stage as a particular (and sometimes peculiar) moment in time. Yet this process also presupposes a dominant aesthetic norm, while the aim of postmodernism was to break open the field of dominant categories. With the fading of these categories, it also becomes more difficult to fulfil a function of transformation.

In the twenty-first century, nearly fifty years after the advent of postmodernism proclaimed the inevitable dissolution of universal standards of beauty and justice, moral and aesthetic categories nevertheless remain entwined. This persistence of a connection between morality and aesthetics suggests an underlying desire for coherence between content and form: even in resisting the simplified binary of good, or beautiful, and bad, or ugly, we continue to navigate the difficult waters of morality and beauty as not-quite-the-same and yet somehow in alignment. In a reflective piece in the *New Yorker*, Vinson Cunningham notes, 'Beauty does more than simply seduce: it masks and perfumes, freezes moral categories in place.'[32]

The salient feature of ugliness in terms of aesthetic development is its *contextual* value: in contrast to dominant aesthetic norms, it pushes against the boundaries, eliciting a response that reflects upon the dominant standard, and herein finds a new lease on life.[33] Ugliness is now more important than ever as an indication of resistance to the all-too-easy acceptance of the 'return to beauty'. Timeless and pleasing aesthetics may be so dominant in our environment that the varying approaches of collision (Zaha Hadid), excessive plastification (Jeffrey Koons) and decay may each be necessary to revive a sense of vitalism.

In recent decades, when visual media have permeated nearly every sphere of life with a proliferation of images, the 'beautiful' no longer is only an aesthetic appreciation; it may equally raise suspicion as 'inauthentic' or superficial. The grating forms of the 'ugly', whether in Brutalist architecture or 'ugly Belgian houses', may in this context of exaggerated aestheticization appeal to a fondness or an appreciation *because* it is ugly. The ugly then becomes a signal of authenticity or vitality, stronger than the intellectual signal of discriminating judgement. The production of ugliness, accompanied by friction and embodying resistance to simulated smoothness and perfection, may well be a political act that is eminently necessary in the age of Instagram.[34] As we post images of a life idealized in a series of perfected moments, the vitality of life as lived is hidden behind the surface of digital projections. Ugliness then might counter this aesthetic of apparent smoothness, asking the viewer to stop and register disharmony, distortion and perhaps even disgust.

In some sense, (pop) music underwent some parallel developments – a number of revolutionary transitions were determined by friction and dissonance, both denoting energy and vitality in a culture gone stale. The early days of rock and roll, punk music and hip-hop each laid claim to an unprecedented energy, which translated in many cases to harsh sounds. In architecture, there are times when a similar urgency is felt to provide alternatives to smoothness. In this sense, Instagram creates a need for the ugly, because smoothness creates a sense of overall similitude. Boredom is in essence the contemporary foil against which ugliness gains value.[35]

If the Romantic era is correct in suggesting that horror and disgust serve to reinforce a sense of vitality, then perhaps this is just what is required in a time where perfection seems paramount. And indeed, as the proliferation of savvy marketing produces ever more categories of sanitized perfection – formerly ignored marketing niches are now being subsumed under such labels as 'plus-size' models, 'mature' employees or even 'imperfect' vegetables – perhaps the *new* ugly and aberrant are to be reinvented as weapons that destabilize such categorization, allowing the fundamental irrationality and messiness of our imperfect humanity to resurface. By interrupting the flow of glances and swipes, much as the sublime did at the end of the nineteenth century, ugliness today might be less about testing the boundaries of aesthetic standards and instead about simply producing a glitch in today's aesthetic economy. Taken in this respect, the plea for ugliness is not so much a desire to violate an aesthetic sensibility, as it is a plea for regular and recurrent renewal of what constitutes beauty, and above all, the recognition that what we crave in the very idea of beauty is the vitality of life itself.

Notes

1 I am indebted to Bart Decroos, Arie Graafland and Kirsten Hannema for comments on and conversations about earlier versions of this chapter. Most notably Umberto Eco, ed., *On Ugliness* (London: Harvill Secker, 2007); Andrei Pop, Mechtild Widrich, eds., *Ugliness: The Non-Beautiful in Art and Theory* (London: I.B. Tauris, 2015); Gretchen E. Henderson, *Ugliness: A Cultural History* (London: Reaktion Books, 2015).

2 Jerome Stolnitz, '"Beauty": Some Stages in the History of an Idea', *Journal of the History of Ideas* 22, no. 2 (April–June 1961): 185–204; Elaine Scarry, *On Beauty and Being Just* (Princeton, NJ: Princeton University Press, 1999).

3 Mary Douglas, *Purity and Danger: An Analysis of the Concepts of Pollution and Taboo* (London: Routledge, 2000), 95–6, 163–4.

4 See, in particular, Dirk van den Heuvel, 'As Found: The Metamorphosis of the Everyday: On the Work of Nigel Henderson, Eduardo Paolozzi, and Alison and Peter Smithson (1953–1956)', *OASE* no. 59 (2002): 52–67.

5 Rosalind Krauss, 'Sculpture in the Expanded Field', *October* 8 (Spring 1979): 30–44. Its continued relevance is most evident in the recent revisiting of the original article: Spyros Papapetros and Julian Rose, eds, *Retracing the Expanded Field: Encounters Between Art and Architecture* (Cambridge, MA: MIT Press, 2014).

6 Charles Jencks, *The Language of Post-Modern Architecture* (New York: Rizzoli, 1977); his work did not stand alone; as early as 1956, the exhibition *This is To-Morrow* (Whitechapel Gallery, London) included numerous elements of pop culture and advertising imagery.

7 'Suspended judgement' in cognitive psychology favours the rational weighing of arguments over immediate moral judgements; yet here I also suggest it also related to the 'suspension of disbelief' that forms a key element in movie scenarios, for example, encouraging the viewer to temporarily suspend his or her critical faculties in order to engage with the narrative. For further reading, see also Douglas Rushkoff, *Media Virus: Hidden Agendas in Popular Culture* (New York: Ballantine Books, 1994).

8 Mark Cousins, 'The Ugly', *AA Files* 28 (Autumn 1994): 61–4.

9   Eco, *On Ugliness*, 16.
10 Particular reference works for this essay include Susan Sontag's 1964 essay 'Notes on Camp' in *Against Interpretation and Other Essays* (New York: Picador, 1966); Herbert Gans, *Popular Culture and High Culture: An Analysis and Evaluation of Taste* (New York: Basic Books, 1999); and Eco, *On Ugliness*.
11 Boris Groys, *On the New* (London: Verso Books, 2014), 102.
12 Vitruvius, *The Ten Books on Architecture* (New York: Dover, 1960), book I, chapter III.
13 Douglas, *Purity and Danger*, 41.
14 Fil Hearn, *Ideas That Shaped Buildings* (Cambridge, MA: MIT Press, 2003), 140–1.
15 Hal Foster, ed., *The Anti-Aesthetic: Essays on Postmodern Culture* (Port Townsend, WA: Bay Press, 1983).
16 Eugène Emmanuel Viollet-le-Duc, *Discourses on Architecture*, trans. Henry van Brunt (Boston, MA: James R. Osgood, 1875), 139.
17 Hanno-Walter Kruft, *A History of Architectural Theory* (Princeton, NJ: Princeton Architectural Press, 1994), 327 9.
18 Elaine Scarry, 'Beauty as a Call to Justice', Lecture, Harvard Thinks Big, Cambridge, MA, 4 May 2011, https://www.youtube.com/watch?v=OHxc1mCiaN8 [accessed 9 July 2018].
19 David Beech, 'On Ugliness', *Art Monthly* 344 (2011): 6–7.
20 Richard Sennett, *The Craftsman* (London: Allen Lane, 2008). Sennett treats this distinction, expressed in the transition from the medieval guild to the artist's studio, as one of the crucial transformations in most of the arts.
21 Tom Wolfe, *The Kandy-Kolored Tangerine-Flake Streamline Baby* (New York: Bantam Books, 1999); Reyner Banham, *Design by Choice* (New York: Rizzoli, 1981).
22 Amy Finnerty, 'Not Pretty', Sunday Book Review, *New York Times*, December 2, 2007, 732.
23 Charles Jencks, 'Pop-Non Pop (1)', *Architectural Association Quarterly* 1, no. 1 (1969): 59.
24 Brian Wallis, 'Tomorrow and Tomorrow and Tomorrow: The Independent Groups and Popular Culture' in *Modern Dreams: The Rise and Fall and Rise of Pop* (London: Institute for Contemporary Arts, 1991), 9.
25 For this line of reasoning, I am indebted to the discussions at an early colloquium on this topic in Brussels on 6 September 2016, particularly with Bart Verschaffel and Wouter van Acker.
26 Alison Smithson, 'But To-Day We Collect Ads', Royal College of Art, *Ark* 18 (November 1956).
27 A 2015 exhibition on the work of Alison and Peter Smithson, centred on Robin Hood Gardens, even took for its title *A Poetry of the Ordinary* (Cambridge, MA: Harvard University Graduate School of Design, September–November 2015).

28 Robert Venturi, Denise Scott Brown and Steven Izenour, *Learning from Las Vegas* (Cambridge, MA: MIT Press, 1972). For a further reflection on their work in particular, see Chapter Nine by Deborah Fausch elsewhere in this volume.

29 Herbert Gans, *Popular Culture and High Culture: An Analysis and Evaluation of Taste* (New York: Basic Books, 1974).

30 Susan Sontag, 'Notes on Camp' in *Against Interpretation and Other Essays* (New York: Farrar, Strouss and Giroux, 1966): 275–92.

31 Charles Jencks, 'Post-Modernism Between Kitsch and Culture' in *Post-Modernism on Trial*, Architectural Design Profile 88 (London: Academy Editions, 1992): 24–35.

32 Vinson Cunningham, 'The Ugly Truth', *New Yorker*, 16 December 2015, https://www.newyorker.com/culture/cultural-comment/the-ugly-truth [accessed 8 July 2018]. Although it is beyond the scope of this article, an interesting television series to study in this light might be *Once Upon a Time* (Dir. Adam Horowitz and Edward Kitsis, 2011–18), which complicates the classic fairytales, blurring the boundaries between good and evil, although all characters other than Rumplestiltskin are more or less beautiful.

33 For how ugliness only has intrinsic aesthetic value in certain contexts, see Matthew Kieran, 'Aesthetic Value: Beauty, Ugliness, and Incoherence', *Philosophy* 72, no. 281 (1997): 383–99.

34 Beech, 'On Ugliness', 8.

35 Christian Parreno, 'Boredom as Space: Episodes of Modern Architecture' (Dissertation, Oslo School of Architecture and Design, June 2017).

CHAPTER FIFTEEN

Ugliness, or the cathectic moment of modulation between terror and the comic in postmodern architecture

Wouter Van Acker

The word 'ugly' comes from an Old Norse word meaning 'to be feared or dreaded', according to the *Oxford English Dictionary*. Gretchen E. Henderson argues that throughout time, what 'we' judge to be ugly, out of fear of certain objects and subjects which we perceive as strange or 'other', has shifted.[1] In a series of publications from the late 1950s and 1960s, modernist architects attributed the horrific nature of the uglification of the urban landscape to the unbridled process of urbanization and suburbanization and a lack of planning regulations. Their wistful aesthetic gaze at the terrifying scenery of urban sprawl was primarily articulated by employing the notion of ugliness, rousing a sensation of anxiety for an uncontrolled and unstoppable commercialization and car-oriented decentralization of the urban environment. In the 1950s, *The Architectural Review* was an outlet where protagonists of the Townscape movement such as Hubert de Cronin Hastings, Gordon Cullen and Ian Nairn proposed picturesque urban design methods to counter the increasing urban blight. In *Outrage* (1955) and *Counter-Attack against Subtopia* (1957), Nairn proclaimed 'a prophecy of doom' about the 'morbid condition' of what he dubbed 'subtopia' or 'the world of universal low-density mess'.[2] In Robin Boyd's *The Australian Ugliness* (1960) and Donald Gazzard's *Australian Outrage* (1966), the authors lamented the degenerate nature of the urban environment and called the profession to arms to brace against this menace of visual decay.[3] In the United States in 1964, Peter Blake published *God's Own Junkyard*, in which he showed with aerial photographs the cancerous breaking down of the original 'beautiful' American landscape into 'the biggest slum on the face of the earth'.[4] The socialist architect Renaet Braem labelled Belgium 'the ugliest country in the world' in his book of 1968 with the same title (in Dutch) that vilified the effects of the 1948 Act in Belgium, passed by the Catholic government, that gave subsidies to families to construct and own their own houses. He fulminated against the lack of planning regulations and the promotion of a suburban, family-oriented model that accelerated the sprawl of detached houses over the countryside and intensified 'land speculation, ribbon development and the rise of ugliness'.[5]

Starting with a discussion of how terror and ugliness were linked in the literature mentioned above, with a focus on Boyd's *The Australian Ugliness*, this essay retraces and analyses how postmodern architects like Denise Scott Brown and Robert Venturi, Maggie Edmond and Peter Corrigan – who founded the firm Edmond & Corrigan in 1975 – and Rem Koolhaas responded to this outrage and indignation over the uglification of the urban landscape. They wrote of ugliness as something other than 'to be feared or dreaded', and in their architectural projects, they demonstrated how one 'must know how to make the best of ugliness itself', to use Koolhaas's definition of the ugly.[6] Through their eyes, I examine the relationships between the ugly, the ordinary and the monstrous, which provided the structure for the two sections of this volume, in the light of a different dynamic, namely the modulation between the terrible and the comic.

Larger than the real: The man-made monster of suburbanization

In the opening line of *The Australian Ugliness*, 'The ugliness I mean is skin deep', Boyd makes clear that the book, published in 1960, is positioned within the debate about ugliness and outrage in response to the degradation of the built environment and the failure of the planning and design profession to steer the forces of modernization in the right direction. Unlike other laments about the effects of the roadside blight on the landscape, Boyd's judgement of ugliness is not only a moral, socio-critical assessment of the trajectory of Australian architecture but also an explicit aesthetic critique of cultural and social behaviour.[7] He argues that, just as we try to hide anxiety below our skin, the commercial veneer that covers the urban landscape camouflages the ugly feeling of anxiety caused by domestic dementia and national self-denial. 'There can be few other nations which are less certain than Australia as to what they are and where they are', Boyd says.[8] To compensate for this absence Australian architecture borrows from 'three remote

FIGURE 15.1 *Robin Boyd, cover of* The Australian Ugliness, *1960.* © *Estate of Robin Boyd, courtesy Robin Boyd Foundation.*

points of the compass': It copies the Georgian style, to display its English origins; it copies the American Californian Bungalow style, and more widely 'the trash which America itself is trying to eliminate', for which he coined the term 'Austerica'; or it follows the Orientalism advocated by the late Hardy Wilson and popular since the 1950s.[9] To escape the identity crisis, ordinary builders inject a mix of snippets from one or several styles into their architecture, resulting in the epidemic of 'prettiness' or 'featurism'.

Despite being the chief spokesperson in Australia for international modernism and against tacky parochialism, Boyd thought that architecture needed to address the real and the ordinary if it was to succeed aesthetically. Architecture could not just be informed by the 'laws of beauty in the works of the great creators', an idea conveyed in the cover image of the book (Figure 15.1) in which a Classical sculpted female torso atop a fluted column rises amid a mare's nest of electric wires and poles. Escaping from this 'gilded prison for the spirit' requires a 'capacity to appreciate the unbeautiful', which will liberate the mind 'from the sirens of beauty, pleasingness, delight', thus enabling it 'to create and to appreciate the real thing, the whole thing'.[10] Honesty in design is 'an intellectual, ethical and emotional exercise' that requires portraying the world as it is, evil and ugly, 'distinct from the way it is represented by the paid or honorary purveyors of Featurism'. Boyd ends his book by stating that the ugliness of Australia begins with fear of reality, denial of the need for the everyday environment to reflect the heart of the human problem, satisfaction with veneer and cosmetic effects. It ends in betrayal of the elements of love and a chill near the root of national self-respect.[11]

The pleasing cosmetics of the Australian ugliness might keep the eyes entertained, but it lacks, Boyd says, the expressiveness, cohesion and clarity of form and ideas required for architecture to be a true work of art. The masquerade, the skin-deep layer of veneer, reflects a timidity to face the psychological complex of feeling dislocated, which in itself was a result from the brutal way in which Australia's land had been colonized.[12] 'Arboraphobia', or the fear of native vegetation, is another of his neologisms that point to the terrors in the national psyche that drove suburbanization and the bulldozing of the original landscape.[13]

In voicing the failure to genuinely express the historic moment, or reality, in architecture, Boyd's work raises the question of how the aesthetic register of ugliness and the terrible relate to one another. Mark Cousins's typologies of the ugly here are helpful.[14] The ugly, he says, is either what is there but should not be, using the example of the stain and the facial wound, or what is not there but should be, invoking the concepts of the ghost and the mask. The ugly appears like a stain, dirt, dust or weed, something that is 'out of place'; a presence that one encounters as an excess of reality. The more we focus on it, the more we become obsessed by the impossibility of cleansing it. The ugly makes its appearance, like a wound, when there is a shift in balance from the exterior face, whose depth we read as an expressive representation of what is inside one's mind – how one is feeling – to the interiority of matter, a shift that inhibits the exterior from behaving as representation. The mask is expressionless because its exterior is static and it has no interior, while the ghost fails to have a body and therefore to represent. Wounds, stains, masks and ghosts are *terrible and ugly* because they are 'existence itself', obstacles that stand in the way of representation and thus of being 'read' by the subject.[15]

Cousins's theory of the ugly – the incapacity of the subject to align interior with exterior in the encounter with an architectural object – helps us understand how the ugliness debate of the 1950s and 1960s find their apotheosis in Koolhaas's writing. From *Delirious New York* (1978) to his 'Generic City' (2000) and 'Junkspace' (2001) essays, he conceptualizes the capitalist detachment of the inside and outside. He characterizes the built production of the ever-expanding, unstoppable growth of Asian monster cities as simultaneously repressing the formal and making the formless proliferate; the age-old paradigm of representation and correspondence between inside and outside is replaced by a hyper-mess, absorbing all that is incompatible into new oxymorons:

> We do not leave pyramids. According to a new gospel of ugliness, there is already more Junkspace under construction in the 21st century than

survived from the 20th ... It was a mistake to invent modern architecture for the 20th century. Architecture disappeared in the 20th century; we have been reading a footnote under a microscope hoping it would turn into a novel; our concern for the masses has blinded us to People's Architecture. Junkspace seems an aberration, but it is the essence, the main thing.[16]

Neologisms such as 'cyber-vomit', 'corpotainment' and 'ecolomy', and the epigrammatic descriptions of airports as glistening 'cyclopic dewdrops' or of Calatrava's bridges as 'grotesquely enlarged versions of the harp' exemplify how Koolhaas tries to come to grips with this engulfing ugliness through a witty, journalistic projection of linguistic nets. Although in its non-judgemental perspicuity, his attitude towards this unconstrained urbanization is different from publications like *God's Own Junkyard*, its dazzling, oxymoronic language does evoke the terror of the all-absorbing monstrous entropy and satanic multiplicity of junkspace. Like the ugliness and outrage discourse of the 1960s, the rapidly changing urban condition is sublimated to monstrous proportions.

This succession of writings from the 1960s to the 1990s casts the scenery of unbridled urbanization not only as terrible but also as *monstrous*. Set against the body of classical aesthetics, as Mark Dorrian summarizes, the monstrous goes against what has been naturalized.[17] It is 'against-nature' and ceaselessly assimilates and appropriates the 'many in the one' in incommensurable and irrational hybrids. The fear triggered by the monstrous is unleashed when the state of normality, all that was distanced and kept apart, collapses in a contagious disease of unreasonable juxtapositions. Monster, or *monstrum*, is linked to the Latin word *monere*, to warn, as well as to *monstrare*, to show. The aforementioned essays strike a disquieting tone when they reveal how a monstrous ugliness is spreading over the urban reality like an alien contagion infecting the earth. For example, Koolhaas portrays the architecture of the 'Generic City' as an 'epidemic of yielding ... through the *systematic* application of the unprincipled', absorbed in a 'parasitic swerve of infrastructure' and the fact that postmodernism '*will always remain*' its style of choice because it 'has succeeded in connecting the practice of architecture with the practice of panic'.[18]

In the literature reviewed above, the planetary scale with which the ugliness and the monstrous forces of urbanization are spreading over the urban reality, from the west to the east, from north to south, moves ugliness towards the sublime. In the negative aesthetic experience of the sublime, we feel overwhelmed by the vast scale and evil forces of nature. 'The experience of the sublime,' Terry Kirk reminds us, 'pushes the limits of human senses and tests the boundaries between known and unknowable.'[19] For Jean-François Lyotard, ugliness can be experienced as sublime if its deviance is shocking. The sublime operates through collective anxiety about the fact that we fail to grasp its extent.

The ugly and the terrible as aesthetic descriptors of urbanization recall Adorno's observation that a 'bourgeois consciousness [that] naïvely condemns the ugliness of a torn-up industrial landscape' reveals in its indignation the bourgeois 'ideology of domination'.[20] Disenchantments with commercial transformed landscapes were doomed premonitions, according to Adorno:

> The reduction that beauty imposes on the terrifying, over and out of which beauty raises itself and which it banishes from itself as from a sacred temple, has – in the face of the terrifying – something powerless about it. For the terrifying digs in on the perimeter like the enemy in front of the walls of the beleaguered city and starves it out.[21]

The heroic, sacred value of a self-sufficient beauty – paralleled by a banishment of all anxieties and everything that is condemned by art and architecture under the formal category of the ugly – was perceived by Adorno to have lost its mythical shield. The postmodernist response to the menacing urban reality found a way of formulating a new (anti-)aesthetic distance by encountering, appropriating and producing a 'pleasure of relief, of delight' in a return to the real and within the ugly that had gone under the skin.[22]

Change of scene: Modulations between the terrible and the comic

The change of scene that announces itself with postmodern architecture's engagement with the 'ugly and ordinary' can be thought of metaphorically through Sebastiano Serlio's sixteenth-century models of a tragic, satirical and comic scene. In opposition to the symmetrical 'tragic scene' and as an inversion of the grotesque 'satirical scene' of a sylvian nature, the following case studies or 'acts' take place on the 'comic scene' (Figure 15.2). As Peter Womack argues, Serlio's comic scene is fundamentally illusionistic and urban in character: its projection of an extreme heterogeneity of architectural styles and building types evokes a 'generic' urbanness, brought under control by subject positioning and linear perspective – the vanishing point of which is concealed. The 'comic scene' is conceived as lower; it accepts its secondariness because comedy deals with 'citizens rather than kings, and with commonplace mishaps and satisfactions rather than heroic crimes and virtues'.[23] The comic scene is a 'mentalistic space' of representation and reflection that separates the material from what is intelligible.

This description of the comic scene as conducive to producing a 'mentalistic' distance applies well to the role humour plays in postmodern architecture. Humour reflexively internalizes the negativity of the preceding thrilling scene in which the expansion of urban ugliness was cast as dreadful. Humour, as Barbara Kruger pointed out, has 'the ability to step outside

FIGURE 15.2 *Sebastiano Serlio, The Comic Scene, from Sebastiano Serlio,* The First [-Fift] Booke of Architecture *(1475–1554; London: Stafford, Simon, 1630), scanned from Columbia University Libraries.*

of it all and still get under its own skin'.[24] As such, humour is an effective defence weapon that obtains pleasure by dissolving 'ugly feelings' such as terror, anxiety, disgust or irritation.[25] A surrealist joke of black humour, used by Freud and quoted by Breton to demonstrate this liberating effect, is 'the condemned man being led to the gallows on a Monday who observes, "What a way to start the week!"'[26] Freud remarks that humour 'refuses to be hurt by the arrows of reality or to be compelled to suffer', that 'it insists that it is impervious to wounds dealt by the outside world, in fact, that these are merely occasions for affording it pleasure'.[27]

Humour's liberating effect results from displacing psychic attention from subordination to a frame of mind that takes control of a situation, elevates it to a state of intellectual pleasure and attacks sentimentality or complaint. It takes energy from unpleasant emotions and then discharges that energy, the expenditure of which generates pleasure. 'In laughter,' Freud says, 'the conditions are present under which a sum of psychical energy which has hitherto been used for cathexis is allowed free discharge.'[28] If the pleasure in humour emerges from an 'economy in expenditure upon feeling',[29] then the pleasure that is experienced through the comic in general results from an 'economy in expenditure upon ideation (upon cathexis)'. A joke isn't a joke without laughter. Laughter indicates the moment when cathexis, or the sum of psychical energy, is discharged. By the hearing of a joke a lifting of inhibitory cathexis takes place.

Boyd used deadpan humour to launch biting assaults on Australia's ornamental deficiencies and car-oriented lifestyle – its 'Cadillac cult' or 'Statler-Hilton culture'.[30] These assaults differ from embracing humour as a productive source for postmodern architectural design, which Edmond and Corrigan, Scott Brown and Venturi, and Koolhaas do in their projects and operative writings. The various tenets of humour that these architects appeal to when dealing with the issue of ugliness are not vehicles of public mockery or polemical tools of caricature, but vehicles that induce an aesthetic sensation of liberation and delight.[31]

In the comic, the mobilization of the cathectic energy often results from expectation.[32] Architecture, which is charged with the cathectic tension of aesthetic expectations, can strike a postmodern pose that intentionally fails to meet modernist expectations. This comic stance is essential to the production of the postmodernist ugliness that often flirted with the performative-oriented notion of 'camp' or the object-oriented notion of 'kitsch'. As Susan Sontag notes,

> Camp proposes a comic vision of the world. But not a bitter or polemical comedy. If tragedy is an experience of hyperinvolvement, comedy is an experience of underinvolvement, of detachment.[33]

Kitsch is about discharging the serious and about making seriousness fail. This detachment from reality is realized by looking at the world as if everything existed on a theatrical stage on which persona appear rather than personalities.

The aesthetic of the comic and, in particular, the comic form of the joke is a recurring passageway through which a confrontation with the negative effects of ugliness passes. For Kuno Fischer, the joke has an aesthetic subjective relation towards its object, which is nothing less than the 'concealed ugliness of the world of thoughts'.[34] Just as the ugly is a judgement, so too is a joke a judgement that, as Fischer says, 'produces a comic contrast'. We can judge a difficult contrast to be ugly *and* comic at the same time, and in this judgement 'the joke' unfolds or attains its form.

Act I: Peter Corrigan's architectural theatre

A comic architectural scene can emanate from a grotesque scene of suburbanization, as illustrated in the work of Edmond and Corrigan. Their projects can be read as a case in point of how the cathexis built up around the laments about the post-war suburbanization can be inverted into a comic scene where architecture is staged as a play about the urban scenography of architecture itself.

Corrigan and Edmond, the antipodean Venturi and Scott Brown, played a seminal role in transplanting postmodernism onto Australian soil and exploring the potential of strategically sampling 'ugly and ordinary' features of the Australian suburbs.[35] After studies at Melbourne University, Corrigan completed a postgraduate course at Yale University under Charles Moore, Paul Rudolph and Vincent Scully. He was there in 1970 when Venturi and Scott Brown held the Learning from Levittown studio, but Corrigan did not participate in it because he found they were too like-minded.[36] Corrigan acknowledged this in an article on the Venturis in 1972, in which he compared the house he designed for Mr and Mrs Kevin McCarthy (1967) to Venturi's house for his mother (1963) (Figure 15.3). Shortly after returning to Melbourne in 1974, he partnered up with Maggie Edmond, who had graduated from the University of Melbourne in 1969 and had worked in several architectural firms in Melbourne. The early projects of Edmond & Corrigan, such as St. Colman's Church (1974) or Keysborough Church (1976), appropriated the pluralistic, tatty mediocrity of urban development, traditionally spurned as antithetical to modernistic values.[37]

Corrigan and Edmond's answer to the issue of 'ugliness' diagnosed by their compatriot Robin Boyd, who had died in 1971, was to pursue a direction unlike the Brutalist strategies and fascination with raw concrete and 'as-found' finishes employed by people like James Birrell. The title of the latter's autobiography, *A Life in Architecture: Looking Beyond the Ugliness*, demonstrates the weight that Boyd's enormous journalistic output, his role in creating model modernist houses and his engagement in public life

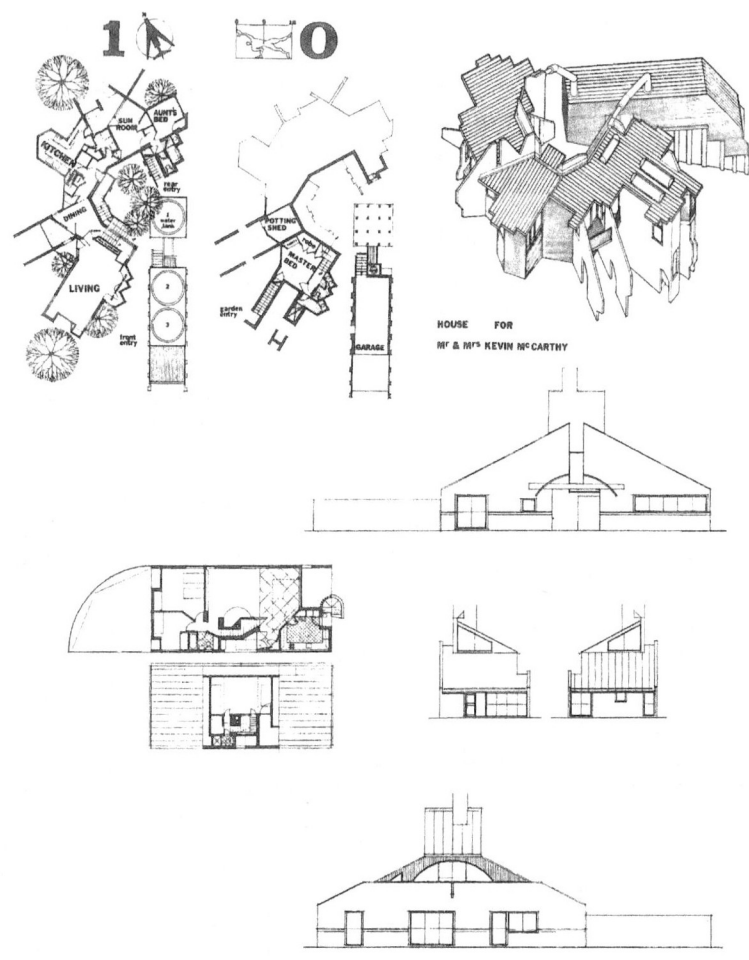

Above is a house by the author, built in 1967, outside Melbourne. It reveals some of the prevailing interests of the sixties, Kahn, Medieval cities, etc. Below it is a house built in 1963 by Robert Venturi for his mother in Philadelphia. While it was designed at about the same time, it displays a new way of looking at form and interior space. Venturi said, "It is a sort of a child's concept of a house." The relatively simple, though sophisticated exterior hides a complex interior; rooms are irregular shapes and the scale is small, in contrast to the oversize facade, which, rumour has it, is in homage to Sir John Vanbrughs' Blenheim Castle. The plan is particularly tight with little net square footage wasted. However, a curved clearstory window leaps up over the dining area, the fireplace is oddly shaped and seems to struggle for space in the central core of the house with a crooked stairway, which is wide at its base but abruptly squeezes to a narrow shape as it approaches the second floor, expressing, says Venturi, the different scales of the downstairs and the more private upstairs.

FIGURE 15.3 *Peter Corrigan, House for Mr and Mrs Kevin McCarthy, Melbourne, built in 1967; compared to Robert Venturi's house for his mother, Philadelphia, 1963. Originally published in* Architecture in Australia *February 1972.*

continued to have within the architectural discourse in Australia, and in Melbourne in particular.[38] Peter Corrigan recapped the liberating effect of postmodernism that followed this Boyd-era:

> Suburbia was ruefully described in the 1960s by Robin Boyd. Subsequently, it has been lucratively mocked by Barry Humphries and the ABC. But the values of the bourgeois Australian dream of a free-standing brick house with a tiled roof on a quarter-acre block of land are being re-examined by a new generation of architects. These values offer no social redemption, but at least they are Australian. They owe nothing to the inner-city, the outback, or the dream-time.[39]

One of the major events that determined the reception of postmodernism in Australia was the *Pleasures of Architecture* conference held in Sydney in 1980.[40] The title hints at the enjoyment of postmodernism that Eco would later express in his text 'Postmodernism, Irony, the Enjoyable' (1983) – replacing laments about the lack of an earnestness with an enjoyment of layered hybridity of urban culture. It is in this context of a lost innocence of abstraction, that during the closing debate of this conference, Koolhaas described Corrigan's work as 'an architecture of fresh transplantations' that is at the same time 'so Australian'.[41]

A notable work of Edmond & Corrigan is their RMIT Building 8 (1993), acknowledged, with notable awards, as a monument of postmodernism but equally vehemently dismissed as ugly, in the *Architectural Review*'s Outrage section and other places.[42] In this building, the functionalist core of John Andrews's Union Building is absorbed into a labyrinth of stairs and corridors, then wrapped by carnivalesque facades that are a collage of design ideas alluding to Melbourne's architectural history and adorned with mirrored-glass trapezoid volumes, causing not only bafflement and disorientation but also laughter through in-jokes about football and suburban culture. In new buildings for RMIT, Lyons architects and ARM have taken up this abundance of architectural contradictions and 'urbaned' it up in the lineage of Edmond & Corrigan.[43] 'Ugly it ain't' is one of the lessons that Ian McDougall, a director of ARM, learned from Corrigan, his former studio teacher, and that transpires from this urban fragment, namely the strategy to pursue 'the familiar and generic, transmogrified into dynamic, strident, agglomerated iconography'.[44]

More than any other building by Edmond & Corrigan, Building 8 is a fragment of their utopia of a 'city of hope' – 'hope' expressing a particular Australian anti-authoritarian sense of liberty that resonated with the postmodern penchant towards cultural inclusiveness and pluralism (Figure 15.4). This joyous tone also radiates from a sense of larrikin humour, an anti-conformist stance towards elitism and a satirical discharge of the prototypical stigmas of existential nihilism and the so-called Australian 'cultural cringe'.[45]

FIGURE 15.4 *Edmond & Corrigan, Building 8, RMIT University, Melbourne, Victoria (1990–4). Photograph by John Gollings, courtesy of Gollings Photography Pty Ltd.*

The comic nature of many projects by Edmond & Corrigan, of which Building 8 is exemplary, has its roots in Corrigan's parallel career as a set designer. In his stage designs Corrigan acknowledges that he aspires to realize a *Verfremdungseffect* – a strange-making effect – the Brechtian technique of unveiling the constructed nature of the theatrical stage. In architecture this effect is conveyed by a shift in balance between the familiarity of the appropriated suburban iconography and its regeneration, engendering a sense of alienation, of the unfamiliar. Architecture is conceived as a theatrical double reality – a real world and a world that exists as a staged representation. When Corrigan writes that 'Brecht presented the stage as a stage',[46] he refers to the simultaneous revelation and collapse of that doubleness, which opens up theatrical reality for social critique. In analogy with the anti-naturalism of Brecht's Epic theatre, John Vaccaro's Theatre of the Ridiculous, and 'poor theatre' more broadly, Corrigan aimed to produce buildings that he regarded as 'poor architecture': a self-assertive layered anti-naturalistic architecture plunging into the mess of the ordinary and the vernacular (much like, as Corrigan says, comic Bette Midler did – 'trash with flash and sleaze with ease').[47]

The satirical nature of Edmond & Corrigan's work conveys not only enjoyment, pleasure and hope but also a sense of anger and aggressiveness. Satire finds an element of ridicule in what it opposes in order to 'evade restrictions and open sources of pleasure that have become inaccessible'.[48] Satire in the work of Edmond & Corrigan is a reflexive reaction, which they direct to expose the latent Eurocentric puritanic model of modernism and of Boyd's generation that followed. This comic exposure calls to mind Fischer's observation that jokes relate to the ugly in the way they 'bring forward something that is concealed or hidden':[49]

> If it [what is ugly] is concealed, it must be uncovered in the light of the comic way of looking at things if it is noticed only a little or scarcely at all, it must be brought forward and made obvious, so that it lies clear and open to the light of day.[50]

If the ugly can become 'the site where multiple cultural tensions are negotiated',[51] then satire as it manifests itself in the work of Edmond & Corrigan, makes the ugly appear clearly as an 'obstacle', inhibiting the interrogation of various models of identity, 'and in that way draws pleasure from a source which the obstacle had made inaccessible'.[52]

Act II: Robert Venturi's irony of the interesting

Because ugliness is unavoidably tied to reality, it lends itself well to being modulated into the horrible as much as into the comic, because both genres depend on imagining what *might be*. The ugly in itself is not funny or terrible, it has to be staged to be experienced as such. The ugly becomes laughable when we read into it a comic human attitude or expression. Henri Bergson acknowledges that while 'a landscape may be beautiful, charming and sublime or insignificant and ugly[,] it will never be laughable. You may laugh at an animal, but only because you have detected in it some human attitude or expression.'[53] Extending Bergson's reasoning, we can say that when we laugh at a building, we are making fun of 'the human caprice whose mould it assumed'.

Similarly to the comic, the horrible is not an objective quality of an object; the subject has to imagine that quality or attribute it to the object. Our reflexive response to ugliness is to dismiss or negate it, and therefore it easily triggers contempt. As Nietzsche observes of contempt, 'There is indeed too much carelessness, too much taking lightly, too much looking away and impatience involved in [it], even too much joyfulness, for it to be able to transform its object into a real … monster.'[54] For ugliness to appear as horrible, then, ugliness has to be magnified to the point where it appears contagious, intolerable and disgusting.

This movement of ugliness – its vivacity – between the comic and the horrible, when instrumentalized in an architectural project, turns into an imbalance. Whether this imbalance is considered to follow the logic of cathexis or catharsis is very much a consequence of discursive interpretation, of the positioning and staging of a project in relation to the spectator or user and the user's capacity for a range of reflexive reactions.

The work of Venturi and Scott Brown intentionally effectuates a failure of dramatic catharsis through a cathectic charge with all the complexities and contradictions that are tied to an urban reality in which their 'boring architecture' is wilfully imbedded.[55] As Emmanuel Petit argues, Venturi followed a model of irony or detachment from ideological prejudice characteristic of a postmodern attitude that was driven by a desire to encapsulate a plurality of contradictory meanings and diverging ways of interpreting the world.[56] A well-known example of this ironic stance is Venturi's non-judgemental inversion of Peter Blake's critical judgement of a typical American Main Street as 'almost all right'.

Irony is a stylistic device that presents both a view and its criticism at the same time, and in its relativism takes on the appearance of self-criticism. The originality of *Learning from Las Vegas* lies, according to Petit, in its way of turning the interpretative methods of literary criticism – reading images as texts – into an operative tool for producing architectural form. This operation consisted of sampling, recycling and recombining images within a field of connotative meanings that went well beyond disciplinary limits, detaching the aesthetic effects of images and photographs from their reality. Such a double-edged appropriation of imagery was based on a New Critic's idea of aesthetic autonomy. This non-judgemental and detached aesthetic stance enabled Venturi and Scott Brown, much like Pop artists in the 1950s and 1960s, to make a cultural pluralism appear in their architecture, exhibitions and writings, though neutralized on the level on communication and mediation.[57] Leaning on George Baird, Charles Jencks and Alan Colquhoun's discussion of architecture as a 'system of communications' and on the work of Pop artists who used unusual juxtapositions of the optical and the symbolic, they developed methods of screening the conventional suburban landscape for what was 'interesting'.[58]

The anti-aesthetic value of 'the interesting' advanced in *Learning from Las Vegas* extended the operational criticism of mannerist examples in *Complexity and Contradiction* (1966) with the richness of communicative qualities found in the 'ugly and ordinary' architecture of signs. Ugliness, when embraced as a resource for artistic and architectural practices, takes a form, as Cousins observes, that offers 'to the undefended spectator or reader a situation which is fundamentally interesting',[59] because its original vivacity is partially lost, and rationalized, through aesthetic control. The interesting as the anti-aesthetic value par excellence is essentially ambiguous: its cultivation of reflexivity is contradicted by an affective relationship to perception. The interesting, according to Jan Mieszkowski, is driven by a 'comparative dynamic' that has no value without comparison.[60] It results from a contradiction of the visible and the mental, a dissonance between knowledge and feeling, between abstract ideas and sensory experience.

According to Mikhail Epstein, 'it is this internal tension between reasonable expectation and the cognitive value of the unexpected or unexpectable that undergirds the category of the interesting'.[61]

Act III: Koolhaas's witty displacements of the historical unconscious

In the 'Relearning from Las Vegas' interview with Venturi and Scott Brown, Koolhaas found that the episode where he and Venturi both presented a competition entry for a hotel for Euro Disney in Paris to be 'a very interesting moment'. The position of Venturi, Koolhaas remembers, 'was sandwiched between demonstrative modernism, on the one side, and demonstrative postmodern form, on the other', a consequence of Venturi's strict adaptation 'of the rules of Las Vegas: a casino is a huge wall with very little articulation except at the top and the bottom'.[62]

Venturi's application of the logic of the decorative shed foreshadowed Koolhaas's assimilation, in his own writings and architecture of metropolitan instability, between the form and function of the skyscraper, as described in the fictional conclusion of *Delirious New York* (1978):

> In the metropolitan archipelago each Skyscraper – in the absence of real history – develops its own instantaneous 'folklore'. Through the double disconnection of *lobotomy* and *schism* – by separating exterior and interior architecture and developing the latter in small autonomous instalments – such structures can devote their exteriors *only* to formalism and their interiors *only* to functionalism.[63]

Koolhaas's retroactive manifesto evoked the clashing of the ideological indifference of the architectural external form of mirror-like or opaque glass facades (as in Mies' drawings of skyscrapers) and the interiorized programme of Manhattanism: 'to live inside fantasy as an autonomous production – was so ambitious that to be realized, it could never be openly stated.'[64] The postmodern ugliness of the 'technology of the Fantastic' that Koolhaas traces back to New York's fun fair in Coney Island is revealed to be the hidden, parallel history of modernism. The disciplinary self-involvement of late modernism and its construction of modernism's history of rational and social transformation is contradicted by a hidden project of modernity: the irrational construction of the reality of individual self-liberation. Koolhaas excavates from history the unconscious underbelly of the rational modernist city, finding it to be a parallel 'city as factory of man-made experience, where the real and the natural ceased to exist'.[65]

The appropriation of the 'technology of the fantastic', discarded to the registers of ugliness by the historiography of Modern architecture, becomes an important source for Koolhaas's anti-representionalist staging and superimposing of clashing doubles: form and programme, rationality and irrationality, reality and unreality – an agenda that is made explicit in Madelon Vriesendorp's Freudian *Flagrant Délit* painting that was used as the cover of *Delirious New York*. Also in his fictional projects, such as the City of the Captive Globe (1972) or the Welfare Palace Hotel (1976), Koolhaas wittely confronts Dali's surrealist paranoid-critical method and Le Corbusier's rationalism, juggling historical layers, to use the words of Jean Paul Richter, as if he were a 'disguised priest who weds every couple'. Or, even better, as Friedrich Theodor Vischer describes it, a jester, somebody who 'likes best to wed couples whose union their relatives frown upon'.[66]

The comic tenet of wit with which Koolhaas superimposes the unconscious and conscious project of modernism together, I propose, can be interpreted through Freud's concepts of condensation and displacement.[67] These two mechanisms, Freud argues, are essential for the formation of both dreams and jokes.[68] First, condensation contracts contrasts in a form of brevity. As Theodor Lipps wrote in his *Komik und Humor* (1898):

> A joke says what it has to say, not always in few words, but in *too* few words – that is, in words that are insufficient by strict logic or by common modes of thought and speech. It may even actually say what it has to say by not saying it.[69]

Freud explains that jokes require wit to reveal hidden similarities between apparent dissimilarities with a surprising rapidity of contrasts and to compress them in a form that brings their conflict into the open. Koolhaas's work demonstrates this aptitude for quick and inventive contractions of architectural historico-institutional types and topoi.

The second witty operation on the ugly, unconscious underbelly of modernism in Koolhaas's work can be theorized through the technical method of displacement in dreamwork and the formation of jokes. The method is directly related to inhibitions and the process of censorship in conscious thinking. In a displacement, the cathexis, the emotional tension, that has built up around an unresolved desire during the day is transferred to that desire. A displacement in dreamwork selects ideas remote from what is objectionable, but are derivatives of the original idea. That idea is allowed to bypass censorship, although when rationally interpreted, such a displacement comes across as irrational.

Displacement in the work of OMA, as in witty jokes, renders allowable inhibitions in architectural history through ambiguity, multiplicity and double-sidedness of meaning, in such a way that the architecture proves that it is not insensible to these inhibitions. In OMA's Guggenheim Hermitage in Las Vegas (2001), the corten-steel wall piercing the ground floor of the facade of the Venetian Hotel operates a displacement, through the technique of the cut-out, invoking multiple historical references such as the theme of the 'wall' and perimeter, which can be retraced to Koolhaas's Berlin Wall 1971 thesis project, the theory of the decorated shed with the name 'Guggenheim Hermitage' functioning as billboard, the identical soccles of the skyscrapers in the City of the Captive Globe, and so on. OMA's cut-out, which ironically presents itself as a form of inhibition, plays a witty game of 'indirect representations' that challenge interpretation through a multiplication of opposites.

Closing the curtain walls of ugliness

The way in which Venturi and Scott Brown, Edmond and Corrigan, and Koolhaas recovered the cathexis, constructed discursively around the ugliness of expansive (sub)urbanization, proved an important source for a postmodern project they shared: restaging modern architecture as what I call a double, comic scene; a condensed, allegorical mis-en-scene of ordinary urbanness that is constructed self-reflexively as an anti-intellectual critique on the place that it will take in the mediated archive of the architectural discipline, where it will be shown, circulated and discussed. This ambiguity and imbalance is what enables architecture to be both terrible and comic. Charles Beaudelaire said, 'Laughter is the revelation of the double';[70] it only comes about when the incompatible contrast between ideas is found to be capable of discharging at a particular moment. This discharge is, however, not to be interpreted as purifying, therapeutic or cathartic but rather as an unresolved non-catharsis that operates through a transition or modulation in tone. Similar to the cinematic modulation of the horrible into the comic by an awareness of fiction, which makes terror and violence bearable and enjoyable because of the fleshliness of its 'cool', low-res visual effects[71] – a demand upon the subject to fill in the image – postmodern architecture finds joy in framing a reflective play on the reality of representation. It complies with architecture's secondary role in the sphere of words and gestures, appropriating and imitating the material world of the everyday that has settled in a state of ennui.

It is at this level of dealing with the incompatible that the postmodern architecture discussed in this chapter operates like a broken mirror, traditionally held to be the metaphor of ugliness, and converges and diverges with the mirror curtain wall, – the recurring trope that characterizes postmodernism. Jameson's analysis of postmodernism as a 'mirror spiral' could be considered a special case of the broken mirror. Unlike the mirror that one looks through, the mirror curtain wall and the broken mirror are to be looked at. Refraction and fracture stand for the discontinuation of the mirror as a metaphor of truth, and by extension, the discontinuation of the modernist episteme of transparency and knowledge as a faithful representation.

Notes

1. Gretchen E. Henderson, *Ugliness: A Cultural History* (London: Reaktion Books, 2015), 17–18.
2. Ian Nairn, *Outrage* (London: Architectural Press, 1955), 373; Ian Nairn, *Counter Attack against Subtopia* (London: Architectural Press, 1957).
3. Donald Gazzard, ed., *Australian Outrage. The Decay of a Visual Environment* (Sydney: Ure Smith, 1966); Robin Boyd, *The Australian Ugliness* (Melbourne: The Text Publishing Company, 2010). See especially Mathew Aitchison on the transatlantic history of the ugliness and outrage debate, in 'The Boyd Ultimatum', *AA Files*, no. 66 (2013): 59–67.
4. Peter Blake, *God's Own Junkyard: The Planned Deterioration of America's Landscape* (New York: Holt, Rinehart, and Winston, 1964), 8.
5. Renaet Braem, *Het Lelijkste Land Ter Wereld* (Brussel: VUB-Press, 1968), 15 (quote translated from the Dutch by Wouter Van Acker).
6. The quote is from the dictionary included in *S,M,L,XL*: 'Ugly. You must know how to make the best of ugliness itself', in Rem Koolhaas and Bruce Mau, *S,M,L,XL* (New York: Monacelli Press, 1997).
7. Naomi Stead, '(Not So) Anti-Architecture', *Places Journal* (October 2017).
8. Boyd, *The Australian Ugliness*, 71.
9. Ibid., 73
10. Ibid., 264.
11. Ibid., 265.
12. Emma Jones, 'Rediscovering *The Australian Ugliness*: Robin Boyd and the Search for the Australian Modern', *sITA Journal* 2 (2014): 94–114.
13. On Boyd as an author, see Philip Goad, 'Robin Boyd and the Art of Writing Architecture' in *Semi-Detached: Writing, Representation and Criticism in Architecture*, ed. Naomi Stead (Melbourne: Uro, 2012).
14. Mark Cousins, 'The Ugly [part 1]', *AA files* 28 (1994): 61–4; Mark Cousins, 'The Ugly [part 2]', *AA Files* 29 (1995): 3–6; Mark Cousins, 'The Ugly [part 3]', *AA files* 30 (1995): 68.
15. Cousins, 'The Ugly [part 1]', 64.
16. Rem Koolhaas, 'Junkspace', in *Content*, ed. Rem Koolhaas (Köln: Taschen, 2004), 162.
17. Mark Dorrian, 'On the Monstrous and the Grotesque', *Word & Image* 16, no. 3 (2000): 310–16.
18. Koolhaas and Mau, *S,M,L,XL,* 1261 and 1262 (emphasis in original).
19. Terry Kirk, 'Monumental', *Perspecta* 40, special issue 'Monster' (2008): 11.

20 Theodor Adorno, *Aesthetic Theory* (London: Continuum, 1997), 61.
21 Ibid., 67.
22 Jean-Francois Lyotard, 'The Sublime and the Avant-garde', *Artforum* 22, no. 4 (1984): 40.
23 Peter Womack, 'The Comical Scene: Perspective and Civility on the Serlian Stage', *Representations* 101, no. 1 (Winter 2008): 41.
24 Barbara Kruger, as quoted in Jennifer Higgie, ed., *The Artist's Joke* (Cambridge, MA: MIT Press, 2007), 15.
25 Sianne Ngai, *Ugly Feelings* (Cambridge, MA: Harvard University Press, 2005).
26 There is much literature on the use of black humour and surrealism, and how it persisted in postmodern literary criticism in the 1960s and 1970s; see, for example, Doug Haynes, 'The Persistence of Irony: Interfering with Surrealist Black Humour', *Textual Practice* 20, no. 1 (2006): 25–47. The quote is from André Breton, 'Partonerre' [Lightning Rod, 1939], in Higgie, *The Artist's Joke*, 46.
27 Ibid., 46.
28 Sigmund Freud, *Jokes and Their Relation to the Unconscious* (London: Penguin Books, 1991), 200.
29 Freud, *Jokes and Their Relation to the Unconscious*, 302.
30 Philip Goad, 'The Critic and the Car: Robin Boyd, Automobiles and Australian Architecture' in *Driving Futures*, ed. Harriet Edquist, Mark Richardson, Simon Lockrey, Proceedings of Automotive Historians Australia, vol. 1 (Melbourne: AHA, 2016), 1–15.
31 For a recent publication on humour as a tool to affect public perception of architecture and the complicity of the profession, see Michela Ross, ed., *Laughing at Architecture: Architectural Histories of Humour, Satire and Wit* (London: Bloomsbury, 2018).
32 Freud, *Jokes and Their Relation to the Unconscious*, 258.
33 Susan Sontag, 'Notes on Camp' in *A Susan Sontag Reader*, ed. Susan Sontag and Elizabeth Hardwick (New York: Vintage Books, 1983), 116, Statement 44.
34 Kuno Fischer, *Über den Witz* (Heidelberg: C. Winter, 1889), 49–51, as quoted in Freud, *Jokes and Their Relation to the Unconscious*, 40–1.
35 For more detailed exploration of the theatrical background of the work of Maggie Edmond, Peter Corrigan and Edmond & Corrigan, see Wouter Van Acker, 'Peter Corrigan, the Bodgie Wolf, and Other Larrikin Tygers of Wrath', *Fabrications* 28, no. 1 (2018): 3–24.
36 Peter Corrigan, 'Reflection on a New North American Architecture: The Venturis', *Architecture in Australia* 61, no. 1 (1972): 55–67.
37 On the 'antipodean' regionalism of the Australian modernists in the 1960s, see Doug Evans, 'Centre and Periphery: Melbourne Regionalism and Its Global Context in the 1950's and 1960's', *Universal versus Individual*, Conference Jyväskylä, Finland, 2002, http://www.alvaraalto.fi/conferences/universal/finalpapers/doug.evans.rtf [accessed 9 February 2016].

38 James Birrell, *A Life in Architecture: Beyond the Ugliness* (St Lucia: University of Queensland Press, 2013), 22.
39 Peter Corrigan, 'A Sub-urbane Culture', *Studio International*, 13 June (1986).
40 Paul Hogben, 'The Aftermath of "Pleasures": Untold Stories of Post-Modern Architecture in Australia' in *Progress*, Papers from the 20th Annual Conference of SAHANZ, Faculty of Architecture University of Sydney, Sydney, 2003.
41 Participants in this debate, besides Corrigan and Koolhaas, were George Baird, Norman Day and Philip Drew. 'Rem Koolhaas', in *Transitions* 1, no. 4 (October 1980): 14.
42 For a discussion of its divergent appreciation, see Neil Clerehan, 'Shiny Beast: Stunning Success or Egotistical Folly? Behind the Facade of RMIT's Building 8', *The Age*, 20 September 1997.
43 See Chapter One by John Macarthur on ARM in this volume.
44 Ian McDougall, '10 Lessons from Corrigan' in *Cities of Hope Remembered: Cities of Hope Rehearsed: Australian Architecture and Stage Design by Edmond and Corrigan 1962–2012*, ed. Conrad Hamann (Port Melbourne: Thames & Hudson Australia, 2012), 12.
45 Melissa Bellanta, *Larrikins: A History* (St Lucia: University of Queensland Press, Penguin, 2012).
46 Peter Corrigan, '*Stage Space*' in *Contemporary Australian Drama*, ed. Peter Holloway (Sydney: Currency Press, 1979), 36.
47 This is one among many references to popular culture in Corrigan's work. Bette Midler is quoted in Will Friedwald, *A Biographical Guide to the Great Jazz and Pop Singers* (New York: Knopf Doubleday, 2010), 661.
48 Freud, *Jokes and Their Relation to the Unconscious*, 147.
49 Fischer, *Über den Witz*, 51, as quoted in Freud, *Jokes and Their Relation to the Unconscious*, 44.
50 Ibid., 40.
51 Naomi Baker, *Plain Ugly: The Unattractive Body in Early Modern Culture* (Manchester: Manchester University Press, 2010), 7.
52 Freud, *Jokes and Their Relation to the Unconscious*, 144.
53 Henri Bergson, *An Essay on the Meaning of the Comic* (London: Macmillan, 1911), 23.
54 Friedrich W. Nietzsche, Walter Kaufmann, ed., *On the Genealogy of Morals* (1887; New York: Vintage Books, 1989), 37. Also quoted in Ngai, *Ugly Feelings*, 336.
55 Robert Venturi, Denise Scott Brown and Steven Izenour, *Learning from Las Vegas: The Forgotten Symbolism of Architectural Form* (Cambridge, MA: MIT Press, 1977), 101.
56 Emmanuel Petit, *Irony or, the Self-critical Opacity of Postmodern Architecture* (New Haven, CT: Yale University Press, 2013), 31–72.
57 Venturi, Scott Brown and Izenour, *Learning from Las Vegas*, 93.

58 Ibid., 130. They quote Charles Jencks and George Baird, *Meaning in Architecture* (New York: George Brziller, 1969), and Alan Colquhoun, 'Typology and Design Method', *Arena, Journal of the Architectural Assocation* (June 1967): 11–14.
59 Cousins, 'The Ugly [part 3]', 68.
60 Jan Mieszkowski, *Labors of Imagination: Aesthetics and Political Economy from Kant to Althusser* (New York: Fordham University Press, 2006), 114.
61 Michail Epstein, 'The Interesting', *Qui parle* 18, no. 1 (2009): 78.
62 Hans Ulrich Obrist and Rem Koolhaas. 'Relearning from Las Vegas: An Interview with Denise Scott Brown and Robert Venturi' in *The Harvard Design School Guide to Shopping* (Köln: Taschen, 2001), 590–617.
63 Rem Koolhaas, *Delirious New York: A Retroactive Manifesto for Manhattan* (Rotterdam: 010 Publishers, 1994), 296 (emphasis in original).
64 Ibid., 10.
65 Ibid.
66 As quoted in Freud, *Jokes and Their Relation to the Unconscious*, 41.
67 I ascribe the comic tenet of 'wit' rather than 'irony' to Koolhaas's work. On how irony takes form in the work of Koolhaas, see the chapter on Koolhaas in Petit, *Irony or, the Self-critical Opacity of Postmodern Architecture*.
68 Freud, *Jokes and Their Relation to the Unconscious*, 222.
69 Ibid., 44.
70 As quoted by Robert Smithson, in Higgie, *The Artist's Joke*, 61.
71 This refers to McLuhan's description of TV and comic books as 'cool' (low-res) media, in opposition to classic 'hot' (high-res), the latter of which requires an aesthetic distance. Marshall McLuhan, *Understanding Media: The Extensions of Man* (Corte Madera: Ginko Press, 1994).

INDEX

Aalto, Alvar 25, 33, 161
abject 26, 42–3, 54, 80
Abramović, Marina 118
Abraxas 95–8, 100–3
Action Architecture 66–7
Ackerman, James 128
Adorno, Theodor 1, 2, 131, 262
aesthetic
   distance 8, 9, 12, 40, 102, 203, 262, 277
   experientialism 25, 111
   of failure 20, 178, 270
   friction 15, 245–7, 251–3
   gaze 7, 39–41, 44, 162, 257,
   judgment 1, 6–7, 9, 13, 21–2, 39, 41, 46–7, 129, 175–6, 246, 248
   pre-aesthetic 44
   taste 1, 6, 11–15, 19–20, 24, 26–8, 40–2, 47, 63, 71, 101, 155, 168–70, 175–81, 186–7, 209, 212–13, 216–17, 247
aesthetic object 1, 7, 13, 45–7, 50–1
   architecture as 1, 46–8
aesthetics
   and disinterest 6–8, 39–41, 44, 155, 163, 175, 233, 239
   Kantian, see *Kant*
   minor 34
   and (a)morality 39, 62, 125–7, 131, 134, 155, 168–9, 180, 210, 215, 217, 227, 231, 234–5, 238, 240, 249, 252–3
   politics of 23, 119
   and visual perception 26, 40, 45, 81, 111, 137, 158, 233, 248
   weak 9, 11–13, 32, 101, 104, 142
affect 6, 12, 21, 25–8, 34, 46, 79, 83, 111, 148, 270
Alberro, Alexander 2, 22, 34

Alchimia 15, 209–13, 215–19
alienation 69, 80, 102, 169, 233, 240, 268
amorphous 98, 109, 142, 147, 242
anthropocentrism 80, 88
anthropomorphism 48, 81
anti-aesthetics
   and aesthetics 22, 34
   and architecture 8, 21, 28, 120
   in art theory 2, 21–5, 29, 270
   in architectural theory 20, 24, 29, 270
   definition of 6, 22
   normative 9, 15, 34
   and postmodernism 3, 5–7, 20–1, 102, 108–9, 112, 223, 226
anti-classicism 125, 127, 129
appropriation
   and collage 32
   of imagery 209, 270, 271
   and the original 32
   as postmodern artistic strategy 21, 28–9, 32, 34–5, 247
   and postmodern theory 6, 22, 24–5, 33, 35
   and property 31–2
   and quotation 31
   of the vernacular 19, 26
appropriateness 10, 32, 125, 128, 216, 247 see also *concinnitas*
ARM, see *Ashton Raggatt McDougall*
as-found 163, 245, 251, 265
asymmetry 98, 137, 147, 149, 247
Ashton Raggatt McDougall 13, 19, 28–34, 267
Assemblage 20
assemblage
   machinic assemblage 82–5, 87–8, 92

INDEX

autonomy
  aesthetic 34, 249, 270
  architectural 20, 224, 238, 271
  artistic 8, 22
  disciplinary 6, 249
  formal 20, 39, 97
Aymonino, Carlo 223, 235, 239

Bacon, Francis 138
bad taste 1, 6, 11, 25–8, 77, 134, 168, 168–70, 175–81, 186–7, 196–7, 213, 216–17
Baird, George 99, 270
Bakhtin, Mikhail 142, 143, 148
balkanology 112, 118–19
banal 7, 15, 28, 47–8, 154, 210, 213–19, 246
Banham, Reyner 28, 61, 64, 68, 103, 109, 227, 250
Bataille, George 10, 26, 43, 54
Baudrillard, Jean 20, 101, 111
BBPR or Ludovico Belgiojoso, Enrico Peressutti and Ernesto Nathan Rogers 223, 227, 230
beauty
  anti-beauty 65
  arbitrary 95, 98–100
  architectural 45, 50, 52, 139, 148, 180, 225, 239, 259
  authentic 51, 113, 249, 262
  classical 72, 128, 246–7
  conventional 9, 63, 250, 252
  easy/difficult 27, 33, 109, 170, 248
  experience of 47, 48, 53, 155, 197
  faded 49
  as fair 193, 249
  humanistic 69
  judgement of 6, 7, 68–9
  as object of desire 52
  pure 7–8, 40, 129
  return to beauty 2, 245, 253
  transcendental 34
  useless 49
beautification 111–12
beautiful
  definition according to Kant 8, 34, 41
  and the non-beautiful 3, 41, 155, 162
  and pleasure 6, 40, 42
  and the ugly, see *ugly and beautiful*

Bellori, Giovan Pietro 129, 133–4
bizarre 127, 227
Blake, Peter 15, 155, 157, 180, 258, 270
Bofill, Ricardo 95, 98, 101–3
Borromini 51, 157
Bosanquet, Bernard 27–8, 33
Boston City Hall 61, 65–70
Boullée, 100–1
Bourdieu, Pierre 24, 175, 252
Boyd, Robin 15, 257–60, 264–5, 267, 269–70
Brecht, Bertolt 233, 248, 268
Brutalism
  American 65–7, 109
  Australian 265
  eclipse of 99, 101–3, 116
  and ethics 61–5, 71
  in general 5, 13, 28, 49, 59–72, 109, 253
  New Brutalism 62–5
  in Skopje 107–20
Bunshaft, Gordon 5, 154, 161
Bürger, Peter 6
Burckhardt 131–2
Burke, Edmund 26, 53
Butterfield, William 19, 21, 26–8, 59–68, 71–2

camp 11, 175–83, 185–7, 191, 245–7, 252, 264
Cárdenas, Randolph 200, 204–5
carnivalesque 116, 267
Casabella 209, 214, 217, 226–7
ch'ixi 203, 205
chola 195–7, 204
collage 31–2, 251, 267
colossal 80
commodification 8, 23, 113
concinnitas 127, 247
confusion 12, 21, 159, 187, 232, 237–9
Collins, Peter 61, 67–9
Corrigan, Peter 258, 264–9, 273
Cousins, Marc 3, 9, 10, 38, 63, 178, 232, 260, 270
Crimp, Douglas 20, 22, 32
Croce, Bernardo 27
criticality 6, 8–9, 20, 23, 215
critical regionalism 20–1, 31

INDEX

daidalon 83–5, 87, 88
Danto, Arthur 36, 156
deadpan 14, 162–3, 168, 170, 264
Decadentism 99–101
decay 25, 43–4, 69, 80, 116, 147, 249, 253, 258
defamiliarization, see *alienation*
Deleuze and Guattari 13, 82, 87, 225, 232–3
Derrida, Jacques 20
Diderot, Denis 53
dirt 10, 48, 247, 260
disgust 2, 3, 7, 12, 43–5, 50, 154–5, 175, 187–8, 239, 253, 269
disharmony 7, 8, 98, 181, 187, 253
Disneyland 118, 252, 271
displeasure 7, 8, 25, 239
Douglas, Mary 10, 245, 247
Dorfless, Gillo 11, 126, 213, 214, 217, 219
Duchamp, Marcel 32, 162, 245
Du Pasquier, Nathalie 210, 212
dust 10, 62, 260
Dvořák, Max 129, 134

ecdysis 143–5
Eckel, see *disgust*
Eco, Umberto 2, 34, 98, 99, 104, 126, 147, 177, 186, 214, 233
Edmond & Corrigan 258, 265–9
Edmond, Maggie 265
empathy theory 25
error, see *ugliness as error*
excessive 9, 10, 14, 43, 48, 77–9, 97, 100, 112, 119, 139, 142, 153, 164, 175–8, 183, 186, 187, 193, 197, 200–5, 214–16, 253, 260
existentialism 64, 73

facadism 108, 112–16
formlessness 9–10, 28, 42, 43, 98, 147, 260
Foster, Hal 5–6, 20–5, 251
Foucault, Michel 20
Frampton, Kenneth 20, 169
Frankenstein 11, 79
Frascari, Marco 83, 89–90, 139, 140, 141
Furness, Frank 157

Gans, Herbert 168
Goldschmidt, Richard 138–9, 141
Guerriero, Alessandro 211
Greenberg, Clement 6, 22, 179
Gothic Revival 19, 25–9, 34, 62, 72, 98, 166
grotesque 2, 11, 38, 62, 77, 79, 98, 127, 142–3, 154–5, 159–62, 234, 246–8, 262, 265

Habermas, Jurgen 20
Haskell, Douglas 179–80
heroic architecture 5, 71, 215, 262
historicism 14, 108, 109, 112–13, 115, 116, 120, 169, 181
horror 10, 15, 43, 78, 80–1, 91, 157, 253
humour 2, 32, 164, 175, 181, 262
Harvey, David 115
Hegel 24–5, 27
Hersey, George 68
Hugo, Victor 68
Huxtable, Ada Louise 70–1
hybridity 6, 22, 24, 29, 83, 84, 98, 115, 118, 119, 157, 164, 195, 261, 267
hyperreal 109, 112
hyper-capitalism 119

informe/informal 7, 26, 98, 101, 196, 201
impure, see *pure and impure*
interesting 6, 8–9, 15, 21, 38, 181, 187, 189–90, 269–71
International Style 66, 68, 211, 218
irony 11, 15, 33, 125, 168, 211, 246, 249, 267, 269–70
Izenour, Steven, see *Venturi, Scott Brown and Izenour*

Jameson, Fredric 7, 11, 20, 109–13, 116, 273
Jencks, Charles 11, 13, 19, 20, 25, 180–1, 211, 246, 250, 252, 270
Johnson, Philip 5, 33, 61, 65, 66, 68, 153–4, 161, 168, 176, 181, 189
joke
  architectural 32, 146, 148, 181
  failed 48
  in-joke 184, 267

surrealist 264
  theory 31, 264–5, 269, 272
Judd, Donald 6

Kahn, Louis 65, 155
Kallmann, Gerhard and Michael
    McKinnell 65–7
Kant, Immanuel
  aesthetics 7–8, 41, 50, 163, 175, 234
  aesthetic pleasure 8, 22, 24, 33, 239
  Critique of Judgment 3, 7, 80, 154
  free play of imagination 8, 239
  sensus communis 6, 22, 42
  subjective taste 6, 27, 176
  and sublime 26, 53, 80
Kerr, Robert 26–7
kitsch 11, 48, 109–10, 126, 169, 179,
    180, 186, 189, 194, 197, 209–15,
    217–19, 245, 247, 252, 264
Konstantinov, Janko 108, 110
Koolhaas, Rem 258, 260–1, 264, 267,
    271–4
Krauss, Rosalind 10, 20, 32, 54,
    143, 246

labyrinth 83–4, 88–9, 93, 132, 267
Las Vegas 163–5, 168, 246, 251,
    271–2
Le Corbusier 31, 33, 51, 64, 141–2,
    169, 250, 272
Lefebvre, Henri 102, 113
Levine, Sherry 32
Libeskind, Daniel 33
Lyons architects 28, 267

Mamani, Freddy 14, 193–5, 198–202,
    205
mannerism 14, 125–36, 155–7, 247–8
maniera 128–9, 131–2
mask/masking 11, 108, 112–15, 117,
    125, 260
McKinnell, Michael
  see Kallmann, Gerhard and Michael
    McKinnell
Mendini, Alessandro 209–20
Memphis 209–19
metabolism 109
Moles, Abraham 210–11, 213–15
Moore, Charles 161, 176, 181–7, 265

monster
  architectural 10, 139–40,
    142
  and becoming 81–3
  and categorization 78, 80
  cities 260
  definition of 77
  and diagramming 83
  etymology 89, 261
  hopeful monsters 14, 138–9,
    141–2
  and inhuman 80–2
  and liminality 78, 81
  as Minotaur 83–4, 89
  and mutant/mutation 82, 138–9,
    141–2, 233
  and normality 43, 50
  and ontology 80–1
  political 109, 118
  and sensorial 78
  and the ugly 77–8, 147
monstrous
  and anxiety 43, 47, 78
  and evolutionary theory 90, 138–9,
    143
  definition of 43, 142, 147
  and posthumanism 13
  as process 82
  and ugliness 11, 45, 77–8, 80, 98,
    138
monumental 59, 60, 66–8, 71, 95–8,
    100–3, 159, 169
  faux monumentality 100–2

Nash, John 26
neo-avant-garde 6, 211, 215, 218, 225,
    237, 250
neo-Andean 193, 195, 205
neo-Gothic, see *Gothic Revival*
neo-baroque 113, 118
neoclassical 3, 14, 96–8, 100–3, 107,
    113, 115–17, 125
neo-rationalist 224–6
Neorealism 223, 225–7, 232–4, 237,
    240
new Andean architecture 205
New International Style 211
niche tactics 14, 137, 148
nomad science 87

INDEX

October 22
ordinary
  architecture 48, 53
  and beauty 42
  and Charles Moore 187
  and Edmond & Corrigan 268
  in general 9, 11, 41, 155, 176, 180, 199, 245–6, 250–2, 273
  and Immanuel Kant 8
  and Robert Venturi 4, 156
  and Robin Boyd 259
  and the Smithsons 251
  ugliness 154, 170
  and ugly, see *ugly and ordinary*
Oppositions 20
Owens, Graig 6, 20, 22, 24, 29, 33

Panofsky, Erwin 136, 141
Palladio, Andrea 51, 127–8
pastiche 11, 31, 98, 101, 108, 111–13, 116, 120, 246
Perrault, Claude 99–100
Pevsner, Nikolaus 59, 68, 129, 132
phenomenology 25, 225–6, 231
picturesque 3, 25–8, 34, 49, 116, 157, 176, 257
Pop Art 14, 156, 162, 164–5, 170, 178, 181, 183, 209, 212–13, 270
Portoghesi, Paolo 130
post-communism 107, 109–12, 115, 119
postmodernism
  and anti-aesthetics 3, 5–7, 14, 23–4, 246, 250–2, 261, 273
  and Brutalism 99
  as cultural theory 1, 100, 110–11
  and mannerism 126, 130
  and modernism 1, 5–6, 24, 33, 265–7
  and the neo-avant-garde 2, 6, 22, 176
  neo-Stalinist 119
post-humanism 20
Price, Udevale 12, 25, 28
Pollock, Jackson 64–5
propriety, *see* appropriateness
Pugin, AWN 26, 250
pure and impure 3, 5, 7–9, 24, 46, 78, 86, 129, 143, 155, 160, 175, 177, 240, 247
putrefaction 43

Quaroni, Ludovico 15, 223, 226, 230–5, 237, 240

Radical Design 209–11, 216–17
reflexivity 5–6, 8, 155, 158, 234, 245, 262, 269–70, 273
Repton, Humphry 26
representation 9–11, 15, 22, 32, 40, 44–6, 79–81, 113, 154, 167, 187, 260, 262, 268, 273
  and medusa strategy 44
Ridolfi, Mario 223, 226, 234–6
Rivera Cusicanqui, Silvia 202–3
Rogers, Ernesto Nathan 15, 223–31, 240
Rosenkranz, Karl 3, 8, 43–5, 54, 98, 147–8, 178, 181, 183, 232
Rossi, Aldo 31, 96, 156, 223–5, 231–3, 237–40
Rudolph, Paul
  Crawford Manor 4, 5
  in general 71, 109, 265
  Orange County Civic Centre 70
  Yale Art and Architecture Building 68
ruin 20, 26, 43, 49, 116, 239, 249
Ruscha, Edward 162
Ruskin, John 26, 27, 62, 249–50

salon de eventos 200–2
Scolari, Massimo 224–5
Schiller, Friedrich 34
Scott Brown, Denise 162–4
  and Venturi, see *Venturi and Scott Brown*
Scully, Vincent 176, 265
semantics 33, 59–65, 71–2, 146, 239, 240
Skopje
  Macedonian 107, 109, 111–12, 115, 116, 118–20
  Macedonian Opera and Ballet 116–17
  Muslim 118–19
  National Archaeological Museum 114
  (new) Old Theatre 115–16
  Ottoman 114, 118–19
  Skopje 2014 107–9, 111–20
  Stone Bridge 113–16
  Yogoslavian 107–9, 118–19

Smithson, Alison and Peter 13, 61–6, 72, 163, 165, 169, 227, 230, 245, 251
Sontag, Susan 176–8, 181, 188, 252, 264
Sottsass, Ettore Jr. 14, 211–13
South Bank Centre 71
Stern, Robert A. M. 176
Stirling, James 65–6, 139–42, 176
sublime 8, 9, 12, 13, 26, 45, 50, 52–3, 80, 248–9, 254, 261, 269
  see also Kant and sublime
Summerson, John 13, 19, 25, 59–68, 71–2, 140
surrealism 98, 104, 264, 272, 275

Tafuri, Manfredo 63, 227, 232, 235
Tange, Kenzo 14, 107–9, 119–20
Tendenza 223–7, 230–1, 233–4, 237, 240
teratology 80, 89–90
terror 2, 12, 15, 43, 257–61, 264, 273
The Architectural Review 64–5, 72, 155–6, 194, 257, 267
Torre Velasca 223, 227–30, 240
Townscape 155–7, 257

ugliness, see also *ugly*
  as aberration 15, 80, 125, 138, 246, 248, 261
  Australian 257–60
  and banality, see *banal*
  camp 176, 178–9, 181, 186–7
  definition of 42
  definition of architectural ugliness 45, 47–9
  and deformity 12, 26, 43, 47–8, 99, 142, 147, 153–4, 178, 239
  as error 48, 103, 132, 139, 249
  as exaggeration 48, 154, 164, 176, 177, 186, 214, 227
  and excess, see *excessive*
  and hybridity, see *hybridity*
  incidental 49
  instrumentalizing 5, 9, 34, 38, 59–61, 68, 72, 137, 223, 234, 269
  literature on 3
  and (ab)normality 41–3, 47, 79–81, 243, 261

ordinary 154, 170
and propriety 10, 32, 125, 128, 216, 247
and psychoanalysis 38, 78, 81
and scale 10, 48, 50, 60, 62–3, 68, 97, 100–1, 103–4, 108, 115–16, 157, 159, 164–5, 167, 183, 249, 261
and sensuous experience 12, 19, 27, 34, 40, 42, 45, 78
social 103
and terror, see *terror*
ultimate 11, 43, 80
and vitality 155–7, 231, 233, 237, 252–4
ugly
  and aesthetic judgement 1, 6, 9, 13, 21–2, 41, 46–7, 126–7, 175, 246–8
  as agent of shock 12, 63, 84, 91, 112, 154, 169, 248, 261
  architecture 47–8, 50, 137, 170, 238–9
  and beautiful 3, 7, 41, 71, 147, 153, 168, 181, 232–3, 237, 239–40, 246, 250–1
  and cleaning 1, 10, 43, 47, 116, 118, 260
  and comic 11, 15, 28, 186, 258, 262–5, 267–9, 271–3
  and convention 5, 9, 60, 62–3, 78, 82, 155–6, 162, 165, 176, 246–8, 250–1
  dissonance 1, 52, 95 97, 205, 249, 253
  and distortion 25, 32, 96–7, 133, 158, 164–5, 253
  duckling 34
  feelings 11–12, 264
  fugly 14
  intersubjective 1, 111, 116, 175
  and mal-proportion 19, 132, 139
  and mannerist, 133, see also *mannerism*
  merely ugly 44
  as moral judgement, see *aesthetics and morality*
  and ordinary 4, 5, 42, 153–6, 160–1, 169, 170, 180, 187, 251
  and rejection 42, 45, 128–9, 134, 231

and ridiculous 44, 48, 268
and taste 1, 26, 71
Ugly Belgian Houses 11, 18, 253
uncanny 43, 52, 90
utopia 102, 119, 211, 217, 231, 267

Valéry, Paul 50, 52–3
Vasari 128–30, 132, 134
Venturi, Robert
  Complexity and Contradiction 155–60, 270
  and Denise Scott Brown, *see* Venturi and Scott Brown
  and Rauch, see *Venturi and Rauch*
Venturi and Rauch (firm) 4, 5, 153, 161
  Guild House 3, 5, 164–5
  and Scott Brown 166
  Vana Venturi house 33
Venturi and Scott Brown
  Duck and Decorated Shed 5, 146, 163–4, 273
  Ironic Column 134
  on Main Street 155–6, 164–5, 169, 270

Signs of Life exhibition 165
'ugly and ordinary' 5, 153–4, 160–1, 262, 265, 270
Wu Hall 165–8
Venturi, Scott Brown and Izenour
  Learning from Las Vegas 4–5, 14, 71, 156, 160–3, 186, 270–1
Venturi and Short (firm) 159–60
Verfremdung, see *alienation*
vernacular (architecture) 5, 14, 19, 26, 29, 61, 154–5, 169, 176, 182, 195–6, 201, 205–6, 237, 250, 268

Warhol, Andy 97, 156, 165, 178, 245
Waugh, Evelyn 62
weird 80
Wittkower, Rudolf 61, 157
Wolfe, Tom 168, 178, 250
Wölfflin, Heinrich 26, 130, 132, 134
Wood, John the Elder 3

Yamasaki, Minoru 67, 179

zany 34
Zevi, Bruno 130, 226, 238–40

www.ingramcontent.com/pod-product-compliance
Lightning Source LLC
Chambersburg PA
CBHW050135240426
43673CB00043B/1677